W9-DBD-774

Globalisation of Accounting Standards

MONASH STUDIES IN GLOBAL MOVEMENTS

Series Editor: John Nieuwenhuysen, *Director, Monash Institute for the Study of Global Movements, Australia*

This series will be an important forum for the publication of new research on global movements sponsored by Monash University. It will present a multidisciplinary perspective on global movements of people, resources and ideas in their diverse economic, social, political and cultural dimensions. The series will make a valuable contribution to our understanding of some of the most important trends and challenges arising in an increasingly globalised world.

Titles in the series include:

Privatization and Market Development
Global Movements in Public Policy Ideas
Edited by Graeme Hodge

Globalisation of Accounting Standards
Edited by Jayne M. Godfrey and Keryn Chalmers

Globalisation of Accounting Standards

Edited by

Jayne M. Godfrey, *Monash University, Australia*
Keryn Chalmers, *Monash University, Australia*

MONASH STUDIES IN GLOBAL MOVEMENTS

Edward Elgar
Cheltenham, UK • Northampton, MA, USA

Published by
Edward Elgar Publishing Limited
Glensanda House
Montpellier Parade
Cheltenham
Glos GL50 1UA
UK

Edward Elgar Publishing, Inc.
William Pratt House
9 Dewey Court
Northampton
Massachusetts 01060
USA

A catalogue record for this book
is available from the British Library

Library of Congress Cataloguing in Publication Data

Globalisation of accounting standards / edited by Jayne M. Godfrey, Keryn Chalmers.
    p. cm. — (Monash studies in global movements series)
  Includes bibliographical references and index.
  1. Accounting—Standards. 2. Financial statements. 3. Accounting. I. Godfrey, Jayne M. (Jayne Maree) II. Chalmers, Keryn, 1961–
    HF5626.G55 2007
    657.02'18—dc22

                                                              2006034672

ISBN 978 1 84542 852 5

Printed and bound in Great Britain by MPG Books Ltd, Bodmin, Cornwall

Contents

v

Figures

Tables

Contributors

Editors

Jayne M. Godfrey, Editor, is Professor of Financial Accounting at Monash University, where she is the Deputy Dean – Research of the Faculty of Business and Economics. For her service to Australian society through business leadership, Professor Godfrey was awarded Australia's Centenary Medal. She has served on the Australian Accounting Standards Board, which sets accounting rules with the force of law for Australian companies, and retains an active interest in the economic determinants and consequences of both national and international accounting standards. Professor Godfrey has been President of the Accounting Association of Australia and New Zealand (now the Accounting and Finance Association of Australia and New Zealand), and has held visiting and advisory appointments at universities throughout Africa, Asia, Australia, Europe and the US.

Keryn Chalmers, Editor, is Associate Professor in Financial Accounting at Monash University. Her research interest is in the financial accounting and financial reporting area, specifically in relation to accounting policy and disclosure choices of management and the role of financial reporting as a governance mechanism. Keryn is a director of the Accounting and Finance Association of Australia and New Zealand, a member of CPA Australia's national education accreditation board and a Senior Fellow of the Financial Services Institute of Australasia (Finsia).

* * * *

David Alexander is Professor of Accounting at the Birmingham Business School, University of Birmingham, England, and is a Fellow of the Institute of Chartered Accountants in England and Wales. He is the co-author of several text books and professional guides in the International Accounting area, and has published numerous papers in academic journals in the European and International Accounting area.

Gordon L. Clark is the Halford Mackinder Professor of Geography and Head of the Oxford University Centre for the Environment, and is a Senior Research Associate with the Worklife and Labor Studies Centre, Harvard Law School, Harvard University. Professor Clark has been UK representative on the European Commission DG Research TMR Panel, is a member of the Advisory Board of the ESRC Centre for the Study of Globalisation and Regionalisation (Warwick University), serves on the strategic advisory board at Lund University (Sweden), and is an Honorary Professor at the University of Melbourne (Australia).

Iain Edwards is the Head of the School of Arts at Monash University, South Africa Campus.

Serge Evraert is a Professor at the University of Bordeaux IV, France. He leads the Centre of Research for International Accounting and Control (CRECCI). Professor Evraert is President of the International Association for Accounting Education and Research (IAAER) and a past President of the European Accounting Association (EAA) and the French Accounting Association (AFC).

James C. Gaa is Professor of Accounting in the Department of Accounting and Management Information Systems at the University of Alberta. Professor Gaa was a board member of the International Accounting Standards Committee (Canadian Board Member), 1997–2000. Other appointments include membership of the Canadian Advisory Group on International Accounting Standards, 1989-2001 and the Accounting Standards Oversight Council (ex officio), Canadian Institute of Chartered Accountants, 2000–2001.

Tessa Hebb is a Senior Research Associate at the School of Geography, Oxford University Centre for the Environment and is a Senior Research Associate with the Worklife and Labor Studies Centre, Harvard Law School, Harvard University where she directs a programme of research on public sector pension fund investment. Dr Hebb is a member of the OUCE's Spaces of Globalisation research cluster.

Chitoshi Koga is Professor of Accounting and International Accounting at Kobe University. He is a member of the Executive Boards of various academic and professional organisations in Japan.

Ian Langfield-Smith is a Lecturer in the Department of Accounting and Finance at Monash University.

De-Ming Lu is the Division Director, Division of Accounting Policy, in the Office of the Chief Accountant of the China Securities Regulatory Commission. Previously, he was in charge of research at the China Accounting Standards Committee.

Wei Lu is a Senior Lecturer in the Department of Accounting and Finance at Monash University.

Pietro Mazzola is Full Professor of Strategic Management at IULM University in Milano and teaches Financial Accounting at Bocconi University in Milano. He is a member of the editorial board of *Family Business Review*, has been involved as scientific advisor in the preparation of two out of four *Listing Guides of the Milano Stock Exchange* (Strategic Plan Guide, 2003 and Investor Relation Guide, forthcoming) and cooperates with the Cox Family Enterprise Center of Kennesaw State University in Atlanta on research on the Cost of Capital for Family Business.

Hans Peter Möller is Professor and head of Department of Accounting at the School of Economics and Business Administration at the Aachen University of Technology (RWTH), Germany.

R. Narayanaswamy is Professor of Finance and Control at the Indian Institute of Management, Bangalore, India.

Norita Mohd Nasir is a Lecturer in Accounting at Monash University, Malaysia campus.

Ruth Picker is Ernst & Young's Professional Practice Director and Partner – National Accounting & Auditing Standards. Ms Picker was a member of the AASB for five years from February 2000 until February 2005, during which time she was Deputy Chairman and Acting Chairman.

Adel Du Plessis is a Lecturer in the Department of Business and Economics at Monash University, South Africa campus.

Lorenzo Pozza is Associate Professor of Financial Accounting at Bocconi University. He is a member of the editorial board of the following journals: *La Rivista dei Dottori Commercialisti, La Valutazione delle Aziende*. He is Director of the graduate degree programme in Law and Business Administration.

Angelo Provasoli is Rector and Full Professor of Accounting at Bocconi University in Milan. At present he is chairman of the Executive Committee of the Italian Standard Setter Body (OIC). From 1973 to 2003 he was chief of the editorial board of the Italian Journal of Chartered Accountants.

Gunnar Rimmel is a Lecturer of Accounting and International Accounting at Göteborg University.

Jean-François des Robert is a specialist in France on the application of international standards to individual accounts. He was the Director of International Partnership and Development for the French profession, and as such worked on the development of International accounting and auditing standards in many transition countries, from Central European countries (Hungaria, Poland, Slovakia, Albania, Bosnia), to Mediterranean countries (Algeria and Morocco), and China, Cambodia and Laos.

Peter Schelluch is Deputy Pro Vice Chancellor, Monash University, South Africa Campus.

Kevin M. Stevenson is a Partner in PricewaterhouseCoopers's Global Capital Markets Group. He was, until May 2005, the Director of Technical Activities for the International Accounting Standards Board (IASB) and Chairman of the IASB's International Financial Reporting Interpretations Committee (IFRIC) in London.

Donna L. Street is the Mahrt Chair in Accounting at the University of Dayton. Professor Street is co-editor of the Institutional Perspectives section of the *Journal of International Financial Management and Accounting* and serves on the editorial board of the *Journal of International Accounting Research* and the *Journal of International Accounting, Auditing, and Taxation*. Professor Street is the Vice President of research of the IAAER and is President of the International Section of the American Accounting Association.

Jean Struweg is a Lecturer in the Department of Business and Economics at Monash University, South Africa campus.

Andrew West is a Lecturer in the Department of Business and Economics at Monash University, South Africa campus.

Dariusz Wójcik is a Lecturer in Economic Geography at University College, London, is a Research Fellow at Jesus College, and is a Research Associate at the Oxford University Centre for the Environment.

Wei-Guo Zhang is the Chief Accountant of the China Securities Regulatory Commission, and the Director General of the Department of International Affairs within the Commission. Previously, he was Head of the Department of Accounting, Shanghai University of Finance and Economics. He has been Secretary General of the China Accounting Professor's Association, and a member of the China Accounting Standards Committee, China Auditing Standards Committee, and National CPA Examination Board.

Aniza Zainol is a Lecturer in Accounting at Monash University, Malaysia campus.

Foreword

The International Accounting Standards Board has as its mission the development of a single set of high quality, understandable and enforceable accounting standards to be applied by countries around the world. This mission is the result of market pressures for a common reporting lexicon. This book charts the past and the present, and suggests some future directions in the accounting standards globalisation process. In doing so, it explains that the effects of globalising accounting standards are far broader and deeper than many would consider. Political, legal, religious and cultural ramifications add to the economic issues most often raised in the accounting standards globalisation debate. All of these issues are discussed in the chapters of this book.

Consistent with its theme, this book is a truly collaborative project. Contributing authors are drawn from around the globe, and from academia and national and/or international standard-setting backgrounds. They apply a range of theories and research methods to provide a wealth of knowledge, experience and insight to issues faced at political, theoretical and practical levels as different countries work towards global accounting standards.

I am told that the brief to the authors was to write about the globalisation of accounting in either a country-specific or an international context. With no constraints, presumably other than word limits, the authors have produced a book that delves deep into national and international issues surrounding the globalisation movement in general and particularly in relation to accounting standards. The significance of this movement to many countries is profound.

Contributing authors address issues such as when, how and why individual countries adopt their particular approaches to financial reporting globalisation. They also examine issues such as the impact of globalisation on capital markets or firms' investment, financing and operating decisions and the appropriateness of conceding national sovereignty over accounting standards. Their exposition of theories of regulation and of legal, political and social influences on policy setting or the effects of globalisation is invaluable in understanding diverse regulatory approaches.

Distinctive features of this book include the fact that its chapters are entirely contemporary works written specifically to the theme of globalisation of accounting standards. The balance of chapters across continents and countries, and across academic and standard-setter perspectives, is unique. Moreover, most of the chapters have been analysed and debated by the team of authors to ensure that the book provides a coherent and comprehensive overview of matters relevant to the future.

I commend this book to all readers seeking insights into the depth and breadth of issues relating to the globalisation of accounting standards.

Sir David Tweedie
Chairman, International Accounting Standards Board

Acknowledgements

This book is the outcome of a project funded through a grant from the Monash Institute for the Study of Global Movements. The Institute's generous support enabled each of the invited academic authors and accounting standard setters from various countries to contribute a chapter on an aspect of the globalisation of accounting standards from a unique perspective. A conference held at the Monash University Prato Centre in Italy also enabled many of the contributing academic authors to present their work and to debate and refine the arguments offered within their draft chapters. We are extremely grateful to the Monash Institute for the Study of Global Movements and its director, Professor John Nieuwenhuysen, whose support and encouragement enabled this book not only to be produced, but to be produced in such an enjoyable and intellectually stimulating manner. We also thank the Monash University Prato Centre for making our conference an academic and cultural experience to remember.

Our colleagues and co-authors, Wei Lu and Ian Langfield-Smith, provided valuable support, especially in the early stages of developing our proposal for this book and in reading and commenting on chapters. Thank you!

As editors, we thank the contributing authors for being such a delight to work with. Their insights, efficiency and cooperation have been invaluable. We are pleased that, in the true spirit of globalisation, many international friendships have been forged through the conference and book editing process.

We also appreciate the editorial support and assistance provided by Liz Rawlings, Elaine Ross and Andrew Parsloe and the staff at Edward Elgar.

To our families – as always, we are truly grateful for all your understanding and support.

Jayne M. Godfrey and Keryn Chalmers
April 2006

1 Globalisation of Accounting Standards: An Introduction

Jayne M. Godfrey and Keryn Chalmers

The 1990s and early years of the twenty-first century have witnessed globalisation on an unprecedented scale. Information technology advances mean that improved communication has led to transactions cost reductions and increased economies of scale. Accordingly, firms have grown not only in size but in geographic dispersion, consistent with the transactions costs theory espoused in the seminal work of Coase (1937). Coase argues that reductions in information costs will see increases in the size of the firm as the marginal costs of organising factors of production and the marginal costs of distributing products to customers through the firm decline relative to the marginal costs for individuals to organise production and distribution of goods and services. Along with the globalisation of business comes globalisation of the language of business: accounting.

One of the most significant and controversial recent trends in business is the commitment of countries to work towards adopting international accounting standards. The year 2005 heralded a new era in financial reporting as many countries adopted International Financial Reporting Standards (IFRS) for the first time.[1] As it is realised, the globalisation trend affects the way that firms worldwide report their financial transactions. Accounting standards globalisation significantly changes the reported earnings and reported financial position of many firms and public sector entities. Accountants, managers, shareholders, politicians and financial statement users will all grapple with the consequences of the globalisation movement in terms of potential effects on capital markets, product pricing, wealth distribution and labour markets.

So why have countries switched from their national accounting standard-setting regimes to a global regime, in some cases without even knowing the final form and content of the standards that they have committed to adopt? What differences exist between the globalisation approaches adopted by various countries, and why are the approaches different?

Nations' globalisation approaches all have aspects in common. Indeed, they must if international convergence is to occur. However, they differ in material ways as countries seek to maintain varying degrees of sovereignty over their regulations and as international differences in economic, political, legal, religious and social characteristics influence national standard-setting agendas.

This book is born of a curiosity as to why countries would relinquish their existing national accounting standard-setting regimes to join the global movement. To what extent are national incentives altruistic, economic, political or social? Who are the winners and losers in the process? The answers vary by country, as is to be expected.

PURPOSE AND SCOPE

The purpose of this book is to provide an analysis of some of the myriad of issues and perspectives of accounting globalisation as perceived by authors from diverse geographical regions. Major regional differences on a range of dimensions explain economic and political imperatives and stakeholder interests in pursuing accounting standards globalisation, and differences between national approaches to accounting regulation.

The book provides exposure to both academic and standard-setter perspectives. Consistent with an aim to draw out theoretical and practical issues, contributing authors include academics with experience in relation to various aspects of international accounting and high profile individuals with experience in the standard-setting arena. Many of the academic authors have current or past involvement in national and international standard setting, particularly during a period of momentum in globalising accounting standards. As such, the book melds both academic perspectives and regulatory insights.

The views represented emerge from countries in the continents of Africa, America, Asia, Australia and Europe. Consistent with the globalisation theme, the issue of accounting globalisation is explored from the perspectives of developed and developing countries, code and common law countries,[2] and countries that vary in terms of ownership structure and investor protection.[3]

INTERNATIONAL AND NATIONAL APPROACHES

While this chapter explains the purpose of the book and how the sequencing enables its attainment, the following chapter offers an overall context from which the book develops. As is evident from many chapters in this book, a key argument that national governments and finance market players have posed in favour of adopting international accounting standards is that doing so frees up capital markets, with corresponding potential macroeconomic benefits. Focusing upon information economics and the demand and supply of global accounting standards, in Chapter 2 Gordon Clark, Tessa Hebb and Dariusz Wójcik draw out the role of accounting information in an increasingly global finance market, and explain the inevitability of the globalisation of accounting standards.

Chapter 3 is the first chapter to focus solely upon accounting standards. In this chapter Kevin Stevenson describes the International Accounting Standards Board's (IASB) progress in globalising accounting standards. He challenges readers to appreciate the issues facing an organisation that almost certainly did not expect the globalisation movement to lead to such rapid acceptance of IASB standards as has occurred. Commensurate with international acceptance of the wording of international accounting standards, a need arises for infrastructure to ensure international understanding and acceptance of the interpretation of those standards. A need also arises for advisory and enforcement mechanisms so that the international standards are applied as intended and in a manner that serves, rather than retards, the globalisation of the language of accounting and the comparability of financial reports.

Chapters 4 to 7 inclusive are written by authors affiliated with the four countries that, at the commencement of the globalisation movement, had already formed their own clique of advanced national accounting standard setters in collaboration with the International Accounting Standards Committee (IASC), which was the precursor to the IASB. The group, commonly known as the Group of 4+1, or G4+1, comprised the standard setting bodies of Australia, Canada, the UK and the US, along with the IASC as observer.[4] It had no formal status, but joining forces in developing discussion papers and debating issues enabled these highly advanced standard-setting bodies to work together to resolve accounting issues.

As a group and individually, during the early 2000s, the G4+1 countries had the most advanced of all sets of national accounting standards. In each case they had also adopted a conceptual basis to developing accounting standards.[5] Similarly, the IASC had commenced the development of a conceptual framework.[6] While the conceptual frameworks were not identical, they had much in common, particularly in relation to their assumption that a key role of reported financial accounting information was to provide relevant and reliable information to users making decisions regarding the allocation of scarce economic resources.[7] Despite having much in common, there were, and still remain, significant differences between countries' approaches to standard setting, from the more extreme 'bright lines' or rules-based approach evident in the US to the principles-based approach preferred in the UK and Australia, with the Canadian approach reflecting its British heritage and US geographic influences.

In Chapter 4, David Alexander provides some controversial analysis of the UK's role in relation to influencing principles versus rules approaches in the development of IFRS, and contrasts the UK approach with that of the US. In doing so, he challenges the sometimes-argued view that IFRS are dominated by Anglo-Saxon approaches. This is followed in Chapter 5 with Donna Street's examination of the influence that the US standard setter, the Financial Accounting Standards Board (FASB), has exerted on IASB activities via the US influence on G4+1 activities. With the largest capital market in the world and probably the most detailed accounting standards in the world, the US has perhaps unsurprisingly been the most reticent of all G4+1 countries to adopt international accounting standards developed outside its jurisdiction. Nonetheless, the FASB is now working jointly with the IASB on all future accounting standards.[8] The nature and extent of the FASB's involvement in the globalisation of accounting standards is significant politically, both in relation to the types of standards likely to emerge from the IASB in the future, and in terms of the survival of particular standard-setting regimes.

As a country with a British heritage and with very strong economic and geographic ties to the US, Canada needs to be mindful of its past, present and future in developing accounting standards. James Gaa provides interesting insights in relation to the historical, cultural, political and geographic influences on the Canadian approaches to global standard setting. In particular, he addresses the tension between the UK principles approach and the US rules approach, and how Canada has resolved that tension in developing its own approach to standard setting as the globalisation movement advances.

Despite being originally the smallest country in the G4+1, Australia has long been perceived as having high quality accounting standards and as being a major contributor to G4+1 deliberations and governance. As such, Australia surprised the world's standard-setting community when its standard-setting oversight body unexpectedly announced in 2002 that Australia would adopt IFRS from 2005. In Chapter 7, which investigates issues arising when a nation leads the charge of advanced national standard-setting bodies to adopt IFRS, Ruth Picker provides insights into why Australia committed so early to adopting IFRS that had not even been developed at that stage. She investigates the consequences of that decision for Australia's national standard setting and enforcement, and for the business and finance communities. Her insights are relevant to all countries that have adopted, or are considering adopting, IFRS.

The next sequence of chapters focuses on issues and experiences of continental European countries in relation to the accounting globalisation phenomenon. As part of the European Union, countries such as Italy, France and Germany had no real choice but to adopt IFRS as a result of the EU's commitment that all its members would do so for listed companies' financial reports ending on or after 1 January 2005. Their reactions to the EU decision have differed, but in each case the adoption of IFRS involves a significant change in the conceptual approach to accounting standards and the role of financial reporting. None of these countries had made significant progress towards developing a conceptual framework for their national accounting standards, nor was it necessarily appropriate since the main purpose of financial reporting was inextricably linked to taxation laws rather than usefulness to investors, creditors, and others making non-tax-affecting economic decisions.

Italy did not take a significant role on the international stage of accounting standard setting prior to 2000. However, as Angelo Provosali, Pietro Mazzola and Lorenzo Pozza explain in Chapter 8, despite its late start, Italy has made rapid and significant progress in its approach to implementing international standards. The authors' account of Italy's increased engagement and readiness to adopt IFRS demonstrates the huge advances that can be made by a nation as it seeks to avoid being perceived as unsophisticated and recalcitrant against the globalisation trend.

The French resistance to IFRS adoption has been widely reported, particularly in relation to accounting for financial instruments. In Chapter 9, Serge Evraert and Jean François des Robert explain some of the significant issues that a nation faces in relation to the globalisation of accounting standards when that nation's culture and language affect not only the interpretation of accounting standards developed in another language, but also the very role of financial reporting.

The third in this sequence of chapters, Chapter 10, reports an exploratory empirical study that assesses a key assumption underlying the globalisation of accounting standards: that capital markets will be better informed. Hans Peter Möller investigates associations between stock properties and financial reporting under IFRS and German GAAP financial reporting standards. His study questions the superiority of international GAAP over German GAAP in providing information that is useful to German capital markets. This conjecture is interesting given the sequence of chapters that investigate why the major trading nations of China, Japan and India might seek to join the accounting standards globalisation movement.

The Italy-France-Germany sequence of chapters highlights that the effects of globalising accounting standards include and extend beyond capital markets. Furthering this line of argument, Keryn Chalmers, Jayne Godfrey, Ian Langfield-Smith and Wei Lu discuss the implications if a nation joins the globalisation movement not only for its private sector, but also for its public sector. Internationally, the two sectors traditionally report under different accounting regimes. Australian accounting standards are sector neutral; furthermore, Australia's adoption of international accounting standards is not restricted to listed entities only. All entities required to prepare financial reports in accordance with Australian accounting standards, including public sector entities, must adopt international accounting standards from 2005. The issues, challenges and rewards faced by Australia as its public sector grapples with rapid change 'ahead of the pack' are relevant to other nations that might contemplate a similar convergence of sector reporting.

China, Japan and India have significant economies that have been insulated in their financial reporting and capital market activities to varying degrees. With increasing involvement in world trade, labour and capital markets and as they emerge from their own individual economic crises, these countries look to join the globalisation movement primarily as a means of assisting their economic reform process. In Chapter 12, Wei-Guo Zhang and Du-Ming Lu describe the history of the development of China's accounting standards from their socialist origins to their current capital market focus. Consistent with themes established in earlier chapters, the authors explain the importance of accounting standards to capital market development and the need for rigorous and effective enforcement of accounting standards.

Given the globalisation trend, Chitoshi Koga and Gunnar Rimmel draw upon diffusion theory to explain what is necessary for the successful acceptance of international accounting standards into a country such as Japan. Chapter 13 explains the theory and surveys senior financial managers of Japan's largest companies in order to determine what areas they perceive would be most affected by Japanese adoption of international accounting standards. Japan's business system of keiretsu groups means that financial reporting in Japan traditionally has not been directed primarily towards investment decisions. Consequently, it is not surprising that managers are sceptical that the benefits of adoption will exceed the costs. The key perceived benefits of adopting international accounting standards relate to the potential to attract international debt and equity.

Similar to China and Japan, India's economic crisis has generated interest in adopting accounting standards that will confer enhanced credibility to financial reporting and contribute to the economic development of India. R. Narayanaswamy discusses in Chapter 14 why India is joining in the globalisation of accounting standards movement to aid its economic recovery and improve India's national standing amongst developed countries.

The final two chapters demonstrate that, while the benefits of globalising accounting standards are generally extolled in terms of the capital market and other national economic gains, implications of the accounting standards globalisation movement can be far wider-reaching and equally profound. Drawing upon the experiences of Malaysia and South Africa respectively, the focus of these chapters extends beyond economics. In Chapter 15, Norita Mohd Nasir and Aniza Zainol explain the role that religion can play in relation to a global approach to accounting standard setting. Information needs in an Islamic community, where concepts such as interest and profit play no role, are incompatible with adopting accounting standards that are developed with underpinning capitalistic values.

South Africa's reasons for embracing the globalisation movement, like those of other countries sampled in this book, have been at least partially to overcome the nation's economic difficulties. However, as Iain Edwards, Peter Schelluch, Adel du Plessis, Jean Struweg and Andrew West explain in Chapter 16, in post-apartheid South Africa the political, racial, and educational implications to a new government of joining the globalisation movement can possibly be even more significant than any economic gains.

THEMES

While each of the chapters from 3 to 16 inclusive is written from the perspective of a particular country, the issues relevant to one region are rarely unique to it. Common themes emerge in relation to a broad range of issues. Some of those themes are discussed in the remainder of this chapter.

Role of Financial Reporting

Two key assumptions relating to financial reporting emerge throughout the book: (1) accounting information is used in decision making; and (2) demand for high quality accounting information has increased over time.

One of the often-assumed fundamental roles of external financial reporting is to provide accounting information that is useful for decision making. This is articulated in the various conceptual frameworks such as those developed by the G4+1 countries: Australia, Canada, the UK, and the US, and evidenced by the reliance on external accounting information for investing and contracting decisions. However, some countries do not have conceptual frameworks (e.g., Japan and Germany) and therefore do not explicitly identify financial reporting objectives.

The second key assumption in the chapters is that demand for high quality accounting information has increased over time. This increase is attributable primarily to the increasing need to attract institutional and foreign investment in increasingly competitive capital markets and to the commensurate increase in the importance of national stock exchanges to countries' economic development. The performance of securities markets relies on the integrity of market information, of which accounting information is an important subset.

As core markets become more efficient, sophisticated investors seek opportunities for higher rates of return in markets that are comparatively less efficient. Accounting information is used in assessing the viability and profitability of investing in new industries and countries. Accordingly, it is in countries' interests to ensure the supply and quality of accounting information satisfies investors' demands.

Catalysts for the Globalisation of Accounting Standards

As reflected in the book, stakeholders in various countries have claimed that the benefits of global accounting standards include increased comparability of financial statements, kudos from becoming more sophisticated in their reporting, transfer of political power, and greater access to capital markets, especially foreign and institutional investment.

Across the countries represented in this book, joining the movement towards global accounting standards generally is justified on economic or political grounds. The move to more globally accepted accounting standards is clearly seen as a mechanism for economic transformation, particularly for developing countries. In this regard, the International Organisation of Securities Commissions (IOSCO) has played a critical role in promoting international accounting standards as it was IOSCO's conditional endorsement of international accounting standards developed by the IASC for multinational corporations' cross-border listings that provided the impetus for the IASC's quality improvements in international accounting standards. IOSCO's recommendation in May 2000 that its members allow multinational companies to use international accounting standards for cross-border listings and capital raisings was a catalyst in gaining acceptance for a global set of accounting standards. It also provided the political ammunition for the acceptance of international accounting standards in various countries.

Generally, globalisation of accounting is a component of a total globalisation package (e.g., globalisation of the economy, globalisation of culture, globalisation of corporate governance). Countries believe that embracing global accounting standards will open up capital markets and either attract, or restrict the loss of, foreign investment. Typically, embracing international accounting developments has post-dated a country crisis and is a legitimising or reputation enhancing action. This is reflected in the chapters describing the growing acceptance of international accounting standards in China, India, Japan and South Africa to promote economic reform; the US working closer with the IASB subsequent to its financial scandals at the start of this century; and Italy eventually embracing harmonisation to enhance its reputation in the accounting standard-setting community.

National Approaches to Globalisation

While many approaches to internationalisation are similar, differences are evident as countries seek to maintain varying degrees of sovereignty over their regulations. In the process of working towards a common set of accounting standards, the countries whose experiences are examined in this book differ in terms of their strategy (e.g., incremental versus big-bang approach), timing (e.g., commencement of convergence, adoption date) and scope (e.g., whether the public sector is included and whether unlisted private sector corporations are required to apply IFRS).

For EU countries, the early move to harmonise can be linked to the Fourth and the Seventh Company Law Directives concerning individual and group accounts respectively.[9] These directives generally improved the comparability of accounts and thus the conditions for cross-border business and allowed the mutual recognition of accounts for the purposes of quotation on securities exchanges throughout the EU. On 7 June 2002, the EU announced the requirement for both companies and building societies with securities traded on EU regulated markets to use IAS in their consolidated accounts for financial years beginning on or after 1 January 2005. By many EU countries, this is still seen as an Anglo-Saxon victory.

For Australia, the initial approach, commencing in 1996, was to selectively harmonise and converge. This is similar to the approach taken in South Africa and Malaysia. What Australia has since done is primarily adopt IFRS verbatim with an effective date of 1 January 2005.

Other countries have formally committed via Memoranda of Understanding with the IASB to converge their national GAAP with IFRS. For example, at their joint meeting in Norwalk, Connecticut, USA on 18 September 2002, the FASB and the IASB each acknowledged their commitment to the development of high-quality, compatible accounting standards that could be used for both domestic and cross-border financial reporting. At that meeting, both the FASB and IASB pledged to use their best efforts to make their existing financial reporting standards more compatible as soon as is practicable, and to coordinate their future work programmes to ensure that, once achieved, compatibility is maintained.

More recently, discussions among the accounting standard setters of China, Japan and Korea recognised that international convergence is an irreversible trend and the nations support the IASB's efforts to develop a single set of high-quality and globally accepted standards. However, they also stipulated that convergence is not necessarily equal to being identical. For example, Australia has promulgated Australian equivalents to IFRS but with differences. A 2005 PricewaterhouseCoopers report documents that only around 50 per cent of about

35 standards receive a 'no significant difference' rating. The EU has also 'tinkered' with standards, as evident by the passage of IAS 39, the controversial standard on financial instruments and 'carve outs' introduced by the EU.

Malaysia provides a different example of a globalisation approach. In Malaysia there is a significant presence of Islamic banks and financial institutions. Islamic Shariah principles and practices differ fundamentally from conventional principles and practices underpinning financial report preparation. For example, Shariah principles define permitted and non-permitted transactions, with interest being prohibited. This fundamentally changes the economic substance of many investing and financing decisions and makes the financial reports non-comparable. This issue has been addressed internationally with the establishment of the Accounting and Auditing Organisation for Islamic Financial Institutions, a private standard-setting body, formed in Bahrain in 1991 because of the inadequacies of international standards to cater for Islamic financial institutions. The organisation has issued approximately 60 standards on accounting, auditing, governance and ethics. To accommodate the unique characteristics of Islamic financial institutions' operations, Malaysia has introduced an accounting standard – MASB FRSi-1 Presentation of Financial Statements of Islamic Institutions.

Issues Emerging from the Implementation Process

Key issues relating to implementation of global standards include the principles versus rules debate, interpretative issues and the adequacy of IAS GAAP knowledge. The role of principle-based versus rule-based standards and the role of professional judgement is a thread common to the UK, Canadian and US chapters. IFRS are often typified as being principles-based, leaving much to the accountant's professional judgement in applying general principles while US GAAP, particularly, is typified as rules-based, with detailed rules prescribing how to account for each of the various events and transactions that fall within broader areas that would otherwise be governed by general accounting principles.

The EU is required to decide on the applicability of individual IFRS within the EU. The decision to adopt is made if it is not contrary to principles of the fourth and seventh Directives; it is conducive to European public good; and meets the criteria of understandability, relevance, reliability and comparability. The true and fair override contained in the EU fourth directive and used by the UK Accounting Standards Board (ASB) to overturn (e.g., in relation to investment properties and the need to depreciate) EU Directives has generated concern that the perception that the IASB is aligning itself with the rule-orientation of the FASB may result in further overrides if the converged standards are seen as lower quality than existing UK standards. The ASB's discontent with IFRS 3 (a joint project with FASB) is an illustration of this: the ASB has publicly expressed reservations concerning IFRS 3, warning that it would not represent an improvement in UK reporting.[10] Thus, the possibility of differential reporting could arise given that the EU directive is not applicable to all UK entities.

Concerns have also been expressed as to whether comparable and consistent financial reports will result from the globalisation of accounting standards, given a perceived lack of interpretative guidance. These interpretative issues are not unique to any particular country, and they are particularly pertinent where countries have come from a position of having standards that permitted limited flexibility. Kevin Stevenson draws out these matters in his chapter examining issues from the perspective of the IASB, which has faced a more widespread and rapid adoption of IFRS than expected. The IASB's interpretative body, the International Financial Reporting Interpretations Committee (IFRIC), reviews accounting issues that are likely to receive divergent or unacceptable treatment in the absence of authoritative guidance. However, many countries demand and require a quick response on an interpretative query and are confronted with at least two potential problems: IFRIC might not consider the issue warrants an interpretation; or the interpretation development may take too long to meet the particular needs of the inquirer. An interpretation takes a minimum due process time of seven months from first appearing on the IFRIC agenda. This has prompted the call (primarily in Europe) for additional mechanisms to provide urgent interpretative responses or additional implementation guidance in order to avoid compromising the consistency of IFRS compliant reports.

In time it will become apparent if firms in countries adopting IFRS are producing high quality applications of IFRS. One of the challenges emanating from the implementation of IFRS is the training of staff (audit firms and reporting entities) to facilitate IFRS compliance. In South Africa, for example, IFRS compliance has been outsourced to the external audit firms. Further, these audit firms have established IFRS conversion consulting businesses (an interesting twist of the notion of auditor independence!).

Labour markets are already feeling the effects of globalisation as senior practitioners in Australia decide that the necessary 'retooling' is not for them in their pre-retirement years, and they retire earlier than otherwise. Meanwhile, graduates face increased demand by virtue of their knowledge of new accounting requirements, but do not have the commensurate experience to fully meet employers' needs.

While removal of global barriers makes a global accounting language appealing, differences between the economic, social, and political characteristics of each country raise questions concerning the ability of all countries to enforce an identical set of regulations. Indeed, cynics have commented that one of the reasons that the French were initially fairly laissez-faire about adopting IFRS was that they did not expect that the adoption would be enforced.

What cannot be forecast with certainty is the future role of national standard setters and how the IASB/FASB alliance will play out. The survival of national standard setters depends on them remaining relevant and being seen to influence the global standard setter's deliberations. The IASB is a powerful global body, and given the spate of US corporate collapses and scandals linked to poor financial reporting in the early 2000s, the FASB was forced to reconsider its 'stand-alone' approach. While the FASB is now working with the IASB,[11] making realisation of a truly global accounting more probable, it is unclear whether that probability will be realised through FASB or IASB dominance.

CONCLUSION

The past decade has seen enormous attention and effort focused upon the convergence of accounting standards. While progress has been substantive, it is important to reflect on the subtleties of the differences (commitment, timing, processes and scope) across countries and to understand that the effects of accounting standards globalisation extend beyond mere reporting to economic, social, political, religious and cultural outcomes. This book provides a step towards that understanding.

NOTES

1   By April 2006, more than 90 countries had adopted International Financial Reporting Standards (IFRS) for the financial statements of domestic listed entities.
2   The common law system relies on legal rules being developed by judges based on general principles and precedents. Civil or code law is written by legislators with judges not venturing beyond the statutes (Coffee 2001).
3   Investor protection (both shareholder and creditor) refers to how the law protects principals from wealth expropriation by managers (La Porta, Lopez-de-Silanes, Schleifer and Vishny, 2000).
4   The group grew to include more than the initial four national standard-setting bodies, but continued to be referred to as the G4+1.
5   For example, refer to the Australian Accounting Standards Board (2004), the Accounting Standards Board (1999), and the Financial Accounting Standards Board (1978, 1980, 1984, and 1985).
6   Refer to the International Accounting Standards Board (2001).
7   For example, refer to IASB (2001) paras 12–14.
8   Financial Accounting Standards Board, Memorandum of Understanding: The Norwalk Agreement, FASB Website, viewed 10 April 2006: www.fasb.org/news/memorandum.pdf
9   Van Hulle (1991) summarises the content of the EU 4th Directive noting: 'The directive itself is a combination of rigidity and flexibility. There is rigidity in: the mandatory layouts for the

balance sheet and profit and loss account; the valuation rules and notably the limited possibility to depart from the historical cost principle; the minimum content of the notes and the annual report; and in the audit and disclosure requirements. There is flexibility in: the true and fair override; the many options both for member states and for companies; the fact that the provisions of the directive are minimum requirements; and the possibility to derogate from certain provisions in exceptional cases provided that disclosures are made in the notes on the accounts' (p.25).

10 Refer to: www.frc.org.uk/asb/press/pub0850.html.
11 Joint projects include business combinations, intangibles, income taxes, segment disclosures and provisions.

ACKNOWLEDGEMENTS

This chapter has benefited from the insights provided by the authors of all chapters in this book. However, errors and omissions remain the responsibility of the authors.

REFERENCES

Accounting Standards Board (ASB) (1999), *Statement of Principles for Financial Reporting*.

Alexander, D. (2006), 'Globalisation of accounting standards: a UK perspective', in Jayne M. Godfrey and Keryn Chalmers (eds), *Globalisation of Accounting Standards*, Cheltenham, UK: Edward Elgar.

Australian Accounting Standards Board (AASB) (2004), *Framework for the Preparation and Presentation of Financial Statements*.

Chalmers, K., J. Godfrey, I. Langfield-Smith and W. Lu (2006), 'Globalisation of accounting: implications for Australian public sector entities', in Jayne M. Godfrey and Keryn Chalmers (eds), *Globalisation of Accounting Standards*, Cheltenham, UK: Edward Elgar.

Clark, G., T. Hebb and D. Wójcik (2006), 'Institutional investors and the language of finance: the global metrics of market performance', in Jayne M. Godfrey and Keryn Chalmers (eds), *Globalisation of Accounting Standards*, Cheltenham, UK: Edward Elgar.

Coase, R.H. (1937), 'The Nature of the Firm', *Economica*, **4** (16), 386–405.

Coffee Jr, J.C. (2001), 'The Rise of Dispersed Ownership: the roles of law and the state in the separation of ownership and control', *Yale Law Journal*, **111**, (1), 1–81.

Edwards, I., P. Schelluch, A. du Plessis, J. Struweg and A. West (2006), 'Globalisation and accounting reforms in an emerging market economy: a case study of South Africa', in Jayne M. Godfrey and Keryn Chalmers (eds), *Globalisation of Accounting Standards*, Cheltenham, UK: Edward Elgar.

Evraert, Serge and Jean Francois des Robert (2006), 'French accounting revolution: implementing IFRS in French companies', in Jayne M. Godfrey and Keryn Chalmers (eds), *Globalisation of Accounting Standards*, Cheltenham, UK: Edward Elgar.

Financial Accounting Standards Board (FASB) (1978), *Statement of Financial Accounting Concepts (SFAC) No.1: Objectives of Financial Reporting by Business Enterprises*.

Financial Accounting Standards Board (FASB) (1980), *Statement of Financial Accounting Concepts (SFAC) No.2: Qualitative Characteristics of Accounting Information*.

Financial Accounting Standards Board (FASB) (1984), *Statement of Financial Accounting Concepts (SFAC) No.5: Recognition and Measurement in Financial Statements of Business Enterprises.*

Financial Accounting Standards Board (FASB) (1985), *Statement of Financial Accounting Concepts (SFAC) No. 6: Elements of Financial Statements (a replacement for SFAC No. 3).*

Gaa, J. (2006), 'The place of Canada in global accounting standard setting: Principles versus rules approaches', in Jayne M. Godfrey and Keryn Chalmers (eds), *Globalisation of Accounting Standards*, Cheltenham, UK: Edward Elgar.

International Accounting Standards Board (2001), *Framework for the Preparation and Presentation of Financial Statements.*

Koga, C. and G. Rimmel (2006), 'Accounting harmonisation and diffusion of international accounting standards: the Japanese case', in Jayne Godfrey and Keryn Chalmers (eds), *Globalisation of Accounting Standards*, Cheltenham, UK: Edward Elgar.

La Porta, R., F. Lopez-de-Silanes, A. Shleifer, and R. Vishny (2000), 'Investor Protection and Corporate Governance', *Journal of Financial Economics*, **58** (1–2), 3–27.

Möller, P. (2006), 'Accounting regimes and their effects on the German stock market', in Jayne M. Godfrey and Keryn Chalmers (eds), *Globalisation of Accounting Standards*, Cheltenham, UK: Edward Elgar.

Mohd Nasir Norita and Aniza Zainol (2006), 'Globalisation of financial reporting: an Islamic focus', in Jayne M. Godfrey and Keryn Chalmers (eds), *Globalisation of Accounting Standards*, Cheltenham, UK: Edward Elgar.

Narayanaswamy, R. (2006), 'The impact of globalisation of accounting standards on Indian accounting standards', in Jayne M. Godfrey and Keryn Chalmers (eds), *Globalisation of Accounting Standards*, Cheltenham, UK: Edward Elgar.

Picker, R. (2006), 'Too special to go global? Too small to be special? An insight into Australia's decision to adopt IFRS and the consequences for its own standard setting and application', in Jayne M. Godfrey and Keryn Chalmers (eds), *Globalisation of Accounting Standards*, Cheltenham, UK: Edward Elgar.

PricewaterhouseCoopers (July 2005), *AIFRS and IFRS – Similar but Not the Same*, PricewaterhouseCoopers, Australia, viewed 10 April 2006: www.pwc.com/extweb/pwcpublications.nsf/4bd5f76b48e282738525662b00739e22/07e0ed696c08c422ca257073007e7962/$FILE/AIFRS_and_IFRS_Sept2005.pdf

Provosali, A, Pietro Mazzola and Lorenzo Pozza (2006), 'The role of national standard setters in the standard development process: the Italian experience', in Jayne M. Godfrey and Keryn Chalmers (eds), *Globalisation of Accounting Standards*, Cheltenham, UK: Edward Elgar.

Stevenson K. (2006), 'The IASB: Some personal reflections', in Jayne M. Godfrey and Keryn Chalmers (eds), *Globalisation of Accounting Standards*, Cheltenham, UK: Edward Elgar.

Street, D. (2006), 'The US role in the globalisation of accounting standards', in Jayne Godfrey and Keryn Chalmers (eds), *Globalisation of Accounting*, Cheltenham, UK: Edward Elgar.

Van Hulle, K. (1991), 'Our Misunderstood and Maligned Directive', *Accountancy*, **107** (1174), 25.

Wei-Guo Zhang and De-Ming Lu (2006), 'Convergence of Chinese accounting standards with international standards: process, achievements and prospects', in Jayne M. Godfrey and Keryn Chalmers (eds), *Globalisation of Accounting Standards*, Cheltenham, UK: Edward Elgar.

2 Institutional Investors and the Language of Finance: The Global Metrics of Market Performance

Gordon L. Clark, Tessa Hebb and Dariusz Wójcik

INTRODUCTION

One way of thinking about global finance is to think of its flows. Every day, huge volumes of traded currencies circumnavigate the globe putting in play the relative value of at least 10 currencies, if not the stability of the global economy. Likewise, portfolio managers trade on home and away stock markets seeking to take advantage of arbitrage opportunities and the greater or lesser efficiency of their home market versus other markets. In the world of market flows and inter-market arbitrage, information is at a premium (Clark and Thrift 2004). In some markets, information is largely public in that it is openly disclosed to market participants according to well-established rules and regulations. In other markets, there is a mixture of public and private information derived, in part, from the historical privileges accorded to inside investors as opposed to outside investors. The fact that information is less than ubiquitous and has a price has implications for market efficiency and the investment performance of portfolio managers (Clark and Wójcik 2003).

Another way of thinking about global finance is to think about its institutions. We could study 'public' international institutions such as the Bank for International Settlements, the International Monetary Fund, and the various coordinating national institutions that meet on a regular basis to manage financial stability. In this chapter, these organisations are hardly ever mentioned except to note that their mandates are less about controlling and regulating the flows of global finance than responding to and coping with the adverse consequences of uncoordinated market action (Cable 1999). Rather, we focus on private institutions such as institutional investors and the market for financial services that has mushroomed over the past 40 years or so to dominate the management of global financial assets (Davis and Steil 2001). We also refer to communal institutions that are, in effect, the building blocks of social practice (Pettit 2002) – in this case, modern portfolio theory and its related progeny.

One of the commonly-made observations exploited in this chapter is that the theory and practice of finance are based upon information (Wilhelm and Downing 2001). Market agents make trades and plan strategies on the basis of observed market prices. By this logic, information not only greases the wheels of global financial transactions, it also goes to the very heart of the practice of finance that has come to dominate investment management itself. We argue that the language of finance has distinctive market-specific characteristics representing its history in the Anglo-American world. We also argue that the language of finance is a language of practice that privileges minority 'outside' shareholders as opposed to majority 'inside' shareholders (the latter being representative of continental European regimes of accumulation and distribution).

Like Lo (2004), however, we also argue that the language of finance seems to have come to a dead end. The TMT bubble and the crisis of confidence in corporate governance during the early 2000s have conspired to undercut the hegemony of the language of finance while simultaneously putting in play a burgeoning market for information that goes well beyond the parameters set by modern portfolio theory. Even those most committed to the theory of efficient markets have conceded that the intellectual scaffolding underpinning the language of finance hardly ever works as expected or desired (compare Fama 1970 with Fama and French 2004). Inevitably, investment managers have sought alternative routes for extracting value from financial markets around the world. One way of doing so requires a better appreciation of the empirical relationships that might be found between corporate governance and market value (however both are measured and described). This empirical world is inevitably and fundamentally information intensive. But it now goes well beyond the reference points of finance theory that held sway for a couple of generations (for example, Ho and Lee 2004).

The chapter is organised in the following manner. The next section provides a potted history of the rise and fall of managerial capitalism. Throughout, we refer to the Anglo-American world with the contrast drawn to continental Europe – a useful way of sustaining our argument. We then move on to the intellectual roots of finance, noting its principles as well as its implications for institutional investors. Thereafter, we argue that this language became hegemonic spreading around the globe and in particular being a means of valuing European institutions. This leads to an analysis of the burgeoning market for information in the face of acknowledged problems with the language of finance, noting its implications for national and international investment practices. In general, our strategy in preparing this chapter has been to identify the 'big' issues rather than reporting original results. We have eschewed technical precision in favour of principles and practices. As a result, the chapter is designed to set a framework for research and a means of understanding what follows in the chapters reporting research concerning various nations' experiences in the accounting standards globalisation movement.

RECENT HISTORY

According to Chandler (1990), by the early years of the twentieth century much of the US economy had assumed the organisational form of managerial capitalism that was to dominate the century. For Chandler, centralised corporate administration combined with vertical integration was the operative solution to the competitive pressures associated with the geographical scope of the continental economy. Whereas financiers played crucial roles in the formation of conglomerates, Chandler argued that their significance was quickly discounted as the expanding scope and scale of corporate activities empowered managerial elites. He compared US managerial capitalism with other forms of capitalism in developed economies distinguishing, for example, between Britain (personal capitalism) and Germany (co-operative capitalism). Most importantly, he suggested that public distrust of banking over the nineteenth century and early twentieth century was such that the US finance industry remained decentralised, fragmented, and the fiefdom of individuals rather than national institutions (in contrast to Germany and Britain).[1]

Over the second half of the twentieth century, financial capitalism overtook managerial capitalism in the Anglo-American world. New kinds of national and global institutions were formed with access to financial resources far-surpassing those available to hitherto largely self-financing manufacturing corporations. Not only were these institutions increasingly important for corporate restructuring on behalf of ambitious corporate raiders, they had become important owners of corporate stocks and bonds in their own right even if their individual holdings were quite small (compared to the German practice of financial institutions holding large blocks of preferential voting stocks in closely-related companies). Most importantly, these financial institutions became increasingly active agents in hostile mergers and acquisitions. In effect, they funded the market for corporate control (Jensen 1993). Instead of supporting entrenched corporate managers, financial institutions focused upon releasing corporate value to stock owners – an organising principle that has taken many forms including 'corporate engagement' in the aftermath of the TMT bubble and corporate governance scandals (Clark and Hebb 2004).

Underpinning the emerging power of financial capitalism has been a set of rules, regulations, and practices. For example, Anglo-American pension funds are governed by the principle of fiduciary duty inherited from the common law of trust, albeit formalised in statute and regulation (Clark 2006). Importantly, regulations requiring the full funding of expected obligations against market value combined with a required (if not always enforced) separation between the financial interests of the plan sponsor or sponsors and plan beneficiaries created large pools of 'independent' investment capital. By contrast, the book reserve system of pension funding left German pension plans largely 'under-funded' and hostage to the interests of corporate managers in adding to physical plant and equipment rather than the interests of employees in investing those assets nationally and internationally (Clark 2003). Furthermore, the enormous growth in pension fund assets combined with an increasing concern for the cost-efficient administration and management of pension fund assets encouraged the development of a global financial services industry centred on the Anglo-American world whose principal clients are neither corporations nor governments (Hayes 1993).[2]

The rules governing the theory and practice of investment have also been transformed over the past 50 years. Bernstein (1992) traced the recent origins of the theory of finance to Markowitz's (1952) seminal paper on 'portfolio selection'. That paper was one of a small number of related papers published around the time that provided both the conceptual apparatus for valuing stocks and the rudiments for optimal portfolio design (see also Roy 1952). One of the implications of Markowitz's paper for portfolio design and investment theory was the recognition that the risk of any investment or asset class should be assessed against the risk profile of the whole portfolio. Moreover, given the demonstrable positive relationship between risk and return, there were objective reasons to take on risk in relation to desired rates of return. The principles of portfolio diversification combined with the removal of implicit and explicit restrictions on investment in certain asset classes and jurisdictions revolutionised financial markets. A global marketplace has developed for financial innovation – key features of modern investment management have extended asset allocation from stocks and bonds to alternative investments such as hedge funds, venture capital, and the like.[3]

A UNIVERSAL LANGUAGE

If the early years of the twentieth century saw the rise of a corporate elite claiming power at the very centre of their organisations, by the end of the twentieth century a new elite had been born operating within and without the modern corporation.

This new elite used the tools of finance to claim control of corporate capitalism. This is a story commonly told about Anglo-American economies. But it is a story increasingly familiar to continental European economies that might otherwise claim a heritage and mode of corporate organisation quite different from their Anglo-American relations.

Here, we take the argument in a slightly different direction, emphasising the practice of finance. One of the most important differences between the financial capitalism of the twenty-first century and the financiers of the late nineteenth and early twentieth centuries is the fact that finance is now an industry populated by many thousands of skilled employees who share, more often than not, a common language about the theory and practice of finance. Whether located in New York, Tokyo, London or Frankfurt and whether employed by Goldman Sachs, the Bank of Tokyo, or Deutsche Bank, they all know about the capital asset pricing model, the Black-Scholes option-pricing theorem, the Sharpe ratio and the information ratio etc. These are elementary reference points in any discussion about modern investment theory. This has had significant implications for understanding the spread of Anglo-American financial practice to distant shores just as it has significant implications for understanding the standards set by institutions such as the International Accounting Standards Board.

The language of finance is built upon three axioms derived from modern portfolio theory (Houthakker and Williamson 1996). First, financial markets are efficient in the sense that they embody all available information relevant to the formation of prices; second, market arbitrage inevitably drives out market imperfections such that market inefficiency is idiosyncratic rather than systematic; and third, market behaviour is rational in the sense that rational agents dominate irrational agents through the exploitation of the latter by the former. Of course, the TMT bubble and the systematic misleading of the market by those with a stake in market speculation have challenged the plausibility of these axioms (Clark et al. 2004; Shiller 2000). Furthermore, the application of the results of experimental psychology to understanding market behaviour has brought to light what appear to be systematic anomalies undercutting the hegemony of the rational actor model (see Hilton 2003 on the implications of these findings for the study of financial markets).

The language of finance is also built upon three stylised facts about the world. First, as core markets become ever more efficient, opportunities for higher rates of return are to be found in markets that are relatively less efficient; second, in a world of economic globalisation, competition is more about industries than countries, suggesting that investment inevitably flows to lower-priced sites of production; and third, there is a premium to be had for those capable of identifying imperfections and being able to move on to new opportunities as the rest of the market catches up. One does not have to be a believer in the 'strong' version of market efficiency to agree that these stylised facts about the world are at least *one* plausible scenario for the future. Each is, of course, quite contentious especially in terms of the claimed declining significance of national borders. Significantly, the combination of axioms and stylised facts provides both a recipe for short-term and long-term investment strategy recognised as such by the Goldman Sachs textbook on investment management as well as the Goldman Sachs report on global growth prospects over the next 50 years (see, respectively, Litterman et al. 2003 and Wilson and Purushothaman 2003).

The language of finance as a shared language of practice has been sustained by the education of financial analysts. Not only is there virtually a common finance curriculum around the world, finance has become a core component of MBA education. Furthermore, when staffing finance functions' institutions often sort amongst applicants according to the extent to which shared education is likely to reinforce the competence of existing teams. Just as importantly, clients have come to expect financial service providers to sell their services according to the expertise assumed to be embodied in certain types of people (their training and education). In many cases, clients do not understand modern portfolio theory. But they are convinced that adherence to its axioms is a measure of quality differentiating between competing financial service providers. Most importantly, the language of finance is almost always the language of ex-post legitimisation – the reference point used to explain how and why investment strategies may or may not have worked as expected.

Most remarkably, the language of finance is English. Whereas 10 or 15 years ago dictionaries of translated financial terms proliferated, as new generations of financial analysts have joined global financial institutions, English has become *the* reference language for texts uniting terms and functions. Dictionaries have become more complex, more detailed and more technical as opposed to conceptual. A commitment to English as the *lingua franca* of finance has made this possible.[4] By contrast, local languages have remained the languages for marketing and client relationships although, even in these circumstances, English terms have found their way into discussions with clients about the latest innovations in financial engineering. This being the case, the language of finance may be thought hegemonic, in ways similar to those Power (2004) attributes to related concepts such as 'enterprise risk management'.

PORTFOLIO DESIGN AND INVESTMENT MANAGEMENT

Like many others who have sought a break point in the post-war record of economic growth, Clowes (2000) identified 1973 as the moment when the balance of power shifted in favour of investment management firms and away from bank trust departments.[5] He suggested that these new institutions had two related goals: achieving higher rates of return in relation to accepted benchmarks and rates of return in excess of that measured by a stock market index such as the S&P500. He contended that bank trust departments offering similar investment functions were often more risk-averse and unwilling to embrace the new language of finance. In any event, by his account at least, bank trust departments clung to their traditional relationships with large manufacturing corporations and failed to respond to the emergence of new kinds of financial institutions shorn of alliances with those kinds of corporations. Similar banking-corporate relationships were to hold sway in much of continental Europe through to the end of the 1990s, at least.

With a recipe for portfolio design and a rapidly growing volume of assets to be invested, investment management became a highly structured exercise. Instead of placing large tranches of assets with selected stocks underpinned by personal or long-term cross-institution relationships with target companies, portfolio designers eschewed past relationships in favour of diversifying investment across the market of traded securities. Of course, there were constraints (as there remain constraints) on this kind of investment strategy. If expected performance is benchmarked against a market index, assets must be distributed such that stocks that dominate the index are appropriately represented in the portfolio. In any event, the smaller the market capitalisation of a company, the lower its market liquidity and consequently the higher the risk of being trapped holding that stock relative to other opportunities. As the investment management industry matured, the practice of investment became subject to scrutiny by peers and clients alike utilising the tools of the new orthodoxy (Litterman et al. 2003).

To illustrate, assume a client has £1 billion in assets to be invested and assume that the client faces the prospect of a net inflow of contributions year-on-year over the foreseeable future. If we also assume the client underwrites the expected value of benefits or in some way provides a capital guarantee, risk and return over the short-run and long-run are crucial metrics in any investment decision-making process. By convention, three types of decisions are made (in the following order): the allocation of assets to different asset classes, the allocation of assets to specific types of investment products or strategies within asset classes, and the allocation of those assets to financial service providers (Campbell and Viceira 2002). We also assume, for the moment, that assets are allocated only to domestic stocks and bonds (as was certainly the case 30 years ago). If there is a 50/50 split of assets between stocks and bonds, the allocation of assets is weighted towards the largest capitalised stocks.[6] This kind of logic works even if we segment the stock market into large cap, medium cap, and small cap components (with their own benchmarks for assessing risk and return).

Also assume total market capitalisation is £1 trillion and that the average large institutional investor has £1 billion to invest. This suggests the following. First, by spreading assets widely across the market (subject to the constraints noted above) the capacity of such institutional investors to monitor the performance of individual stocks is very limited. Second, by spreading assets across the market, few institutional investors will own a significant portion of any stock. Notwithstanding the allocation of assets by market capitalisation, only the largest institutional investors are likely to hold more than 200 basis points of any traded company security. Third, by spreading assets across the market, institutional investors inevitably rely upon the market for pricing the value of traded securities – in turn, the pricing of any market security relies upon investors responding to positive and negative market signals as to its current and expected value. Since information is very expensive if sought for the entire portfolio, the cheapest strategy is to trade on publicly available information (Davis and Steil 2001).

By this logic, the integrity of market information is an essential ingredient in the performance of investment managers and for the performance of entire securities' markets. If information were private, if it flowed first to large shareholders and then were distributed to the market *after* its meaning had been digested, there would be enormous advantages in being an 'insider' as opposed to an 'outsider'. It is hard to imagine how the recipe for portfolio design owed to the pioneers of modern financial theory could survive such a harsh reality. Not only would market pricing be thoroughly distrusted, but the rebalancing of market portfolios would always lag the real state of play in the company stock that made up those portfolios. Enormous attention would be focused upon the largest capitalised stocks leaving behind even medium-sized stocks to fend for themselves. In such circumstances, the stock market could shrink in terms of the number of listed companies and the volume of transactions. This is one way of accounting for the relatively concentrated structure of most continental European stock markets and, by contrast, the growth of Anglo-American stock markets over the past 30 years or so.[7]

However, it would be misleading to suggest that the Anglo-American regime of information disclosure has been without fault. The volume of disclosure has been such that a market for information processing and valuation has developed matching the interests of the largest institutional investors. Ironically, because of the cost of processing information, smaller investors have been sidelined in the market for information, being reliant upon the free-to-air, cable, and print media and all their foibles with respect to the competition for market share and the like (see Clark et al. 2004). In these circumstances, many of the largest institutional investors have sought to exploit the enormous volume of public information believing that superior computing capacity and analytical routines allow for the identification of arbitrage opportunities that go unrecognised in the day-to-day flow of information.

ON TO THE REST OF THE WORLD

Institutional investors have come to dominate Anglo-American stock markets, and through them the nature and practice of corporate governance, especially amongst the largest firms. They represent a new form of capitalism; one where financial institutions are privileged over production and the financial circumstances of the investing middle-class flow directly into macroeconomic indicators. From 1973, the flow of assets into financial markets became a virtual tidal wave. For example, over the 1990s pension fund assets in Canada, the UK, and the US grew from (respectively) 31 per cent, 55 per cent and 47 per cent of GDP in 1991 to 48 per cent, 66 per cent and 63 per cent of GDP in 2001. Even allowing for the effects of the bubble economy, it is clear that the financial foundations of these economies are very different from their European counterparts (Chan-Lau 2004).

Institutional investors have sought to extract stock value from incumbent managers and their relationships with other groups inside and outside of the corporation. There has been widespread debate about this strategy, recognising that the long-term growth of large corporations may require short-term sacrifice in terms of less than optimal earnings and stock price value. Equally, it has become an article of faith amongst many academic and industry analysts that corporations are a club for a well-paid but underperforming corporate elite. It is clear, whatever the merits of each argument, in making corporate elites the object of institutional investor strategy the futures of many firms and industries have become issues of market speculation. Furthermore, cross-market information on corporate performance, assets and liabilities has become essential to the process of relative valuation. In this regard, the demand for common reporting practices has been part and parcel of the emerging global market for corporate control.

The future of capitalism has also become the object of investment decision making. Whereas focus upon the firms of the S&P500 and the FTSE100 is often an exercise in reassigning corporate value from managers (income) to owners (stock price value), institutional investors have also sought to anticipate the next frontier and the next set of market opportunities. It is arguable that the TMT bubble was an extreme instance of this process of looking forward. But it is characteristic of financial institutions to anticipate the creation of value especially in circumstances where there are high potential pay-offs compared to the hard graft associated with extracting value from mergers and acquisitions.

In fact, it is arguable that Anglo-American financial markets are so efficient that only those institutions with the biggest investment in data-processing technology, talent, and organisational capacity are able to systematically add value. Even in the best of circumstances, relatively low expected rates of return and the squeeze on the equity premium suggest that Anglo-American financial markets have become difficult environments in which to add value (and claim a premium on fees).

In this context, institutional investors have moved towards either information intensive or relationship intensive sectors like hedge funds, venture capital, and related forms of alternative investment. Equally, fleet-of-foot investment in areas outside the core competence of most market agents has also become an important refuge from low rates of return in conventional markets. One consequence has been a shift of geographical focus from an overwhelming concentration upon Anglo-American markets to a renewed interest in the rest of the world. All kinds of investment strategies have been deployed, including conventional portfolio investment in continental European stock markets and private placements in China. The tension apparent in these strategies is a tension between information intensive data processing (portfolio investment) and third-party relationship management (growth-based strategies in far-off markets). If executed efficiently, the costs of the former are far lower than the costs of the latter.

Using many of the theories and investment strategies honed in Anglo-American markets, investment houses have treated European markets 'as if' they were amenable to these types of methods and techniques. So, for example, investment firms have built virtual investment portfolios across Europe focusing upon firms and industries rather than firms and countries. Here, the European single market has been taken as the current and future reference point for information-intensive capital market investment strategy. Likewise, active investors have taken larger stakes in local firms hoping to precipitate corporate restructuring, mergers and acquisitions on the scale experienced in Anglo-American markets (Clark and Wójcik 2003). National governments have been resistant, however, to the idea of 'putting in play' their national champions. Notwithstanding lower rates of economic growth in much of continental Europe over the past few decades, nation states have been, more often than not, defensive in terms of the European Commission's campaign to accelerate capital and labour market integration. Nevertheless, there are high fees to be had and potential windfall profits to be gained from anticipating the pricing of changes in past relationships.

Anglo-American financial institutions have sought information and data resources consistent with their experience and investment philosophies. This has prompted the growth of private information and corporate ratings agencies, as well as a drive within the European Commission to encourage European adoption of international financial accounting standards consistent with the needs of global portfolio investment managers. As information has become more readily available across markets built upon accepted metrics, portfolio managers have used their data-processing capacities to exploit hidden market inefficiencies. In part, this has forced 'insiders' to act more like 'outsiders' in that their own investment strategies have come to replicate rival Anglo-American corporations rather than reinforcing practices associated with bank-based insider capitalism. By discounting cross-holdings, old loyalties have been put in play in response to the actions of global financial players (Wójcik 2007).

Here lies, of course, one of the objections to the increasing role of portfolio managers in continental Europe. Not only is continental capitalism the object of portfolio managers, the language of finance is the language of shareholder capitalism rather than continental stakeholder capitalism. This has significant implications for the status of the various classes of corporate stockowners and bondholders, while discounting the union, community and regional alliances that have traditionally underpinned industrial corporations. For critics of financialisation, the language of finance is all about the putative global hegemony of Anglo-American institutions and practices affecting the economy, society, and culture (Jameson 1997). If there is regret about the passing of an era, there is also resistance to the claims of privilege of the new global financial elites relative to those pushed aside by the imperatives of portfolio management.

The TMT bubble precipitated a crisis of confidence in Anglo-American financial markets and, by extension, confidence in the theory of finance honed and articulated over the second half of the twentieth century (Lo 2004). The basic premise underpinning the TMT bubble was the emergence of a 'new economy' based on technology-driven labour productivity and new forms of industry and organisation. As speculation took over stock-by-stock valuation, companies like Microsoft claimed an increasing share of total market capitalisation being, at one point, valued more than half a dozen of the largest industrial corporations including GE, GM, Ford, etc. Many in the market believed there was a free ride to be had on the momentum of the market, subject to claimed superior techniques of market timing, entry and exit. At the height of the bubble, advocates of the new economy peddled rosy forecasts of unending growth and a Dow Jones Industrial Index of 36,000. Although there were some analysts, at the time, who suggested that the bubble would collapse, it is clear that neither market prices nor the language of finance provided adequate reference points for attributing 'value' to firms and industries.[8]

Although much has been written about the consequences of the TMT bubble, it is worth emphasising that at its height Anglo-American markets attracted enormous inflows of capital, particularly from European and Asian investors.

The assumed integrity of market prices combined with widespread confidence in American financial accounting practices and regulations gave investors a false sense of security. And underpinning this confidence was confidence in the language of finance which is, in so many respects, a home-grown institution built upon the success of Anglo-American markets over the past few decades. It was common to see investment company 'roadshows' in continental Europe and East Asia dominated by young American analysts featured as knowing representatives of the new economy. They were perceived to be representatives of a world of finance far superior to the indigenous. By contrast, the future of non-Anglo-American markets seemed in doubt.

The collapse of the bubble and the crisis of confidence in corporate governance prompted significant legislative and regulatory responses (Coffee 2003; Gordon 2003). Indeed, it could be argued that the resulting Sarbanes-Oxley Act on corporate disclosure standards re-established American standards of corporate governance as the global market leader. Furthermore, the current valuation of stock options, so often disputed through the 1990s run-up in American markets, has been part of the reform process, notwithstanding continuing objections from Silicon Valley. These initiatives have focused on the integrity of disclosure including the nature, volume, and certification of the quality of market-sensitive information. Significantly, reforms were concerned to reassure national and international investors of the integrity of market signals as expressed through relative pricing even if there have been doubts about the practical value of the language of finance in the real world.

Investors have also sought other kinds of metrics not so obviously derived from the language of finance. Most importantly, ratings firms have discovered a large and growing market amongst institutional investors. In part, institutional investors use these ratings firms to synthesise and sort the available information, thereby circumventing the heavy costs associated with making sense of the avalanche of information disclosed. But, as well, recognising the limitations of market prices, there has been growing interest in empirical relationships rather than theoretical logic. For example, institutional investors have sought information about the relationship between the measured quality of corporate governance, long-term performance and market value. There has also been increasing interest in the geography of finance in that the scoring of governance practices has had a significant comparative component – using the metrics to evaluate firms in their home jurisdictions against the standards now expected by global investors (Wójcik et al. 2007).

The crisis of confidence in corporate governance has been one element driving the expanding range of metrics used to judge corporate performance. Perhaps just as important, has been the response of institutional investors to increasing pressure to be responsible investors in the sense of actively voting their proxies in annual general meetings. If this appears to be an issue only relevant to the Anglo-American world, we should take care not to underestimate the growing interest of continental European regulators in encouraging such notions of responsibility. In effect, as portfolio investors have moved on to the rest of the world they have also carried with them the responsibility to act in other jurisdictions in ways that go beyond simple entry and exit strategies. Responsibility is sometimes assessed against corporations in their home jurisdictions with respect to their actions in other jurisdictions. At the same time, experience with voting proxies in the US has encouraged foreign institutional investors to look again at related practices in their home jurisdictions. Inevitably, given the range of the issues now considered in annual general meetings, more information is needed than might be found in the disclosure documents of the companies concerned. This has prompted the development of ratings companies that specialise in assessing these issues of corporate social responsibility and providing informed judgment as to the proper course of action.

The attempts of investor activists to use annual general meetings to hold companies to account for their actions in Third World jurisdictions have been significant. Here, coalitions of institutional investors have provided activists with a platform to raise searching questions about the environmental and social standards used by companies where legislative frameworks are poor or non-existent (Clark, Salo and Hebb 2006). The language of finance as inherited from the portfolio investment is silent on these issues or even hostile to raising them. Here again, measuring performance, providing justifiable metrics by which to judge performance, and assessing performance against accepted and justifiable environmental and social reference points have prompted institutional investors to seek third-party providers of those metrics (Clark and Hebb 2005). As a consequence, there is a market for a broad range of global metrics, and those metrics must be certified. By contrast, more often than not, there is little in the way of agreed robust 'public' standards through which to judge these issues.

IMPLICATIONS AND CONCLUSIONS

Modern portfolio theory is widely acclaimed as the most important innovation in finance theory over the twentieth century (Bernstein 1992). It provides a rationale for diversifying risk through spreading investment across a broad range of market securities. It provides a model for option pricing with many sophisticated versions developed over the past 25 years. It also provides a recipe for public policy, especially for enhancing the quality and quantity of information on traded securities such that market pricing is more efficient. On these grounds alone, it became *the* language of finance, squeezing out traditional forms of investment as well as challenging models of industrial organisation that privilege insiders over outsiders. For some, it threatens the very future of continental European inherited systems of accumulation and income distribution. For others, it is thoroughly modern and a normative reference point for the future – where economic agents, whatever their home jurisdictions, will converge on the most efficient form of economic and social organisation.

Being a recipe for investment, the language of finance relies very heavily upon the quality and quantity of information provided to market agents. But information processing costs money. Indeed, it could be argued that one comparative advantage of institutional investors over individual investors is the capacity of the former to process information in ways that can uncover arbitrage opportunities hidden from individuals who have neither the computing power nor the analytical tools to make sense of the available data. More importantly, information need not lead market pricing but can be a form of ex-post rationalisation which explains how and why an investment strategy may have succeeded or failed. We must take care not to idealise investment strategy as if it is always led by information as opposed to being subject to information channelling according to institutional imperatives. Finally, as information reflects past, current, and expected events, information must be valued. The most obvious point of reference in valuing information is a theoretical conception of market performance.

However, this was precisely the problem revealed by the TMT bubble and the crisis of confidence in corporate governance. Not only are markets different from one another in terms of their underlying political economies, for all the arguments in favour of convergence to one ideal form of the market, economic and political interests remain embedded in those markets such that adaptation is the more likely response rather than wholesale structural change (Sassen 2004). This is apparent in the cross-listing of firms from one market to another. It is also reflected in the geographical inertia of some types of market agents compared to others. In any event, markets are quite unstable over time in terms of the motive forces or imperatives driving market trading. Therefore, information may be more or less relevant for trade between different markets, and more or less relevant over time for trade within markets. Inter-jurisdictional differences in market structure combined with unanticipated shifts in market-specific sentiment are likely to mean that disclosure is always less than optimal and is always being 'reformed' in relation to past failings.

We have argued in this chapter that the language of finance has given way over the past few years to a more complex and empirically based investment practice. While it remains as a test of legitimacy for any investment professional, it is widely acknowledged to be at once too abstract and at another level too often exclusive of market relevant actions and sentiments (Shleifer 2000). At the limit, it suggests that there is only one kind of market where, in fact, other kinds of markets have persisted even if they have been challenged by the power and influence of Anglo-American markets. If quietly developed in the shadow cast by the language of finance, in the aftermath of the TMT bubble these new approaches to investment management have come out into the open. Using information asymmetries between market agents who have access to nominally the same information is an important element in market arbitrage. Likewise, being fleet-of-foot in relation to unpredictable and unanticipated shocks has become one response to the apparent difficulties of sustaining superior performance.

Recognising these trends, there is a burgeoning market for third party information processing and valuation. There are many kinds of service providers in this market, some of which focus upon quantitative scoring while others focus upon qualitative assessment. In between, there are all kinds of ways of combining qualitative and quantitative information such that institutional investors' interests in tailored information products can be met. By this logic, the rules and regulations governing information disclosure simply set the stage for market agents that specialise in information processing rather than representing sufficient quality for market agents to trade in their own right. If so, national and international accounting standards relevant to financial markets may have a public benefit but be much less than that required for market agents to be competitive. By this logic, as the language of finance crumbles into an immense array of investment strategies, information itself will become increasingly variegated and private. Ironically, institutional investors may use their market power to claim the privileges accorded 'insiders' of an earlier era.

NOTES

1. Recent research on the 'varieties of capitalism' has resuscitated this kind of characterisation (see generally Hall and Soskice 2001). As we shall see, however, our argument is not entirely sympathetic to this literature in that we argue theoretically and empirically that the past is not *ipso facto* the future – all kinds of economic agents have an interest in making the future in their own image (see Clark and Wójcik 2005).
2. These developments have been described in various ways. Most importantly, Clark (2000) suggested the phrase 'pension fund capitalism' while Hawley and Williams (2000) referred to these developments as 'fiduciary capitalism' (compare with Drucker 1997 where he first raised the prospect of 'pension fund socialism').
3. We should take care not to exaggerate the innovation potential of financial markets. Just as the 'efficient markets hypothesis' prompted the development of one kind of market-pricing theory, it also denied the relevance of other kinds of market-pricing theories. There is a cost to be borne from the hegemony of one kind of theory – innovation can be stifled in these circumstances (witness the resistance to non-Bayesian notions of probability) whatever the virtues of competition (compare Baumol 2002).
4. Reinforcing our point was the announcement in late 2004 that the Deutsche Börse would adopt English as the 'official' language of the Frankfurt market, to be used in all shareholder communications, trading and announcements. No doubt this announcement was spurred by the take-over offer for the London Stock Exchange. Equally, it reasonably reflects the actual practice of the global financial industry.
5. In much of the academic literature, 1973 is seen as the end of the post-war 'golden era' and the emergence of a new regime of accumulation commonly referred to as post-Fordism (see Amin 1994). We are agnostic on this notion of a binary structural transformation while agreeing with Clowes that the rise of financial capitalism and the decline of managerial capitalism can be conveniently captured by a date such as 1973 – the point where two trends cross over one-another (see also Webber and Rigby 1996).
6. For a useful analysis of this type of simple formula for asset allocation, and its consequences for investment returns, comparing 1987 with 2004, see Ambachtsheer (2004).
7. Of course, the growth and development of Anglo-American stock markets is also due to the inflow of financial assets from funded pension plans prompting more efficient systems of capital allocation and, at the limit, higher rates of real economic growth (Davis and Hu 2006)
8. In fact, Dale (2004) argues that over confidence in the metrics of market valuation combined with an inability or unwillingness to recognise discrepancies in market pricing is characteristic of all speculative bubbles. His research focused on the South Sea bubble, drawing instructive lessons and commonalities with the TMT bubble.

ACKNOWLEDGEMENTS

This chapter is based on a larger project on institutional investors and global financial markets funded, in part, by a Canadian Social Sciences and Humanities Research Council project at the University of Toronto, drawing upon previous research funded by the European Science Foundation and the UK Economic and Social Research Council. We would like to thank our colleagues for their interest and comments on these projects including Lisa Hagerman, Rob Bauer (ABP), Jamie Salo, Kendra Strauss and Adam Tickell (Bristol). The first-named author also benefited from a conversation on Europe and related topics with Jeffrey Gordon (Columbia). None of the above should be held accountable for the views and opinions expressed herein.

REFERENCES

Ambachtsheer, K. (2004), 'Our 60-40 asset mix policy advice in 1987: wise or foolish?', *The Ambachtsheer Letter*, Toronto: KPA Advisory Services.

Amin, A. (Ed.) (1994), *Post-fordism: A Reader*, Oxford: Blackwell.

Arnott, R.D. (2004), 'Is our industry intellectually lazy?', *Financial Analysts Journal* 60(1), 6-8.

Baumol, W. (2002), *The Free-Market Innovation Machine*, Princeton: Princeton University Press.

Bernstein, P.L. (1992), *Capital Ideas: The Improbable Origins of Modern Wall Street*, New York: Free Press.

Cable, V. (1999), *Globalization and Global Governance*, London: Royal Institute of International Affairs.

Campbell, J. and L. Viceira (2002), *Strategic Asset Allocation*, Oxford: Oxford University Press.

Chandler, A. (1990), *Scale and Scope: The Dynamics of Industrial Capitalism*, Cambridge MA: Harvard University Press.

Chan-Lau, J. (2004), Pension funds and emerging markets, WP/04/181, Washington DC: International Monetary Fund.

Clark, G.L. (2000), *Pension Fund Capitalism*, Oxford: Oxford University Press.

Clark, G.L. (2003), *European Pensions and Global Finance*, Oxford: Oxford University Press.

Clark, G.L. (2006), 'Pension fund governance: models of regulation and accountability', in *The Oxford Handbook of Pensions and Retirement Income* edited by G.L. Clark, A, Munnell, and M. Orszag, Oxford: Oxford University Press, p. 483–500.

Clark, G.L. and T. Hebb (2004), 'Corporate engagement: The fifth stage of capitalism', *Relations Industrielles/Industrial Relations*, **59**, 142–69.

Clark, G.L. and T. Hebb (2005), 'Why should they care?', *Environment and Planning A*, **37**, 2015–31.

Clark, G.L. and N.J. Thrift (2004), 'The return of bureaucracy: managing dispersed knowledge in global finance', in *The Sociology of Financial Markets* edited by K. Knorr Cetina and A. Preda, Oxford: Oxford University Press, p. 229–49.

Clark, G.L., N.J. Thrift, and A. Tickell (2004), 'Performing finance: the industry, the media, and its image', *Review of International Political Economy* **11**, 289–310.

Clark, G.L., J. Salo, and T. Hebb (2006), 'Shareholder activism in the public spotlight', 2001–2004, WPG 06-02, Oxford: Oxford University Centre for the Environment.

Clark, G.L. and D. Wójcik (2003), 'An economic geography of global finance: ownership concentration and stock price volatility in German firms and regions', *Annals, Association of American Geographers*, **93**, 909–24.

Clark, G.L. and D. Wójcik (2005), 'Path dependence and the alchemy of finance: the economic geography of the German model, 1997–2003', *Environment and Planning A*, **37**, 1769–91.

Clowes, M. (2000), *The Money Flood: How Pension Funds Revolutionized Investing*, New York: Wiley.

Coffee, J.C. (2003), 'What caused Enron? A capsule social and economic history over the 1990s', available at ssrn.com (abstract 373581).

Dale, R. (2004), *The First Crash: Lessons from the South Sea Bubble*, Princeton: Princeton University Press.

Davis, E.P. and B. Steil (2001), *Institutional Investors*, Cambridge MA: MIT Press.

Davis, P. and Y-W. Hu (2006), 'Saving, funding and economic growth', in *The Oxford Handbook of Pensions and Retirement Income* edited by G.L. Clark, A, Munnell, and M. Orszag, Oxford: Oxford University Press, p. 201–18.

Drucker, P. (1995), *The Pension Fund Revolution*, Piscataway: Transaction Books.

Fama, E. (1970), 'Efficient capital markets: a review of theory and empirical work', *Journal of Finance*, **25**, 383–417.

Fama, E. and K R. French (2004), 'The capital asset pricing model: theory and evidence'. *Journal of Financial Perspectives*, **18**, 25–46.

Gordon, J.N. (2003), 'Governance failures of the Enron board and the new information order of Sarbanes-Oxley', Working Paper 416, Cambridge MA: J.M. Olin Center for Law, Business and Economics, Harvard University.

Hall, P.A. and D. Soskice (eds) (2001), *Varieties of Capitalism: The Institutional Foundations of Comparative Advantage*, Oxford: Oxford University Press.

Hawley, J.P. and A.T. Williams (2000), *The Rise of Fiduciary Capitalism*, Philadelphia: University of Pennsylvania Press.

Hayes, S. L. (ed.) (1993), *Financial Services: Perspectives and Challenges*, Boston: Harvard Business School Press.

Hebb, T. and D. Wójcik (2005), 'The institutional investment value chain: CalPERS' emerging markets strategy', *Environment and Planning A*, **37**, 1955–74.

Hilton, D.J. (2003), 'Psychology and the financial markets: applications to understanding and remediating investment decision-making', in I. Brocas and J. Carrillo (eds), *The Psychology of Economic Decisions, Volume 1: Rationality and Well-Being*, Cambridge: Cambridge University Press, p. 273–97.

Ho, T. and S.B. Lee. (2004), *The Oxford Guide to Financial Modeling*, Oxford: Oxford University Press.

Houthakker, H. and P.J. Williamson (1996), *The Economics of Financial Markets*, Oxford: Oxford University Press.

Jameson, F. (1997), 'Culture and finance capital', *Critical Inquiry*, **24**, 246–65.

Jensen, M. (1993), 'The modern industrial revolution, exit, and the failure of internal control systems', *Journal of Finance*, **48**, 831–80.

Litterman, B. et al. (2003), *Modern Investment Management*, New York: Wiley.

Lo, A. (2004), *The adaptive markets hypothesis: market efficiency from an evolutionary perspective*, Cambridge MA: Laboratory for Financial Engineering, MIT.

Markowitz, H.M. (1952), 'Portfolio selection', *Journal of Finance*, **7**, 77–91.

Pettit, P. (2002), *Rules, Reasons, and Norms*, Oxford: Oxford University Press.

Power, M. (2004), 'Enterprise risk management and the organization of uncertainty in financial firms', in K. Knorr Cetina and A. Preda (eds), *The Sociology of Finance*, Oxford: Oxford University Press, p. 250–68.

Roy, A.D. (1952), 'Safety first and the holding of financial assets', *Econometrica*, **20**, 431–49.

Sassen, S. (2004), 'The embeddedness of electronic markets: the case of global capital markets', in K. Knorr Cetina and A. Preda (eds), *The Sociology of Finance*, Oxford: Oxford University Press, p. 17–37.

Shiller, R.J. (2000), *Irrational Exuberance*, Princeton: Princeton University Press.

Shiller, R.J. (2003), *The New Financial Order*, Princeton: Princeton University Press.

Shleifer, A. (2000), *Market Inefficiency*, Oxford: Oxford University Press.

Webber, M.J. and D.L. Rigby (1996), *The Golden Age Illusion: Rethinking Postwar Capitalism*, New York: Guilford.

Wilhelm, W.J. and Downing, J.D. (2001), *Information Markets: What Business Can Learn from Financial Innovation*, Boston MA: Harvard Business School Press.

Wilson, D. and R. Purushothaman (2003), 'Dreaming with the BRICs: The Path to 2050. Global Economics Paper 99', New York: Goldman Sachs.

Wójcik, D. (2003), 'Change in the German model of corporate governance: evidence from blockholdings 1997-2001', *Environment and Planning A*, **35**, 1431–1458.

Wójcik, D. (2007), 'Convergence in corporate governance: empirical evidence from Europe and the challenges for economic geography', *Journal of Economic Geography* (forthcoming).

Wójcik, D., Clark, G.L., and Bauer, R. (2007), 'Corporate governance and cross-listing: evidence from European companies', *Competition and Change* (forthcoming).

3   The IASB:
Some Personal Reflections

Kevin M. Stevenson

INTRODUCTION

The first of April 2006 is the fifth anniversary of the formation of the International Accounting Standards Board (IASB). For many, the remarkable globalisation of financial reporting and the activities of the IASB over that five-year period are inextricably entwined. But, of course, the IASB itself is part of a much longer historical movement towards achieving global financial reporting standards. This chapter reflects on the first five years of the IASB and looks forward to the next five years and the challenges ahead.

GLOBALISATION = IASB?

With nearly 100 countries requiring or allowing application of international financial reporting standards (IFRS) by either 2005 or 2007, it would be fair to say that the IASB has been remarkably successful in its short life. That success has been demonstrated by the decisions of Europe, Australia, Canada, New Zealand, South Africa, China and many other countries to either adopt IFRS or to harmonise with them. Further, the agreements of the FASB and IASB to converge their programmes, project teams, conceptual frameworks and accounting standards[1] has ensured that the main drivers for future change are being aligned. Most of these developments could not have been expected to have occurred within the first five years of the IASB's existence.

However, at the end of the day, the IASB is a private sector entity, orphaned at birth, with a small complement of people, no equity and no long-term finance. Moreover, it has no authority over any auditor, preparer or regulator. How then can it be so influential?

The answer to this question, and the lie in equating globalisation of financial reporting with the IASB's activities, is that there has been a long held view among influential auditors, preparers and regulators that global accounting standards were essential. In other words, the existence and influence of the IASB are the result of market demand.

DEMANDS FOR GLOBAL STANDARDS

But was that demand necessarily altruistic? It seems not. In Europe, the globalisation of financial markets had in the 1990s led several high profile entities to elect to adopt US GAAP. Many in Europe either feared the demands of US GAAP or resented the intrusion of the US. To those who feared the spread of US GAAP, the standards of the IASB's predecessor, the International Accounting Standards Committee (IASC), represented a softer alternative. The IASC's standards were beaten out of consensus between people from a large number of countries. IASC products, and the processes for arriving at them, had been evolving since 1973.[2] They were known, not particularly feared and perhaps thought to be capable of being influenced through concerted representational efforts. It will be offensive to some, but it must be said, that some in Europe probably felt that they could, to an extent, manage the IASC's discussions with no resulting calamities. In contrast, many other conscientious Europeans and many from other countries were professionally motivated and prepared to put in enormous efforts for the discipline in which they believed.

Whether any parties could actually manage the IASC for their own purposes is highly doubtful. Nonetheless, in the author's experience at least, some in Europe considered they had influence in IASC circles.

For some preparers and auditors, the establishment of global accounting standards offered considerable convenience. It promised to reduce the number and complexity of systems used across borders, increase the mobility of staff, and reduce the confusion caused by reporting multiple results for the same entity. No doubt, in some domestic environments, the adoption of international standards also promised a slowing down, and perhaps a blunting, of the increasingly difficult demands of domestic standard setters.

At an international regulatory level, the enticements of the International Organization of Securities Commissions (IOSCO) to the IASC to work for the removal of foreign registrant reconciliation requirements for cross-border activity were attractive to multi-national companies, large accounting firms and, in pursuit of their own objectives and recognition, members of the IASC. IOSCO had indicated that it would consider accepting IASC standards for cross-border registration purposes if those standards were of an acceptable level. The IASC in its later years engaged in an improvements programme to try to reach that level.[3]

Beyond these interests were the truly professional aspirations of those who wanted to see financial reporting requirements better serving the needs of users. These people were present among all of the groups involved with the setting, application and enforcement of financial reporting requirements. Their numbers were not great, but their persistence and foresight could not be faulted.

Ultimately, the efforts of the IASC to put in place a set of core standards that could meet IOSCO's needs demonstrated two things: (a) the goal was not impossible, but (b) the structure and resources of the IASC were inadequate to allow the goal to be met in the short run. The IASC's 'volunteer' model, that is, a model in which professionals from around the world donated their time to attending meetings and preparing or reviewing papers, needed to be replaced by a model of considerably greater resources and efforts.

The realisation that the IASC needed a dramatic makeover opened the way for debate as to what the replacement model should look like. A great schism came into being between those who wanted an expert, independent structure similar to that of the FASB (but without the presence of an SEC) and those who wanted what may be termed a bicameral parliamentary model in which representationalism was key.

History shows that the expert, independent model won out, due to the efforts of those with professionalisation of standard setting in mind. Thus, the congruence of vested and altruistic forces that gave the opportunity to form the IASB broke down at the last and there was no turning back – it was too late. A good deal of bitterness at the outcome survived the formation of the IASB and seems to have often surfaced in later interchanges between the IASB and some from Europe. Those who failed to achieve the bicameral model did, however, have influence over regulatory arrangements in Europe. They chose to support the legal backing by Europe for IFRS, but nevertheless worked to create the 'upper house' of their preferred model in the form of the European endorsement process. This explains much of the difficulty faced by the IASB in achieving endorsement of the 2005 stable platform of standards.

As the IASB has developed and established a working relationship with the FASB, it has become evident to those who regarded the international standards to be a soft alternative that they are now confronted by a global version of the FASB. This version is focussed on user needs and not upon preparer, auditor or regulatory convenience. This was demonstrated by the IASB issuing a standard on share-based payments that broke through decades of preparer resistance in the US.

LEGITIMATE BIRTH?

It can be said that the first five years of the IASB were the culmination of the efforts of many over a very long period. However, the motivations of those supporting the IASB's formation were mixed, as have been the responses of regulators in giving authority to those standards.

This is not the firmest grounding for the IASB. A coalition of parties opposed to the IASB's requirements could see a future splintering of the efforts to achieve global standards. That coalition may not be so forthright as to cause a replacement body to come into being, but it could significantly harm the IASB through patchy endorsement of standards, or by entering the process of interpretation. There have been signs that some in Europe see interpretation as an area in which influence may be regained.

The danger to global accounting standards is, therefore, that political realities are not understood or evident and that subversion of the efforts of the IASB may come from those who do not have a user focus. Some of these parties may not even realise that they have a vested interest and probably would object to assertions that they do. It must be stressed that the motivations of many parties may seem appropriate to their roles, but still not be user focussed. Regulators seeking rules that suit enforcement, accounting bodies concerned about their self-regulatory responsibilities, domestic standard setters seeking to maintain their influence, firms confronted by difficult clients and many others have vested interests that are not always evident to themselves or to others, but are nevertheless inconsistent with users' needs.

But are the standard setters, and in particular the IASB, themselves free from criticism of vested interests? The existence of legal backing for IFRS has no doubt increased the focus upon and influence of the IASB, and even domestic standard setters. A strong impression has been created that the IASB has been prepared to enter into significant and prolonged dialogue with the European Union (EU) when confronted by the threat of non-endorsement. The brinkmanship of the EU in its move to IFRS has, unfortunately, risked the value of the brand it has chosen, IFRS. That brinkmanship has taken the form of partial endorsement of the financial instruments standards and the continual threat of the European Financial Reporting Advisory Group (EFRAG) voting down the endorsement of standards.[4] It has also raised speculation that Europe has either much to hide or has a low capacity to understand or comply with IFRS. The IASB's own image has probably also suffered from the endorsement process. It is perhaps being seen to be prepared to 'trade horses' or to be preoccupied with Europe when compared with its attention to other domestic situations in which IFRS has been adopted. Indeed, the IASB itself intensely dislikes being characterised as the European standard setter.

TECHNICAL PROGRESS

In assessing the first five years of the IASB it is easy to be diverted by the political side-show of Europe and the high-profile battles that the IASB has had with the European Commission, EFRAG, central bankers and vocal opponents from French banks and insurance companies.[5] The more critical question to address is whether the IASB should be happy with the way in which it is trying to improve the lot of users of financial reporting.

Almost certainly the board would not be content with its technical progress. It came together revelling in the prospect of developing high quality standards in a professional, independent and progressive manner. There were many issues that Board members wanted to see addressed and they felt they were free from past constraints. There was almost a naivety among the Board that led it to believe that the only significant hurdle to progress was obtaining the right number of votes at its own table.

But were the expectations at the beginning realistic? Would setting standards at the IASB ever have been free from exactly the same forces as experienced by domestic standard setting? Would there have been no additional frustrations to deal with on the global stage? The answer to all these questions is undoubtedly 'no'.

The IASB first had to discover and deal with differences in culture, expectations, knowledge and approach among its own membership and between the Board and the few staff that it inherited. All boards take time to settle. The IASB was an uncomfortable group in its first year or two, often considered to be 'loud', sometimes seen to be culturally inept and too often to be out of touch with the consequences of its demands upon its staff. Outsiders tended to think the Board was US dominated and that it was ideologically driven and preoccupied by a desire for measurement reform.

However, boards do take time to come together and it does take time to build professional staff capacity. By late in 2003, many were doubtful that the Board could produce the standards that were needed for 2005. However, the Board was by then a much more cohesive body and the staff very dedicated. History shows that huge productivity was achieved by the March 2004 cut-off for the 2005 stable platform. Soon the cry was 'too much' rather than 'when will they ...?'.

The revision of many of the old IASs and the issuance of the first seven IFRS, together with the establishment of the International Financial Reporting Interpretations Committee (IFRIC) and the issuance of its initial interpretations, has in fact been a great achievement in less than five years; but still the Board would be unhappy. Why? The answer is that the Board is comprised of people who are not content to recycle matters that have been addressed over many years and are not the stuff of innovation. And, indeed, their abilities go far beyond that level of challenge.

The Board has reformed the accounting for business combinations and share-based payments, but even these complex areas have not required enormous innovation. Rather they have represented achievement through finalisation of past thinking. The Board has spent much time on financial instruments and has achieved standards that have been in gestation for over a decade. Again, the performance has been in achieving closure of an important stage in the life of financial reporting for financial instruments.

However, whilst the Board can feel rightly that business combinations and share-based payments are topics well on their way to better future standards, they are less than happy about financial instruments. They see the standards as being complex, arbitrary, anti-abuse oriented, internally inconsistent and inconsistent with the conceptual framework. They are unhappy with the classifications of financial assets and liabilities, the inconsistent measurement bases between such classifications, the lack of logic in hedge accounting, the failure to make progress on de-recognition and the difficult and inaccessible nature of the two standards (IAS 32 and IAS 39).[6]

In other major projects, insurance, revenue and related liabilities and performance reporting, the Board has laboured long and hard without much reward; hence the frustration that the Board feels about its own performance. Some of that frustration is misplaced and some of it self-induced. The Board, for all its ability, has found it difficult to establish a working pattern that sees it make steady progress in clear directions on difficult topics. In large part that has been due to the distractions of putting the stable platform to bed, dealing with spirited and politically inspired opposition and just trying to do too many things at once.

PAR FOR THE COURSE?

The Board's frustration reflects the personality of the Board and the standards that it sets itself. As indicated above, the achievements of the Board over the first five years, the achieved spread of IFRS and the likely future of IFRS in China, South Korea, Russia and many other countries all mean that the Board has achieved much more than could have been expected in 2001.

But the frustrations of the Board are important. Their removal is essentially the legitimate target of the Board over its second five-year plan – the period in which major individual projects will characterize the Board's endeavours.

Nevertheless, it behoves all standard setters to clearly recognise that managing change is their main task, and a complicated one when performed on a world scale. Devising new and insightful solutions is the attraction for those who take on standard setting, but not often the actual opportunity on a day-to-day basis.

THE CONCEPTUAL FRAMEWORK

The 'sleeper in the pack' in terms of assessing the IASB is how well it handles the development of a new conceptual framework. Few boards operate for any length of time without feeling the need to establish or revise the conceptual framework. Both the IASB and FASB have felt this need and are now working to replace their existing frameworks with a single new framework – a framework equally recognised within their respective GAAP hierarchies. The outside world, and maybe even the two Boards themselves, underestimate the potential of this project.

In terms of stylistic ambition, the conceptual framework is the means by which creativity can be expressed – creativity based on the depth of experience of both the IASB and FASB. That depth is a 'once-in-a-lifetime' opportunity as it will probably be impossible in the future to assemble so many experienced and talented people. The demise of domestic standard setting will mean that the avenues that have been used by those people to reach where they are today will not be available to future generations. New pathways need to be developed.

THE OTHER SIDE OF THE FENCE

One of the more subtle but most important strategies of the IASB has been to accentuate principles and not rules. They have forcibly rejected the role of 'street vendor in the market for excuses'. The Board has not found it hard to get support for this principles-based approach – though many misunderstand what the Board means by that phrase. Some assume that latitude is being given. However, the Board intends that each standard is explicitly connected to the Framework by a clearly stated principle or principles. They see this approach as being a means of achieving coherence, completeness and integrity, without a mountain of guidance. The Board reasons that preparers by and large have the ability to faithfully apply principles, that principles are not so easily engineered out of the way and that numerous rules are in fact counterproductive. A set of standards that articulates well with a Framework would be a very powerful tool.

In the US, the conceptual framework project could lead to a change in status for the Framework. The endeavour is to have it come within the GAAP hierarchy, in the manner already set down in IFRS. The FASB is also committed to a principles-based approach but it is also the keeper of a considerable heritage that is excruciating in its detail in some areas. As the FASB manages the revision of GAAP it will face the possibility of old and new forces pulling against one another. If the Framework becomes authoritative and the culture has not fully adjusted to a principles-based approach, it would appear that considerable tension could emerge. Under Sarbanes Oxley requirements what will the reaction be to addressing the new GAAP (i.e. including the Framework) for previously unregulated areas?

The pressure by the IASB to have the market take charge of its own destiny when interpreting standards seems to have worked far better than anyone has realised or would admit. At the very least, the major firms now have global consulting and quality control mechanisms in place. Also, they do not now turn automatically to formal interpretation as the means to an answer. They realise that they have to 'call' issues based on their reading of the standards and the principles involved. Furthermore, the intellectual capability now applied to issues is considerably more than was ever applied to domestic GAAP, including US GAAP. Now every part of large firms has to be concerned with how issues are handled.

The author strongly suspects that this is also having a beneficial indirect effect on the consistency of auditing. No longer is there the cloud of domestic requirements that would induce a foreign reviewer to hesitate in being critical about how an issue is handled.

More fundamentally, there has been a renaissance in the importance of technical knowledge and training within firms. Now there is the scale and opportunity for consistent training in financial reporting issues, as well as the need for accounting issues to be resolved consistently across borders.

Some seem to fear that this is establishing further barriers to entry that favour the Big Four. They have the means to come to sophisticated answers on a global basis, but who answers the questions of the smaller firms or the preparers that consider the Big Four are wrong on an issue? Some domestic standard setters have suggested that they need to engage in interpretation for this very reason. However, it seems to be doubtful logic that interpretation should be the means for ensuring equality of ability across practising firms. Education may take up that cause, but it does not seem to be a valid basis for interpretation. Otherwise, the most inept in the market will drive the level of interpretation. The game is complicated and if entities are going to hold themselves up as competent they must be able to understand the principles and standards in play and they must establish the means of obtaining assurance about the views they develop.

No doubt at some point there will be failures in entities that reveal liberal interpretations of standards and there will be the inevitable calls for tightening standards.[7] However, it will be interesting to see how the courts use explicitly stated principles to question the actions of preparers and auditors. It may be less acceptable that the letter of standards is followed but not the principles.

In this regard, practice is bracing itself for the activities of securities and other regulators. Those regulators will take time to adjust to the subtlety of principles-based standards and may be disconcerted when it becomes evident that there may be more than one acceptable way to meet the requirements of a principle. Some early mistakes by regulators could cause knee-jerk reactions that set back the cause of re-establishing professional judgement.

It is this author's experience that large firms are devoting enormous reserves to ensure consistent and proper application of accounting principles, and that decision making on complex issues is being upgraded significantly. Now issues are not handled in ad hoc ways – they are checked against world databases, discussed by expert subject and industry panels and resolved much more consistently than in the past when the need for dialogue and consistency just did not exist. Interestingly, this pressure for consistent answers exists under principles-based standards, but did not exist to anywhere near the same degree under domestic standards.

NEW FRONTIERS

The remaining chapters in this book document developments in various places around the world. However, it is worth examining how the IASB's original strategy of working with eight liaison standards setters has evolved.[8] Now five of those countries are either IFRS adopters or are about to be (Australia, New Zealand, France, Germany and the UK), one has signalled its intention to withdraw from establishing domestic standards in favour of moving to converged US and IFRS standards (Canada) and the US is working solidly with the IASB in the major convergence programme. Japan also has a convergence programme but is the laggard of the group.

The IASB has therefore widened its communications focus to take in other standard setters, recognising that the task has changed from five years ago. The new frontiers are in the subcontinent, Asia, South America, Africa and in Russia. China is proving to be a conscientious improver of its standards and intends to ensure consistency with IFRS in 2006. Korea is hoping to change in 2008. Few Asian countries of any size will not be on IFRS by 2008 or 2009. Russia is also on the move and South America has shown signs of changing. Some African countries have been longstanding supporters of international standards and others have plans for change.

Indeed, by the end of the second five-year term of the IASB, it is now a reasonable hope that IFRS will have been accepted on a fairly universal basis. That seemed unlikely five years ago.

BUT WHAT OF THE US?

If we suppose that nearly all major countries will have adopted IFRS by 2010, will that include the US? It certainly seems reasonable to expect that in five years' time there should be an established track record of the IASB and FASB handling major projects together. Hopefully, they will have issued a new single Framework, issued several common standards on major projects (including leases, pensions, revenue, performance reporting, aspects of financial instruments and insurance) and have a more clearly integrated approach to interpretation. But would US GAAP be formally replaced by IFRS in the US, albeit with the FASB remaining as the local face of international standard setting?

My personal view is that five years is too short a time frame for this to happen. Indeed, if the list of projects above is finished the Boards will have been both very productive and very persuasive on the world stage. The latter may be the greater accomplishment as those projects will involve much more technical development of financial reporting than has been achieved in IFRS to date.

As the IASB, FASB and SEC embark on their roadmap towards removal of the need for foreign registrants to reconcile to US GAAP, there will be diversion from the major projects. In some respects that roadmap represents another catch-up or improvements period, similar to the last five years.

It is not clear to the author that the removal of the reconciliation requirement is as important as seems to be generally accepted by the IASB and many others. It would be a boon for preparers and auditors in terms of convenience, but would it remove a spur for developing financial reporting? Once the prize was achieved, would there be extreme reluctance to further develop financial reporting via IFRS? Also, is there as much to be gained by the FASB in the removal of the requirement? Or will they see it as a diversion from users' needs for the sake of foreign registrants' convenience?

There are no easy answers to these questions, but it is to be hoped that in five years the successful completion of the projects mentioned will make the reconciliation largely irrelevant. Then the culture of continuous improvement and the focus on users' needs will exist more evidently.

Nevertheless, there remains the need for the US to significantly overhaul the baggage it carries in the form of old GAAP, written in different eras and in different styles. The FASB is aiming to recodify GAAP, but the sense is that there is a long way to go and probably a need for a major project to be established that gives recognition to the size of the task.[9]

In practice, we do see evidence that detailed US GAAP is accepted by default as IFRS when IFRS does not explicitly cover some issue. This is sometimes highly dangerous as in some instances non-US preparers are not fully appreciating the context of the US GAAP. Over time this could mean that a hybrid form of informal GAAP is created in a manner that inhibits reform by giving too much recognition to the literal reading of standards and not enough to the application of principles.

THE IMPORTANCE OF THE CADRE

Comments were made above about the opportunity that exists today to use the impressive talent of the IASB. It was also indicated that the Board took time to come together and to develop a working approach. To this point, only two members of the IASB have left the Board (Bob Herz, to chair the FASB, and Harry Schmidt, who retired after many years of service to the IASC and IASB). But others have limited terms to run and the next five years will end with quite a different population on the Board (or at least a different population about to come onto the Board).

It is to be hoped that the efficiency of the Board is at its peak over these next five years so that its inherent abilities and its communal knowledge are fully utilised.

It is also to be hoped that the Trustees continue to be alert to the qualities needed of future Board members and that they are not the victims of concerted efforts to have representatives of vested interests appointed to the Board. The author was surprised in his time with the Board at the ambition of some groups and individuals in this regard.

CONCLUSION

The IASB should be delighted with its first five years of operations. They have led to a platform from which high quality global standards can be expected to be developed over the next five years.

The first five years saw considerable political pressures come to bear. The ways in which they were handled were not always optimal, but no lasting damage seems to have resulted.

However, the next five years will require the Board to achieve outcomes that will be judged on more technical grounds – grounds based on user needs. In the author's view, a preoccupation with removal of reconciliation requirements for foreign registrants in the US would be unfortunate. If it is achieved by serving users' needs through completion of major projects, the IASB and FASB will have been very successful. The Board must not become embroiled with regulators in that exercise in any way that looks like the experiences with Europe and it must continue to ensure that its relationships around the world are balanced and informed. Neither the US nor Europe is the proxy for the world and the European Commission is not, no matter how much it protests, a 'customer' of the Board.

NOTES

1. FASB (2002)'The Norwalk Agreement' and its extension in March 2004.
2. Its formation year.
3. See website www.iasplus.com/restruct/restiosc.htm.
4. Brackney K.S and P.R. Witmer (November 2005), 'The European Union's Role in International Standards Setting: Will the Bumps in the road to Convergence Affect the SEC's Plans?', *The CPA Journal* (online).
5. Ibid.
6. The IASB has formed a working group to consider how IAS 32 and IAS 39 might be fundamentally improved in the future. See www.iasb.org/docs/projects.
7. Watts, R. and J. Zimmerman (1978), 'Towards a Positive Theory of the Determination of Accounting Standards', *The Accounting Review*, **53** (January), 112–34.
8. USA, UK, Japan, Canada, France, Germany, Australia and New Zealand.
9. Smith, L.W. (2005), 'The FASB's Efforts Toward Simplification', *The FASB Report*, February 28, Norwalk, FASB.

4   Globalisation of Accounting Standards: A UK Perspective

David Alexander

INTRODUCTION

Two simple but significant points need to be remembered concerning accounting harmonisation. These are firstly that it is a dynamic and long-term process, and secondly that the need for harmonisation implies pre-existing differences. To understand the nature of the harmonisation process and of the UK's pivotal but problematic position in that process, it is necessary to explore the main characteristics of the starting position. A helpful framework within which to do this is that established by Nobes (1983). Eschewing the already developing statistical cluster analysis tradition (e.g. Nair and Frank, 1980), Nobes attempted an analysis and classification based on investigation and appraisal. He gave detailed consideration to 14 countries, and the essence of his conclusions is shown in Figure 4.1.

Nobes postulated a fundamental class dichotomy related to the purpose for which financial information is likely to be used, which he labelled micro/fair/ judgemental, and macro/uniform. *Micro* implies an emphasis on the individual reporting entity. The economic decisions needing to be made, and which the financial statements provide information to assist, relate primarily to the reporting entity, to its use of resources and demand for finance. This is consistent with a finance market emphasising equity investors. In order to produce information relevant to each specific reporting entity in its own specific circumstances, the reporting system needs to be flexible enough to adapt to the relevant specifics. This implies the need for *judgement*. This judgement, which by definition cannot be applied precisely or objectively, needs at least to be applied *fairly*.

Macro implies an emphasis on the wider economy and on broader economic planning. The economic decisions needing the reported financial information as inputs into the decision-making process will be less concerned with financial

Figure 4.1 Groupings of some major countries in 1980

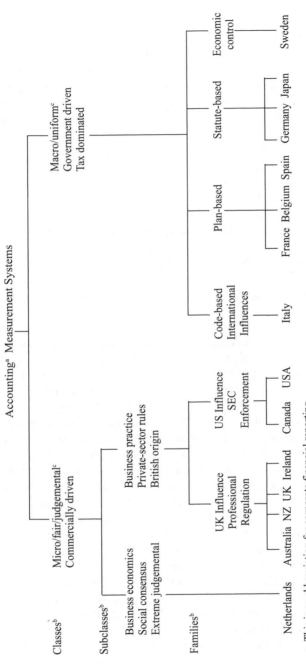

Accounting[a] Measurement Systems

Classes[b]: Micro/fair/judgemental[c] Commercially driven | Macro/uniform[c] Government driven Tax dominated

Subclasses[b]: Business economics Social consensus Extreme judgemental | Business practice Private-sector rules British origin | Code-based International Influences | Plan-based | Statute-based | Economic control

Families[b]:
- Netherlands
- UK Influence Professional Regulation: Australia NZ UK Ireland
- US Influence SEC Enforcement: Canada USA
- Italy
- France Belgium Spain
- Germany Japan
- Sweden

a This is an abbreviation for corporate financial reporting.
b These terms, while borrowed from biology, should be interpreted merely as loose labels.
c The terms at these and other branching points are merely labels to be used as shorthand to try to capture some of the attributes of the members of the accounting systems below them.

This classification has been prepared by a UK researcher and may contain usage of terms that will mislead those from other cultures.
Source: Adapted from Nobes 1983.

47

investments into the individual entity by individual investors, and more with industry or economy-wide planning. This implies less need for local relevance, and a greater importance for additivity and *uniformity*. If entity-specific finance is largely provided from internally-generated, or family, sources, then any resulting irrelevance to a potential equity investor wishing to appraise a particular entity is not a problem, *ceteris paribus*. If finance is significantly provided by lending institutions such as banks, then again there is no problem as such institutions are big enough to demand private inside information. Throughout, this chapter refers to countries as being micro countries or macro countries, according to whether the national financial reporting imperatives are micro or macro, as described above.

The essential rationale behind Nobes (1983) is the very simple one of fitness for purpose. This author sees an analogy with Darwinian principles. See, for example Vorzimmer (1970), but for a warning against possible dangers of applying Darwinism to the social sciences, see Jones (1999). Accounting has developed in response to the environment in which it found itself. Since different countries provided significantly different environments, accounting at the national level developed in significantly different ways. Nobes (1983) suggested a number of causes of the differences and classification which he espoused. These have since been developed and modified, not least by Nobes himself (Nobes 1998). Detailed discussion is unnecessary here but the Nobes analysis maps well with some other considerations. One of the most significant, and central, to the arguments put forward in this chapter to explain developments from the 1970s to date, concerns sources of finance. Gearing (leverage) ratios are historically generally higher in Nobes' macro countries than in the micro. For example, pensions are more likely to be internally funded (by large long-term provisions) in the macro than the micro countries, and banks are more likely to play a major role, in entity management as well as entity financing, in macro rather than micro countries. This is all consistent with the focus on prudent balance sheet valuation traditionally found in the macro countries, designed to ensure that debt can always be repaid out of existing assets, rather than on 'fair' profit reporting, designed to support economic decision making, which is the traditional focus in the micro countries. Numerous country or comparative studies support these general contentions.

Of even longer historical importance, legal systems seem to be significant. Two fundamental systems exist, Roman law and common law. The Nobes macro countries map remarkably well with the Roman law tradition developed from and through the codification by Justinian in the fifth century AD and recodified by Napoleon at the turn of the nineteenth century. Perhaps another way of putting this is that those countries invaded by Napoleon tend to be macro countries. The micro countries map largely with the common law tradition which was created in the UK after the Norman conquest of 1066. The Roman law tradition emphasises centralist specification by one means or another. The common law tradition emphasises the establishment of principles, leaving their application to be considered by individual actors and jurists in particular situations. At least two important areas need to be added to the original Nobes analysis, which would in 1983 perhaps have been referred to as Soviet command economies and underdeveloped countries, and would today be referred to as emerging economies and developing countries, respectively.

DEVELOPMENTS FROM 1970 TO 2000

It is difficult now to appreciate just how significant the differences between country practices and philosophies, encapsulated in the previous section, actually were. Also, ignorance across countries was significantly greater than today. This led, at minimum, to mutual suspicion on a grand scale. German reported earnings were significantly tax-driven and, further, were smoothed almost out of meaningful recognition, often by the use of secret reserves. Consolidated accounts in Germany usually excluded all subsidiaries outside German borders. UK financial statements followed a variety of inconsistent (though often reasonably transparent in principle if not in quantification) policies selected by management and approved by auditors. The author recalls seeing a set of US financial statements from the early 1970s presenting (as a genuine voluntary extension of information disclosure) a section on 'minorities', defined as 'blacks, Hispanics and women'. It really was a different world.

It is from such a starting point that moves towards harmonisation began. Given our focus on the UK in this chapter, only two contexts need extensive consideration here, namely the European Union (EU) and the International Accounting Standards Committee (IASC), which is now the International Accounting Standards Board (IASB). We consider the EU (variously European Economic Community [EEC] and European Community [EC] in earlier years, but for convenience EU throughout this chapter) first.

The eventually successful (second) attempt by the UK to join the EU began in the early 1970s, leading to membership in 1973. The original six members were France, Germany, Luxemburg, Belgium, Austria and Italy. All are from the macro classification in Figure 4.1. The UK, Iceland and Denmark joined at the same time. The crucial point, amply demonstrated by Figure 4.1, is that the UK, in terms of the very role and conception of financial reporting, was in a minority.

The most significant effort at that time to introduce a common European dimension to financial reporting was the Fourth Directive (EEC, 1978), covering formats and rules of accounting. Its creation, originally one-sided (macro), but eventually a highly uneasy compromise involving much optionality (and therefore a low degree of harmonisation), was problematic.

The Fourth Directive's first draft was published in 1971, before the UK, Ireland and Denmark had joined the EU. This initial draft was heavily influenced by German company law, particularly the *Aktiengesetz* of 1965. Consequently, for example, valuation rules were to be conservative, and formats were to be prescribed in detail. Financial statements were to obey the provisions of the Directive.

The UK, Ireland and Denmark joined the then 'common market' in 1973. The influence of Anglo-Saxon thinking was such that a much amended draft of the Fourth Directive was issued in 1974. This introduced the concept of the 'true and fair view'. Another change by 1974 was that some flexibility of presentation had been introduced. The process continued and, by the promulgation of the finalised Directive, the 'true and fair view' was established as a predominant principle in the preparation of financial statements (Article 2, paragraphs 2–5). In fact, it was an overriding requirement that accounts prepared in accordance with the Directive gave a 'true and fair view'. If, 'in exceptional circumstances' the only way to give this is to ignore a specific Directive (i.e. legal) requirement, then such requirement *must* be ignored. In addition, the four basic principles (accruals, prudence, consistency and going concern) were made clearer than they had been in the 1974 draft (Article 31).

Over the next few years, this Directive was enacted, more or less, in the various member countries. This process involved difficulties of language, difficulties of conceptual understanding and deliberate minimisation of the effects of the Directive. A considerable literature emerged (see, as examples, Ordelheide, 1990; 1993; 1996; Alexander, 1993;1996; Nobes, 1993; Aisbitt and Nobes, 2001). The process is now in train all over again with the latest influx of EU membership in 2004 (see Dragneva and Millan, 2003; Garrod and McLeay, 1996).

The UK has a good record of enacting the requirements of European agreements. For example, it enacted the Fourth Directive into UK Company law in 1981 (the same year as Denmark). This was two years before the next countries and ten years before Italy. Further, it enacted it properly and in full, although maximising its use of the optionality enshrined therein. However, the UK, mainly through the Accounting Standards Committee (ASC), but within the implications of a common law tradition, proceeded on a number of occasions to overturn its effects. An early and archetypal example was SSAP 19 on Investment Properties issued in 1981. The Directive, and UK Company law since 1981 (but not before), contain a requirement that 'fixed assets with a finite useful life shall be depreciated'. SSAP 19 says in effect, that the nature of investment properties, as fixed assets, means that depreciation would fail to give a 'true and fair view'. Accordingly the UK Standard *requires* that the UK and EU legal requirement is ignored, citing the (legal) 'true and fair view' override as, in effect, requiring it to so require. The Accounting Standards Board (ASB) repeated the argument more recently with goodwill in FRS 10 Goodwill and Intangible Assets. Roman lawyers and Brussels bureaucrats were not impressed.

Part of the EU response seems to have been to push for the development of European Accounting Standards, *additional* to national and international standards, although a more positive rationale for this could theoretically be provided: European Union implies European (single) market, and single market implies a set of European-level regulations. The UK apparently had little difficulty in preventing such a development, until such prevention became unnecessary in 1995, as discussed later in this chapter. Given that the EU working group charged with developing a harmonised definition of a sausage eventually gave up and voted to disband itself, the UK success at procrastination is not surprising.

It is unlikely to be coincidental that the International Accounting Standards Committee was formed in London in 1973, the very year of the UK's accession to the EU (Hopwood, 1994:243). The original members were the accountancy bodies of nine countries: Australia, Canada, France, Germany, Japan, Mexico, Netherlands, the UK (with Ireland) and the US. It is instructive to consider this list in the context of Figure 4.1. It is immediately clear that, unlike the situation in the European Union, the UK philosophy does not seem to be in a minority here. This is likely to be true if you count the countries. It is even more likely to be true in terms of the overall economic power represented. The continental European economy could not outgun the UK, North America and Australasia combined.

There is no space here to describe the history of IASC between 1973 and 1995. The key point is that as a private club, with no statutory or pseudo-statutory enforcement powers, its standards were full of options, and of distinctly limited influence. The route to a higher level of influence emerged in 1995 with the IASC's agreement with the International Organisation of Securities Commissions (IOSCO) designed to lead to an improved single set of international standards being accepted instead of national standards for listed enterprises on stock exchanges throughout the world. As is well known, the agreement was reached, albeit with significant provisos from the US, in 2000.

Meanwhile, in the EU, something stirred. It should be recalled that the rationale for the development and survival of the 'continental' accounting and reporting system was that the finance needs of national enterprises could be met within the nation. The development of a global finance market (the supply side) raised questions over the continuation of this assumption. A rapid expansion of finance needs, with further industrialisation and the creation of larger and larger multinational enterprises (the demand side) rendered such continuation impossible. The catalyst seems to have been the unification of Germany in 1991, necessitating vast quantities of finance in the former East German Länder which the German economy could not provide. At the time, the German finance needs *required* access to US equity finance which in turn *required* the preparation of full US GAAP financial statements. The continental dyke was breached in 1993 when Daimler-Benz produced US accounts and applied for listing on the New York Stock Exchange. The message for Europe was that the inevitable result of the pursuit of a Eurocentric policy would be the widespread usage by European companies of US GAAP, over which Europe would have no influence whatever. This is the reality behind the EU decision in 1995 to drop the concept of European standards and to actively support the IASC, as the lesser of two evils. This is made very clear by the Commission itself (European Commission 1995).

> With its Communication, the Commission wants to offer a clear prospect that companies seeking listings on the US and other world markets will be able to remain within the EU accounting framework and that US GAAP (Generally Accepted Accounting Principles), over which they and their governments can exercise no influence, is not the only option.

The UK was undoubtedly delighted, although it would have been unhelpful to say so at the time.

When the IASC/IOSCO agreement was reached in 2000, the EU put its policy of supporting the IASC into practical operation. It announced the intention of *requiring* the use of IAS GAAP for the consolidated accounts of all enterprises listed on a European (strictly European Economic Area) stock exchange. A senior EU official described this move, in private conversation with the author, as the saving of the IASC (from the Americans). This claim has genuine merit, but the reverse would seem also true: this was perhaps the only way to give the EU any influence over anything that mattered. Certainly the EU has set up formal 'endorsement' and influencing mechanisms, designed to act as a counterweight to the US/SEC influence on the IASB.

The EU has given final approval to its regulation on the application of International Accounting Standards. Unlike an EU Directive, the Regulation has the force of law and no further action is required by member states before the Regulation comes into effect. This means of course that they have no possibility of rejecting it. The Regulation applies in all EU member states plus Iceland, Norway and Liechtenstein.

While the regulation requires the publication of IAS consolidated financial statements, the European Commission is required to decide on the applicability of individual IASs within the EU. It may adopt an IAS only if:

• It is not contrary to the principles of the EU Fourth and Seventh Directives.
• It is conducive to the European public good.

- It meets the criteria of understandability, relevance, reliability and comparability required of financial information needed for making economic decisions and assessing stewardship of management.

In relation to this first requirement, however, the two Directives have been amended in a number of respects to remove inconsistencies with existing or emerging IAS requirements. Readers who regard the 'true and fair view' concept as dangerously vague are invited to produce an operationally watertight definition of 'the European public good'! Member states have the option of extending the application of the regulation to unlisted companies and to legal entity, as opposed to consolidated, financial statements.

The IASB has found itself in a difficult tactical position. It recognised the need for rapid developments as regards new, and some existing, standards. It recognised that the distinctly partial and qualified support that it received from the US SEC in 2000, which insisted on continuation of a compulsory reconciliation for companies listed in the US from IAS to US GAAP, represented in effect a direct challenge to the IAS to negotiate bilaterally with the US and seek direct convergence. It also recognised that the EU, which only supported IASs from 1995 because it believed that it could, and should, be allowed and encouraged to influence them, was determined to increase its influence, and (unlike the US) was committed to actually using that which it was seeking to influence. Finally, it recognised that the countries of the EU (25 of them now) had an enormous conversion job to do in order to be ready to produce consolidated financial statements for years beginning on or after 1 January 2005 under full IAS requirements, together with comparatives for the previous year on that same basis.

The first three points require an extended programme of change and development, although they do not necessarily imply a clear or consistent direction. The fourth logically requires the opposite. The IASB's policy was to push through very significant changes with an intended final publication date of 31 March 2004, all required to be followed by 1 January 2005, but to define the resulting requirements as a 'stable platform', not to be changed or extended before 1 January 2006. This policy was only partially successful, the problem being caused by the financial instruments issue, as discussed later in this chapter.

THE ISSUE OF POLITICAL INFLUENCE

There is a large well-established literature on the issue of the economic consequences of accounting decisions, going back at least to Zeff (1972). The essential point is the belief, or at least the suspicion, that accounting policies *per se* (independent of management-induced transactions) may have economic effects by directly or indirectly affecting cash flows. What is relevant from this line of research is that governments may seek to influence accounting policies and accounting regulations in the belief that those policies could produce actions or cash-flow effects contrary to government wishes. Further, actors may petition governments so to act, as for example with the 'stock option' saga in the US, and elsewhere, and the financial instruments IAS 39 furore centred in Europe, which is discussed immediately below.

The point at issue here is the extent to which governments should be *allowed* to influence accounting regulations. In some senses, it is obvious that they should. The *quality* of financial reporting, in a corporate governance/investor protection/fraud prevention sense, is clearly a government responsibility. But the direction and technical content arguably is not.

There is a long and often strong tradition in the US of interference, or attempted interference, in such technical content. The accounting for executive stock options is just one example of where the US government has intervened in the accounting arena to require the mandating of a particular accounting policy (see Zeff, 1997). More to the point here, the US regulatory system, and the role of Congress, seems to facilitate, if not actively encourage, such interference.

The idea that, however indirectly, accounting regulation outside the US could be significantly determined by US political interference seems to many unacceptable in principle. This brings us back to the EU and its negotiating position with the IASB. The EU, through the Commission, was determined to set up its own mechanism to act as a counter-balancing political influence. The formal requirement is that it is IAS GAAP as, and to the extent that it has been, 'endorsed' by the EU procedures, which is required by European listed consolidated accounts from 1 January 2005, not IAS GAAP *per se*. This has odd practical effects. For example, a revised IAS Standard only replaces the earlier version for EU purposes after endorsement by the EU, whether or not such date is consistent with the IASB's own effective date as applicable in, for example, Australia.

More fundamentally, of course, it creates a mechanism crying out to be lobbied, as in the highly politicised and public shenanigans relating to IAS 39 Financial Instruments: Recognition and Measurement. Many banks, especially the more secretive continental European ones with a long history of income-smoothing, objected to aspects of IAS 39, as the letter of 4 July 2003 from the President of France to the President of the European Commission makes abundantly clear. Failing to persuade the IASB to make the fundamental changes they desired, they have worked through the EU and its endorsement mechanism instead. The effects are firstly that the IASB has been forced to make a series of rushed amendments throughout 2004, which have seriously disturbed the so-called stable platform. And secondly, that the Commission endorsed a *different version* of IAS 39 from that required by IAS GAAP proper.

It is not unreasonable to suggest that the general UK reaction to this has been incredulity. The ASB quickly announced its endorsement of the full IAS 39, and its incorporation into UK GAAP. Whether it has (or whether even the UK parliament would have) the authority to require, or even allow, the use of the full IAS in group accounts of enterprises listed on, for example, the London stock exchange, is unclear. The EU believes not. The formal position of the EU is that the provisions, which are directly related to the accounting treatment of portfolio hedging, should not be adopted for mandatory use. However, the EU version of IAS 39 does give companies the option to apply these provisions, and therefore to apply all hedge accounting provisions of IAS 39. But in the second case, regarding the option to use full fair value for all financial assets and liabilities, the EU version of IAS 39 claims to prevent the possibility of applying this approach as far as financial liabilities are concerned (Commission Regulation (EC) No.2086/2004 of 19 November 2004, at paras 10 and 5). As this book goes to press, in 2006, agreement is apparently being reached so as to remove this anomaly, with the requirements backdated to 1 January 2005.

In this author's view, the European Commission took a major wrong turning when it set out to create its own machinery to give it political (as opposed to technical) influence over the contents of IAS GAAP. They had their motivations. Firstly, as already discussed, it was a reaction to US intervention. Secondly, democratic principles were advanced. The essential argument was that the State (read: European Union) must have control over that which is required in its name. Although the point may not be invalid in principle, the implication that unelected officials controlled by an unelected Commission can provide democratic validity, is highly questionable.

Doubtless, political theory can produce relevant arguments in both directions. The essence of this author's view is that the technical detail of accounting regulation is too important *not* to be left to accountants. Whatever one's views on the principles involved here, the effect of the EU's actions is to create practical outcomes which are highly problematic for the progress, and likely the reputation, of the IASB.

AN ANGLO-SAXON TRIUMPH?

It is a statement of the obvious that the philosophy of the IASB is to focus on the needs of the capital market. Indeed, it is only the existence of an international capital market that creates a logical need for international reporting standards in the first place. It is also obviously true that the micro/fair/judgemental class of the original Nobes classification (see Figure 4.1) essentially embraces the Anglo-Saxon world, and also that it is precisely the broad approach of this class which underlies the IASB and its works. The reason for this relationship has nothing to do with voting rights or power politics. The point, at its simplest, is that a national system designed to meet the needs of investors is likely, again on the Darwinian principle, to be highly suitable as the basis for an international system which is designed to meet the needs of investors.

Alexander, Archer and Nobes discussed the 'Myth of Anglo-Saxon Accounting' in a series of papers in the *International Journal of Accounting* (Alexander and Archer, 2000; Nobes, 2003; Alexander and Archer, 2003b). The emphasis of much of the detailed argument in the first two papers seemed to point in opposite directions. But behind this some clear elements of agreement emerged. Alexander and Archer state in the final note (2003b:503), on which Nobes had privately commented several times during drafting, as follows:

> All three authors seem agreed that [Anglo-Saxon accounting] while of important historical interest, is in diagnostic terms an outdated notion.

Much of the detail of the arguments in these papers has moved on. But it is submitted here that the prognostication of the above quotation has been amply justified by recent and upcoming events.

The view that US financial reporting regulation in the 20 years or so up to 2000 was focussed on detail has been widely argued. See for example Alexander (1999), Zeff (1995), Benston (2003) and Alexander and Archer (2000). The practical situation was that 'present fairly in accordance with [US] GAAP', meant 'follow US GAAP', where GAAP meant the regulatory hierarchy specified in SAS 69 (AICPA, 1992). US auditing philosophy seems less clear-cut on the matter, under rule 203 of SAS 69, but the 'rules' were, as far as practical financial reporting is concerned, supreme. See for example Van Hulle (1997), discussing the creation of the 1997 version of IAS 1.

> ... Canada and the United States came out strongly against the override. [They] were not in favour of the override because they feared abuses ... The representative of the SEC argued that – although there is an override test in the auditing standards in the US – *no* registrant with the SEC had *ever* applied the override in its financial statements (emphasis added).

Sir David Tweedie, then chairman of the UK ASB, made his view of the debate quite alarmingly clear, according to *Accountancy* (1997, August, 17).

IAS1, *Presentation of Financial Statements,* was approved but not without the usual argument over the true and fair override which has been left in the standard. Essentially the US, Canada and Australia do not believe in it but the UK and most European countries do. The SEC's Mike Sutton made his disapproval of the final standard clear at the meeting, though he had already written to the IASC to say that the true and fair override was unacceptable to SEC staff. "Are you prepared to sign off accounts that you know are wrong?" Sir David [Tweedie] asked the US. "They said yes because that's what the rules say, and we were just rolling around on the floor at this stage – it's bizarre what the US does."

The apotheosis of this US approach is of course the Enron story. Complex rules relating to the creation, and non-consolidation, of special purpose vehicles permitted Enron both to inflate revenues and to hide borrowings as far as the consolidated accounts were concerned. The labyrinthine nature of such detailed rules is wonderfully illustrated by a US publication of the period (Williams et al. 2000:11.15) which, by its very volume, is too long to quote.

Benston (2003), giving an American view (with some advantage of hindsight), is forthright:

When some scandal uncovered financial accounting that appeared misleading or inadequate, public, press, and political criticism led to more rules. The FASB, in turn, was established to write such rules, and it did so assiduously. Its propensity to develop rules with extensive and detailed illustrations, interpretations, and instructions resulted, I believe, from its having both a large budget and a professional full-time staff. GAAP then develop into a set of specific rules, not unlike the tax code, which must be followed to the letter, but not necessarily (or at all) according to its intent.

The danger having been recognised, consideration of change emerged. The US situation since 2000 is complex, and of course ongoing. No attempt at comprehensive coverage can be made here, but some important points can be highlighted through quotations. The outcome is extremely important for the future of international reporting, and indeed for the coherence and validity of the IASB.

The FASB (2002) quotes Tweedie (as chairman of the IASB) as testifying before a US Senate Committee as follows:

We favour an approach that requires the company and its auditor to take a step back and consider whether the accounting suggested is consistent with the underlying principle. This is not a soft option. Our approach requires both companies and their auditors to exercise professional judgement in the public interest. Our approach requires a strong commitment from preparers to financial statements that provide a faithful representation of all transactions and a strong commitment from auditors to resist client pressures. It will not work without those commitments. There will be more individual transactions and structures that are not explicitly addressed. We hope that a clear statement of the underlying principles will allow companies and auditors to deal with those situations without resorting to detailed rules. [February 14, 2002].

Schipper (2003), writing in her individual capacity, but being a member of FASB, has a different emphasis:

> In this commentary, I have argued that US financial reporting standards are in general based on principles, derived from the FASB's Conceptual Framework, but they also contain elements – such as scope and treatment exceptions and detailed implementation guidance – that make them also appear to be rules-based. I discuss the effects on comparability, relevance, and reliability of these rules-based elements, with special attention to the effects of detailed implementation guidance. I emphasize that detailed guidance is intended to achieve comparability and pose an empirical question: How much comparability actually exists in US financial reporting? An assessment of the potential sacrifice of comparability that some believe would surely accompany the adoption of principles-based standards requires, first, an understanding of the current state of comparability.

Careful examination of these two extracts makes it clear that Schipper's point of view is different from that expressed explicitly by Tweedie and implicitly by the FASB. Tweedie talks about requiring 'the company and its auditors to take a step back and consider whether the accounting suggested is consistent with the underlying principles … without resorting to detailed rules'. Schipper argues that US standards are generally *based* on principles and then discusses advantages of having detailed implementation guidance.

Tweedie (2005) reiterates and emphasises the difference in attitude:

> It may be that the US says 'we need lots of guidance'. Well fine – put it in an appendix. We suspect that a lot of auditors will go to the US standards and head for the appendix. But the fact is that you won't have to under international standards – you will be able to use your judgement.

Pursuant to Section 302 of the Sarbanes-Oxley Act (2002), the SEC (2002) specified the form of wording required by certification, in certain defined circumstances, in a number of situations.

There are three key points in this certification. First, achievement of fair presentation in the financial statements is to be confirmed. Second, as an additional and quite separate requirement, confirmation is required that the annual report is not misleading either through an untrue statement *or through omission*. Third, certification that GAAP has been followed is *not* required. The Section 302 requirement relating to non-misleadingness seems, to this author, specifically, and deliberately, undefined. This is the Tweedie version of 'principles-based', not the Schipper version.

In July 2003 the US SEC released a *Staff Study Report Prepared by the Office of the Chief Accountant and the Office of Economic Analysis on the Adoption of a Principles-Based Accounting System* (SEC, 2003).

The SEC Report concludes that neither US GAAP nor international accounting standards, as currently comprised, are representative of the optimum type of principles-based standards. The Report urges a principles-based approach that clearly establishes the objectives of an accounting standard. Therefore, to distinguish the SEC Staff's vision of a principles-based approach to standard setting from those proposed by others, they refer to it as an *objectives-oriented* standard setting. According to the Report, the objectives-oriented standard is based on an improved and consistently applied conceptual framework and provides sufficient detail and structure so that the standard can be operational and applied on a consistent basis. The standard, however, should avoid providing too much detail such that the detail obscures or overrides the objective underlying the standard. Standards should set out the accounting objective 'at an appropriate level of specificity' with 'an appropriate amount of implementation guidance'. Furthermore, the objectives-oriented standard should minimise exceptions from the standard and avoid the use of percentage tests, known as bright lines. Such bright lines allow for technical compliance with the standard while evading the intent of the standard.

The Report explicitly rejects the 'true and fair view' override as a necessary component of a principles-based or objective-oriented standard setting system. We quote below part of point III(G).

> Some have suggested that a necessary component of principles-based standards is the inclusion of a "true and fair override". A true and fair override would permit a company to depart from accounting principles established by the standard setter (thus "overriding" those standards) if the override results in a "true and fair" presentation of the company's financial position, results of operations and cash flows. [This last sentence is incorrect. Rather, a true and fair override would *require* such departure if the original requirements did *not* result in a true and fair presentation.]
>
> While we believe that it is important for preparers and auditors to determine that the financial statements clearly and transparently provide information to investors that allows them to evaluate the company's financial position, results of operations, and cash flows, we do not believe that a "true and fair override" is a necessary component of a principles-based or objectives-oriented standard-setting system. In fact, we would expect that an objectives-oriented standard-setting regime should reduce legitimate concerns about the established standards not providing appropriate guidance, as the standards should be based on objectives that would almost certainly not be met by a presentation that was not "true and fair".

In this statement, the SEC staff makes the standard setter (the FASB) fully responsible for developing such accounting standards that, when properly applied, would always present a 'true and fair view' of an economic entity. Surprisingly, however, in another part of the study (IB) the following passage can be found:

> Furthermore, through the PCAOB, the audit process and auditors will be more closely scrutinized. As the evaluation of auditors shifts from one of "peer review" to that of PCAOB inspection, it will place an additional premium on the auditors' ability to evaluate both compliance with generally accepted accounting principles ("GAAP") and the adequacy of a company's disclosures in light of the underlying economic substance of the company's transactions.

This statement clearly suggests that being in compliance with GAAP and adequately disclosing the underlying economic substance of the company's transaction is not necessarily one and the same (!).

We find the 'objectives-oriented approach' problematic. Requiring 'an appropriate level of specificity' does not give a clear indication of a new philosophy. The distinction between the need for some general undefined requirement (such as non-misleadingness), which we regard as crucial, on the one hand, and some form of *override*, as in the UK tradition, on the other, which is more debatable, is well recognised. However, it is of major concern that the body given responsibility by Congress to control US financial reporting has difficulty expressing what a 'true and fair override' is. Further, as shown above, the Report seems inconsistent with itself on the capacity of standards (GAAP) to provide adequate measures of economic disclosure.

The reason why all this is so important is not, directly, because it matters what the US does or doesn't do. Rather, it is the input to the IASB developments that the US seeks to have, which is crucial. The signs from the ongoing convergence project between the IASB and the US are highly disturbing in the context of the above discussion. There is evidence that the convergence process is leading the IASB towards a practical acceptance of the detail approach. IFRS 5 on the classification of non-current assets as held for sale is an obvious example (Alexander and Archer, 2005). This standard establishes a general criterion that a sale must be 'highly probable', but then proceeds to specify, in considerable detail, the evidence needed to suggest that a high probability exists. The likelihood, therefore, is that it is this detailed evidence which will be appraised, and not the general criterion of 'high probability' in its own right.

CONCLUSION

We conclude from the above discussion that the US is entering a period of debate on the desirable approach to regulation and standard setting. There are forces seeking to move away from the previous emphasis on rules. There is also significant evidence of a lack of understanding of the issues within the US decision-making organs, and of a reaction against real change. The UK has never subscribed to the US-style rule-making tradition, and has resisted earlier EU attempts to impose it, with considerable success. UK participants in the international standard-setting process are still rigorously arguing for the UK's traditional position (FRC 2005).

The crucial area of debate is at the IASB. This author argues that it is vital that the IASB is allowed and encouraged to develop its international standards based on principle, on coherent intelligent application, and on the recognition that intelligent application of *common* principles in different contexts and cultures may lead to *different* detailed outcomes. He contends that the UK should be actively arguing for such an approach with every opportunity and at every turn. It may still be a long struggle.

ACKNOWLEDGEMENTS

Some of the raw material for this paper came from joint work being conducted with Eva Jermakowicz and Sylwia Gornik-Tomaszewski and I acknowledge this input with thanks, although the use made of the material in this paper, and all opinions expressed, remain the sole responsibility of this author. I am also grateful to the two editors of the book, to all participants at the Globalisation of Accounting Standards Conference in Prato, Italy in May 2005 and for the support of the Monash Institute for the Study of Global Movements.

REFERENCES

Accountancy (1997), SEC Miffed at 'UK Victory' – August p.17. ICAEW, London, UK.

Alexander, D. (1993), 'A European true and fair view?', *European Accounting Review* **2** (1), 59–80, London: Routledge.

Alexander, D. (1996), 'Truer and fairer: uninvited comments on invited comments', *European Accounting Review* **5** (3), 483–493, London: Routledge.

Alexander, D. (1999), 'A benchmark for the adequacy of published financial statements', *Accounting and Business Research*, **29** (3), 239–253.

Alexander, D. and S. Archer (2000), 'On the myth of "Anglo-Saxon", financial accounting', *International Journal of Accounting* **35** (4), 539-557.

Alexander D. and Archer S. (2003a), *European Accounting Guide*, 5th ed., New York: Aspen.

Alexander D. and Archer S. (2003b), 'On the myth of "Anglo-Saxon" financial accounting: a response to Nobes', *International Journal of Accounting*, **38** (4).

Alexander D and S. Archer (2005), *Miller International Accounting/Financial Reporting Standards Guide*, Chicago: CCH.

AICPA (1992), *The meaning of present fairly in accordance with generally accepted accounting principles in the independent auditor's report* (SAS 69), New York: AICPA.

Aisbitt, S. and C. Nobes (2001), 'The true and fair view requirement in recent national implementations', *Accounting and Business Research*, **31** (2), 83–90.

Benston, G. (2003), 'The regulation of accountants and public accounting before and after Enron', *Emory Law Journal*, **52** (3), 1325–1351.

Cooke T and Nobes C. (1997), *The development of accounting in an international context*, London: Routledge.

Dragneva R. and E. Millan (2003), 'Transposing the "true and fair view" concept in the legislation of Hungary and Poland in the context of EU enlargement', *Review of Central and East European Law*, 2002–3, No. 2,183–209, The Netherlands: Kluwer Law International.

EEC (1978), Fourth Council Directive 78/660/EEC of 25 July 1978 in the annual accounts of certain types of companies, *Official Journal*, L222 14.08.1978, Brussels.

European Commission (1995), Commission proposes a new strategy for the improvement of the financial reporting framework for companies in Europe; IP(95) 1234, 14 November, Brussels.

FASB (2002), Proposal for a principles-based approach to US standard-setting (ref 1/ 25001), New York: FASB.

FRC (2005), The implication of new accounting and auditing standards for the 'true and fair view' and auditors' responsibilities, 9 August, www.frc.org.uk.

Garrod, N. and S. McLeay (1996), *Accounting in transition*, London and New York: Routledge.

Gray, S. (1988), *Towards a theory of cultural influence on the development of accounting systems internationally*, March: Abacus.

Hofstede, G. (1980). 'Culture's consequences: international differences in work-related values.' Beverley Hills, CA: Sage.

Hopwood (1994), 'Some reflections on "The harmonization of accounting within the EU"', *European Accounting Review*, **3** (2) 241–253, London: Routledge.

Jones, S. (1999), *Almost like a whale: the origin of species updated*, Doubleday.

Nair, R. and W. Frank (1980), 'The impact of disclosure and measurement practices on international accounting classifications', *Accounting Review*, July.

Nobes, C. (1983), 'A judgmental international classification of financial reporting practices', *Journal of Business Finance and Accounting*, Spring.

Nobes, C. (1993), 'The true and fair view; impact on and of the Fourth Directive', *Accounting and Business Research*, **24** (Winter) 35–48.

Nobes, C. (1998). *Towards a general model of the reasons for international differences in financial reporting*, Abacus, **34** (2).

Nobes, C. (2003) 'On the myth of Anglo-Saxon accounting: a comment', *International Journal of Accounting*, **38** (1), 95–104.

Nobes, C. and R. Parker (2003), *Comparative international accounting*, 7th ed., London: Prentice Hall.

Ordelheide, D. (1990), 'Soft transformation of accounting rules of the Fourth Directive in Germany', *Les cahiers internationaux de la comptabilité*, Paris.

Ordelheide, D. (1993), 'True and fair: a European and a German perspective', *European Accounting Review*, **2** (1), 81–90, London: Routledge.

Ordelheide, D. (1996), 'True and fair: a European and a German perspective II', *European Accounting Review*, **5** (3), 495–506, London: Routledge.

Schipper, K. (2003), 'Principles-based accounting standards', *Accounting Horizons*, **17** (1), 61–72.

SEC (2002), *Final rule: certification of disclosure in companies quarterly and annual reports* (S7-21-02; RIN 3235-A154), Washington DC.

SEC (2003), *Study Pursuant to Section 108(d) of the Sarbanes-Oxley Act of 2002 on the adoption by the United States financial reporting system of a principles-based accounting system*, Washington DC.

Tweedie, D. (2005), 'Take it from the top', Feature Interview by Caroline Biebuyck, *A Plus*, June.

Van Hulle (1997), 'The true and fair override in the European accounting directives', *European Accounting Review*, **6** (4), 711–720.

Vorzimmer, P. (1970), *Charles Darwin: the years of controversy*, Philadelphia: Temple University Press.

Williams J., J Carcello and J. Weiss (2000), *Miller GAAP implementation manual*, San Diego: Harcourt.

Zeff, S. (1972), *Forging Accounting Principles in five countries: A history and an analysis of trends*, Champaign, Ill: Stipes.

Zeff, S. (1995), 'A perspective on the US Public/Private approach to the regulation of financial reporting', *Accounting Horizons*, **9** (1), 52–70.

Zeff, S. (1997), 'Playing the Congressional card on employee stock options: a fearful escalation in the impact of economic consequences lobbying on standard setting', in T. Cooke and C. Nobes (1997), *The development of accounting in an international context*, London: Routledge.

5 The US Role in the Globalisation of Accounting Standards

Donna L. Street

INTRODUCTION

In the United States (US), the Financial Accounting Standards Board (FASB) and Securities Exchange Commission (SEC) are both presently committed to promoting and assisting in the development of one set of high quality accounting standards that are globally accepted. To achieve this objective, the FASB is working in cooperation with the International Accounting Standards Board (IASB) and other national accounting standard setters. The FASB's commitment to converging US generally accepted accounting practices (US GAAP) and International Financial Reporting Standards (IFRS) is formalised via a Memorandum of Understanding (MOU) with the IASB. To strongly encourage the development of high quality global standards, the SEC has issued a 'Roadmap to Convergence'. The Roadmap, issued in 2005 in collaboration with the European Commission, aims to eliminate the SEC's 20-F reconciliation requirement for foreign issuers using IFRS by 2009.[1]

This commitment to achieving high quality global standards represents a relatively new paradigm for the US. During the 1970s and 1980s, the US followed a very different philosophy as the FASB, alternatively, viewed comparability almost exclusively from a domestic perspective. Accordingly, during its first two decades, the US Board achieved harmonisation with other major accounting standard setters in very few areas (Street and Shaughnessey 1998). This lack of harmonisation may be associated with limited agenda coordination and cooperation between the FASB and other major standard setters. Fortunately, the situation began to improve in the 1990s when the FASB issued the Board's first strategic plan for international activities and, additionally, became a member of the G4+1 working group. With the announcement of the MOU between the FASB and the IASB in 2002, the pace of convergence between US GAAP and international accounting standards has accelerated.

This chapter reviews the US evolution to a global focus in regard to accounting standard setting. Topics covered include the FASB's first strategic plan for international activities, its role as a member of the G4+1 and the Board's resulting collaborative efforts with other English speaking standard setters and the International Accounting Standards Committee (IASC), the FASB's role in encouraging the restructuring of the IASC, and its MOU with the IASB. Finally, the SEC's recent Roadmap agreement with EC is discussed as well as the Roadmap's impact on the convergence efforts of the FASB and the IASB. Overall, the review reveals that during the last two decades the FASB has undergone a major transformation. The FASB no longer focuses exclusively on domestic issues. Instead, the FASB is presently fully committed to collaborating with the IASB and other national standard setters to achieve one set of high quality globally accepted accounting standards.

THE FASB'S FIRST STRATEGIC PLAN FOR INTERNATIONAL ACTIVITIES

In 1991, the FASB formulated its first strategic plan for international activities, thereby signaling the beginning of a new era in accounting standard setting. The plan represents the genesis of the FASB's commitment to harmonisation or convergence as it focused on achieving greater comparability between US accounting standards and those issued by other national standard-setting bodies and the IASC. The FASB's strategic plan recognised the IASC as the logical focal point for harmonisation efforts. In line with the Board's strategic objectives, the FASB served on the IASC Consultation Committee, and a FASB Board member attended the IASC meetings as an observer. According to then FASB Chair Beresford, the plan was to move US standards a 'little closer to the IASC and UK way of doing things' in order to achieve broad standards requiring more professional judgment in their application (Kelly 1997).

As set forth in the strategic plan, the FASB would begin to engage in joint multi-national standard-setting projects. The goal of these joint endeavors would be to arrive at separate national standards that were in substantial agreement with one another. Additionally, the strategic plan noted that the FASB would compromise and consider adopting IASC or foreign national accounting standards if it deemed them to be superior to their US counterparts. While examples of the latter did not materialise, in 1997, the FASB did issue a new standard to simplify the computation of earnings per share (EPS) and to make the US standard more compatible with the EPS standards of other countries and with those of the IASC. Indeed the FASB pursued its EPS project concurrently with the IASC to help achieve international harmonisation of standards for computing EPS. While the resulting US and international standards were not identical, the provisions were substantially the same.[2]

During the 1990s, the FASB also developed a segment-reporting standard jointly with the Canadian Accounting Standards Board, and the IASC revisited segment reporting at the same time. In an effort to achieve similar, if not identical, standards, a member of the IASC Segment Reporting Steering Committee participated in the FASB meetings during the re-deliberations of the North American Exposure Draft, and FASB members participated in meetings of the IASC Segment Reporting Steering Committee. Many constituents encouraged the North Americans to work closely with the IASC to achieve similar standards. Today the North American and international standards are similar but not identical.[3]

In line with the Board's strategic plan, throughout the 1990s, the FASB continued to seek out additional ways to cooperate with other accounting standard setters to achieve comparability of standards. The formation of the G4+1 working group of accounting standard setters proved to be the best way forward to advance this important initiative.

THE FASB COMBINES FORCES WITH THE G4+1

Beresford (2000) recalls that in June 1988, while serving as Chair of the FASB, he addressed the IASC and proposed a conference of accounting standard setters from around the world, including the IASC. According to Beresford, the time was ideal for 'discussing how to work cooperatively on new issues and eliminate some of the accounting differences between countries'. He recommended that 'the conceptual framework underlying the accounting standards in the various countries should be the main topic of discussion'. Beresford suggested sharing respective 'objectives of financial reporting, accounting terminology, and other basic notions before moving to specific topics'. In June 1991, the IASC, the FASB and the European Federation of Accountants (FEE) jointly hosted the first accounting standard setters' conference in Brussels. A year later the FASB hosted a similar meeting of about 40 standard setters. The standard setters' meeting became an annual event until it was abandoned in the late 1990s.

Beresford (2000) explains that, while the FASB found the standard setters' meetings useful for improving communication, the Board believed the meetings would probably yield limited progress on eliminating accounting differences. Group size was problematic, and more importantly, many countries did not share the FASB's objectives of financial reporting. While the US user-based focus is to 'provide unbiased information to enable investors, creditors and others to make economic decisions', many other countries view social or political objectives as being more important. The FASB, therefore, determined that a more productive endeavor would be to meet periodically with a smaller group of standard setters that shared the US accounting philosophy. The G4+1 working group represented the ideal solution.

In 1992, Beresford hosted a meeting with Tweedie (then Chair of the UK Accounting Standards Board) and Denman (then Accounting Standards Director of the Canadian Accounting Standards Board). Based on their discussions, the standard setters realised their countries shared problems with provisioning and agreed to cooperate in addressing these issues. According to Tweedie, this agreement represents the first step in the development of the 'Group of 4' or G4.

In October 1992, the FASB hosted the second meeting of world standard setters and announced that the US Board had recently agreed to consider a strategic plan focusing on its relationship with other national standard setters. Then the US, UK and Canada extended an invitation for other national standard setters to join their working group. The group would address leading-edge issues and conduct associated research. The Australians joined immediately. This decision by the English-speaking standard setters to form the G4 may be explained by each member's keen interest in international financial reporting and a desire to solve accounting problems using the concepts set forth in the Framework.

The IASC also accepted an invitation to participate in the working group; accordingly, the group became known as the G4+1. The G4 participants believed that the IASC's participation was very important as the group wanted to make it crystal clear that the major English-speaking national standard setters were not keeping secrets from the rest of the world. In 1996, New Zealand (NZ) became the sixth official member of the G4+1.

The initial purpose of the G4+1 was to ensure standards were harmonised among members. The G4+1's orientation was a conceptual, capital market-based, transparent accounting philosophy. The group did not aim to set standards but attempted to agree to broad principles instead. Each G4+1 member was then encouraged to develop its own policy taking into consideration the group position (Tweedie 1997). Thus, G4+1 discussions and papers were soon viewed as 'coming attractions' for the sponsoring standard setters' agendas (Beresford 2000). Former US G4+1 member Leisenring explains, 'we started to look at agendas to see what issues were going to be prevalent down the road'. Therefore, a review of the order of G4+1 discussion papers enabled identification of the evolution of the problems each G4 standard setter was facing (Street 2005).

Membership in G4+1 required active participation and agreement that all debates be based on the Framework. The requirement that members commit to the G4+1 shared objectives meant many national standard setters could not join. The publication of the G4+1's objectives in 1997's *International Review of Accounting Standards Specifying a Recoverable Amount Test for Long-Lived Assets* signalled two important messages (Beresford 2000). First, the G4+1 members were 'pledging a long-term commitment to work toward truly international accounting principles'. Second, 'there is strength in numbers, and each body gains support to make improvements in its own country by taking positions consistent with those elsewhere'.

THE FASB'S ROLE IN THE G4+1

The FASB was a major contributor to G4+1 debates and the US Board's staff served as the lead authors of several G4+1 discussion papers. Accordingly, several G4+1 projects signalled forthcoming changes in US GAAP. For example, the FASB took the lead in developing the 1995 report *Major Issues Related to Hedge Accounting*. At the time, hedge accounting was a hot topic at the FASB, and other standard setters were also keenly interested as there was an absence of guidance on accounting for, or disclosure of, derivatives and other hedge accounting issues (Beresford 2000). Although its members could not reach a consensus on hedge accounting, the report revealed that all G4+1 members were in agreement that derivative financial instruments should be recognised and measured at fair value. According to Beresford (2000), 'by itself, that statement signalled a major change in what was being considered by the FASB and others'. Consistent with the G4+1 paper, the FASB's 1998 Statement of Financial Accounting Standards (SFAS) 133 *Accounting for Derivatives and Hedging Activities* requires that all derivatives be recognised at fair value.

In 1998, *Methods of Accounting for Business Combinations: Recommendations of the G4+1 for Achieving Convergence* was published. This report was the first distributed by G4+1 members as an Invitation to Comment and was of particular importance to the North American members. Reflecting on the G4+1's most significant contributions to practice, Leisenring stated, 'we do not do pooling of interest anymore' (Street 2005). According to O'Malley (former Canadian Accounting Standards Board G4+1 participant), prior to the G4+1 project Canada was under tremendous pressure to adopt Accounting Principles Board (APB) Opinion 16.[4] Fortunately, the FASB realised APB 16's limitations and knew the US standard was imposing considerable pressure on Canada. Accordingly, the FASB supported Canada's efforts to defend its existing standard by indicating the US was out of step with the rest of the world. More importantly, the FASB placed Business Combinations on the Board's agenda. O'Malley explains that:

Jenkins[5] was very astute in recognising ... he was going to have a political issue. He was managing the political process right from the day they [FASB] decided to put that project on the agenda. Then they used the G4+1 discussion document as the thought piece for the FASB project (Street 2005).

Following the US and Canadian decisions to eliminate pooling, with the issuance of SFAS 141 and Handbook Section 1581, respectively, the press heralded a new era of international accounting standard setting. The *Financial Times* (1999) reported, 'A pattern is emerging'. Difficult decisions about the future of accounting are being made at an international level in a forum where standard setters are free from the pressures of dealing directly with constituents. Then each jurisdiction edges towards the agreed goals. While the procedure is complex, it works. *Accountancy* (1998, p. 16) added that *inter alia* the issuance of Invitations to Comment suggested the G4+1 had evolved from 'think tank' to 'embryonic standard setter'.

As illustrated by the G4+1 project on business combinations, the working group ultimately began to tackle projects intended to result in standards in a shorter period of time. While the G4+1's initial papers were thought pieces and much more conceptual, some of the group's later projects began to address specifics about topics of concern or difficulty to FASB and the other participating standard setters.

It is important to acknowledge that other G4 members also made major contributions to the G4+1. For example, the UK led the development of 1995's *Provisions: Their Recognition, Measurement, and Disclosure in Financial Statements*; 1999's *Reporting Financial Performance: A Proposed Approach*; and 2000's *Accounting for Share-based Payment*. The UK and US jointly directed the project that produced 1998's *Reporting Financial Performance: Current Developments and Future Directions*. Australia spearheaded the efforts that produced *Accounting for Leases: A New Approach* in 1996; *International Review of Accounting Standards Specifying a Recoverable Amount Test for Long-Lived Assets* in 1997; and *Leases: Implementation of a New Approach* in 2000. Canada took the lead in developing 1999's *Reporting Interests in Joint Ventures and Similar Arrangements*. New Zealand led the effort that yielded 1999's *Accounting by Recipients for Non-Reciprocal Transfers, Excluding Contributions by Owners: Their Definition, Recognition, and Measurement (Non-Reciprocal Transfers)*.

During its brief existence, the G4+1 issued 12 discussion papers and, in cooperation with other national standard setters, the G4 (the G4+1 excluding the IASC) wrote a draft standard for the IASC on financial instruments.[6] All the former documents were authored by staff of the G4 standard setters. The IASC's 'observer' status in the working group was limited and eventually certain

G4 members, most notably the FASB, began to publicly question the IASC's viability as a global standard setter.

THE FASB AND ITS G4 PARTNERS QUESTION THE IASC'S VIABILITY AS A GLOBAL ACCOUNTING STANDARD SETTER

While the G4+1's objectives clearly indicated each member had to participate and contribute, most G4 members viewed the IASC's contribution to debates and projects as minimal. The general view was that the IASC delegates normally 'dropped an odd thought in' (Street 2005). The IASC's limited contributions can largely be explained by severe resource constraints. Specifically, the IASC did not have the staff resources required to lead a G4+1 discussion paper. Additionally, during the late 1990s, the IASC's main focus was completion of the core standards project and pursuit of an endorsement by the International Organisation of Securities Commissions (IOSCO). Thus, with few exceptions (i.e. provisions), the G4+1 was not addressing the types of issues that the IASC could place on the Board's agenda. Futuristic issues, like those debated at G4+1 meetings, were normally not on the IASC's radar screen. Nonetheless, despite the IASC's limited contribution, the initial G4 position was that including the IASC as an 'observer' was crucial to appease anxiety (particularly within continental Europe) regarding the G4's intentions.

Eventually 'turf battles' between the IASC and certain G4 members further strained the relationship. From the FASB's perspective, a highly notable illustration is the manner in which the IASC distributed a G4+1 discussion document on Reporting Financial Performance. While on secondment from the FASB in 1996, Johnson visited the UK Accounting Standards Board to assist with the first of two G4+1 discussion papers on Reporting Financial Performance. The IASC suggested the G4+1's position should be exposed to a wider audience. Accordingly, the Johnson paper was given to the IASC for distribution as a comment document. In a manner that stunned G4 members, the IASC simply replaced 'G4' with 'IASC' and released the document as an IASC staff paper. No reference was made to Johnson or the G4. In response to instances of this nature, G4 members were livid and determined to send a strong message to the IASC that this type of behaviour was to be terminated. The G4 members made it very clear that, in the future, the IASC should proceed with great caution.

Adding fuel to the fire, at a time when the FASB was facing harsh criticism from the SEC, the Financial Executives Institute (FEI), and others, then IASC Chair Sharpe began to describe the existence of different national standards as 'untenable' and the work of national standard setting bodies as 'crazy'. Sharpe claimed that the IASC was the appropriate body to deliver high quality accounting standards that meet the needs of international capital markets. Some leading national standard setters viewed Sharpe's statements as the 'declaration of a turf war' that could undermine recent efforts to establish a close working relationship between the IASC and national standard-setting bodies (Cairns 1996).

With the sovereignty of certain national standard setters threatened, some G4 members questioned whether the IASC was trying to 'put them out of business'. If so, perhaps the IASC should leave the working group. At one G4+1 meeting, during a heated discussion, Leisenring indicated that if certain jurisdictions were looking for a global standard setter to set their national standards, similar offers could be made from Washington, D.C., and other G4 bases.

Some within G4, therefore, began to speculate about alternatives to the IASC (for example G4, an expanded G4, or even an expanded FASB). Fortunately, Sharpe and then IASC Secretary General Carsberg realised the severity of the mounting tensions and decided to appoint the Strategy Working Party to consider various options and develop the blueprint for a quality international accounting standard setter. Today's IASB represents the outcome of the Strategy Working Party's efforts.

ROLE OF US AND THE G4 IN THE RESTRUCTURING OF THE IASC

While views varied a bit, most G4 members believed that, as then structured, the IASC was not a viable international accounting standard setter and was not up to the task of setting the type of standards capital markets demand. Too many people were at the IASC table, and some delegations included individuals with no interest in, or talent at, standard setting. Approval of an International Accounting Standard (IAS) required 75 per cent of the votes. Thus, international standards became riddled throughout with the compromises necessary to achieve passage. Furthermore, many IASC delegations were not committed to the Framework and were willing to abandon it when the resulting answer was not in line with their view. G4 members, alternatively, insisted that jurisdictional and other special interest should be set aside and that international standards should be based on the Framework. As a result, discussions of the IASC's future began to surface more prevalently at G4+1 meetings.

In private conversations, some G4 members began to consider the future of international accounting standard setting. Discussions focused on problems with the structure and processes of the IASC, lack of resources at the IASC, the need to restructure the IASC, and the demonstrable need for a body to take the next step and produce high quality accounting standards that had explicit support from a much wider international community. A viable international accounting standard setter needed resources and had to do more than assimilate national standards. Facing criticism from certain G4 members including the FASB, as well as IOSCO and the US SEC, the message was unmistakable. To become 'the global standard setter', the IASC had to move into the FASB's league.

To overcome these concerns and become the standard setter it wanted to be, the IASC appointed the Strategy Working Party to reconsider its structure. The Strategy Working Party was to propose an infrastructure that would enable the IASC to bring about convergence between national accounting standards and practices and achieve high-quality global accounting standards (IASC 1998). *Inter alia* the FASB's (1999) *International Accounting Standard Setting: A Vision for the Future* served as a catalyst for change by suggesting that, if the IASC did not satisfactorily restructure, perhaps the FASB or the G4 could transform itself into the global standard setter.

In September 1997, the G4+1 met with the Strategy Working Party to discuss replacing the existing IASC board with representatives of the G7 standard setters (the G4 plus France, Germany and Japan). At the meeting hosted by the FASB, a bicameral structure was considered. The proposal called for a 'technical committee' of eight to 11 responsible for setting standards and a larger 'supervisory board' that would approve the standards. The technical committee would include representatives of several national standard setters. According to *Accountancy* (1997), 'G4 made it clear they may not be interested in making a commitment to the committee if the board retained the supervisory power to veto their work'.

Following a 1998 G4+1 meeting, *Accountancy* (1998, p. 16) reported that recent G4+1 activities, including the issuance of Invitations to Comment (business combinations), provided evidence that the working group had evolved from simply debating accounting concepts in order to agree to broad principles to actually developing draft accounting standards. Furthermore, according to G4+1 participants, the next step could be joint exposure drafts and common standards. *Accountancy* additionally stated:

> This is reinforced by the amendments the G4+1 has made to its memorandum of understanding. This could be interpreted as a clarification of the rules for potential new members of the G4+1, such as Germany. G4 standard-setters have made it clear that their preference is to work within a new IASC structure. However, their beefed-up activity and move towards common standard-setting is a clear signal that the group will invite new members in and make a bid to become the global standard-setter if the IASC board fails to agree restructuring proposals (*Accountancy* 1998, p. 16).

Publication of the *Accountancy* report coincided with the release of the Strategy Working Party's initial restructuring recommendations based on a bicameral structure.

The FASB and other G4 members immediately challenged the right of the restructured IASC Board to veto standards produced by the Standards Development Committee. A joint comment letter by the FASB and the Financial Accounting Foundation stated, 'Establishing a high-quality international accounting standard-setting structure and process is key to the development and long-term success of international accounting standards' (FASB and FAF, 1999). The joint letter further stated that the Standards Development Committee should be an 'autonomous and independent decision making body'. The Standards Development Committee should have full and final authority to set its own agenda and to approve exposure drafts and standards. Representatives of the Standards Development Committee should be highly qualified, technically competent individuals and independent of outside affiliations.

In *International Accounting Standard Setting: A Vision for the Future*, the FASB (1999) clearly set forth the criteria the US Board deemed necessary for a quality international accounting standard setter. The FASB noted that establishment of such an organisation could take place in several ways:

- The IASC could restructure.
- A successor international organisation could build on what the IASC had done, perhaps based on the G4+1.
- The FASB could be modified to become more internationally acceptable.

The FASB's paper sent a strong signal that the IASC needed to restructure properly or an alternative plan would be set in motion. Specifically, the proposed Standards Development Committee should have the power to issue standards on its own right. A quality international standard setter should have:

> ... full authority to set standards. That is, it is independent from other decision-making bodies, it has the power to innovate, and its decisions are not subject to approval of another body that could veto decisions based on self-interested objectives (FASB, 1999, p. 26).

The FASB favoured a full-time, small, independent international board with membership based on technical expertise. Any other solution would result in the pursuit of alternative solutions by the FASB.

The SEC position mirrored that of the FASB. The SEC's views were set forth in the Commission's 1999 concepts release and in a September 1999 letter to the Strategy Working Party. Then SEC Chief Accountant Turner clearly specified in the letter that a transformed IASC should be structured along the lines of the FASB. Specifically, Board members should be independent technical experts. Turner further indicated that a focus on geographic representation was misguided. In an October 1999 speech, then SEC Chairman Levitt (1999) reiterated that the US experience revealed that, to be credible, members of an accounting standard-setting body should be selected based primarily on technical competence and devotion to the public interest.

The IASC restructuring was further discussed at a September 1999 meeting of the G4 and then SEC Chief Accountant Turner. Following the discussion, the G4 endorsed the SEC position that eventually became the basis of the current IASB structure. The G4 concurred with the SEC that the IASB should be a full-time board. Like the SEC, the G4 strongly opposed the EC's geographic representation proposal.

As the debate continued G4 members unanimously, some more passionately than others, communicated to the IASC that the SEC proposal was clearly the way to go. A heated battle developed towards the end when the SEC and EC entered a fervent debate regarding geographic representation versus independence. This polarisation between the SEC and the EC made the resulting negotiations extremely difficult.

In the end, the US SEC position prevailed. An IASC (1999) press release dated 19 November announced that the Board had unanimously approved a new structure. A single Board would include 12 full-time members and two part-time members. The foremost qualification for membership would be technical expertise. Up to seven of the Board Members would have direct liaison responsibility with one or more national standard setters.

A primary problem with the IASC was the perception that it had a lot of vested interest. This is most likely why the SEC, which was privy to the FASB's views, was adamant that the new board be independent and comprised of full-time members. The SEC totally refused the EC proposal of a geographically representative, part-time board.

In selecting the SEC expert model, the technical press suggested that a key strategic issue was that financial statements prepared utilising international standards should be accepted on stock exchanges worldwide (Walton 2004). With the primary target being US financial markets, the SEC expert model was chosen.

During a recent review of the IASB Constitution, the Trustees of the IASC Foundation reconsidered the EC's position that achieving geographic representation should play a primary role in the selection of IASB members. After considering the alternatives, the Trustees reaffirmed support for the expert group model. Specifically, the Constitutional Review Committee concluded that:

... adding specific criteria regarding geographical representation on the IASB would be inconsistent with the Constitution's aim of encouraging independent, unbiased and expert participation, aiming towards international convergence. The Trustees point out that the logic of the organisational arrangements is that decision-making is delegated to professional standard-setters, who do not make the decision as representatives of particular countries, but on the basis of the technical merits and broad practicality of a particular argument with the objective of worldwide application of a standard (IASCF 2005, p. 39).

In March 2005, the IASC Foundation Trustees accepted the Committee's recommendation and determined that the Constitution would not be amended to require explicit geographic balance. Despite this victory for the SEC and other proponents of the expert group model, the battle will likely continue with the EC exerting pressure on the Trustees to move back towards a standard setter geographically representative of countries using IFRS.

CURRENT ROLE OF THE US IN THE INTERNATIONAL ACCOUNTING STANDARD-SETTING ARENA

Following the formation of the IASB, the G4 announced in January 2001 that the working group would no longer meet. Alternatively, the FASB and the other G4 national standard setters would work in partnership with the IASB via liaison representatives. Today the FASB remains committed to convergence with the IASB leading the way to the development of a single set of internationally accepted accounting standards. Former G4 participant Leisenring holds the US liaison seat on the IASB,[7] and the FASB is formally committed to achieving convergence with IFRS via the MOU.

In July 2002, board member Herz left the IASB to become the new FASB Chair. The appointment of Herz to lead the US standard-setting body sent a strong unmistakable signal that the US is fully committed to achieving the convergence of US GAAP and IFRS. In October 2002, the FASB and the IASB formalised their commitment to convergence and jointly issued a MOU known as the Norwalk Agreement. In the MOU, the two boards pledge their best efforts to (1) make existing standards fully compatible as soon as practicable and (2) coordinate future work programmes to ensure that once achieved, compatibility will be maintained. The MOU includes both short-term and long-term convergence initiatives.

Fulfilling the MOU's short-term initiatives, as of fall 2005, the FASB had issued several new standards to eliminate differences with IFRS (for example, SFAS 151, Inventory Costs; SFAS 153, Asset Exchanges; and SFAS 154, Accounting Changes and Error Corrections), and additional changes to US

GAAP were anticipated in regard to Earnings Per Share (an exposure draft was issued in September 2005), Income Taxes (an Exposure Draft was anticipated by the first quarter of 2006), and Research and Development. Furthermore, SFAS 123, Accounting for Share Based Compensation had been amended to move more in line with IFRS.

Addressing the long-term initiatives set forth in the MOU, the FASB and the IASB are pursuing several joint projects including Financial Performance Reporting by Business Entities (with the UK Accounting Standards Board), Revenue Recognition and Liability Extinguishment, and Business Combinations (Applying the Acquisition Method). Additionally, the two boards are investing significant resources aimed at the development of a common Framework. Indeed, as the FASB strives to achieve the goals of the MOU as well as the goals set forth in the SEC's recently issued 'Roadmap to Convergence', the US Board's agenda is presently, and will most likely continue to be, exclusively focused on joint projects with the IASB aimed at either:

1) achieving convergence of existing standards; or
2) replacing existing US and international national standards with higher quality alternatives.

SEC ROADMAP TO CONVERGENCE

During his testimony before the Trustees of the IASC Foundation, former SEC Chief Accountant Nicolaisen (2004) stated:

> … part of achieving high quality financial information is to have information that enables investors to make valid comparisons among reporting companies. This raises the issue of the SEC reconciliation requirements for foreign registrants, and the convergence work that is being done to reduce differences between IFRS and US GAAP. … My personal view is that if things continue as they have been going – if the IASB operates as a strong independent standard-setter, if the commitment to quality application of IFRS remains, and if good progress is made in accounting convergence and the development of an effective global financial reporting infrastructure – then 'in this decade', the SEC will be able to consider eliminating the reconciliation. I assure you that I am eager to embrace IFRS because I believe our investors will benefit.

In line with Nicolaisen's comments, then SEC Chairman Donaldson and EU Internal Market Commissioner McCreevey announced, in April 2005, the establishment of a Roadmap to Convergence aimed at eliminating the SEC's reconciliation requirement for foreign issuers using IFRS. The SEC is adamant that accomplishing this goal is contingent, *inter alia*, on continued progress towards converging US GAAP and IFRS. Achievement of high quality accounting standards must remain a cornerstone. Additionally, the SEC will carefully review the faithfulness and consistency of foreign issuers' application of IFRS and their reconciliations to US GAAP from 2005 forward. The roadmap, accordingly, basically represents an iterative set of reviews on the convergence process that will continue until the SEC staff decides whether and when it can recommend to the Commission that the IFRS to US GAAP reconciliation be eliminated. The target date for elimination of the reconciliation is between now and 2009.

The IASB and the FASB are joining forces to respond to the roadmap. The Boards' resulting discussions with the SEC have focused on determining the minimum amount of change required to enable the Commission to consider removing the 20-F reconciliation. During these discussions, the SEC staff has directed the IASB and the FASB to not only focus on achieving the Boards' convergence objectives but to also devote resources to the improvement of accounting standards over time. Specifically, the SEC insists that the two Boards should not focus on eliminating differences between standards that need significant improvement (for example, pensions and leases).

To achieve convergence of existing standards, the FASB is working to eliminate differences with IFRS associated with Investment Properties and the IAS 39 Fair Value Option. In the same vein, the IASB plans to eliminate differences with US GAAP on segment reporting (the IASB has tentatively agreed to adopt SFAS 131), government grants, borrowing costs and joint ventures. Additionally, the FASB and the IASB are jointly researching Impairment.

Responding to SEC concerns regarding areas where both boards' existing standards are questionable (not high quality), the FASB and the IASB will limit their short-term convergence initiatives going forward. Alternatively, the Boards will focus on areas where both US GAAP and IFRS standards require improvement. Joint agenda items, as of late 2005, in addition to those cited previously, included Liabilities/Equity, De-recognition, and Fair Value Measurement Guidance. In November 2005, FASB also added a project to its agenda aimed at comprehensively reconsidering accounting for pensions and other post-employment benefits. In conducting the project, the FASB plans to work with the IASB and other standards setters. The SEC has additionally identified some issues of concern that are not on the FASB and IASB joint agendas. These include Consolidations, Leases, Intangible Assets, Financial Instruments, the feasibility of reporting all financial instruments at fair value, and Disclosure.

CONCLUSION

As illustrated in this chapter, the FASB's issuance of a strategic plan for international activities in 1991 marks the genesis of the US commitment to contributing to the development of a single set of globally recognised, high quality accounting standards. Throughout the 1990s, the FASB endeavors aimed at achieving comparability or harmonisation of accounting standards worldwide escalated as the Board formed a partnership with other English speaking national standard setters and the IASC. The resulting working group, known as the G4+1, contributed significantly during its brief existence to accounting thought and practice and eventually evolved from 'think tank' to 'embryonic standard setter'.

In the late 1990s, the FASB and the SEC voiced concern over the IASC's cumbersome structure and served as key catalysts in persuading the IASC to restructure. The FASB and the SEC believed that establishment of a quality international accounting standard-setting structure held the key to the long-term success and development of high quality international accounting standards. If the IASC were to become a viable international accounting standard setter, it had to make substantial change and move into the same league as the FASB. A quality international accounting standard setter had to be characterised by traits including an independent decision-making structure, adequate due process and sufficient technical capabilities. The result of the restructuring was the formation of today's IASB.

Following the establishment of the IASB in 2001, the US joined forces with the new international standard setter to work toward the development of one set of high quality global accounting standards. In 2001, the FASB and the IASB formalised their commitment to converge US GAAP and IFRS in a MOU known as the Norwalk Agreement. Accepting the challenges set forth in the SEC's 2005 Roadmap to Convergence, the two boards further accelerated their efforts to not only converge existing standards but also to cooperate in developing high quality standards to replace existing standards deemed by the Commission not to be of high quality. Indeed, the current agenda criteria of the FASB require that all topics considered for addition to the US agenda need to be assessed for the possibilities for cooperation with the IASB (or another standard setter). As illustrated in this chapter, the FASB has undergone a metamorphosis during the last two decades. The FASB is no longer focused exclusively on domestic issues. Instead, today's FASB is fully committed to collaborating with the IASB and other national standard setters to achieve one set of globally accepted high quality accounting standards.

NOTES

1   Currently foreign issuers listed in the US are required to file form 20-F with the SEC which includes a reconciliation of net income and shareholder's equity with US GAAP.
2   In September 2005, FASB issued an Exposure Draft proposing changes to move the US EPS standard even more in line with the international approach. Further discussion is presented in the section on the MOU.
3   In January 2005, IASB discussed the approaches of the international and North American approaches to segment reporting and decided to converge with the North Americans in the form of a new IFRS. Further discussion is provided in the section on the MOU.
4   The Canadian standard was much more restrictive on the pooling of interest method than APB 16.
5   Jenkins was Chair of FASB when accounting for business combinations was revisited.
6   The IASC never adopted the position set forth in the draft standard authored by the group of national standard setters known as the Joint Working Group. Instead, International Accounting Standard 39 is based on the US's SFAS 133.
7   In 2005, the IASB Constitution was revised to eliminate reference to the seven national liaison seats. The constitution now simply states that 'IASB will, in consultation with the Trustees, be expected to establish and maintain liaison with, national standard-setters and other official bodies concerned with standard-setting in order to promote the convergence of national accounting standards and International Accounting Standards and International Financial Reporting Standards' (IASCF 2005, p. 25). Hence, only time will tell how the partnership between IASB and its current liaison national standard setters will function in the future.

ACKNOWLEDGEMENTS

This chapter benefited greatly from the cooperation of several members of the G4+1 working group. The author thanks Sir David Tweedie, Sir Bryan Carsberg, David Cairns, Warren McGregor, Patricia O'Malley, Robert Rutherford, Alex Milburn, Elizabeth Hickey, James Leisenring, April Mackenzie and Andrew Lennard for their assistance. The author also gratefully acknowledges financial support provided by the P.D. Leake Trust (a charity associated with the Institute of Chartered Accountants in England and Wales).

REFERENCES

Accountancy (1997), 'G4+1 pledge to support IASC', 19 November, 12.
Accountancy (1998), 'Tactic warning from G4', 15 December, 16.
Beresford, D.R. (2000), 'G4+1: A newcomer on the international scene', 1 March, *The CPA Journal*, **70** (3), 4–19.
Cairns, D. (1996), 'Accountancy – time for turf warriors to reach a peace accord', *Financial Times*, 16 May, 12.
FASB (1999), *International Accounting Standard Setting: A Vision for the Future*, Norwalk, Connecticut: FASB.
FASB and FAF (1999), Comment letter on Shaping IASC for the Future, March 10.
Financial Times (1999), 'Removing the transatlantic divide', 16 September, 32.
IASC (1998), *Shaping IASC for the Future* (A discussion paper of the Strategy Working Party of IASC), December, London: IASC, p. 52.

IASC (1999), 'IASC board reaches momentous decision on its future Structure' (IASC Press Release), 19 November.

IASCF (2005), *Changes in the IASCF Constitution: Report of the IASC Foundation Trustees*, London: IASCF, July.

Kelly, J. (1997), 'IASC/IOSCO – a hand on the brake', *FT World Accounting Report*, April, 2–4.

Levitt, A. (1999), Speech to Economic Club of New York, 18 October.

Nicolaisen, D.T. (2004), Prepared statement of Donald T. Nicolaisen, Chief Accountant, US Securities and Exchange Commission, at the Public Hearing on the IASC Constitution Review.

Street, D.L. (2005), *Inside G4+1: the working group's role in the evolution of the international accounting standard setting process*, London: ICAEW Centre for Business Performance.

Street, D.L. and Shaughnessy, K.A. (1998), 'The quest for international accounting harmonization: a review of the standard setting agendas on the IASC, US, UK, Canada, and Australia, 1973–1997', *Journal of International Accounting, Auditing, and Taxation*, **7** (2), 131–161.

Tweedie, D.P. (1997), Personal letter, 15 May.

Walton, P. (2004), 'IAS 39: Where different accounting models collide', *Accounting in Europe*, **1**, 5–16.

6   The Place of Canada in Global Accounting Standard Setting: Principles Versus Rules Approaches

James C. Gaa

INTRODUCTION

One of the major issues in financial reporting today, both internationally and in North America, is the degree to which financial accounting standards should be formulated in terms of general principles as against specific rules. Since its formation, the Canadian accounting profession has been heavily influenced by its cultural and historical ties to the UK and by its geographical and economic ties to the US. The result has been a tension between the two sources of influence, both generally and with respect to accounting standards. Generally speaking, the influence of the UK results in a preference for standards which leave significant space for the exercise of professional judgement. On the other hand, the influence of the US for standards that contain a significant amount of detailed guidance of various sorts limits professional judgement. Given the dual influences on Canadian accounting standard setting, it is not surprising that Canadian accounting standards and standard setting have taken a middle course between standards expressing principles and standards containing very detailed rules.

Thus, accounting standard setting in Canada is an interesting example of the tension between the two approaches to accounting standard setting. The purpose of this chapter is to describe how and explain why accounting standard setting in Canada has taken a middle course between the two, both in general and with respect to the issue of the degree to which accounting standards should be 'rule-based' or 'principle-based'.

The first section briefly recounts the basic structure of domestic standard setting in Canada. The second section is a summary of the Canadian involvement in the development of international accounting standards which have, for the most part, leaned in the direction of requiring professional judgement. Following that, the third section examines the relationship between US and Canadian standard setting. The fourth section is a discussion of Canadian standard setting, with respect to the question of the extent to which accounting standards should be based on principles and/or rules. The chapter ends with a summary and conclusion.

CANADIAN ACCOUNTING STANDARD SETTING

The early years of Canadian corporate governance closely followed the developments in the UK (Zeff 1971, p. 272). As with the American accounting profession, the creation and evolution of the Canadian accounting profession grew from the roots of the profession in the UK in the mid-1800s. However, the profession developed in parallel in the two countries, due in large part to Canada's history as a British colony until 1867 and as part of the Commonwealth after that. For example, the Companies Acts of 1897 and 1907, in the province of Ontario, were closely modeled on the Companies Acts passed earlier in the UK. Both provided for the disclosure of income statement and balance sheet information, and the 1907 Act called for a balance sheet audit. Although there was no standard-setting body at that time, the disclosure requirements in the 1907 Act were copies of the recommendations of the Institute of Chartered Accountants of Ontario (the ICAO), and were one of the first instances of professional influence on mandatory disclosure. Possibly because of this influence, these provisions were much more advanced than similar legislation in the UK and the US (Murphy 1986, p. 40).

Although the profession continued to make recommendations relating to new legislation over the next several decades (Murphy 1986, pp. 42–4), the profession did little in the way of making policy pronouncements. In 1934, the Institute created a Committee on Terminology. The committee did little until 1937, when it began producing a loose-leaf dictionary that was published in 1938 (Zeff 1971, p. 276). In 1938, the profession created a Research Committee (renamed the Accounting Research Committee).

The publication in 1940 of Regulation S-X by the US Securities and Exchange Commission (with extensive disclosure requirements) caused the Institute to take action because of the obvious imbalance between the two jurisdictions and the consequent threat that some other body might begin to make policy pronouncements (Zeff 1971, p. 277). This resulted, in 1946, in the creation of a research department and in granting the authority to the Accounting Research Committee (renamed the Accounting and Auditing Research Committee in 1946) to develop and publish reports (Zeff 1971, p. 278).[1] Bulletins No. 1 and No. 2 were published in 1946 and 1947. Showing again the influence of the Institute on regulation, even in the absence of a formal standard-setting function, the Bulletins were quickly adopted as policy by the Ontario Securities Commission (Zeff 1971, p. 279).[2] A total of 26 bulletins (covering both accounting and auditing topics) were published at the rate of approximately one or two per year until 1967.

The Canadian Institute of Chartered Accountants (CICA) created the CICA Handbook in 1968 by incorporating the Bulletins. Until the early 1970s, the pronouncements of the Accounting Research Committee (both the Bulletins and the contents of the Handbook) were mandatory only insofar as they were specifically adopted by the provincial securities commissions. In 1972, the Canadian Securities Administrators[3] issued National Policy Statement No. 27. While this did not have the force of law (Murphy 1986, p. 51) – for example, the Ontario Securities Act was not revised in this way until 1978 – it did require that financial statements prepared under the jurisdiction of the Securities Commissions would be prepared in accordance with generally accepted accounting principles, as contained in the CICA Handbook. The official status of the CICA Handbook was further enhanced in 1975, with the passage of the Canadian Business Corporations Act. The Act mandated that financial statements of corporations chartered under the Act be prepared in accordance with GAAP and the Regulations to the Act specified that the CICA Handbook was the primary source of GAAP in Canada. This delegation of power to the Accounting Research Committee was essentially without any restrictions (Murphy 1986, p. 53). It is perhaps notable that the Handbook provisions were not mandatory for any members of the CICA (i.e., outside the domain of the Corporations Acts and the Securities Commissions) until about this time, when the Code of Conduct of the Ontario Institute was revised in 1973 (Murphy 1986, p. 45).

Although several changes have taken place since 1975, the basic structure of standard setting in Canada has remained essentially the same. That is, the Accounting Standards Board (AcSB) is a committee composed of volunteers, mostly from the accounting profession, whose work is supported by CICA staff members. The Board is formally a committee of the CICA, although it publishes its standards under its own authority. For a number of years, it has been the only accounting standard-setting body in the world that is part of the profession (CICA 1998, p. 4). Some changes were made in its structure upon the recommendation of the 1998 Report of the CICA's Task Force on Standard Setting (CICA, 1998).

THE ROLE OF CANADA IN INTERNATIONAL STANDARD SETTING

Canada's participation in the setting of international accounting standards dates to 1966, when professional accounting bodies in Canada, the UK and the US agreed to create the International Accounting Study Group. The IASG, which was concerned with both accounting and auditing matters, was formed in the following year. The first of 20 studies published between 1968 and 1977, was a comparison of inventory accounting in the three countries (Deloitte & Touche, n.d.). Subsequently, the IASC was formed in 1973, on the base of the IASG (which continued to exist as a separate body until 1977).[4] Canada was a founding member of the IASC and was a Board member throughout its existence.

In addition to being an active member of the IASC Board, Canada provided staff support to the IASC. The most notable area was in relation to financial instruments, where the IASC and the CICA began a joint project in 1988. This work eventuated in the promulgation of IAS 32 (Financial Instruments: Disclosure and Presentation) in 1995 and IAS 39 (Financial Instruments: Recognition and Measurement) in 1998, together with implementation guidance on IAS 39.

In addition, the AcSB staff supported the work of the Joint Working Group of Standard Setters on Financial Instruments and Similar Items (which published its draft standard in 2000). Also, the Accounting Standards Board was an active participant in the G4+1 Group of Standard Setters from 1994 to 2001. Since the creation of the IASB in 2001, a Canadian has been a member of the IASB, with liaison responsibilities to the AcSB. As part of this activity the Accounting Standards Board has been a party to a formal agreement among the IASB and the eight major national standard setters. The relationship among the IASB and national standards setters is currently the subject of a draft memorandum of understanding (IASB, 2005a).

In spite of Canada's active participation in international standard-setting activities over many years, international accounting standards have not until now had much effect on Canadian accounting standards. The most obvious example of this is accounting for financial instruments. Although the AcSB staff did most of the work leading up to IAS 32 and 39, the draft standard published by the Joint Working Group of National Standards and a Canadian standard on presentation and disclosure were promulgated at the same time as IAS 32. However, standards on recognition and measurement similar to IAS 39 were not approved until 2005 – six years after IAS 39 and 12 years after the passage of the FASB's Statement No. 115.

Until very recently, little attention was paid to international accounting standards or the IASB/C, outside of the standard setting group of the CICA.[5] As Skinner and Milburn (2001, p. 48) observe, 'The chief impact of international standards on Canadian standards to date has probably resulted from the interaction that occurs when the same subject is being studied by both Canadian and international standard setters'. This indirect impact is the result of participation of the AcSB Staff (and, more recently, the IASB liaison to the

AcSB) in the work of the IASC, the G4+1 and the IASB. Nevertheless, Skinner and Milburn conclude that, as of 2001, 'Overall, the impact of IASC standards on Canadian practice has not been very noticeable' (2001, p. 48). What little impact has occurred recently has met with mixed response. According to the Report of the Council of Senior Executives' Strategic Planning Task Force (CICA, 2004, p. 19), the response has split along the lines of whether companies are domestic or multinational: 'Members and firms operating only in Canada view the trend to international standards as irrelevant or detrimental, while the largest Canadian CA firms are increasingly multinational and controlled from outside this country.'

CANADIAN AND US ACCOUNTING STANDARDS

The primary reason for the relative disinterest in international accounting standards has been the close economic and cultural ties between, and Canadian dependence on, the US. As discussed above, the origins of the Canadian accounting profession go directly back to the UK. However, in the early years of the twentieth century, the influence of the US increased. Zeff (1971, p. 272–3) suggests two reasons for this. One was that American accounting textbooks began to be more influential in Canada than British texts. Second, and more important, was a rapid increase in American investment in Canadian business. Before the First World War, most of the capital required was supplied from the UK, with consequent reporting (accountability) in the context of UK requirements. The periods following the First World War, and again after the Second World War, experienced capital influx, so that by 1962 80 per cent of the foreign capital invested in Canada was from the US (Zeff 1971, p. 173). As Zeff points out, since much of this was direct investment, the influence of American accounting (and auditing) standards was consequently significant.

Thus, a major factor influencing accounting in Canada is its proximity and close economic ties to the US. Currently, the US is roughly 10 times larger than Canada in terms of both population and the size of the economy. Furthermore, especially since the passage of the North American Free Trade Agreement (NAFTA), trade between the two countries has increased dramatically. According to Statistics Canada (2005), in 2004, 82 per cent of exports of goods were to the US and 69 per cent of imports of goods were from the US. In addition, Canada's total trade balance was negative for all countries and regions, except for trade with the US, with the result that 152 per cent of the total trade balance in goods was due to trade with the US (Statistics Canada, 2005).

In addition, because of the integration of businesses across the border, the capital markets are relatively integrated. Canadian capital markets are estimated to constitute 2 per cent of the world market, and are too small to finance all of the Canadian economy. With the world's largest capital market next door, many Canadian enterprises naturally seek financing there. Thus, a number of the largest Canadian enterprises are subsidiaries of American corporations, SEC registrants (because their securities are traded in the US markets) or obtain private financing in the US. In summary, the importance of American capital markets has made it necessary for Canadian financial reporting to be sensitive to the information needs of American investors and resulting pressure for accounting standards to be similar, if not the same, in the two countries.

Because of this pressure and consistent with Canada's traditional preference for independence of the US, the perceived need for a Canadian standard-setting body and distinctive Canadian standards was explicitly stated at least as far back as 1961. The following is from a report in that year by the CICA Executive Committee, quoted in the CICA's Special Committee on Standard Setting (SCOSS) Report to the Board of Governors (CICA 1980):

> Research is being carried out in other countries by responsible professional accounting bodies; if the Canadian profession does not develop its own body of research material, our members, and the Canadian business community generally, will be compelled to accept many, if not most, of the standards recommended from outside Canada. Since Canadian laws, customs and economic conditions are sufficiently different from those of other countries, it is essential that we develop our own body of material even though this may involve some duplication of the research activities of accounting bodies in other countries. In addition, the Canadian business community is more likely to accept and put into practice the recommendations put forth by an authoritative Canadian source rather than by a foreign organisation. Moreover, if the accounting profession's views are not authoritatively stated on all important accounting and auditing matters, governments may feel it necessary to step in and regulate many such matters themselves.

This opinion was re-affirmed in 1967, and endorsed again by the CICA Executive Committee in 1980 (CICA, 1980). An interesting example of this distinctiveness was the promulgation in 1982 of sec. 4510 of the CICA Handbook, which was a voluntary guideline for measuring and disclosing the effects of changing prices. Although it was similar to the FASB standard (SFAS 33), it called for disclosure of the financing adjustment (for the sources of capital) that was contained in the UK standard. The result was 'a smorgasbord of supplementary current cost and general price level disclosures' (Skinner and Milburn, 2001, p. 563).' As discussed below, the primary difference between US and Canadian standards has been the degree to which judgment is required in their application.

Beginning in the early to mid-1980s, the attitude that Canadian accounting standards should be distinctive gave way to the recognition of the importance of the close economic ties between Canada and the US. This shift reflected gradual changes in attitudes and economic relations during this period, which eventuated in the signing of the North American Free Trade Agreement. Accordingly, there was a shift towards the idea that standards in the two countries should be the same or similar, unless specific differences were called for. Thus, the burden of proof was transferred to advocates of differences between US and Canadian standards. This position was advocated in the 1998 Final Report of the CICA's Task Force on Standard Setting, in the context of harmonising standards internationally:

> Our task force views standards as being harmonised when they have been arrived at following a process of input and negotiations among the relevant standard-setting bodies, and it is in this sense that we use the term in our report. This interpretation still allows a national body to set its own standards, but assumes it will do so only in the event it can clearly demonstrate that its country's circumstances are unique (CICA 1998, p. 12).

Subsequent to, and following from, the publication of this report, the Accounting Standards Board adopted two constraints in the development of Canadian accounting standards:

> Convergence with the highest quality of US and international accounting standards – that is, working with the FASB, IASB and other national standard setting bodies to agree on much needed improvements to existing standards, and the development of new standards; and harmonisation with US GAAP – that is, elimination of significant unjustifiable differences with FASB standards. (http://www.acsbcanada.org/index.cfm/ci_id/193/la_id/1.htm)

The CICA's Task Force on Standard Setting (TFOSS) report (CICA 1980) clearly predicted the eventual globalisation of accounting standards, from one source. For a period starting in the late 1990s, surrounding the transition from the old IASC to the new IASB, it appeared that there would be a struggle as to whether US GAAP or IAS GAAP would become the global standard; it was reasonably clear that there was not room for both. These constraints show clearly the desire, if not the need, for the AcSB to perform a balancing act between the twin objectives of moving towards and being an active participant in the development of international accountings standards and also needing to align itself with US GAAP. This mixed approach was explicitly recognised by the AcSB:

> The course set by TFOSS recognised Canada's strong business ties with US markets and the important ultimate goal of global standards. It kept our options open while enabling us to make important improvements domestically and contribute to the enormous progress of the International Accounting Standards Board (IASB) (Cherry 2004).

During this period, the need to conform to US GAAP caused the AcSB to pass a standard that conformed with US GAAP, even though it viewed the result as inferior. In the stock-based compensation controversy, the AcSB promulgated a new standard (Sec. 3870) that matched US GAAP (SFAS 123). Although it stated that it was not interested in 'inadequate standards', it did so nevertheless.

> The AcSB views the intrinsic value based method [allowed by the FASB standard] as being flawed. ... Nevertheless, in accordance with its policy of harmonisation with the US, the AcSB felt that it was essential that Canadian enterprises be given the same choice as US companies, and concluded that it could not mandate the fair value based method for employee transactions (CICA 2001).

The AcSB eventually issued a standard mandating fair valuation of stock compensation, in line with the IASB standard; and the FASB eventually followed suit, thus turning this episode into an instance of Canada leading US standards. However, Skinner and Milburn described the normal state of affairs: 'Canadian standards are similar to US standards for obvious reasons. And the US has usually gone first, with the AcSB following up' (2001, p. 45). An example of this, in which the AcSB adopted the US view instead of the IASB view, was the impairment or disposal of long-lived assets, for which the two standard setters differed in their approaches to the problem.[6] The AcSB decided that it would converge to US GAAP (SFAS 144) because it was conceptually sound.

By early 2003, it was possible for the Chair of the AcSB to announce that most major differences between Canadian and US GAAP had been eliminated or were on the verge of being eliminated (Cherry 2003). The only major differences were those where US standards were judged to be inferior (such as research and development costs)[7] or where a global convergence project was planned.[8]

Canadian securities market regulators have required that all domestic issuers prepare financial statements in accordance with Canadian GAAP (CSA 2001). Since approximately 1990, Canadian issuers have increasingly obtained financing in the US. The effect of this has been that the SEC and Canadian regulators have, in combination, required these firms to report in accordance with Canadian GAAP (with either a detailed reconciliation to the numbers that would have been produced through the use of US GAAP) or to publish two complete sets of financial statements. In order to provide more comprehensible information for the two jurisdictions, a number of companies (e.g., the Royal Bank of Canada and CN Rail) chose the second option and began to publish two complete annual reports, one using US GAAP and one using Canadian GAAP (CSA 2001, para. 13).

As a result, there was increasing pressure from SEC registrants for Canada to adopt US GAAP or at least to allow SEC registrants to use US GAAP without reconciliation. Their argument was that the US capital markets were their primary constituency, and that their information needs therefore should be given priority. This was not a universal opinion, since domestic issuers (who were not SEC registrants) had no need for what they viewed as a set of more extensive and detailed standards. Writing in 2001, Skinner and Milburn observed that:

> [o]n the one hand, there is likely to be significant pressure for some Canadian companies that raise capital in the US for the US standard to be accepted in Canada. On the other hand, other enterprises may resist the complex and restrictive US accounting [for financial instruments], and may wish to pick and choose which parts of SFAS 133 they would like to adopt (2001, p. 355).

Following comments on its 2001 Discussion Paper 52-401 'Financial Reporting in Canadian Capital Markets' (CSA 2001), the CSA decided in 2004 to allow Canadian SEC registrants to use US GAAP, without reconciliation to Canadian GAAP (CSA 2004).[9] Ironically, in April 2005, the Royal Bank decided to stop publishing its US GAAP statements in favour of using Canadian GAAP. The reason given for this was that Canadian and US GAAP had converged to the point that separate statements were no longer required.[10] Whether this trend will continue is difficult to predict at this time. However, the strategic plan of the AcSB (CICA 2005a) makes it clear that SEC registrants will continue to be able to use US GAAP.

PRINCIPLES VS. RULES

One of the major issues in the standard setting arena today is the question of whether to adopt 'principles-based' or 'rules-based' standards (e.g., AAA 2003; SEC 2003; Nelson 2003; Schipper 2003). As an over-generalisation, it is sometimes said that international accounting standards are principle-based, whereas US standards are rule-based, and that this difference (in both style and substance) has been one of the main bones of contention between the two points of view. Part of the movement towards international convergence is due to movement in the US by the SEC (2003) and the FASB (2004a, 2004b), to recognise that 'principle-based' standards have some important advantages (as well as disadvantages) over 'rule-based' standards. The agreement between the FASB and IASB in 2002 (FASB 2002), to work towards the convergence of US and IASB standards was a precursor to this, in the sense that convergence requires an agreement between the two parties, at least on a case-by-case basis, as to the degree to which a standard contains rules. The development of Canadian standards and standard setting is an interesting lens through which to view this issue, since it has (as described above) played the middle ground between

American and British/IASC styles of accounting standard. First, it shows that this issue is long-standing; second, it brings out some of the fundamental issues that may be downplayed in the current debates.

Discussion of this issue has suffered from a good deal of miscommunication and misunderstanding, due in part to a lack of definition. Nelson's (2003) definition, which is similar to that of the SEC Study (2003) is that a principle-based standard is one that is based on 'the framework of principles articulated in the FASB's concepts statements' (2003, p. 91). Nelson then defines rules 'broadly to include specific criteria, "bright lines", thresholds, examples, scope restrictions, exceptions, subsequent precedents, implementation guidance, etc.' (2003, p. 91). In slightly different terms, according to Schipper, 'to the extent that US GAAP is aimed at providing comparable, relevant and reliable financial reporting, it is principle-based' (Schipper 2003, p. 63). Based on these definitions, all FASB standards are principle-based, with varying degrees to which they are also rules-based. That is, the issue of 'rules vs. principles' is based on a false dichotomy, with the major issue being the degree to which they include rules. Then, it may be seen that a 'principled' approach to accounting standards would be to minimise or at least limit, the degree to which rules are included in a standard.[11]

The Canadian approach to standard setting is interesting in this context. One might conclude from the recent convergence of US and Canadian GAAP that the two sets of standards are highly similar, if not identical. This is true to a large extent; but major differences do persist and in fact have recently been extended. The key to this puzzle is how Canada can maintain its traditional principled approach, and still converge to US (and international) GAAP.

In the most recent formulation of its views (dated July 2003) in the CICA Handbook, the AcSB has this to say in its Introduction to Accounting Recommendations: 'Accounting Handbook Sections emphasize principles rather than detailed rules and, therefore, cannot be phrased to suit all circumstances or combinations of circumstances that may arise (CICA, n.d.).' This policy distinguishes the more rules-based approach of the US, in that Canadian standards have traditionally required a greater degree of professional judgment than US GAAP (Skinner and Milburn 2001, pp. 45–46).

Although the 1961 report of the CICA Executive Committee advocated a distinctive set of Canadian accounting principles, it also saw the possibilities of mediating the conflict between these two styles of standards:

> A distinctive Canadian research program is also needed because we are in the unique situation of being able, if we will, to effect a balance between positions taken in the US and Great Britain. By looking from a different viewpoint at problems which have been studied elsewhere, we can make a valuable contribution to the growth of a

useful and recognised body of precepts and practices for the accounting profession (quoted in CICA 1980).

Presumably, these balanced positions would have been principle-based, but also contain some rules as in US GAAP. Convergence may have been implicit in this view, at least in the sense that Canadian standards would be regarded as superior to both US and UK GAAP by picking the best parts of their standards.[12] But, it was improbable even at that time that UK and US GAAP would converge to Canadian standards.

If the idea had been that Canadian accounting standards would be a combination of principles and rules, this changed by 1980. In that year, the CICA published a research study by Edward Stamp, a British academic. The purpose of the study was to advise the Institute about corporate reporting in the future. He strongly opposed the emphasis on rules:

> One of the most disquieting trends in standard setting in recent years in North America has been toward the development of 'books of rules' that attempt to define in great detail how every conceivable problem that the standard setting body can think of should be dealt with. This trend is of course consistent with the decision by the FASB to attempt to construct a series of definitions of the various elements of financial statements from which further rules can be developed (Stamp 1980, p. 92).

Partially in reaction to the FASB's approach of developing standards from its Conceptual Framework and also publishing standards with many rules, Stamp advocated an 'evolutionary' approach. Stamp's approach is not actually a principle-based approach, as defined above. Since it was based on an analogy with the common law, the principles implicit in standards would be discovered in them as they evolved and then applied to new issues. According to Stamp (1980, p. 88), the principle-based approach, as it is currently (in 2005) understood, rests on a false analogy to science. Thus, Stamp's point of view is the opposite of the principled approach discussed by AAA (2003), Nelson (2003), Schipper (2003), the SEC (2003) and the FASB (2004), where standards are consistent and derived from the principles in the Conceptual Framework (SEC, 2003). Rather, 'they evolve as a result of intelligent people thinking deeply about the problems that have to be solved, and doing their thinking against a conceptual background that commands the respect and support of the community' (Stamp 1980, p. 91). The test of standards would be their practicality and usefulness, rather than their logical relationship to a FASB-style conceptual framework.

The 1980 report of the CICA Special Committee on Standard Setting (the SCOSS Report) agreed with Stamp (1980) in a number of ways. First, it recommended that standards 'should be written in terms of general principles rather than detailed rules', and that the standards sections 'should contain only such background/explanatory material as necessary for a reasonable degree of comparability in applying the principles therein' (CICA 1980, p. 27). Second, although the report 'generally support[s] the idea of a conceptual framework, and would encourage efforts to develop such a conceptual framework' (CICA 1980, p. 28), it recommends that 'standards should continue to be formulated with primary regard for usefulness and practicality, and hence for their acceptability among users and preparers of financial statements' (CICA 1980, p. 28). Third, 'examples and illustrations should be minimised ... unless they add significantly to the lucidity of principles expressed ... and should be published separately from' the standard itself. The intent of this was that these rules (following Nelson's (2003) definition) should not have the authority of the standard (CICA 1980, p. 37). This is contrary to the contemporary view of standards containing both principles and rules.[13] As with Stamp's study, principles are implicit in standards and new standards should be developed with an eye to these principles. Thus, the report advocates a form of principle-based standards and of standard setting, but not the kind being discussed currently.

The SCOSS Report advocated general standards (i.e., standards without detailed rules) on the grounds that it leaves preparers and auditors with considerable latitude to make professional judgments about the appropriate accounting treatment in a given circumstance. The CICA Special Committee on Standard Setting was aware of several reasons for including rules in accounting standards. In particular, it mentions pressure on auditors in the absence of specific guidance (CICA 1980, p. 13). However, in its opinion, general standards are desirable because of the required professional judgment. At the same time, it recognised that detailed rules may be necessary at some point:

> If any significant number of auditors are prepared to accept these instances [of poor or dishonestly applied judgment] as precedents or to claim 'judgment' as the rationalization for inappropriate presentations by their clients, the pressure on other auditors to accept similar presentations by their clients can become intense. Detailed and inflexible rules may then be seen as the only defence against accounting practices being set at the lowest level that any auditor can be found to accept (1980, p. 13).

In addition, legal liability was a significant issue, where compliance with strict rules could be viewed as a defence. Also, bureaucracies may want standards containing rules as a way of avoiding criticism. In spite of these pressures, the Report advocates general standards. 'If we are proven wrong, detailed rules can be drafted and adopted: but once we abandon principles for detailed rules, it may be impossible to turn back' (CICA 1980, p. 13).

Although the Report seems a bit out-of-date in some ways, it did recognise the major issues being discussed at the present time; and while it seems a bit naïve, the emphasis on general standards may have been a reasonable approach to standard setting at that time. Indeed, in a way it may have been ahead of its time. On the other hand, the current focus on principle-based standards (i.e., standards that are derived from a clear conceptual framework) was in its beginning stages in the US and not yet acceptable in Canada.

Although the 1998 report of the CICA's Task Force on Standard Setting contemplated the goal of a single set of internationally accepted accounting principles, it did not address how the Canadian preference for principle-based standards would work itself out. The position of the report, as discussed above, was to work towards convergence with US GAAP (at least in the short run) and to work for the development of international standards in the long run. Converging with the more rules-based standards of the US and retaining the principle-based approach seem to be incompatible. But the solution is fairly simple: eliminate differences between Canadian and US GAAP in such a way that compliance with US GAAP guarantees compliance with Canadian GAAP, while allowing that the reverse might not be true – i.e., compliance with Canadian GAAP does not guarantee compliance with US GAAP (ACSOC 2001, p. 6). Essentially, this is a continuation of the traditional approach of the AcSB with respect to US GAAP, as described by Skinner and Milburn:

> The Canadian recommendations are normally shorter and less detailed than the American. In part this simply reflects the fact that the all-volunteer Canadian board does not have the resources to explore every subject to the same extent as does the FASB. In part also, it reflects a Canadian policy to leave more room for the exercise of professional judgment as to the best accounting in each situation (2001, p. 46).

An example of this is the standard on the measurement and recognition of financial instruments (CICA nd., Sec. 3855), which is consistent with both IAS 39 and SFAS 115 and 133, but contains less detailed guidance. Nevertheless, Section 3855 is quite detailed, and does not appear to be a principles-based standard (in the sense that it lacks extensive rules). The Chair of the AcSB addressed this point in 2003, in general terms:

> Some might fear that the financial instrument proposals [eventually approved by the AcSB in 2005] signal a shift from principles-based standards to complex, detailed rules. Not at all. The AcSB has steadfastly resisted this trend … (Cherry 2003).

Earlier, the AcSB had approved an accounting guideline on accounting for special purpose entities that was highly rule-oriented. Nevertheless, the AcSB position was that 'the AcSB continues to favour accounting standards that emphasise clearly articulated principles, and will resist excessive detail' (Cherry 2003). In very general terms, this corresponds to the view of standard setting according to which standards should be based on principles (i.e., a conceptual framework), and should contain only as many and as detailed rules as necessary. Seen this way, the primary difference between the US and the Canadian approaches to standard setting is that they differ as to how much detailed guidance, in the form of rules, is deemed to be required.

CONCLUSION: THE FUTURE OF CANADIAN ACCOUNTING STANDARDS

A major topic of discussions of accounting standard setting today concerns the relative merits of 'principle-based' vs. 'ruled-based' standards, where the two approaches either emphasise or downplay the importance of professional judgment. This chapter examines Canadian accounting standard setting as the product of the influence of historical, cultural and economic ties to the UK and the US.

The Accounting Standards Board recently published a proposed plan for its activities over the next five years (CICA 2005a). The plan calls for the Board to focus its attention on the convergence of Canadian GAAP with IASB GAAP global accounting standards. To this end, the Board will do two things. First, it will amend or replace Canadian standards that do not conform to International Financial Reporting Standards produced by the IASB (IFRSs), and adopt new IFRSs as they are promulgated. Second, in accordance with the draft agreement among the IASB and eight national standard setters (IASB 2005a), the AcSB will continue to work with the IASB and the FASB to ensure that Canadian perspectives on the issues are taken into account. In so doing, it will cease to set domestic standards, except in cases where unique Canadian circumstances require it.[14, 15] Since the CICA has been calling for the international convergence of accounting standards, and for Canada's active participation in it, since at least the publication of the TFOSS report in 1998 (CICA 1998),[16] the approval of the plan in 2006 is essentially the announcement that the time has come for Canada to move forward, rather than to continue hanging back. But, in another way, it may signal that the Canadian approach to standard setting has been accepted – i.e., a principled approach that requires significant professional judgment, and adds sufficient rules to achieve the objective of setting the standard in the first place.

NOTES

1 The Accounting and Auditing Research Committee was renamed the Accounting Standards Board (AcSB) in 1991.
2 In fact, the Bulletins were adopted even before Bulletin No. 2 was formally adopted (Zeff 1971, p. 279).
3 The CSA is an informal association of Provincial securities regulators. For historical and political

reasons, Canada does not have a national securities regulator. Instead, Canadian capital markets are regulated by each province. For several reasons, it is important for the provincial regulators to act in concert. The CSA is the vehicle for that communication and cooperation.

4 The other signatories to the newly formed International Accounting Standards Committee were: Australia, France, Germany, Japan, Mexico, Netherlands, United Kingdom/Ireland and United States.

5 The informal group of people on the standard setting group of the CICA consisted of members of the research staff of the AcSB, the Canadian members sitting on the IASC Board, the Canadian Advisory Group on International Accounting Standards and a few others. The Canadian Advisory Group met before each IASC Board meeting to review the agenda and to develop an informal position on the issues. This group worked mostly in isolation (due to general indifference among Canadian preparers and auditors), and so provided most of the domestic input to the Canadian representatives to the IASC Board. However, Board members were not bound to the views developed by the Group. This group was created jointly by the CICA, the Certified General Accountants Association of Canada, the Society of Management Accountants of Canada and the Financial Executives Institute.

6 An AcSB staff report comparing Canadian and IASB GAAP identifies the impairment of assets as a significant difference. IAS 40 requires that the net recoverable amount be determined by discounting, while the Canadian standard (Sec. 3063.05) specifies that the net recoverable amount is the sum of the undiscounted future cash flows (CICA 2005c; IASB 2005b).

7 According to SFAS 2, research and development costs are expensed as incurred, while Sec. 3450 of the CICA Handbook states that development costs should be capitalised if they meet a number of criteria that capture the definition of an asset.

8 One major item, measurement and recognition of financial instruments, was largely worked out by 2003, but was not finally approved until February 2005.

9 In addition, foreign issuers seeking capital in Canada were allowed to use Canadian GAAP, US GAAP or International Financial Reporting Standards.

10 Canadian banks had been active proponents of US GAAP, on the grounds that their financial information had to be closely comparable with their American competitors. In particular, they were dissatisfied with the Canadian standard (Section 1581, as revised in 2001) that effectively prevented enterprises from accounting for business combinations as pooling of interests. To this end, they lobbied for a relaxation of the Canadian standard, to what is generally regarded as an inferior standard (i.e., APB 18). The eventual outcome was that SFAS 141 eliminated the use of pooling of interests accounting in 2001, thus converging US GAAP to the Canadian/IASB view.

11 See also AAA 2003, p. 81.

12 Convergence through selection of the best parts of US and UK standards was clearly the idea behind the guideline (Section 4510 of the CICA Handbook) on accounting for price changes in the early 1980s, mentioned above.

13 The SEC Study (SEC 2003) defines a third category of standard, 'principles-only' standards, which do not contain any rules. The study rejects this possibility on the grounds that they would not provide sufficient structure for accountants to make judgments.

14 An example of the need to preserve some autonomy is the recent adoption of the standards for the measurement and recognition of financial instruments. The FASB standard requires that a hedging instrument be a derivative financial instrument. However, the Canadian capital market is not complete enough to provide a sufficient variety of derivatives for hedging purposes. Therefore, Canadian companies may use non-derivative financial instruments as hedges of foreign currency risk exposure (Sec. 3865.07(e)).

15 The AcSB also recognises the controversy over whether public and private companies need to prepare financial statements in accordance with the same set of accounting principles. As such, over the next several years, it plans to study the needs of the users of the financial information of private enterprises, with a view to considering whether a separate set of accounting principles is needed.

16 The earlier report (CICA 1995) mentions continuing to work with international standard setters and reducing differences with other standards. However, it was given a relatively low priority at that time.

REFERENCES

Accounting Standards Oversight Council (ACSOC) (2001), 'Annual Report', Toronto, CA: Accounting Standards Oversight Council.

American Accounting Association (AAA) Financial Accounting Standards Committee (2003), 'Evaluating Concepts-Based vs. Rules-based Approaches to Standard Setting', *Accounting Horizons*, **17**(1), 73–89.

Canadian Institute of Chartered Accountants (n.d.) *CICA Handbook*, Toronto: The Canadian Institute of Chartered Accountants.

Canadian Institute of Chartered Accountants (1980) CICA Special Committee on Standard Setting Report to CICA Board of Governors, (SCOSS Report), Toronto, CA: The Canadian Institute of Chartered Accountants.

Canadian Institute of Chartered Accountants (1995) Report of the CICA Task Force to Review the Recommendations of the AICPA Special Committee on Financial Reporting (1995)', Extracts from Section V, Summary of Task Force Views, viewed 27 December 2005. www.cica.ca/multimedia/Download_Library/Standards/Accounting/English/DPappendices.pdf

Canadian Institute of Chartered Accountants (1998) 'Final Report of the CICA Task for on Standard Setting' (TFOSS) Toronto, CA: CICA. Extracts from the Executive Summary, viewed 27 December 2005. www.cica.ca/multimedia/Download_Library/Standards/Accounting/English/DPappendices.pdf

Canadian Institute of Chartered Accountants (2001) 'FYI Newsletter, Special Edition 2001', viewed 27 December 2005. www.acsbcanada.org/multimedia/Download_Library/Standards/Accounting/English/e_FYIspecial01.pdf

Canadian Institute of Chartered Accountants (2004), Report of the Council of Senior Executives' Strategic Planning Task Force, viewed 27 December 2005. www.cica.ca/multimedia/Download_Library/About_the_Profession/StratPlanReport_E.pdf

Canadian Institute of Chartered Accountants (Accounting Standards Board) (2005a) 'Accounting Standards in Canada: Future Directions – Draft Plan', viewed 27 December 2005. www.acsbcanada.org/multimedia/Download_Library/Standards/Accounting/English/e_AcctStdsDraftStrategicPlan.pdf

Canadian Institute of Chartered Accountants Accounting Standards Board (2005b) Responses to the Invitation to Comment, viewed 27 December 2005. www.cica.ca/index.cfm/ci_id/21845/la_id/1.htm

Canadian Institute of Chartered Accountants Accounting Standards Board (2005c) Comparison of Canadian GAAP and IFRSs, viewed 27 December 2005. www.acsbcanada.org/multimedia/Download_Library/Standards/Accounting/English/e_IFRS.pdf

Canadian Securities Administrators (CSA) (2001) 'Discussion Paper 52-401: Financial Reporting in Canadian Capital Markets', viewed 27 December 2005. www.osc.gov.on.ca/Regulation/Rulemaking/Current/Part5/cp_20010316_52-401.jsp

Canadian Securities Administrators (CSA) (2004) 'National Instrument 52-107: Acceptable Accounting Principles, Auditing Standards and Reporting Currency', viewed 27 December 2005. www.osc.gov.on.ca/Regulation/Rulemaking/Current/Part5/rule_20040416_52-107_ni.jsp

Cherry, P. (2003) 'Message from the Chair', *FYI Newsletter*, April, viewed 27 December 2005. www.acsbcanada.org/multimedia/Download_Library/Standards/Accounting/English//e_fyi403.pdf

Cherry, P. (2004) 'Message from the Chair', *FYI Newsletter*, April, viewed 27 December 2005. www.cica.ca/multimedia/Download_Library/Standards/Accounting/English/e_FYI0404.pdf

Cherry, P. (2005) 'Message from the Chair', *FYI Newsletter*, January, viewed 27 December 2005. www.acsbcanada.org/multimedia/Download_Library/Standards/Accounting/English/e_FYI0105.pdf

Deloitte & Touche (n.d.) 'Chronology of IASC and IASB', viewed 27 December 2005. www.iasplus.com/restruct/chrono.htm

FASB (2002) 'Memorandum of Understanding: "The Norwalk Agreement"', viewed 27 December 2005. www.fasb.org/news/memorandum.pdf

FASB (2004a) 'FASB Response to SEC Study on the Adoption of a Principles-Based Accounting System', viewed 27 December 2005. www.fasb.org/response_sec_study_july2004.pdf

FASB (2004b), 'On the Road to an Objectives-Oriented Accounting System', *The FASB Report*, August 31.

International Accounting Standards Board (IASB) (2005a) 'Draft Memorandum of Understanding on the role of Accounting Standard-Setters and their relationships with the IASB', viewed 27 December 2005. www.iasb.org/uploaded_files/documents/8_38_DraftMoUFeb2005.pdf

International Accounting Standards Board (IASB) (2005b) 'Comparison of Canadian GAAP and IFRSs at 31 March 2005', viewed 27 December 2005. www.iasplus.com/country/0503canadaifrs.pdf

Joint Working Group of Standard Setters (JWG) (2000), 'Draft Standard and Basis for Conclusions, Financial Instruments and Similar Items', London: International Accounting Standard Committee.

Murphy, G.J. (1986), 'A Chronology of the Development of Corporate Financial Reporting in Canada', *The Accounting Historians' Journal* (Spring): 31–62. Reprinted in Murphy (1993), pp. 519–50.

Murphy, G.J., ed. (1993), *A History of Canadian Accounting Thought and Practice*, New York: Garland Press.

Nelson, M.W. (2003), 'Behavioral Evidence on the Effects of Principles-Based and Rules-Based Standards', *Accounting Horizons*, **17**(1), 73–89.

Schipper, K. (2003), 'Principles-Based Accounting Standards', *Accounting Horizons* **17**(1), 61–72.

Securities and Exchange Commission (SEC) (2003) *Study Pursuant to Section 108(d) of the Sarbanes-Oxley Act of 2002 on the Adoption by the United States Financial Reporting System of a Principles-Based Accounting System*, viewed 27 December 2005. www.sec.gov/news/studies/principlesbasedstand.htm#1c

Skinner, R. M. and J. Alex Milburn (2001), *Accounting Standards in Evolution*, 2nd ed. Toronto: Prentice-Hall.

Stamp, Edward (1980), Corporate Reporting: Its Future Evolution (CICA Research Study) Toronto, CA: The Canadian Institute of Chartered Accountants.

Statistics Canada (2005) 'Imports, exports and trade balance of goods on a balance-of-payments basis, by country or country grouping', Viewed 27 December 2005. www40.statcan.ca/l01/cst01/gblec02a.htm

Zeff, S.A. (1971), *Forging Accounting Principles in Five Countries*, The University of Edinburgh Arthur E. Andersen & Co. Lecture Series, Champaign, IL: Stipes Publishing Co.

7 Too Special to Go Global? Too Small to be Special?
An Insight into Australia's Decision to Adopt IFRS and the Consequences for its own Standard Setting and Application

Ruth Picker

INTRODUCTION

In July 2002, the then Chairman of the Financial Reporting Council (FRC),[1] Mr Jeffrey Lucy, announced that the FRC had issued a strategic directive to the Australian Accounting Standards Board for the adoption by Australia of international accounting standards issued by the International Accounting Standards Board (IASB) by 1 January 2005. This announcement took the entire business community by surprise.

In many ways the adoption by Australia of International Financial Reporting Standards (IFRS) mirrors any normal human reaction to significant change – shock, denial, anger, acceptance and coping. The reaction by various sectors differed – some drove the change initially and then reacted when they realised the extent of the implications; others resisted the change initially and then moved to acceptance fairly quickly once they developed coping mechanisms. Others remained in denial for a long time. This article explores particularly the reaction of the Australian Accounting Standards Board (AASB), the business community, the accounting profession and the corporate regulator in this tumultuous time in Australia's financial reporting history.

THE CHANGE

The Media Release issued by the FRC provides clues to the reasons behind the

FRC's decision:

> Mr Lucy said he understood that the 1 January 2005 timing is somewhat later than the Government would have liked. However, it is determined by the decision of the European Union to require EU listed companies to prepare their consolidated accounts in accordance with IASB standards from that date, in support of the EU single market objective. 'Australia certainly cannot afford to lag Europe in this regard', Mr Lucy said. He also expressed his support for efforts to encourage the United States to further converge its standards with IASB standards with a view to eventual adoption.
>
> Mr Lucy was pleased to note that the Chairman of the IASB, Sir David Tweedie, had issued a statement in London welcoming the FRC's decision. Sir David said that the FRC's announcement demonstrates growing support for the development and implementation of a single set of high quality global accounting standards by 2005.
>
> 'This vote of confidence is a reflection of the leadership role that Australia continues to play in standard-setting and will increase momentum for convergence towards high quality international standards. The input and active participation of interested parties in Australia and the Australian Accounting Standards Board (AASB), under the leadership of Keith Alfredson, are and will remain a vital element in ensuring the IASB's success. It is through national standard-setters, such as the AASB, and the members of our various committees that we are able jointly to develop high quality solutions to accounting issues, leverage resources to research topics not yet on the international agenda so as to expedite conclusions, reach interested parties throughout the world and better understand differences in operating environments, thus fulfilling our role as a global standard-setter.'
>
> Mr Lucy noted that implementation issues would also need to be considered by the FRC (to the extent they did not involve the content of particular standards) and the AASB between now and 2005. These could relate, for example, to the timing of introduction of particular IASB standards in Australia before 1 January 2005 (which would be AASB standards until that date), as well as to issues of interpretation.
>
> Mr Lucy also confirmed that Australia would be making a substantial financial contribution, through the FRC, to the International Accounting Standards Committee (IASC) Foundation in 2002–03.[2]

Prior to the FRC's strategic directive the AASB had been progressing its IASB harmonisation programme over several years. However, there was a fundamental difference between harmonisation and adoption. Under the harmonisation strategy, the AASB considered the relevant international standard when developing its own. Where it determined that the provisions of the international standard were appropriate and of sufficient quality for incorporation into the Australian standard, then it picked up the requirements of the international standard and included those in the Australian one. However, where the AASB did not agree with what the international standard said, or where it considered that the existing Australian requirements were superior to the international rules, it retained the Australian ones. The AASB also developed its own requirements. The Australian standards had their own unique numbering system and there was no alignment between the title or number of the AASB standard and the equivalent IASB standard/s. The AASB acknowledged that there were still several IASB standards for which Australia did not have an equivalent – notably on financial instruments, intangible assets and post-employment benefits. In those areas, the AASB was preparing to develop its own standards using the harmonisation strategy.

Shock

The reaction of AASB members to the FRC's strategic directive was one of shock. Board members were summoned to an urgent teleconference and informed of the decision. Members asked, why had the AASB not been consulted? What about the public sector – were they included in this directive? What about IASB standards that were clearly inferior to Australia's – such as those on government grants and related party disclosures? What about the problem of alternative accounting treatments being permitted by certain IASB standards where the AASB had determined previously not to permit options within its standards? What about all of the areas where the Australian standard provided detailed guidance and worked examples where the equivalent IASB standard was short and vague? How would interpretations of global standards work in practice? Wouldn't all of this lower the quality of financial reporting in Australia?

The FRC's response was that the AASB had to work all of that out but the directive was clear – adoption meant adoption, not harmonisation.

The FRC was responding to the call by the International Organisation of Securities Commissions (IOSCO) for countries to adopt a single set of global standards for the purposes of a more efficient capital market. Securities exchanges around the world permitted domestic entities to raise capital based on financial statements prepared in accordance with the home exchange's accounting standards. When a cross-border capital market transaction occurred, the lodgement of financial statements based on different accounting standards became a problem. Some exchanges accepted the company's home country standards, some required reconciliation to the stock exchange country's domestic standards and some accepted the use of IASB standards or a reconciliation to those. The European Union's decision to adopt IASB standards for all listed companies was in direct response to this call to develop a single, more transparent European capital market.

Few could dispute the validity of IOSCO's approach. The business community in Australia had expressed its frustration for some time at the requirement to prepare multiple sets of financial statements for capital raising purposes or for regular listing requirements. In July 2001, the United States' Financial Accounting Standards Board (FASB) issued SFAS 141 'Business Combinations' and SFAS 142 'Goodwill and Other Intangible Assets'. Among other things, these statements prescribed the initial and subsequent accounting treatment for intangible assets (including goodwill) acquired as part of a business combination. In particular, the FASB prescribed an impairment only (no amortisation) approach to goodwill. Amortisation of goodwill had been controversial for many years and the FASB's standard was ground-breaking. The Australian business community immediately called for Australia to follow the US. Indeed, as it became evident that the IASB was going to modify its standard on goodwill to align with the US, the first calls for adoption of international accounting standards began – not from the regulators or standard setters – but from the business community. It is fair to say that at the time those calling for adoption did not envisage the subsequent practical difficulties this would cause.

Two arguments began to emerge. The AASB's was that Australia had given up its sovereign right to set its own standards and, in so doing, would become powerless to set its own high quality standards. If the AASB disagreed with an IASB standard or a part of it, there was nothing it could do other than to write to the IASB and express its view. If the IASB did nothing, the AASB had to accept the standard and prepare it for adoption in Australia. The AASB's major concern was that the quality of financial reporting would fall. It accepted that Australia lagged behind in a few areas (mentioned above) but it felt hard-pressed to give up its own higher quality standards in many areas. Whether or not these standards were indeed of higher quality may have been debatable, but they were perceived by the AASB to be superior because they contained more detailed guidance, were more precisely written and did not permit alternative accounting treatments. Where the AASB decided to remove an option contained in the equivalent IASB standard or to include additional required disclosures, the AASB received advice from the IASB that this would not result in nonconformity with IFRS. This was because the minimum requirements of the relevant IASB standard were met – the AASB's requirements for additional disclosures or the removal of an option were regarded as a strengthening of the minimum standard. However, this 'strengthening' by the AASB was controversial as many Australian users considered, for example, that they could be disadvantaged by having to make disclosures not required by their European counterparts. The second argument thus followed that Australia was a small player in world markets and what right or need did it have to go out on its own and claim to be better? What was necessary was a compromise of the quality of standards for the greater good – the higher objective of achieving global consistency.

The fact that the public sector and all unlisted reporting entities had also been caught up in the net of the FRC's strategic directive was an issue peculiar to Australia. In Europe only listed companies were to adopt IASB standards by 2005. In Australia all reporting entities were caught – private, public, listed, unlisted, corporate and non-corporate. Interestingly, this issue initially attracted less debate than one might have expected. Later, as reporting entities came to terms with the impact of the changes, smaller entities began to call for deferral of the requirement or even for complete relief. Also, later, as the impact on the public sector became more apparent, the AASB began to include special provisions for not-for-profit entities in the standards specifically to cater for government departments and the like. By the time this occurred the FRC appeared to accept that public sector compliance with IASB standards was not always achievable or indeed necessary, given that entities such as government departments were not competing in global capital markets. A similar argument could be put for the smaller unlisted reporting entities; however the most that these entities achieved, after calling for relief and/or deferral, was an extension of time for lodging their first Australian Equivalents of International Financial Reporting Standards (A-IFRS) financial report with the Australian Securities and Investments Commission (ASIC).[3]

Denial and Anger

On 7 and 8 August 2002 the AASB met for the first time after the FRC's strategic directive. As with any person dealing with change, after the first reaction of shock, some denial crept in. The Board grappled with how it would implement the strategic directive. Would any Australian-specific standards still be issued? Would the Board adopt the IASB's numbering and paragraph referencing? Would the Board retain Australian guidance? Would the Board strike out alternative accounting treatments permitted by an IASB standard such that only one method would be acceptable in Australia? Initially the Board tried to retain as much as it could of its proud heritage of standard setting, but over time it gradually accepted that adoption of IFRS meant exactly that – the same standard, with no modifications or additions. It took years before this finally happened, albeit with additional paragraphs for not-for-profit organisations not covered by IFRS and with some additional guidance in the Australian standards.

For example, when the Board initially approved a draft Pending Standard, AASB 119, the Australian equivalent of IAS 19 *Employee Benefits*, in February 2004, it prohibited the 'corridor approach' option,[4] and therefore required full recognition of actuarial gains and losses in relation to a defined benefit liability in the period in which they arose. There was considerable outcry at this decision. Why should Australian reporting entities be disadvantaged relative to their overseas counterparts who were allowed to use the corridor approach which tended to smooth reported earnings? Why should Australian standards be stricter than their equivalent IASB standards? The Board stood by its decision until November 2004. At its meeting on 11 November, the Board considered the proposals in ED 131 'Request for Comment on IASB ED Amendments to IAS

19 *Employee Benefits: Actuarial Gains and Losses, Group Plans and Disclosures'*. In light of the IASB's decision to adopt a third option of accounting for actuarial gains and losses in relation to defined benefit funds directly through retained earnings, the AASB decided to amend AASB 119 to adopt all three options in accounting for defined benefit funds, consistent with IAS 19. Thus, the AASB reversed its previous decision of not adopting the corridor approach. By then the Board felt that the IASB was being unhelpful by adding further optional treatments in its standards and for an Australian standard setter to select one of three available options was untenable.

The Board did, however, stick to some of its early decisions, such as the decision to prohibit the indirect method for the preparation of the Statement of Cash Flows. This was relatively uncontroversial.

In late 2003, as entities realised the extent and costs of the change, some began to push for deferral of the adoption of A-IFRS. Others expressed concern about repeated and late amendments to the standards, especially IAS 39 *Financial Instruments: Recognition and Measurement*. The Group of 100, which represents most of Australia's largest companies, called for a deferral of at least a year.[5]

The Financial Reporting Council investigated the reasons behind the call for deferral and decided to recommit to its original directive. In March 2004 the chairman of the FRC, Charles Macek, issued a Media Release stating that the decision not to amend the transition timetable had been driven by several factors, including reinforcement by the IASB Chairman that the timing of the release of the 'stable platform' of IASB standards would be met and views obtained on the current state of play of transition activities in Europe.

In delivering this message, the FRC stated:

> … the Council came to unanimous in-principle agreement to proceed with the current Australian timetable for adoption of international accounting standards from 1 January 2005. However this is subject to receiving assurance from the AASB that the set of international accounting standards issued by the IASB is complete and meets the requirements of the Australian market place and that the AASB will be able to make available on its website the corresponding versions of Australian standards by 30 June 2004. This will provide a complete, robust and stable set of financial reporting standards in Australia, which are compliant with IASB standards. The Council has taken this decision conscious of the need to provide Australian companies with more certainty for their short term planning needs.[6]

Acceptance

Those who had accepted the change and had begun to prepare were not in favour of deferral. Indeed, many large companies had put in place A-IFRS project teams and had been actively working on the implementation of A-IFRS for over a year by the time the request for deferral arose. However, it was generally agreed that a final set of standards was imperative so that reporting entities could adequately prepare. This is why the commitment of the IASB to issue the final standards and to stop altering them, was of paramount importance.

While the AASB itself had now moved towards acceptance of its changed world it realised that it had a role to play in moving the business community, especially those reporting entities outside the top listed companies, along. In October 2003, the AASB had agreed that it would issue an Accounting Standard requiring reporting entities to disclose the expected impact of adopting Australian equivalents of IFRS in their 2004 and 2005 financial reports. The key reason behind the AASB's decision was to shift reporting entities into acceptance of their changed world. This standard was issued as AASB 1047 *Disclosing the Impacts of Adopting Australian Equivalents to International Financial Reporting Standards* (AASB 1047), in April 2004. This standard was fundamental in ensuring that reporting entities began to unearth the implications of A-IFRS adoption for themselves so that they could make the disclosures required by AASB 1047. The approach by the AASB was softly-softly: In the first year of its application, AASB 1047 did not require quantitative disclosures of the impact of adoption of A-IFRS. However, in its second year, it did require quantification unless the reporting entity had valid reasons for not being able to quantify. ASIC also used the AASB 1047 disclosures as a mechanism for enforcing the change. In June 2004 ASIC announced that AASB 1047 would be the major area of focus for the ASIC surveillance of 2004 financial reports.[7] ASIC continued to review the AASB 1047 disclosures in the succeeding year.

On 15 July 2004, almost exactly two years after the FRC's strategic directive, the AASB issued the so-called stable platform of A-IFRS. They were made as legal instruments and became law, subject to parliamentary disallowance. These standards were titled and numbered consistently with their IASB counterparts. Their paragraph referencing was identical. Where the AASB had added material, such as the application paragraphs, additional disclosures or paragraphs specific to not-for-profit entities, these paragraphs were identified with the prefix 'Aus'. Where deletions were made by the AASB, these were identified as '[Deleted by the AASB]'.

By this stage it was evident that the AASB had largely accepted the change to its own powers in relation to standard setting. It was no longer a free standard setter. It had lost its powers to set its own standards, other than those of purely a domestic nature, which were few. It continued to attempt to influence the IASB in various ways such as by writing letters and attending meetings. It had even accepted permitting options within standards. However, it still retained Australian guidance in some of the standards. Pressure began to mount from some sectors – in business and the accounting firms – for removal of that guidance on the basis that it might inadvertently cause non-compliance with IFRS. The accounting profession, in particular the large accounting firms, had organised themselves globally to cope with the new world. They had accepted that they could not work in isolation interpreting local IFRS-equivalent standards. A client in France in the same industry as a client in Australia, with the same transaction, needed to be advised consistently. Inconsistent interpretations of IFRS posed a risk not only to the audit firms but to the companies as well. In addition, the regulator would be reviewing companies' adoption and interpretation of IFRS and would investigate apparent inconsistencies. At one point the Chief Accountant of ASIC famously stated that there could only be one correct interpretation of A-IFRS.[8]

As the accounting firms mobilised globally, the European way crept in to Australia. If the global head office stated that there were two possible ways of accounting for a particular transaction or event, and published that in its internal and/or external literature, the Australian firm would follow unless the local regulator clearly disallowed the alternative. The Interpretations War had begun.

Coping – the Interpretations War

Once A-IFRS had become law, the Australian business community set about trying to apply the standards. The adoption of IFRS had been hard fought and resistance had endured for nearly three years. Australia had finally succumbed, in varying degrees and at varying times, to globalisation of accounting standards. However, the real war had just begun. Those who had accepted the change relatively early on, such as those in big business and the large accounting firms, were well advanced in dealing with the issue of interpretations. Indeed, as the implementation of IFRS across the world is occurring, the difference in interpretations between countries is emerging as a major concern to be managed.

Large accounting firms have developed mechanisms to cope with this challenge, although no one would claim that those mechanisms provide all the solutions. However, from the perspective of the accounting profession as a whole, standard setters, regulators and accountants in different countries are still grappling with this issue. In Europe, for example, there has been talk of establishing a European interpretive body, although the European Commission has publicly stated that it would not favour such a move. In Australia the AASB has suggested that it should be able to issue interpretations where the IASB's official interpretive body, the International Financial Reporting Interpretations Committee (IFRIC) has declined to address a particular issue. However, in its Paper on the Role of National Standard Setters, the IASB has indicated that there should be no local interpretations of IFRS.[9] Local interpretations would defeat the original purpose of global adoption of IFRS. The question of turf has arisen. Who should be determining IFRS interpretations – the standard setters, the regulators, the accounting profession or the business community? Each group has been claiming their stake. Also, the US Securities and Exchange Commission (SEC) stated in mid-2005 that it expects the accounting firms to ensure that IFRS is interpreted consistently amongst US SEC Registrants that are Foreign Private Issuers. The SEC will review the US GAAP to IFRS reconciliations of Foreign Private Issuers and will investigate discrepancies between companies in the same industry.[10] Not surprisingly, the auditors contend that the SEC directive makes it clear that IFRS interpretations are the auditors' problem and therefore their turf. Accordingly, the auditors of such entities have had to ensure that they work cooperatively globally, within their firms and between firms, to try to reach consensus on as many issues as possible. However, this is not always achievable and the potential for market inconsistencies continues, despite the best intentions of the parties involved. It is important to note though, that financial statements are not prepared by auditors and auditors cannot insist on best practice but in the last resort can only stand out against accounting that definitely is not in compliance with IFRS.

CATERING FOR THE PUBLIC SECTOR

Because the AASB made certain changes to the content of IFRS in developing A-IFRS, there is the potential for nonconformity with IFRS. Given the objectives of adopting IFRS globally, any nonconformity with IFRS created by A-IFRS would pose numerous problems for Australian reporting entities – primarily that they would not be able to make an unreserved statement of compliance with IFRS, as required by IFRS 1 *First-Time Adoption of International Financial Reporting Standards* and IAS 1 *Presentation of Financial Statements* (and their Australian equivalents). Accordingly, the AASB was careful to ensure that reporting entities other than not-for-profit entities would be able to make that statement of compliance. The only significant[11] content changes that result in nonconformity with IFRS are those specifically related to not-for-profit entities. The AASB determined that this would be unlikely to jeopardise such entities because they would not be competing in the global capital markets, whereas Australian listed entities, for example, would.

A not-for-profit entity is defined in the relevant standards as 'an entity whose principal objective is not the generation of profit'. Examples of such entities include charitable organisations and many entities in the public sector, such as government departments, that form part of the so-called budget sector and receive appropriations from government to fund their operations.

The main areas where the content of A-IFRS has been amended specifically for not-for-profit entities are:

- inventories
- property, plant and equipment
- government grants
- segment reporting
- related party disclosures
- interests in joint ventures
- impairment of assets
- intangible assets
- agriculture
- business combinations
- disposal of non-current assets and presentation of discontinued operations

In most cases the amendments cater for circumstances where the recognition and measurement rules are determined by the reporting entity's generation of cash flows. For example, impairment testing under IAS 36/AASB 136 has regard to the extent to which assets generate cash flows through use or sale. In government departments assets often do not generate cash flows but are supported by appropriations from governments so that the assets may be used for community or other social purposes. The 'Aus' paragraphs in AASB 136 thus alter the requirements for impairment testing for not-for-profit entities in circumstances where assets do not generate cash flows.

THE WAY FORWARD

As the interpretations battle rages, some trends are beginning to emerge which indicate a way forward. Firstly, there is increasing acceptance that there is not always one right answer and that two or more methods of applying an international standard in a particular circumstance may be acceptable to companies, their auditors and even to regulators. This is, of course, provided the rationale for the answer selected is fully supported by the literature. Secondly, the role of national standard setters as interpretive bodies is unlikely to eventuate unless the IASB asks them to tackle a selected issue on behalf of IFRIC. This is improbable. Sir David Tweedie's words regarding the important contribution by national standard setters when he welcomed Australia's decision to adopt IFRS in July 2002 appear, in retrospect, incongruous: In agreeing to adopt IFRS all national standard setters set themselves on a path to their own redundancy. Third, the SEC is becoming increasingly interested in IFRS interpretation and standards development; an ironic outcome given that the US is one of the few countries in the world not to have adopted IFRS. Fourth, and following from the third trend, the IASB is converging its standards with those of the FASB at an increasing rate, paying less regard to the views of national standard setters than to those of the FASB. Ultimately, it could be expected that IFRS will become fully aligned with US GAAP. National standard-setters will cease to exist and finally, once US GAAP has become the global accounting language, even the IASB's days may be numbered. Some have suggested that the world's accounting interpretations could ultimately be issued by the SEC. Was this the original intention of IOSCO? Perhaps so. If this is the ultimate outcome, then unlisted reporting entities in Australia will be pushing for their own standards and interpretations. A second securities exchange may even emerge for listed entities that do not operate beyond Australia. Globalisation is fine for those that operate globally, but not for the rest, they may well argue. If the not-for-profit entities have their own rules relevant to their circumstances then so should that large group of reporting entities that do not operate in global markets. With the creation of a second securities exchange we may see changes made to the Corporations Act to recognise new categories of companies. Differential financial reporting will return. At that time a new Australian standard-setting body may well emerge. Let's hope that by then Australia has not lost all its best accounting talent to London or New York.

NOTES

1 Roles of the Financial Reporting Council include strategic oversight of the accounting standard setting process.
2 Media Release issued by the Financial Reporting Council, 3 July 2002.
3 The relief is given under Class Order [CO 05/0637] *Additional month for first financial reports under AIFRS*.
4 This approach permits the spreading of actuarial gains and losses over a period of time, rather than immediate recognition in the Income Statement.
5 Reported in the *Australian Financial Review*, 12 March 2004.
6 Media Release issued by the Financial Reporting Council, 5 April 2004.
7 ASIC Media Release 04-158.
8 This Statement was made at a meeting of the AASB's Consultative Group in late 2004.
9 Draft Memorandum of Understanding on the role of Accounting Standard-Setters and their relationships with the IASB, February 2005.
10 Office of Chief Accountant Speeches, Washington D.C., 6 December 2004.
11 There are circumstances where, if a for-profit entity avails itself of the disclosure relief for parent-entity information, it would not be IFRS compliant. The relevant Standards are AASB 127 *Consolidated and Separate Financial Statements*, AASB 130 *Disclosures in the Financial Statements of Banks and Similar Financial Institutions* and AASB 132 *Financial Instruments: Presentation and Disclosure*. In such circumstances the entity would make an explicit and unreserved statement of compliance for only the consolidated financial statements.

REFERENCES

Alexander, D. and S. Archer (1996), 'Goodwill and the Difference Arising on First Consolidation', *European Accounting Review*, **5** (2), 243–69.

ASIC Media Release 04-158, 26 May 2004, Financial Reports Held to Account, Australian Securities and Investments Commission, Australia, viewed 12 January 2006. www.asic.gov.au/asic/asic_pub.nsf/byheadline/04-158+Financial+reports+held+to+account?openDocument

Barth, M.E. and G. Clinch (1996), 'International Accounting Differences and Their Relation to Share Prices: Evidence from UK, Australian, and Canadian Firms', *Contemporary Accounting Research*, **13** (1), 135–70.

Draft Memorandum, February 2005, Understanding on the Role of Accounting Standard-Setters and Their Relationships with the IASB, International Accounting Standards Board, London, viewed 12 January 2006. www.iasb.org/uploaded_files/documents/8_38_DraftMoUFeb2005.pdf

FRC Bulletin 2002/4, 3 July 2002, Adoption of International Accounting Standards by 2005, Financial Reporting Council, Australia, viewed 12 January 2006. www.frc.gov.au/bulletins/2002/04.asp

FRC Bulletin 2004/2, March 2004, Financial Reporting Council, Australia, viewed 12 January 2006. www.frc.gov.au/bulletins/2004/02.asp

FRC Bulletin 2004/3, April 2004, Financial Reporting Council, Australia, viewed 12 January 2006. www.frc.gov.au/bulletins/2004/03.asp

Lainez, J.A., J.I. Jarne, and S. Callao (1999), 'The Spanish Accounting System and International Accounting Harmonization', *European Accounting Review*, **8** (1), 93–113.

Powell, S. (2003), 'Accounting for Intangible Assets: Current requirements, key players, and future directions', *European Accounting Review*, **12** (4), 797–811.

Townsend, R. (2004), 'It's Time to Embrace Accounting Standards', *Australian Financial Review*, 9 March, 63.

8 The Role of National Standard Setters in the Standards Developing Process: The Italian Experience

Angelo Provasoli, Pietro Mazzola and Lorenzo Pozza

INTRODUCTION

Until recently, Italy has experienced inertia in relation to the process of convergence towards international accounting principles (Zambon and Saccon 1993, p. 272). When in 2000 the European Commission announced its intention to require firms listed on the stock exchanges within the European Union to use International Accounting Standards (IAS), now known as International Financial Reporting Standards (IFRS), for their group accounts from 1 January 2005, Italy faced difficulties in managing the harmonisation process. Firstly, the Italian accounting practice and philosophy differed greatly from those proposed by the International Accounting Standards Board (IASB) in that Italian standards were mainly government driven, tax dominated and code-based (Hagigi and Sponza 1990, pp. 237–238; Nobes 1983, pp. 3–4). Secondly, the former national standard setter, the *Commissione Paritetica per la Statuizione dei Principi Contabili* (Joint Commission for the Adoption of Accounting Principles), was not regarded as legitimate among all parties potentially interested in financial reporting (Zambon and Saccon 1993, p. 265). And, thirdly, Italy played a marginal role in the international standard-setting context, having participated in only four of the 46 IASC's Technical Steering Committees from 1973 to 1989 (Wallace 1990, p. 7).

Yet, since 2000, Italy has undergone an impressive acceleration of the convergence process towards IFRS. This is due primarily to the foundation of a national standard setter, the OIC (*Organismo Italiano di Contabilità*), which has contributed significantly to the definition of challenging objectives and of the boundaries and contents of the process. The OIC managed to achieve a high institutional legitimacy thanks to a clear mission, its governance and the opportunity for interested parties to be involved in the standard-setting process (Wallace 1990, p. 11–14). It is worth noting that, following the national legislator's orientation, Italian firms will probably adopt different sets of accounting principles. Large international firms with financial instruments distributed among the public will probably adopt IFRS for their financial accounts, either because they are obliged to or on a voluntary basis. Small and medium non-listed firms will possibly use national accounting principles for their financial accounts and will choose – where possible – between 'traditional' and 'harmonised' options, the latter resulting from national compliance with the Directive 2003/51/EC.[1]

This chapter is organised as follows. The first section offers an overview of the evolutionary path of financial reporting in Italy, focusing on the most significant steps in the process of convergence towards IFRS. The second section describes the foundation of the OIC and its mission statement, governance and funding. It also explains how the OIC has gathered institutional legitimacy through time. The third section investigates closely the role the OIC has played in the convergence process towards IFRS and suggests the OIC's future courses of action. This is followed by a conclusion.

The second and third sections rely on an extensive review of the OIC's internal documents, for instance pre-foundation and post-foundation reports and letters to international standard setters and authorities, as well as public documents, for example the *Guida Operativa per la Transizione ai Principi Contabili Internazionali – IFRS* (Handbook for the Adoption of International Accounting Standards) published in October 2005.

Hence, the chapter provides insights into the process of convergence towards IFRS in Italy and the contributions provided in this respect by different entities, the national standard setter among them.

THE ITALIAN ACCOUNTING FRAMEWORK: TOWARDS AN INTERNATIONAL PERSPECTIVE

From a general point of view, pre-IFRS Italian accounting practice is internationally regarded as civil law based, tax driven, and conservatively oriented (Hagigi and Sponza 1990, pp. 237–8; Nobes 1983, pp. 3–4). This view is rooted in Italy's socio-economic conditions, whereby regulations are based on civil law, the number of small and medium firms is high, ownership is usually concentrated and firms often finance their growth through debt (Zambon and Saccon 1993, pp. 270–75).

Since Italy is a civil law country and financial reporting is conceived as a 'macro-function' (Alexander and Archer, 2003; Nobes 1983, pp. 3–4; Nobes and Parker, 2003), financial reporting in Italy has been principally in harmony with ordinary regulations, the most important of which are probably the accounting rules included in the Civil Code of 1942. These regulations, which were the forerunners to those contained in the former Commercial Code, governed the minimum content of balance sheets and dictated several valuation rules. In this respect, another regulation worth mentioning is the law no. 216 of 7 June 1974, which defines the format and minimum content of income statements and directors' reports.

A further step in the evolution of accounting legislation in Italy was Decree no. 127/1991, which implemented the Fourth and the Seventh EC Directives by introducing new accounting principles to be adopted by all firms, except for banks, financial institutions and insurance companies, which were to follow special regulations. At the same time, the Decree brought in new formats for balance sheets and income statements, dictated more precise accounting principles and valuation criteria, and specified the contents of notes to accounts and reports on operations. Accounting regulations contained in the Civil Code have been substantially integrated – and interpreted – through civil, criminal and tax jurisprudence. In Italy, precedents, though not legally binding, do indeed affect accounting practice.

Besides ordinary and extraordinary regulations and jurisprudence, accounting principles issued by professional associations have played a significant role. In 1975, the *Consiglio Nazionale dei Dottori Commercialisti* (the authoritative Association of Accountants) began issuing accounting principles, joined from 1983 by the *Consiglio Nazionale dei Ragionieri* (another important Association of Accountants). The principles were meant, on the one hand, to clarify and integrate the accounting regulations contained in the Civil Code, as the Code cannot deal with every specific problem concerning accounts; and, on the other hand, to provide the necessary reference points for the accountancy profession (Caratozzolo 1998, p. 879–94; Sfameni 2001, pp. 14–32).

The legal authority of the profession's accounting principles has largely been discussed elsewhere (Colombo 1994, p. 211; Zambon 1999, p. 71; Zambon and Saccon 1993, pp. 249–50). In summary, legal authority seems to be recognised in two ways. The first way is through article four of the Presidential Decree no. 136 of 1975, which introduced compulsory external audit for listed firms. The second way is through the Consob Ordinance no. 83/03583 of 1983 (modified and integrated by the Ordinance no. 87/2794 of 23 February 1987), which made explicit reference to accounting principles to be applied in the audit of firms' accounts.

Through the above mentioned Decree no. 127/1991, which implemented the Fourth and the Seventh Directives, the legislator changed the previous principle of *chiarezza e precisione* (clearness and precision), implementing into Italian accounting regulations the principle of 'true and fair view', and ordered the *correttezza* (fairness) of firms' accounts. Moreover, by means of the Decree, the legislator clearly recalled the relevance of the accounting principles issued by the Association of Accountants. In the report containing the opinions expressed by all parliamentary committees about the Decree it is written that:

> like in the previous version of article 4 of the Presidential Decree no. 136 of 31 March 1975, asserting that firms' values are to be correctly registered, an explicit recall of accounting principles dealt with in that Decree has been made, clarifying at the same time that they have to be considered as technical principles to integrate and interpret accounting regulations.

Consequently, accounting principles issued by the Associations of Accountants have played a fundamental role in integrating and interpreting accounting regulations, influencing accounting practice and being a point of reference for accounting jurisprudence. Following the Decree no. 127/1991 and the relevance acknowledged to accounting principles, the Italian situation began moving in line with other continental European countries (Zambon 1999, p. 71).

In this respect, Italy has undergone the harmonisation process indicated from the European Union. In 2000, as part of its Financial Services Action Plan, the European Commission announced its intention to require IFRS for use in the group accounts of all firms listed on the stock exchanges within the European Union from January 2005. This intention was consistent with the idea that comparability of financial reporting across time and space is necessary to build the European markets. Two years later, with Regulation (EC) No. 1606/2002, the European Commission made a decisive step in its endeavour to increase the comparability of published financial statements as part of its vision to achieve a level economic and social playing field within the EU. The Regulation requires the adoption of IFRS for the consolidated accounts of listed firms from 2005, while each European country can decide whether to extend the adoption of IFRS to non-listed firms and/or to individual accounts. With the Decree no. 38 of 28 February 2005, the national legislator requires the adoption of IFRS for consolidated accounts of listed firms, banks and insurance companies from 2005 and for individual accounts of listed firms and banks (not of insurance companies, unless they are listed and do not prepare consolidated accounts) from 2006. The legislator permits firms other than those explicitly requested to adopt IFRS, except for small enterprises which draw up shortened accounts in conformity with the article 2435-bis. In addition, by modernising the Accounting Directives (i.e. Directive 78/660/EC, Directive 83/349/EC and Directive 1991/674/EC) through the Directive 2003/51/EC, the European Commission opened up the

Fourth and Seventh Directives to allow accounting treatments available under IASB standards (Haller and Eierle 2004, p. 27). So far the Italian Government has not yet complied with the Directive, as the national complying regulation is still underway.

THE FOUNDATION OF THE OIC: THE NEED FOR INSTITUTIONAL LEGITIMACY

In order to appreciate the contribution provided by the national standard setter to the harmonisation process depicted above, at least three features characterising Italy prior to 2000 should be considered. Firstly, the Italian accounting practice and philosophy differed greatly from the ones the IASB proposed (Zambon 1999, p. 71; Zambon and Saccon 1993, pp. 270–75). In Europe, with the exclusion of the UK and the Netherlands, accounting systems were mainly government driven and tax dominated (Haller and Eierle 2004, p. 30). In Italy, the situation was worsened by the fact that, in spite of international influences, accounting principles were, as referred above, substantially code-based, providing references to the Italian Civil Code (Hagigi and Sponza 1990, pp. 237–8; Nobes 1983, pp. 3–4). In stark contrast, the accounting system designed by the IASB appears to be financially driven, rooted in business practice and principle-based.

Secondly, until 2000 the Italian standard setter was the *Commissione Paritetica per la Statuizione dei Principi Contabili*, a private part-time body controlled by the *Consiglio Nazionale dei Dottori Commercialisti* and the *Consiglio Nazionale dei Ragionieri* (Italian Associations of Accountants) with the Consob as observer (FEE 2000, pp. 18–19). The Associations were neither highly legitimised in Italy among all parties potentially interested in financial reporting (Colombo 1994, p. 211) nor greatly internationally oriented (Zambon and Saccon 1993, pp. 265–9) since the principles had to be compliant with the coded rules, not yet subject to the harmonisation project.

Third, despite having a board member in the IASC, Italy played a very marginal role in the international standard-setting context, with only four participations out of the 46 IASC's Technical Steering Committees from 1973 to 1989 (Kenny and Larson 1993, pp. 534–6; Wallace 1990, p. 7). In 2000, following the reorganisation of the IASC, a smaller committee (the IASB) was created with mostly full-time members and with a much larger technical staff. The newborn IASB held regular meetings with its 'liaison group', a group of national standard setters including at that time eight countries (France, Germany, UK, US, Canada, Japan, Australia and New Zealand) to discuss its programme and particularly current and prospective joint projects. Italy was not a member of the 'liaison group' and was thus involved in the IASB's work only during the annual meeting with all national standard setters (Gornik-Tomaszewski and McCarthy 2003, pp. 53–4; Whittington 2005, pp. 131–2; Zeff 2002, p. 44).

Although the socio-economic context of Italy described above displayed a substantial inertia, it is important to consider the impressive changes that have occurred in Italy since 1990. These include the development of the financial market in terms both of dimensions and maturity; the increasing relevance of institutional investors, in general, and of private equity, in particular; the progressive internationalisation of the economic system as a result of Italy being part of the European Union; and eventually improvements in the accounting culture (Coda 2002, pp. 13–19; Hagigi and Sponza 1990, p. 235).

In light of all these institutional and socio-economic elements, between 2000 and 2005, Italy laid the foundation for major changes in accounting practice and philosophy, taking cutting-edge positions among European countries. A fundamental contribution to these changes was offered by the OIC, the new national standard setter founded in 2001. In the founders' minds, the new body had to:

1. lead the convergence process towards an accounting system whose assumptions were different from those of the national system;
2. represent all the parties potentially interested in financial reporting rather than only the accountancy profession;
3. play a more active role in the standard developing process, enhancing its authority among the national standard setters (OIC, 2000a).

To address these issues, in 2000 an ad hoc working group – the so-called '*Forum Assonime sui Principi Contabili*' (Assonime's Forum for Accounting Principles) – was formed. The group's work followed a three-step process (OIC, 2000a). The first step was to reach a common position as regards accounting principles among large firms. Backing by large firms was needed because large firms are more likely to lobby both directly and affecting associations' line of conduct: on the one hand, lobbying is costly and only large firms can derive sufficient benefits to justify the cost; on the other, lobbying is a means to mitigating political costs borne by large firms (Kenny and Larson 1993, p. 537). As a second step, the working group enlarged its boundaries to embrace all the parties potentially interested in financial reporting, such as the Ministries of Finance, Justice, Industry and Treasury, the *Banca d'Italia* (Bank of Italy), the Consob, the Isvap, accountancy firms and organisations, and academics. The main idea is that all those potentially interested in financial reporting should be represented within the organisation and have sufficient opportunities to be heard and to raise issues. In turn, this enhances the legitimacy and credibility of the national standard setter (Johnson and Solomons 1984, p. 174; Wallace 1990, p. 11). The third step concludes with the foundation of a stable national standard setter.

During 2000 the working group was involved in heavy planning and strategising, and in November 2001 a stable national setter, the OIC, was founded. The OIC's characteristics in terms of objectives, membership, structure, governance and funding are presented below, as they contributed mainly to the legitimisation of the national standard setter (Kenny and Larson 1983, pp. 538–9; Wallace 1990, pp. 11–14). In turn, this explains to a great extent the major role the OIC played in the convergence process.

Objectives

In its first meeting on 5 December 2000, the working group stated that the future national standard setter should:
1. cooperate systematically with the EFRAG (European Financial Reporting Advisory Group) and the IASB, while fostering at the same time high quality research on relevant national accounting issues;
2. help national regulators enact regulations consistent with the European Directives;
3. develop national accounting standards to be adopted by non-listed companies, non-profit organisations and public administration (OIC, 2000b).

These goals were proposed after the members of the working group had examined national standard setters of other European countries, including France and Germany (OIC, 2000a), and read many documents, among which a report entitled 'Accounting Standard Setting in Europe' by the *Fédération des Experts Comptables Européens* (Federation of European Accounting Experts) provided general information about the accounting standard setting bodies in Europe (FEE 2000, p. 4). This seems consistent with the explanation of mimetic institutional influence (DiMaggio and Powell 1983, pp. 154–6), suggesting that organisations try to model themselves after other organisations that they perceive as successful or legitimised because to do so enhances their own legitimacy and reduces their exposure to environmental uncertainty. Since other European standard setters were born before the OIC and were more fully legitimised, the mimetic institutional influence explanation might predict that the rational strategy for the OIC to take was to benefit from other national standard setters' successful experiences.

In the meeting of 3 April 2001, it was suggested that the contribution provided by the OIC to the IASB and the EFRAG would consist of comments on discussion papers and exposure drafts of proposed standards and interpretations, as well as by proposing problems which are to be considered carefully. In the same meeting, the working group specified also the rationale of the second objective, which is to be found in the need for European countries to make national regulations conform to European standards (OIC, 2001b).

In the meeting of 4 June 2001, a new goal was added, namely providing guidance for the adoption of IFRS (OIC, 2001d). The inclusion of this new goal is not secondary, since accounting scholars have suggested that the demand for detailed implementation guidance for applying IFRS will increase dramatically after 2005. As the number of firms applying IFRS increases and those firms become more heterogeneous in terms of jurisdiction, size, capital structure, ownership structure and degree of accounting sophistication, the number of application questions will also increase. If the IASB declines to provide that guidance, preparers and auditors applying IFRS in the European jurisdiction after 2005 will turn to other sources for guidance (Schipper 2005, p. 103–6), for example national standard setters.

Since 2001, the OIC's objectives have not been modified substantially but merely restated and specified; thus the third article of the Statute of the Foundation (OIC, 2001h) encompasses the following goals:

1. developing accounting principles for firms that are not required to adopt IFRS;
2. issuing national accounting principles to be used by non-profit firms and public administrations;
3. providing guidance for the adoption of IFRS in Italy, taking IFRIC's interpretations into the highest consideration;
4. interpreting national accounting standards, and more generally resolving issues not addressed by the accounting principles;
5. helping the national legislator enact accounting regulations, to conform national regulations to European Directives and standards;
6. contributing to the IASB's and the EFRAG's work through:
   a. comments to Discussion Papers and Exposure Drafts of proposed standards and interpretation;
   b. spotting possible inconsistencies among national regulation, European Directives and IFRS;
   c. the promotion of relevant accounting issues to be discussed by international standard setters;
7. promoting accounting culture in Italy by means of documents, accounting research, meetings, conferences and working groups.

As from the objectives above, the OIC's mission is meant to foster: 1) convergence between national regulations and European standards and Directives (first, third, fifth and sixth objectives); 2) a national leadership in the evolution of the Italian accounting framework (second and fourth objectives); and 3) modifying the Italian accounting culture, responsible to a great extent for the accounting inertia of Italy (Zambon and Saccon 1993, pp. 271–2) (seventh objective).

Such a mission seems indeed to be consistent and synergistic with the IASB's mission, encompassing three broad objectives: improvement, convergence and leadership (Whittington, 2005, pp. 132–4). 'Improvement' means specifically the improvement of existing standards, which are those the IASB inherited from the IASC and formally adopted at its first meeting in April 2001. 'Convergence' means reducing international differences in accounting standards by selecting the best practice currently available, or, if none is available, by developing new standards in partnership with national standard setters. 'Leadership' means developing new accounting standards to deal with problems not yet addressed adequately by the international standard-setting community.

Membership

According to institutional theory, organisations strive to be legitimised by becoming or remaining acceptable within the social environment (Dowling and Pfeffer, 1975; Meyer and Rowen, 1977; Meyer and Scott, 1983; Oliver, 1990). In this context, organisations such as the OIC must remain acceptable to their constituencies to survive (Kenny and Larson 1993, pp. 538–40). That is why, from the very beginning, many institutions were involved in the foundation of the national standard setter: accountants' organisations (*Assirevi, Consiglio Nazionale dei Dottori Commercialisti* and *Consiglio Nazionale dei Ragionieri*), preparers (*Abi, Ania, Assonime* and *Confindustria*), users (*Aiaf* and *Assogestioni*), the Italian Stock Exchange and the Regulation Authorities (*Banca d'Italia, Consob* and *Isvap*). Italian Ministries of Justice and Finance also supported the OIC foundation (OIC, 2000b). In the meetings of 5 January 2001 it was recognised that the OIC's legitimacy with international standard setters should derive from the capability of the OIC to represent all parties potentially interested in financial reporting (OIC, 2001a). To better achieve this goal, members of the Steering Committee, created inside the working group to specifically address issues related to the foundation of the national standard setter, were themselves members of all the institutions interested in financial reporting, as shown in Table 8.1 (OIC, 2001a).

In the meeting of 26 July 2001, it was stated that the high number of members could limit the autonomy and action of the OIC (OIC, 2001g). Yet, the participation of all parties potentially interested in financial reporting was deemed necessary to legitimise the organisation nationally and internationally, and to ensure an adequate and impartial opportunity for interested parties to provide input into the standard-setting process (Johnson and Solomons 1984, p. 174; Wallace 1990, p. 11).

Despite representing different categories of stakeholders, the OIC should be independent from its constituencies, since independence garners credibility (OIC,

Table 8.1 Members of the Steering Committee up to 3 April 2001

Preparers	Accountants	Users	Authorities
Abi	Assirevi	Aiaf	Banca d'Italia
Andaf	Commercialisti	Assogestioni	Consob
Ania	Ragionieri	Borsa Italiana	Isvap
Assilea			Ministry of Justice
Assonime			Ministry of Treasury
Confapi			
Confcommercio			
Confindustria			
8	3	3	3 + 2

Total: 17 members (+2 Ministers) + 1 President = 18 members

Source: OIC, 2001b.

2001a). This view is consistent with the idea that the decision-making process of the organisation should be impartial and objective and each exercise of authority should bear a direct relationship to the organisational goals (Johnson and Solomons 1984, p. 173; Wallace 1990, p. 11).

Structure and Governance

Several accounting studies have highlighted the relevance of providing standard setters with adequate governance structures and mechanisms (Canfield 1999, p. 132–3; Wallace 1990, p. 11–14; Whittington 2005, p. 130–32). During the OIC's foundation, the founders paid great attention to the governance structures and mechanisms of the national standard setter (OIC, 2000b, 2001a).

On 20 July 2001, the basic principles guiding the OIC's governance were established (OIC, 2001f): they have remained the same over time and can be read nowadays through the Statute, from art. 7 to art. 17 (OIC, 2001h). The main idea is that the OIC can be legitimised nationally, on the one hand, and cooperate with international institutions, for example the EFRAG and the IASB, on the other hand, only if its governance structures and mechanisms assure that: 1) all the parties potentially interested in financial reporting (firms, accountants, analysts, stock exchanges, etc.) are represented; 2) expert and independent members are appointed; 3) the decision-making process is transparent and provides an adequate opportunity for interested parties to have their views and

Figure 8.1 The OIC governance from 20 July 2001

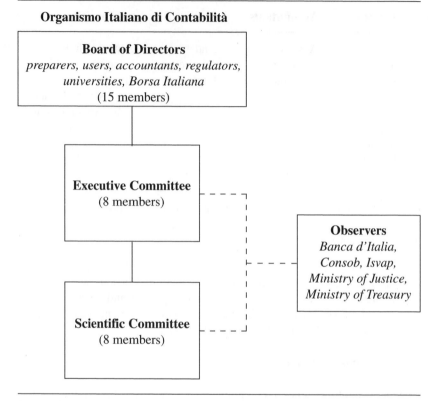

Source: OIC, 2001e.

evidence heard (OIC, 2001f).

To assure the OIC the highest membership and the broadest independency, it was suggested its governance structures would include (Figure 8.1):

1. a Board of Directors;
2. an Executive Committee;
3. a Scientific Committee (OIC, 2001f).

The Board of Directors has 15 members, six of whom are appointed by accountants, five by preparers, two by users, one by the Italian Stock Exchange and one by the Ministry of Treasury (OIC, 2001h). The Board is therefore the body through which all the parties potentially interested in financial reporting should be represented and heard, its role being similar to that of an Assembly of constituencies.[2] Board members are appointed 'among people of proved honour, authority, competence and independence', the last being further specified as 'the Board members do not represent the parties they were appointed by and do not operate on behalf of them' (OIC, 2001h). In this respect, the OIC's intended orientation seems consistent with the more stringent position of the FASB, whose full-time Board members are required to relinquish previous employment ties and comply with the restrictions FASB imposes upon their investing activities (Canfield 1999, pp. 132–3). The OIC's orientation also appears to be coherent with the new IASB structure where Board members are full-time and selected for their skill and knowledge, not as representatives of any group or constituencies. Yet, also in this case, the restrictions imposed by the IASB are stricter than those of the OIC, since the IASB's members are required to resign from their previous employment, with no commitment to re-employment when their Board term ends (Whittington 2005, pp. 130–32). Nevertheless, the OIC's governance decisions seem consistent with mimetic institutional influence (DiMaggio and Powell 1983, pp. 154–6).

In the Executive Committee and, even more, in the Scientific Committee, full membership seems to be less important than expertise and independence. Although two members out of nine of the former must be accountants, no other obligations exist with regard to the Committee composition. Members of the Committee are to be highly qualified since they are responsible for ordinary and extraordinary management, as well as approving national accounting principles issued by the Scientific Committee.[3] Yet, to assure that all parties potentially interested in financial reporting can express their views, the Executive Committee's key decisions require approval by at least six of the nine Committee members and must be examined by the observers (Bank of Italy, Consob, Isvap, Ministries of Justice and of Finance) before being approved. Also, the Scientific Committee members are not appointed following their relationship to institutions interested in financial reporting, but as experts to carry out technical duties.

To ensure transparency and participation in the decision-making process, and consistent with the need for due-process legitimacy (Wallace 1990, pp. 11–14), the OIC allows the Scientific Committee to apply whatever rules it considers appropriate and to form 'ad hoc working groups', and requires it to be assisted by observers (OIC, 2001h). As the proposals of the Scientific Committee are discussed, possibly modified and then approved by the Executive Committee, this forward-and-back process is part of the procedure meant to guarantee that finally approved documents are satisfactorily received by all interested groups. The discussed process is time-consuming and has often been debated. Yet, it has been voluntarily confirmed since it is conceived as a guarantee of equilibrium in decisions and can prevent single constituencies from significantly affecting decisions. Eventually, it is worth noting that a technical staff was created aside from the Scientific Committee, comprising a majority of full-time members (Canfield 1999, pp. 132-

3; Whittington 2005, pp. 130–2).

The governance structures and mechanisms discussed above recall survival strategies of organisations seeking legitimacy (Wallace 1990, pp. 11–14). The more evident analogies are:

1. the weight given to institutional competence, both in terms of expertise and independence, within each organ of the national standard setter, as it results clearly from the organisation's statute (OIC, 2001h);
2. the recognition that, lacking a clear mandate, legitimacy can be garnered through competence and independence. Like the IASC (Wallace 1990, pp. 11–12), the OIC lacks a clear mandate: since its foundation, it was underlined that the OIC would acquire legitimacy through its competence and independence (OIC, 2001e);
3. the willingness to satisfy its diverse constituencies, providing them with the opportunity to find representation within the Board of Directors and to be safeguarded through qualified majorities and open hearings (OIC, 2001h);
4. the decision to dilute the concentration of accountants on the Board, specifying the number of Board members assigned to each constituency (OIC, 2001h).

Funding

Following resource dependency (Oliver, 1990; Tolbert, 1985), the successful competition for scarce resources enhances the organisation's legitimisation and increases its survival likelihood (DiMaggio, 1988; Dowling and Pfeffer, 1975; Oliver, 1990). In the case of the OIC, resources consist primarily of contributions and to a lesser extent rhetoric support (Kenny and Larson 1993, p. 539–40). Regarding the former, it was initially assumed that the OIC would be a private foundation, with a starting Endowment Fund whose returns would have covered operational costs (OIC, 2000b). The starting Endowment Fund would have been provided by the preparers (23 per cent), the regulators (23 per cent), the accountants (5 per cent), the Italian Stock Exchange (4 per cent) and the State (45 per cent) (OIC, 2001a).

Afterwards, in addition to a lower Endowment Fund than that initially assumed, constituencies decided to provide a contribution for a three-year period, more than 60 per cent of which was awarded by the preparers (Table 8.2). This choice boosts the need for legitimisation of the OIC; and the weight of the preparers' contribution stresses the need for governance structures and mechanisms able to safeguard effective membership and independence in decision making.

Table 8.2 Contributions provided by the constituencies of OIC
(up to November 2005)

Preparers	Percentage
Abi	15.070
Andaf	0.240
Ania	10.345
Assilea	1.100
Assonime	2.170
Confagricoltura	7.870
Confapi	0.725
Confcommercio	10.760
Confindustria	<u>15.070</u>
	63.350

Accountancy Profession	
Assirevi	8.330
Dottori Commercialisti	8.330
Ragionieri	<u>8.330</u>
	24.990

Users	
Aiaf	0.415
Assogestioni	0.830
Centrale dei Bilanci	<u>0.415</u>
	1.660

The Italian Stock Exchange	<u>10.000</u>
	100.000

Source: OIC, 2005c.

THE ROLE OF THE OIC IN THE LIGHT OF INTERNATIONAL AND NATIONAL REGULATIONS

As discussed in the previous section, the main objectives of the OIC can be summarised as follows:
1. helping national legislators enact financial reporting regulations that foster convergence between national regulations and European Directives;
2. providing guidance for the adoption of IFRS in Italy taking IFRIC's interpretations into the highest consideration;
3. developing and interpreting national accounting principles;
4. cooperating with international standard setters.

As far as the first objective is concerned, the OIC has contributed to the Italian accounting system harmonisation in at least two ways. With reference to the Regulation (EC) No. 1606/2002 of the European Parliament and of the Council, the OIC has promoted the adoption of IFRS also for individual accounts of listed companies. With the Decree no. 38 of 28 February 2005, the national legislator espoused the OIC's suggestion and established that listed firms are to adopt IFRS for their individual accounts by 2006. The legislator considered the adoption of IFRS for consolidated and individual accounts of listed firms, which is necessary to compare firms and consequently to promote market efficiency (OIC, 2005a). Eventually, this argument prevailed over arguments against the application of IFRS for individual accounts (for an extensive discussion of arguments in favour and against the adoption of IFRS for individual accounts, see Haller and Eierle 2004, pp. 35–8). As a consequence of the OIC's contribution, Italy is one of the few European countries that will require the adoption of IFRS in the individual accounts of listed firms, together with Greece and some countries previously under the influence of the former Soviet Union. The preparers have now to cope with this requirement, whose importance has, to some extent, been underestimated and passed over in silence.

With respect to the Directive 2003/51/EC of the European Parliament and of the Council, which the Italian Government has not yet complied with, the OIC has been playing an advisory role supporting the national legislator. In this respect, it seems likely that the national legislator will allow firms to adopt either traditional accounting principles or new principles 'harmonised' with IFRS. More precisely, it could be argued that the harmonisation of the accounting principles included in the Civil Code should mainly concern the disclosure of firms' values. In the same way, it seems possible that the regulation intended to give priority to the substance rather than to the contractual form of operations will be extended to all firms. In contrast, it could be assumed that accounting principles regarding fair value measurements – or at least the most challenging ones – will be optional.

If the Italian compliance with the Directive 2003/51/EC follows this path, Italian firms will probably adopt different sets of accounting principles, resulting in poor comparability of financial accounts and firms' performance (Haller and Eierle 2004, pp. 35–7). On the one hand, large, international firms with financial instruments widely distributed among the public will probably adopt IFRS for their financial accounts, either because they are obliged to (this is the case for Italy from 2006) or on a voluntary basis. In contrast, small and medium non-listed firms will possibly use national accounting principles for their financial accounts and will choose – where possible – between 'traditional' and 'harmonised' options, judging if the potential benefits arising from higher quality reporting outweigh the costs arising from accounting system changes (Haller and Eierle 2004, pp. 35–7).

As far as the OIC's second objective is concerned, firms that have been required to adopt IFRS have been increasingly seeking guidance (Schipper 2005, p. 103–6). Guidance seems to be even more necessary in Italy than in other European countries, since Italy has experienced a stronger acceleration in the adoption of IFRS for financial reporting than other European countries. Indeed, the need for guidance may be considered particularly pressing in Italy in that the Italian legislator has settled on the obligation for listed firms, firms with financial instruments widely distributed among the public, as well as banks, to adopt IFRS for their individual accounts by 2006. Their compliance is critical as individual accounts are used, as in other European countries such as Germany (Haller and Eierle 2004, p. 35), for tax computation, dividend determination and loss assessment to reduce equity if necessary. In this respect, the OIC has played a role of guidance, providing guidelines for IFRS adoption in Italy, taking IFRIC's interpretations into the highest consideration. In October 2005 the OIC published a complete and detailed guidebook to help firms adopt IFRS. The guidebook should prove useful for listed firms required to adopt IFRS for their individual accounts from 2006 (OIC, 2005a).

With reference to the OIC's third objective, for firms that do not adopt IFRS and whose main normative reference is thus represented by the Civil Code, the OIC focuses upon developing – and subsequently interpreting – national accounting principles to integrate and clarify the principles of the Civil Code, which will be modified following the Directive 2003/51/EC.

As far as the OIC's fourth objective is concerned, the national standard setter has been contributing to the definition process of the structures and mechanisms of cooperation between national and international standard setters. So far, this process has reached its peak with the publication by the IASB of the 'Draft Memorandum of Understanding on the Role of Accounting Standard Setters and their Relationships with the IASB' (MOU) in February 2005, which was received by the OIC on 18 February 2005 (IASB, 2005a). On 27 April 2005, the Board of

Directors of the OIC approved the comments on the Draft MOU prepared by the Scientific Committee and, on 28 July 2005, sent the IASB its comment letter. The letter highlights the OIC's attitude on some important issues, such as (OIC, 2005b):

1. the relevance of the role national standard setters are to play in the IFRS issuing process. Using the OIC's own words, '[...] a widespread use of IAS/IFRS, or at least a convergence towards IAS/IFRS, is unthinkable unless the IAS/IFRS issuing process is agreed with by the NSSs (which must be actively involved in said process)';

2. the idea that the structures and mechanisms of cooperation between national standard setters and the IASB must be rethought to provide the opportunity for a deeper involvement of national standard setters in the IFRS developing process. Literally: '[...] it is necessary to review the process of forming the organs of the IASB, their make-up and their representativeness';

3. the belief that the relationships between national standard setters and the IASB cannot be defined without taking into account the role of the European Union. More precisely, 'Italy's membership of the EU means that the OIC, in its relations and role with the IASB, cannot leave aside the relationships and role of the EU with the IASB [...]';

4. the willingness to join international projects; for instance '[...] the OIC views the IASB project concerning NPAEs very favourably and can only be very interested in participating in said project'.

The OIC's comment letter, together with another 62 comment letters received by the IASB (IASB, 2005b), has been examined by the IASB in depth and has resulted in the 'Draft Statement of Best Practice Concerning the Relationship between the IASB and other Accounting Standard-Setters' (IASB, 2005c), published by the IASB in September 2005.

CONCLUSION

Until recently, Italy's experience in the process of convergence towards international accounting principles was one of inertia. When in 2000 the European Commission announced its intention to require IFRS for use in the group accounts of all firms listed on the stock exchanges within the European Union from January 2005, Italy faced difficulties in managing the harmonisation process as firstly, the Italian accounting practice and philosophy differed from the IASB proposals, in that they were mainly government driven, tax dominated and code-based; secondly, the former national standard setter was not highly legitimised among all parties potentially interested in financial reporting; and thirdly, Italy played only a marginal role in the international standard setting context. Yet, since 2000, Italy has undergone an impressive acceleration of its convergence process. This was due primarily to the foundation of the OIC as a national standard setter that has contributed significantly to the definition of challenging objectives and of the boundaries and contents of the process, having achieved a high institutional legitimacy. As a consequence of the results the OIC has already attained, it can be argued that in the future it will play an important role in the convergence process, particularly in helping to reduce international differences in accounting standards (especially for private and non-listed companies) and obtaining national leadership in guiding the evolutionary path of Italian accounting culture, thus reinforcing indirectly the IASB's leadership.

NOTES

1   This is Directive 2003/51/EC of the European Parliament and of the Council of 18 June 2003, amending Directives 78/660/ECC, 83/349/ECC, 86/635/ECC and 91/647/ECC on the annual and consolidated accounts of certain types of companies, banks and other financial institutions and insurance undertakings.
2   The Board of Directors appoints the members of the Executive Committee and approves the organisations' strategic plans, budgets and accounts (OIC, 2001h).
3   More precisely, the Executive Committee appoints its President; appoints the President and the members of the Scientific Committee; appoints the General Secretary; proposes organisation's objectives and plans to the Board of Directors; approves Scientific Committee's work plan; approves national accounting principles, their interpretations and opinions about accounting regulations; approves the attitude the Scientific Committee suggests towards the cooperation with international standard setters; suggests nominees for members of the EFRAG, of the IASB or of other international institutions; prepares organisations' budgets and accounts; and assures the broadest membership among the Scientific Committee (OIC, 2001h).

REFERENCES

Alexander, D. and S. Archer (2003), *European Accounting Guide*, New York, US: Aspen.
Canfield, C. (1999), 'FASB v. IASC: Are the Structure and Standard Setting Process at the IASC Adequate for the Securities and Exchange Commission to Accept International Accounting Standards for Cross-Border Offerings?', *Northwestern Journal of International Law and Business*, **20**(1), 125–45.
Coda, V. (2002), 'Il Legame tra Strategia e Comunicazione Economico-Finanziaria' (tr. The Relationship among Strategy and Financial Communication), in Di Martino S. (ed.), *Investor Relations, Corporate Governance e Valore d'Impresa (tr. Investor Relations, Corporate Governance and Enterprise Value)*, Milan: Egea, pp. 13–19.
Carattozzolo, M. (1998), Il bilancio d'esercizio *(tr. The Annual Report)*, Milan: Giuffré.
Colombo, G. E. and G. B. Portale (1994), *Trattato sulle società per azioni (tr. Dissertation on limited companies)*, Turin: UTET.
DiMaggio, P. (1988), 'Interest and Agency in International Theory', in Zucler L. (ed.), *Institutional Patterns and Organizations*, Cambridge, MA: Ballinger Press, pp. 3–21.
DiMaggio, P. and W. Powell (1983), 'The Iron Cage Revisited: Institutional Isomorphism

and Collective Rationality in Organizational Fields', *American Sociological Review*, **48**, 147–60.

Dowling, J. and J. Pfeffer (1975), 'Organisational Legitimacy: Social Values and Organisational Behaviour', *Pacific Sociological Review*, **18**(1), 122–36.

FEE – Fédérations des Experts Comptables Européens. (2000), *Accounting Standard Setting in Europe*.

Gornik-Tomaszewski, S. and I.N. McCarthy (2003), 'Cooperation Between FASB and IASB to Achieve Convergence of Accounting Standards', *Review of Business*, **24**(2), 52–60.

Hagigi, M. and A. Sponza (1990), 'Financial Statement Analysis of Italian Companies: Accounting Practices, Environmental Factors, and International Corporate Performance Comparisons', *The International Journal of Accounting*, **25**(4), 234–51.

Haller, A. and B. Eierle (2004), 'The Adoption of German Accounting Rules to IFRS: A Legislative Balancing Act', *Accounting in Europe*, **1**, 27–50.

IASB – International Accounting Standards Board. (2005a), Draft Memorandum of Understanding on the Role of Accounting Standard Setters and their Relationships with the IASB (MOU).

IASB – International Accounting Standards Board. (2005c), Draft Memorandum of Understanding on the Role of Accounting Standard Setters and their Relationships with the IASB – Comment Letter Summary.

IASB – International Accounting Standards Board. (2005c), Draft Statement of Best Practice Concerning the Relationship between the IASB and other Accounting Standard-Setters.

Johnson, S.B. and S. Solomons (1984), 'Institutional Legitimacy and the FASB', *Journal of Accounting and Public Policy*, **3**(3), 165–83.

Kenny, S.Y. and R.K. Larson (1993), 'Lobbying behaviour and the development of international accounting standards', *European Accounting Review*, **2**(3), 531–54.

Meyer, J.W. and B. Rowan (1977), 'Institutionalized Organizations: Formal Structure as Myth and Ceremony', in Meyer J. W. and W. R. Scott (eds), *Organizational Environments*. Beverly Hills, CA: Sage, pp. 45–67.

Meyer, J.W. and W.R. Scott (1983), *Organizational Environments*. Beverly Hills, CA: Sage.

Nobes, C. (1983), 'A Judgemental International Classification of Financial Reporting Practices', *Journal of Business Finance and Accounting*, **10**(1), 1–19.

Nobes, C. and R. Parker (2003), *Comparative International Accounting*, London: Prentice Hall.

OIC – Organismo Italiano di Contabilità. (2000a), Principi contabili: situazione attuale e proposte operative (tr. Accounting principles: present situation and operational proposals).

OIC – Organismo Italiano di Contabilità. (2000b), Promemoria incontro del 5 dicembre 2000 in tema di Istituto Nazionale di Contabilità (tr. Memorandum for the meeting of 5 December 2000 regarding the National Accounting Institute).

OIC – Organismo Italiano di Contabilità. (2001a), La costituzione dell'Organismo Italiano di Contabilità (tr. The foundation of the Italian Accounting Body).

OIC – Organismo Italiano di Contabilità. (2001b), Nota per la riunione del 3 aprile p.v. (tr. Memorandum for the meeting of 3 April 2001).

OIC – Organismo Italiano di Contabilità. (2001c), Steering Committee per la costituzione di un Organismo Italiano di Contabilità. Verbale della prima riunione del Segretariato (tr. Steering Committee for the foundation of an Italian Accounting Body. Report of the first meeting of the Secretariat).

OIC – Organismo Italiano di Contabilità. (2001d), Nota per la riunione dello Steering Committee per la costituzione di un Organismo Italiano di Contabilità del 4 giugno 2001 (tr. Memorandum for the meeting of the Steering Committee for the foundation of an Italian Accounting Body of 4 June 2001).

OIC – Organismo Italiano di Contabilità. (2001e), Steering Committee per la costituzione di un Organismo Italiano di Contabilità. Verbale della seconda riunione dello Steering Committee (tr. Steering Committee for the foundation of an Italian Accounting Body. Report of the second meeting of the Steering Committee).

OIC – Organismo Italiano di Contabilità. (2001f), Proposte in tema di compiti e governance dell'Organismo Italiano di Contabilità (tr. Proposals regarding the role and governance of the Italian Accounting Body).

OIC – Organismo Italiano di Contabilità. (2001g), Steering Committee per la costituzione di un Organismo Italiano di Contabilità. Verbale della terza riunione dello Steering Committee (tr. Steering Committee for the foundation of an Italian Accounting Body. Report of the third meeting of the Steering Committee).

OIC – Organismo Italiano di Contabilità. (2001h), Statuto della Fondazione (tr. Foundation's statute).

OIC – Organismo Italiano di Contabilità. (2005a), Guida Operativa per la Transizione ai principi contabili internazionali (IFRS) (tr. Guidebook to the Adoption of International Accounting Principles).

OIC – Organismo Italiano di Contabilità. (2005b), Comment letter on the 'Draft Memorandum of Understanding on the Role of Accounting Standard Setters and their relationships with the IASB'.

OIC – Organismo Italiano di Contabilità. (2005c), Contributi erogati dai soci (tr. Contributions provided by the constituencies).

OIC – Organismo Italiano di Contabilità. (2005d), Planned implementation of the IAS Regulation (1606/2002) in the EU and EEA.

Oliver, C. (1990), 'Determinants of Interorganizational Relationship: Integration and Future Developments', Academy of Management Review, 15(2), 241–65.

Schipper, K. (2005), 'The Introduction of International Accounting Standards in Europe: Implications for International Convergence', European Accounting Review, 14(1), 101–26.

Sfameni, P. (2001), 'Le fonti della disciplina e del bilancio delle società' (tr. Sources of regulations and annual report), in Bianchi L.A. (ed.) La disciplina giuridica del bilancio d'esercizio (tr. Regulations on annual report), Milan: Il Sole24 Ore.

Tolbert, P. (1985), 'Institutional Environments and Resource Dependence: Sources of Administrative Structure in Higher Education', Administrative Science Quarterly, 30(1), 1–13.

Wallace, R.S.O. (1990), 'Survival Strategies of a Global Organization: The Case of the International Accounting Standards Committee', Accounting Horizons, 4, 1–22.

Whittington, G. (2005), 'The Adoption of International Accounting Standards in the European Union', European Accounting Review, 14(1), 127–53.

Zambon, S. (1999), 'On the Verge of Change. Accounting Regulations and Practice Have Undergone a Unique Evolution in Italy', Accountancy, 123(1270), 71–76.

Zambon, S. and C. Saccon (1993), 'Accounting Change in Italy. Fresh Start or Gattopardo's Revolution?', European Accounting Review, 2(2), 245–84.

Zeff, S.A. (2002), '"Political" Lobbying on Proposed Standards: A Challenge to the IASB', Accounting Horizons, 16(1), 43–54.

9 French Accounting Revolution: Implementing IFRS in French Companies

Serge Evraert and Jean-François des Robert

INTRODUCTION

Pushed by the European Union (EU)[1] globalisation initiatives and constraints, in 2003 France imposed a 2005 deadline for the mandatory implementation of International Financial Reporting Standards (IFRS) by French listed companies. Simultaneously or progressively, IFRS will also be adopted by unlisted French entities. The new set of now Anglo-Saxon accounting rules endorsed by the EU may not in the first place significantly affect firms other than those stock exchange listed companies drawing up consolidated accounts and their subsidiaries, but they convey serious changes in accounting policy and methods, some of them already impacting the whole set of annual accounts. This unusual shift in a Code Law country, although having been anticipated for a long time, can nevertheless be qualified as sudden.

In order to appreciate the magnitude of the subsequent operating changes, a flashback is useful to help recall the striking features of the French accounting model as it has operated. The current shifts will then be presented along with their economic, legal and tax consequences and the likely reactions of many stakeholders, given these impacts.

BACKGROUND

Setting and implementing modern accounting principles, while preparing business enterprises and the accounting profession for global trends, has been a constant concern for French public authorities and the accounting profession over the past 50 years.

During the twentieth century, public authorities made little effort to promote accountancy as a strong and necessary management tool, with the exception of the period commencing after the Second World War. In the 1940s, France had neither reliable industrial statistics nor had it implemented a set of national accounts and a mandatory accounting system for business enterprises. This probably reflected the economic reality of a country still dominated by agriculture with its myriad of small and medium enterprises using ad hoc management practices. During this period a step forward for organising modern company accounting occurred under the German occupation. But the real effort was made during the 15 years following 1945 and the end of hostilities establishing the foundations of the principles still existing for French accountancy. During this period new institutions were created, including the National Accounting Council (NAC), the French standard-setting body. Also, a uniform chart of accounts with many industry and business variants was established. The initial 'Plan Comptable' dating from 1947 was updated in 1957 and extended to include cost accounting recommendations and techniques. With the help of tax authorities and on a voluntary basis, by 1960, the French Comptable had been successfully adopted and implemented by French companies for the drawing up of annual accounts.

From its origin, the French accounting model characteristics featured attachment to an organised and detailed accounting scheme, fidelity to a uniform chart of accounts and the influence of tax on annual accounts. In addition to this, the initial design choice gave a strong analytic emphasis exemplified by a strict codification for accounts and a classification of expenditures reported by nature rather than by destination. This was completed in 1983 by a functional presentation of the accounting elements recognised in the income statement and in the balance sheet. This rational form of the French accounting model was not necessarily conservative with strong emphasis on compliance with accounting law, nor could it be depicted as showing a traditional and well accepted French 'centralisation perspective'. It is fair to say that the French standards setting body, from the very beginning, strived to set rules by consensus. This was reflected by its representative composition of a large variety of stakeholders. But, contrary to Anglo-Saxon countries, the organisation of the accounting profession was always supervised by the State and the profession itself, as in other Code Law countries, never had the primary responsibility for setting accounting rules.

Tailored to the needs of after-war reconstruction and to the economic structure of the French economy with State and banking intermediation and moderate market influence, the system functioned well and the ongoing process of standards harmonisation which took place in the EU throughout the 1960s did not alter it.

THE BIG CHANGES: COMPLIANCE WITH THE EU AND THE IASB RULES

Enormous changes, certainly unforeseen, were to come with the adoption of the 1983 seventh EU directive on consolidated accounts. The directive was permissive, with numerous accounting method options. Under UK influence, the introduction of the true and fair view concept and override, along with mandatory footnote information disclosures, increased that permissiveness. Those changes, incorporated in the French Code of Commerce in 1983, were probably inevitable as the full extension of the economic and financial markets under the new Libre Echange Perspective carried forward by the EU since 1985 shows. Modern market economies possibly need more transparency and to be driven by economic values rather than by legal perspectives to ensure accounting serves stakeholder interests. But one should not exaggerate the distorting effects conveyed by the legal and taxation system on corporate accounts. Such effects do also exist elsewhere. However they arose, throughout the reconstruction phase of the postwar period and after, these effects did not hinder the process of building a new, modern and competitive economy supported by more and more national and multinational continental enterprises. Company accounts were restated by financial analysts and auditors when necessary, and until the early 1980s the growth of private and public investment and the restoration of the liquid assets of firms would not rely on products and shares sold on the financial markets.

Furthermore, the National Accounting Council and French public authorities played the game with initial adherence to International Accounting Standards (later replaced by International Financial Reporting Standards and hereafter referred to as IFRS) promulgated by the International Accounting Standards Committee (IASC, now the International Accounting Standards Board, IASB), screening for discrepancies between IFRS and French standards and giving encouragement to France's major companies for early adoption of IFRS. In the 1990s France acted voluntarily as a precursor to adopting IFRS by changing its national chart of accounts (1993), reforming the national standard setter, the Conseil National de la Comptabilité (CNC) to incorporate new 'technical' organisational devices and methods inspired from Anglo-Saxon practice[2] and creating a new institution the CRC (Comité de la Réglementation Comptable[3]) for the future endorsement and implementation of IFRS. From this, it can be seen that France, as a member of the EU, fully accepted the organisation and necessary consequences of a unified and complete, enlarged European market.

THE NEW ACCOUNTING CHALLENGE: IFRS IMPACTS AND CONSEQUENCES

As a consequence of the EU Council regulation mandating that approximately 8700 listed European companies, representing about 25 per cent of the world market capitalisation implement IFRS from fiscal year 2005,[4] all French CFOs and CPAs and their colleagues in other EU countries face the dilemma of changing their accounting model. It is clear that the cost will be high and it is growing with the extension of the amount of the accounting information to be recognised, disclosed and finally released with uncertain benefits to the public at large who will ultimately bear the cost of the incremental supply of information. Will the benefits offset the costs?

More than 1,100 groups currently listed in France will have to use IFRS for their consolidated financial statements. This represents 29,000 individual subsidiaries belonging to these groups and a further 1,800 groups under foreign control. Later, if all 5,000 parent companies presenting consolidated financial statements have to use IFRS, it will be 40,000 companies that will be affected.[5] If all enterprises have to do so, this will be almost 2 million enterprises in total. The French accounting standards have already been changed to incorporate new provision as discussed below.

Will the changes outperform the Plan Comptable experience? Will the growing emphasis on market values be a superior resource for decision making to the old historical cost and continental model? Will financial accountancy be more reliable and relevant? Will the continental accounting professions be able to challenge accounting principles developed by the US/UK accounting systems makers? These questions are unanswered and the future net benefits are probably impossible to assess. At this stage, we can only consider the impacts of the change in accounting methods and try to imagine the organisational arrangements.

THE NEW REPORTING APPROACH IN FRANCE

Providing more information to investors is the core of the new international GAAP, IFRS. Since the IASB's Reduction of Options Project and the tentative convergence project which began with IOSCO and now, under the IASB's new constitution with FASB, the idea always seems to have been two-fold: getting listed companies a full set of accounting standards accepted on stock exchanges worldwide, without any reconciliation constraints, and providing investment companies with an understandable and unique set of accounting standards from which benefits would flow for financial investment and lending purposes.

The main consequences for the French accounting system are likely to be:

- Market-based versus stakeholders and tax-based reporting: French enterprises and all stakeholders will have to change their conception of financial statements and accounting, which are still specially and almost completely based upon tax.
- Transparency: Currently, financial statements are complex, mainly for outsiders, but this complexity is well understood by accountants and practitioners because it is based upon the Plan Comptable, which corresponds not only to tax regulations and to national statistics needs, but also to management and financial needs. For instance, the French Income Statement shows the Value Added, which is necessary for the production of statistics at a national level, and even for the computation of GNP, which is estimated by addition of all the added values of French enterprises. Moreover, the intermediary management indicators (like EBE ('Excédent brut d'exploitation') and VA ('valeur ajoutée') are considered as important tools for management and financial evaluation. Consequently, the statistical computation of value added, which needs not only the individualisation of salaries and fringe benefits and depreciation, but also of external services and consumptions, must appear in the financial statements and should be presented in a note, in addition to IFRS.
- Timely information: Large French companies, especially listed groups, have made progress towards producing financial information soon after the end of reporting periods. While SMEs have to respect the legal and tax obligations of delay (three months and six months), this obligation will probably be reduced so that the French financial information, especially for SMEs, is no longer considered as superseded and outmoded when it is produced.
- Added recognition and increased number of financial statements: The number and style of financial statements will not change much because all the models of financial statements required by IFRS exist in the French system; only the statement of change in equity, which is not very widespread amongst SMEs will have to be developed. The number, quantity and quality of notes will increase, too.
- Added disclosure will be probably the main impact in terms of financial statements. This will not be at the level of balance sheet and income statement, where disclosures will probably be reduced if compared with the official French presentation, but because the cash-flow statement and notes will be developed. The cash-flow statement, from being optional in France in most cases, will become compulsory and more detailed. Companies will have to choose between the indirect method, which is still the only rule in

France, and the direct method. For this issue, most French companies will prefer to retain the indirect method, which starts from net income. Then, if they are obliged to use the direct method, they will prefer to have a reconciliation table between cash flow from operations and net income. As to the notes, very detailed notes exist in the French accounting system, but they have a rather formal content, and are produced often by the 'cut and paste' method. The notes will need to become clearer, stricter, longer and more significant.

FRENCH ACCOUNTING RULES COMPARED WITH IFRS

There are numerous discrepancies between IFRS and French accepted accounting principles from a philosophical, methodological and practical perspective.

From a philosophical and legal point of view, the French approach to accounting is still based upon the Civil and Commercial Code, and on the patrimonial nature of accounting. The balance sheet is the representation of the patrimony of the firm, and must show assets which guarantee creditors' rights. Consequently, such principles as substance over form seem totally inapplicable. Thus, the registration of assets of items which do not belong to the company as a legal person, such as financial leases, are totally contrary to the basic principle that only properties must appear as assets on the balance sheet. This recognition of non-owned assets is accepted for consolidated financial statements, but not for legal individual accounts, which are considered distinct from group accounts, which are supposed to convey only a monetary value without any legal consequence.

Differences also arise from a methodological point of view: As accounting is only considered to be a branch of the Law often called the 'algebra of Law' in France, the approach of IFRS, which do not show 'what must be done, but what should be done' is totally incompatible with the legal approach of the 'Plan Comptable', based upon a complex edifice of laws, decrees, and by-laws. The French system does not accommodate the difference between standards which are supposed to be optional, and become 'norms' only when they have been accepted by a group of entities, and 'rules' when they are enforced by the law. These subtleties do not correspond at all to the French legal concepts, and it is fair to say that most of the concepts of IFRS have no equivalent in French legal terminology. For instance fair value has been translated as 'juste valeur', i.e. just value, impairment of assets as 'dépréciation d'actif' (depreciation of assets), and even the terms income or expenses do not have the same signification as 'produits' and 'charges'. Furthermore, the methodology of IFRS, based upon definitions, objectives, options and other standardisation mechanisms is not understandable at first by a French lawyer, and consequently by a French accountant, with a legal and fiscal background. Even the system of having IAS numbered from 1 to 41, with numbers 2, 3, 4, 5, 6 and 13 missing, superseded or completed by IFRS with the same rank of numbers seems very strange in the country of Descartes. Although the French specialists are able to understand this Anglo-Saxon approach, they are not anxious to abandon their old and familiar logical system, dating from the Romans and Napoleon, just for the apparent reason that the Anglo-Saxon system has come to dominate the accounting world.

Nonetheless, the European and, after that, the French authorities, decided in 2003 to adopt IFRS, and make them compulsory for group accounts from 2005. Most accountants and specialists consider that they do not need to be applied to individual accounts, especially for SMEs.

Excluding group accounts that are actually very close to IFRS, a number of differences do exist between French accounting rules and IFRS applicable at 2005. Some are significant, and all of them will probably be clarified and/or disappear:

- The IFRS conceptual framework accounting principles and conventions are almost all already adopted in France (only neutrality, substance over form and completeness are likely to be problematic).
- The five elements of financial statements already exist and have just to be made compulsory (especially the Statement of Change in Equity).
- Deferred expenses, training and education and R&D expenses may be capitalised in France. In IFRS, only development costs may be recognised as assets, and the others are expensed as incurred.
- The approach by constituents for depreciation, as well as impairment tests and evaluation of fixed assets has been already introduced in 2004,[6] but the principle of provision for large repairs remains accepted in France.
- Investment grants will not have to be included in owner's equity, as is the case in France, but registered as conditional loans.
- The use of the completion method for construction and long-term contracts is preferred, but not compulsory, in France as the alternative method is permitted. Also, deferred tax is permitted but not compulsory.
- Capital leases are not recognised as assets, nor lease rentals as equivalent liabilities (IAS 17). As long as the French Law does not permit capitalisation of un-owned assets in company accounts, the IFRS on financial lease will not be accepted in France.
- Employee benefits are registered as provisions, and not compulsory, but the system of pensions and retirements is different, thus the issue is not material, except for very large organisations, like public entities.
- The concept of errors (fundamental or not), or the treatment of changes in

accounting principles, is not applied in the same way by IFRS and French regulations, where the opening balance must correspond to the former closing balance, without any direct entry on capital or reserves.

- The Income Statement will possibly be presented by function in IFRS, although de facto, only the presentation by nature exists in France, and the presentation by function would need a reconciliation table of expenses by function, into expenses categorised by nature.
- Prepaid expenses and deferred revenues will have to be integrated to debtors' and creditors' accounts, and not shown separately, when IFRS are applied.
- The use of fair value is not yet recognised in France, and the system of financial instruments has no equivalent for individual accounts. The fair value principle does not apply to revaluations of assets or to biological assets.
- The 'off balance sheet accounts' at the moment reported at the end of the balance sheet will be transferred to the notes.
- In France, there is no glossary, as in IFRS, but there is a detailed designation and functioning of compulsory accounts, with a precise list including recommended accounts and coding.
- The French Financial statements models are not just examples but standards compulsory for tax purposes.

From this it appears that with possible exceptions relating to tax influence, leased assets, some principles and valuation bases, many practical differences can be dealt with by convergence of the French Law towards IFRS.

PROCESS FOR CHANGE AND POSITION OF STAKEHOLDERS

Although some stakeholders are still fighting in France against IFRS, most of them consider that it is time now to adapt international standards in the French regulations. The process of change is relatively slow because the stakeholders existing in France in the field of accounting standards are somewhat different from what they are considered to be in the conceptual framework of IFRS. Other stakeholders exist who have to be convinced of the necessity of adopting IFRS for all enterprises.

The Tax Administration has a very strong role to play, because there is absolutely no likelihood in France of disconnecting accounting from taxation. Tax forms for profit tax are still considered by most SMEs as the official presentation of financial statements, because they include a balance sheet, an income statement and a tax reconciliation showing the difference between accounting profit and tax profit. These documents are in accordance with the

Plan Comptable. The main issue is that in France the tax administration is sovereign and has the power to insist that companies make their accounting entries in accordance with the tax law. Some years ago, the management of this very strong administration did not want to know about international standards, because it is difficult in a Code Law country to imagine that standards elaborated by an association in the UK could have any effect on the accounting and tax regulation of an independent state. Recently they changed their mind, as there is no way to fight against the European Commission. Furthermore, they realised that they had to understand the differences between the two sets of rules if they wanted to maintain the connection between accounting and tax accounts. Moreover, tax authorities may now consider that, if IFRS were the basis of accounting in France, the tax revenue would be higher, because companies should report with more completeness and accuracy, and consequently the declared revenues and profits which are the basis for taxation would be higher.

The NAC, which is in charge of elaborating not only standards but also regulation, has begun also to take the real measure of the problem. Some of its representatives considered some years ago the alternative of giving up the elaboration of accounting standards plus trying to offset their adverse effects. At this time they were in accord with the French President, Jacques Chirac, who wrote a letter to the President of the European Commission, Mr Romano Prodi, arguing that it was hazardous and quite impossible to apply IAS 32 Financial Instruments: Disclosure and Presentation and IAS 39 Financial Instruments: Recognition and Measurement because of their resulting volatility on performance evaluation and financial condition of all French banks and financial institutions. Now this 'French exception' manifestation has generated a widespread view that probably before the end of a decade, IFRS will be extended to all individual and company accounts. As a consequence, several committees created by the NAC and regrouping practitioners, firms' accountants and public office servants, including tax officers, have begun to work on such important subjects as IFRS and law, IFRS and tax, and IFRS and SMEs, with the aim of convergence between the two systems and of step-by-step introduction of IFRS into French law. As an early result starting with fiscal year 2005, French accounting regulation was rushed to incorporate into company accounts the provisions of IFRS concerning fixed assets and depreciation (e.g., impairment tests) and acquisition of property in accordance with IAS 16 Property, Plant and Equipment and IAS 36 Impairment of Assets. IAS 17 Leases cannot be applied for individual accounts because it is still contrary to the law, although it can be used for consolidated financial statements. But this subtle distinction between economic and legal financial statements will certainly vanish in the near future as consolidated accounts have de facto a legal effect, being the basis for financial contracts and even for dividends and stock market values.

Progressively, financial reporting will overtake accounting but in France, there is no prospect that the connection will be lost with civil, commercial and fiscal law.

The French accounting profession (CPAs and the Auditors Institute) have played a positive role in the acceptance of IFRS in France. On the eve of the twenty-first century, the French profession was generally not in favour of changing standards as no important change had occurred since 1993–94, and they were particularly concerned about the likely economic consequences associated with fees and costs. On realising the change was inevitable, some of the 17,000 CPAs (very few at first) courageously began to organise a new system of training specialised IFRS. As at end of 2005, there had been long-term training programmes representing 150 hours of work. Several hundred CPAs have claimed their IFRS graduation and more that 60 per cent of practitioners claim to be IFRS fluent. In reality, very few of them have the opportunity to practice, because only 1,000 large groups have to draw up consolidated financial statements, 90 per cent of them being audited and advised by four big firms. Some small firms have access as consultants to the real world of IFRS, but the majority of practitioners, who work in very small accounting firms (less than 10 persons), are not directly affected. However, progressively, the situation of the legal accounting system is evolving towards IFRS, as has already happened with the CNC regulation 2004-15 for fixed assets and depreciation and accountants need to be informed about the fundamental changes that have begun, and their possible tax impact. In order to permit this evolution, the French Accounting Institute has created a new internet site, FOCUS IFRS, and promoted several books about IFRS, some of them specially devoted to the issue of introducing IFRS in SMEs, which is the most important problem in France.

The associations of enterprises like MEDEF (French Enterprises Organisation) and CCIP (Chamber of Commerce of Paris), which represent nearly one million enterprises, are cognisant of the IFRS phenomenon. The ad hoc committees and associations created in 2004 have taken positions in favour of the convergence with IFRS, on the basis that they will permit better transparency and better comparability for financial information in France. The CCIP proposed in a report (dated 23 December 2004) first to consider the impact of IFRS on SMEs, second to reinforce the representation of French enterprises on the standard-setting body and third to promote a simplified system for SMEs, especially for the notes to financial statements. In addition to that, the two associations consider that priority should be given to master the fiscal consequences of the convergence with IFRS. The main objective is to maintain the connection between accounting and taxation because this principle offers simplicity and tax security, as much for enterprises as for the tax administration. The main issue is to incorporate into the law the present oral position of the tax administration in favour of the neutrality of the application of IFRS. The fear of most enterprises in France is that the convergence will increase their tax burden by widening the tax basis, for instance by decreasing the amount of accepted provisions and applying the fair valuation of different assets.

The role of the stock exchange and Financial Market Authority will also have an impact on the development of IFRS, because more than 1,000 listed groups, including all Banks and Insurance companies (also listed) will present their financial statements in line with IFRS at the end of 2005. The French financial analysts and brokers have not placed much faith in financial statements, even certified by two auditors, and they have a tendency to prefer to complete their information on the listed companies from other sources. The Financial Market Authority has not yet begun to play its role of financial police in the area, because it has not yet had to make a large judgement on the application of IFRS. The last big issue with Vivendi Universal (VU) was rather a problem of mixed application of US GAAP and French GAAP. Until now, less than 20 French groups have chosen IFRS as a standard for their consolidated financial statements.[7] For this reason, 80 per cent of the French listed firms, compared with 87 per cent at the European level, declared themselves to be completely prepared for the transfer to IFRS at 15 April 2004. According to the same survey[8] the majority of them (around 55 per cent) had informed their stockholders of the impact of IFRS and started to train their staff while subcontracting the implementation of the new standards; only a minority (25 per cent) considered the new financial statements to be more transparent and comprehensive and two thirds of them did not expect improved comparability between countries. On the other hand, 79 per cent tended to minimise the impact of the anticipated accounting change. No majority considered that benefits would offset costs. Thus, there is doubt with 60 per cent of the French groups thinking IFRS are not relevant to their activity segment and that IFRS are likely to offer a larger margin of interpretation than before. Enthusiasm and scepticism are mixed together, and again, at the stock exchange, nobody seems certain that IFRS will have a positive effect on investment, except perhaps that it will encourage American investment versus European investment. As to the stockholders, most of them are not very interested, because the financial market is not popular with the public at large and the real investors, the institutional investors, either master the main issues or consider that IFRS will not have a material effect on dividends and on market values. However, nobody believes that there is a choice other than fully-fledged IFRS, and now that the machine has been launched, those who do not embark will be left alone on the tarmac.

SMALL AND MEDIUM SIZE ENTERPRISES: THE TWO TIER SYSTEM?

Of course the main problem in France is about SMEs, which represent 70 per cent of the GNP, and have a special need for simplification. IFRS were created in the abstract for public linked companies and they were not scheduled to be applied to SMEs. They were conceived to be applied by large companies in order to facilitate good capital market investment decisions. The July 2002 decision of the European Commission to give to the member states the possibility to authorise or to oblige all or certain of their listed and non-listed companies to prepare their individual or consolidated accounts on the basis of IFRS, is not acceptable for the SMEs in France for the following reason. First, as explained above, the application of full IFRS at individual accounts level implies an in-depth reform of fiscal, commercial, accounting and even civil law. Second, a complete application of IFRS will transform management systems of SMEs, and will affect not only the accounting, but all the departments of the companies (e.g., Purchase Department, Sales Department, Treasury Department, Human Resources Department) and all the management software and systems. The cost of introducing IFRS would be a burden such that, even if the practitioners believe that they will profit from IFRS adoption, it is not clear that SMEs will want to pay for it. Another reason is that the enterprise must and will still have a chart of accounts, and that the direction taken by the French standards setter is to revise progressively this general chart of accounts, which has already been renewed in 1999, and will continue to be used by all individual companies. A prefiguration was made in a book published in late 2004 describing the frame of a new Plan Comptable in line with IFRS but preserving the chart of accounts.[9] In that contribution, the definitions in the IFRS glossary replace the former definitions (e.g. assets, liabilities and depreciation). Similarly for the conceptual framework and all the mechanisms of evaluation and registration which supersede the former French standards. Only matters irrelevant for the SMEs like IAS 32, IAS 39, detailed notes and segment information (IAS 14 Segment Reporting) were not mentioned in the proposed system.

The new IFRS Enterprise Accounting System keeps its peculiarity of having a precise nomenclature of accounts, registration mechanisms of accounting entries, with a debit and a credit, a list of accounts with 3, 4 or 5 position numbers inspired from the present system, including some new accounts like deferred taxes (assets, liabilities, expenses and revenues) and proposes models of financial statements which comply with IFRS. The system must include tables of reconciliation between the new IFRS-based accounting system and the French system, but this already existed in the former system, so only such items as deferred taxes or legally-based provisions or depreciation will have to be added.

This new chart of accounts will permit full application of IFRS, except the fact that, where it exists for financial instruments or other difficult areas, the accountant will have to refer to the one thousand pages of the future IFRS Accounting Guide, which currently is perplexing for many of those associated with SMEs. Practically it is unlikely that France could wait until the IASB produces IFRS for SMEs. The new enterprise accounting system must include a special very small entities system, on a cash basis, which will be at least consistent with IFRS, thanks to the fact that it will produce a simplified balance sheet, an income statement, a cash-flow statement and short notes.

CONCLUSION

In conclusion, France is not in the lead pack (with, for example, Germany, the Netherlands and Spain) for the application of IFRS nor is it a complete laggard. There has been a huge movement of conscience in the last three years, encouraged by the authorities, the Financial Market Authority, the two institutes of practitioners, auditors and accountants (CNCC and OEC), the financial institutions, and even the educational system. All dispositions have been taken in order to permit large listed groups to produce IFRS financial statements at the end of 2005, or in 2006 for companies closing before the end of the year. A large number of people have been trained, but it still represents only a small portion of people to be trained. France has chosen the path of a painless change, with a progressive adaptation of the law permitting the convergence to IFRS. The tax administration has begun to accept the measure of the problem, but promises that the tax burden effect of IFRS will be neutral. Only an accounting evolution, not a revolution, will occur, starting with the presentation of consolidated accounts of listed companies, banks and financial institutions by 2005 and 2006.

NOTES

1   Regulation EU (CE no. 1606/2002 [Parliament], 19 July 2002 [European Council], JOCE 11 September 2002.
2   Decree of 26 August 1996 for the CNC.
3   Law of 6 April 1998 for the CRC.
4   Ricol, R. (2003), Les IFRS à terme pour tous? IFRS 2005 Divergences France/IFRS, Editions Francis Lefebvre, p. 1910.
5   Vermersch, Frédérique et Lys, Olivier, 'Nouvelles Normes Internationales IFRS/IAS' Ouverture, No 53, Ordre des Experts Comptables (OEC) France – 'IFRS, Révolution dans l'Entreprise' Les Echos, 13 mai 2004, p. 29.
6   CNC no 2004/15, 23 June 2004.

7   Against 26 under US GAAP.
8   'IFRS Standards: France: Apathic Support' Mazars, IFRS European Survey, 556 enterprises, 2005.
9   Normes IFRS et PME.

REFERENCES

CNCC, OEC, Pilot Study (2003), 'Enterprise Accounting System consistent with international accounting standards (IAS/IFRS) designed for small and medium-size enterprises', International Conference, Warsaw, January 2003, p. 126.

Hoarau, Christian (1998), Accounting in France, in Peter Walton, Axel Haller and Bernard Raffournier, *International Accounting*, London: Thomson.

Richard, Jacques and Colette Christine (2005), *Système Comptable Français et Normes IFRS*, Paris: Dunod, p. 633.

des Robert, J.-F., Méchin, F. and Puteaux, H. (2004), *Normes IFRS et PME*, Paris: Dunod, p. 340.

Scheid, Jean Claude and Walton, Peter (1992), *European Financial Reporting*, France and London: Routledge, p. 357.

10 Accounting Regimes and their Effects on the German Stock Market

Hans Peter Möller

INTRODUCTION

More than a century ago, Germany's codification of the details of external reporting for stock companies was regulated by the Reichstag – later by its successor, the Bundestag. The codification brought to stock companies a century of quite stable and conservative accounting rules. Over time, the degree of conservatism has diminished due to different interpretations of the code as well as legal changes in the years of 1937, 1965 and 1985. The 1985 rules involved most of the German rules becoming a part of European law. The basic valuation principles were preserved within the European context, with historic cost as the maximum basis for asset measurement and as the minimum basis for debt measurement. Apart from additional disclosure requirements, only the amount of allowable future provisioning has been reduced.

This situation changed from 1992 on, when increasing numbers of stock companies began to voluntarily prepare – additional to their financial statements according to German Commercial Law (HGB) – a second set of financial statements prepared according to either US Generally Accepted Accounting Principles (US GAAP) or International Financial Reporting Standards (IFRS) encompassing their predecessor International Accounting Standards (IAS). For convenience, both sets of international standards are referred to as IFRS throughout this chapter. Also, the German stock exchange has introduced for stock companies of the former so called *Neuer Markt*, a subset of the *Geregelter Markt*, the obligation to disclose financial statements according to US GAAP or to IFRS in addition to European/German regulation (HGB) statements.[1] The Commercial Code was modified in 1998 so that stock companies were generally allowed to apply any internationally accepted accounting regime instead of HGB for the preparation of their consolidated financial statements. This was not allowed for non-consolidated financial statements. The modification of the code preceded a European Union regulation which required stock market companies to apply IFRS for consolidated statements from 1 January 2005.

It is interesting to picture the fiscal year 2002, prior to the requirement to adopt IFRS. Seven hundred and thirty stock companies have financial reports disclosed in Germany and have shares listed at one of the eight German stock exchanges: 133 of these reports follow US GAAP, 232 apply IFRS and 365 still apply HGB. The trend not to use HGB for consolidated financial statements is extremely strong among the large corporations. The stock market orientation of many German companies is accompanied by a preference of their managements for non-HGB financial statements. In the move to IFRS, the suspected lack of shareholder orientation of HGB statements is regarded as an important argument. In addition, it is contended that this presumed lack of shareholder orientation causes information which is inferior to IFRS or US GAAP information and therefore leads to a higher cost of capital than the information given under IFRS or US GAAP.[2]

What is the explanation for the regulatory requirement to adopt IFRS from 2005 on? Has it to do with the quality of the European/German regulations or with the image of these regulations? Is European-based law less effective than other laws or standards? Have German companies been so discontent with their traditional HGB codification that they even accepted the burden of accounting under two different regimes for a certain time span? Which of the claimed advantages of US GAAP or IFRS hold in reality? Are there disadvantages to these standards? Which of the supposed HGB disadvantages or advantages can be found in reality? Are, for Germans, the expected advantages of foreign and therefore less known regimes really higher than the disadvantages of the familiar German accounting laws? This chapter details an exploratory study contributing to addressing these questions.

It is consistent with theory that accounting delivers, in a world of incomplete markets under uncertainty, some of the information that shareholders need to make rational investment decisions. In particular, the financial reports governed by accounting regulations in national systems and in international standards generally, aim to ensure that firms provide information useful to financial statement users who do not have the ability to demand specific purpose reports, and who have no direct influence on the management of a firm. Beaver (1998) explains in detail that, under such conditions, accounting-based owners' equity, income, assets, debt, revenues and expenses are elements of the information needed by these shareholders.[3]

The assumption that shareholders use financial data for decision making is especially important and requires that the information delivered is relevant and reliable. The information provided by management is relevant for shareholders if it allows them to learn something about future changes in the value of the company and about future dividends and capital flows. The information is reliable if the numbers are objective and do not depend on undisclosed views and management intentions. The basic question then is whether the different accounting regimes mentioned above, vary in their relevance and reliability. Unfortunately, these two properties of financial reports often compete with each other.[4]

Within the international investment community, it is strongly believed that financial statements according to US GAAP or IFRS are relevant and reliable. This can be read in the introductory conceptual frameworks of these standards. The details of financial statements according to HGB, on the contrary, are widely unknown to this community. If at all, it is known that such statements are conservative and that the management of a German corporation has great discretion. It is often forgotten that the image of German accounting in the literature stems from times with different rules, which have long passed. So, at first glance, it is not clear for a non-German investor whether HGB statements are relevant or reliable. There is no primary source describing to investors the purpose of HGB accounting and no primary source which explains that HGB statements are relevant or reliable. For people accustomed to a common law country with its privately developed standards, it seems hard to understand that accounting rules are codified, and that this codification relies on some basic principles.

In addition, much of the literature on German accounting stresses the importance of creditor protection as one of the objectives of HGB.[5] From these descriptions some authors conclude that investor protection is missing. Those who know the HGB rules would, however, doubt that such a view is caused by the quality of the rules. A far more natural explanation is that the international investment community consists mainly of people who have been brought up in common law countries without any codification of accounting and who therefore know much better how to interpret standards (US GAAP and IFRS) than reports which follow codified regulations. If a company wants to raise finance from this community, it has to present financial statements that this community understands. Up to now it has been largely unknown which of the three regimes delivers more relevant and more reliable numbers. However, many people from the investment industry regard either US GAAP or IFRS as preferable to HGB.

The content of financial statements varies according to the different regimes. One can expect that different sets of financial statements will provide different information for investors. If shareholders analyse the information and act always in the same way, one can also expect that the market properties of financial statements vary according to whether the statements are prepared using HGB, US GAAP or IFRS if these accounting regimes vary. In order to avoid such a variation by different sets of accounting rules, the US Securities and Exchange Commission (SEC) forces foreign companies whose shares are listed at a US stock exchange, to deliver their financial statements according to US GAAP or to present a reconciliation. The London stock exchange requires foreign companies to provide financial statements that follow IFRS. The internationally relatively unimportant role of the German capital market makes it understandable that German HGB is internationally not highly regarded for investment purposes. As at 2005, any of the three above mentioned sets of accounting information may be used in Germany for consolidated financial statements.

It is interesting that many German companies voluntarily moved to non-HGB accounting reports long before the European Union suggested such a change even though they did not plan to use a foreign capital market. Without additional research, it is not possible to establish definitely the reasons for this change. The hope of obtaining capital at a lower cost could be one reason. The expectation that management can present itself in a more positive way (with consequences for any income dependent remuneration) may be another. The chance to reduce the burden of any enforcement (i.e., can German auditors really assure that US GAAP or IFRS have been applied correctly?) can be another reason. It is also interesting that Deutsche Börse AG prescribed financial statements according to US GAAP or IFRS for the relatively small companies at the Neuer Markt, without solid empirical evidence about the advantages of these regimes over HGB statements.

The superiority of US GAAP or IFRS accounting over HGB accounting for stock market information may be queried,[6] and it is not clear that US GAAP or IFRS accounting produce better stock market properties than the continental European HGB-based accounting. Theoretically, it would undoubtedly be possible to find reasons for some standards to be regarded as superior to HGB rules, and *vice-versa*. It is mainly a question of the criteria applied. Overall, though, we have to accept that we do not know much about the effect of different accounting rules on the stock market. This is especially true if investors in different countries analyse financial data in different ways. Most studies to date rely only on small data sets of prior time periods, and the generalisability of the results is either limited or unclear.[7] In contrast to prior studies, this study uses nearly all German stock corporations and covers multiple years. The results are important to price-taking shareholders and also relevant for the institutions that deal with regulation and standardisation of accounting.

The rest of the chapter is organised as follows. The next section describes the limitations of HGB accounting relative to US GAAP and IFRS accounting. As the chapter seeks to demonstrate empirically that present HGB accounting is not necessarily as uninformative to investors as is generally thought, it is not necessary to describe theoretically the advantages of HGB accounting. The chapter then presents results from other studies before describing original and independent research conducted by the author and forming the basis for the tentative conclusions presented in the final section.

LIMITATIONS OF HGB COMPARED TO US GAAP AND IFRS

For managers as well as for shareholders, HGB accounting seems to have only limited attractiveness.[8] Four reasons are often mentioned: (1) the prudence principle, (2) the explicit discretion left to management in defining income, (3) the influence of tax law and (4) the lack of additional information which goes beyond balance sheet and income statement. The importance of the last reason has meanwhile been reduced for stock companies, as stock companies have been required by law to present a cash-flow statement, a statement of owners' equity and a segment report since 1999. Nonetheless, if any or all of these four reasons are important, they are also reasons that could reduce the relevance of HGB statements for shareholders relative to statements according to other accounting regimes.[9]

The prudence principle of the German HGB implies the application of the realisation principle as well as the anticipation of future expenses in the present period. In turn, the realisation principle reflects worldwide the idea that revenues should be recognised when the enterprise delivers work to a market partner. The definition and the interpretation of this principle are in contrast to the IFRS and US GAAP standards which reflect in present reports contracts which enclose a production that ends after the end of the present accounting period.[10] The treatment of such long-term contracts is, however, not a question of the realisation principle, but one of the treatment of future payments in the present income statement. It is a general question of whether future payments should be anticipated in the present period as revenues or expenses. It is often seen as a limitation of HGB accounting that future payments are only reflected if they relate to expenses, and that they are not reflected if they relate to revenues. HGB does not define any probability for future payments to be treated as expenses. This might lead to a reduction of comparability between the financial statements of different firms. It certainly leads to an asymmetrical definition of revenues and expenditures.[11] On the one hand, it is fair to say that excessive or inconsistent anticipation of future expense payments distorts the information content of financial statements and may lead to unintended or inappropriate stock pricing or outcomes of contracts based on accounting numbers. The same is true for the anticipation of future revenue payments. On the other hand, the quality of financial statements presumably rises if the possibilities to build and use these reserves are diminished.

The second reason for HGB criticisms refers to the discretionary items that enable management to influence the annual earnings number. The different possibilities offered in HGB to account for goodwill illustrate this. According to the German code, companies may either deduct goodwill immediately from owners' equity or depreciate it over four years or depreciate it over its useful life. It is generally argued that a regime which (explicitly) allows for high levels of discretion diminishes comparability between firms and over time. Thus, a regime like the German one with its (explicit) discretion will be regarded by shareholders as worse than a regime which does not explicitly offer discretion. Additionally, German HGB did not require, until 1998, statements other than the balance sheet and income statement, management's report included.[12] In this discussion it should, however, be mentioned that the German HGB allows for discretionary items mainly with respect to future expense payments which are anticipated in the current financial statements. US GAAP or IFRS do not offer such high levels of explicit discretion. However, given that US GAAP and IFRS standards (and IFRS standards in particular) refer, contrary to the codified accounting rules, to a few of many situations and problems, it is very probable that due to the incompleteness of standards details there are areas without any standards that offer much discretion. This is, at least, the result of a detailed analysis of US investors of European/German companies.[13] Other chapters in this book address the extent to which each of these accounting regimes is rules-based or principles-based.

A close relation between tax accounting and financial accounting is also mentioned as a limitation of German HGB accounting. This relation may enable a valuation apt for tax purposes in disclosed financial statements. Originating at a time shortly after the First World War when tax rules were just developing in Germany, the principle of the dominance of HGB rules (Maßgeblichkeitsprinzip der Handelsbilanz für die Steuerbilanz) has still survived for cases when there are no tax rules. Today, sometimes tax rules require that for HGB statements the same valuation is chosen as for tax purposes (umgekehrtes Maßgeblichkeitsprinzip). This principle gives management an incentive to apply tax minimising rules instead of stock market relevant rules. It should be mentioned, however, that tax rules have developed in a way that today there are only a few cases left when tax rules require values that are less than HGB values. It is important to note that this third reason only holds for unconsolidated legal entity financial statements which are the basis for taxation. Its importance is irrelevant for consolidated statements of the economic entity.

The final argument, concerned with a lack of information in excess of balance sheet and income statement, has, as described above, also lost its relevance in 1998 with the requirement to prepare a cash-flow statement, from 1999.

Overall, one has to admit that several reasons formally reduce the importance of German HGB accounting for shareholders, as compared to US GAAP or IFRS. However, the German accounting regime offers with its discretion and with its completeness a flexibility that the other regimes lack. One also has to question whether prudent income measurement that corrects for false expectations is better than an overly optimistic income measurement that possibly relies on wrong expectations. The critique concerned with HGB is very similar to the critique which could be attached to financial statements of other European countries, as Germany is subject to European regulation. A consideration of the US accounting scandals of the start of this century as well as the speed with which generally accepted US accounting principles concerning goodwill have been totally changed, create doubt about the assumed stock market superiority of US GAAP and IFRS accounting.

STUDIES OF DIFFERENT ACCOUNTING REGIMES IN GERMANY

It should be stated from the outset that empirical research on the consequences of different accounting regimes for the stock market is quite rare in Germany, as compared to the studies using US data. Comparative studies of different accounting regimes including the HGB regulations are largely limited.[14]

Most studies using German data reflect either historic periods or a small data set. Some of the historical analyses come to the conclusion that there is a big difference between German and US data, while others suggest similar results between Germany and the US. More recent research concentrates on one fiscal year or on the very large stock companies. It is difficult to learn much from an analysis of prior research with German data about the different accounting regimes for an actual description of what is going on today. Therefore, this chapter abstains from a description of this research. The possibility to explore different accounting regimes in the same stock market still offers research possibilities. This chapter exploits one of these possibilities by using a large sample that reflects all segments of the German stock market.

STATE-ORIENTED APPROACH

A stock market may be described by the prices paid for shares. It is possible to aggregate the share prices of a firm to variables that provide information about the whole market. We mainly think of parameters that describe the distribution of prices. One of the approaches for the measurement of the market properties of different accounting regimes is to examine these variables before and after a change in the applied regime. Such event studies assist in evaluating the relevance of the event. Problems always arise, however, when there are several events happening close to each other, or when not all events are reported.

Another approach for measuring the stock market properties of different accounting regimes is to distinguish between different market segments according to the accounting regimes used by firms. An analysis of differences between the distributions of share prices in the different segments might inform us about the relevance of the different regimes. Under such an approach events are less important. As we describe states instead of changes we could call this a state-oriented approach.

The central problem of both approaches is to control for factors with additional influences on the stock market or factors which are still unknown. An argument against event studies is the fact that they can only include firms which have experienced the event. There is no room for all those firms that have applied only one accounting regime, e.g., firms that did not change their accounting or new firms that applied only one regime. This chapter concentrates on the state-oriented approach. However, it is recognised that there are likely to be omitted variables that adversely influence the results obtained under this approach. In particular, the main constraint upon interpreting the results from the study reported in the remainder of this chapter is the fact that it cannot control for the reasons why firms voluntarily use US GAAP or IFRS and the possibility that those reasons may be related to the capital market characteristics of the firms that are the focus of the study.

HYPOTHESES

The aim of this chapter is to challenge the widely held view that US GAAP and IFRS contrast with the HGB regime insofar as they better fulfil the needs of the stock market. We therefore undertake a state-oriented analysis comparing the stock market variables for HGB firms with those of US GAAP or IFRS firms.

A comparison of different distributions is normally undertaken by a comparison of the moments of the distributions. As we do not argue that the location parameter should vary and as we want to keep it simple, we compare the disturbance parameters of the three distributions. The null hypotheses tested are:

H_1: For the whole market as well as for each size segment (Amtlicher Handel versus Neuer Markt), the market variables are less risky for US GAAP or IFRS firms than for HGB firms.

H_2: For firms of the Amtlicher Handel, the market variables are less risky for

US GAAP or IFRS firms than for HGB firms.

H$_3$: For firms of the Neuer Markt, the market variables are less risky for US GAAP or IFRS firms than for HGB firms.

OPERATIONALISING THE HYPOTHESES

If possible, buyers find on a market a rich offer of diverse goods or services at fair prices and if the cost to participate in the market is low, they tend to fulfil their wishes on that market. Sellers of goods or services will meet their goals and go to the market (again) if they find enough buyers for their goods or services and if the cost to participate in the market is low.

In markets for physical goods, the participants can generally evaluate the quality of the offered goods quite well. Therefore buyers and sellers can easily evaluate whether the price for goods is fair. In contrast, the qualitative properties of the goods offered on the stock market are not obvious. They depend mostly on expectations of future payments from a share, be it future dividends or payments from the sale of the share. Stock market participants have to rely to a great extent on the information provided by the firm, knowing that management will not always disclose everything correctly to other parties. Whether the ask price of the seller or the bid price of the buyer are regarded as fair depends, even in the absence of information asymmetry, on the way these expectations are built. It is generally assumed that in this situation accounting information is at least helpful. Theoretical and empirical research has shown that the ideas of the Capital Asset Pricing Model (CAPM) might be able to explain a part of reality.[15] Reflecting this model, the variance of the abnormal prices would be relevant.

The degree of volatility of prices on adjacent days might be seen as an indicator of the uncertainty of the market as to the correct value of shares. Greater volatility occurs because of greater uncertainty as to what constitutes a fair price. If the price volatility depends on the accounting regime, then this volatility can be used to evaluate the quality of different accounting regimes, *ceteris paribus*.

The difference between the bid and the ask prices also reflects uncertainty about the value of shares. The greater the uncertainty of buyers and sellers, the greater might be the dispersion of these prices. Again, if these prices depend on accounting information, they can be used to evaluate different accounting regimes, *ceteris paribus*.

We also test for the significance of the differences between different regimes. We apply a non-parametric Wilcoxon test. This test does not assume any special distribution of the variables. The statistics of this test, however, are approximately normally distributed numbers which can be evaluated by reference to the density function of a normal distribution.

Risk Measured by the Volatility of the Prices (Returns) of a Security

Variation in the prices of a security over time shows that market participants have changed their expectations about the value of future payments related to the share. Such variations may be induced by many causes, including a change in the attitudes towards risk or new information about value-relevant events, e.g. information contained in accounting numbers. As far as events become known from accounting numbers, expectations may also be influenced by the type of reporting. A detailed, precise and reliable report presumably influences the expectations of the market participants differently from a report which allows for multiple interpretations. It seems safe to assume that the former informs shareholders better than a short, unclear and less reliable report. As a consequence, the volatility of prices should be smaller if the quality of accounting improves. We can therefore regard the standard deviation of prices of a share i, $s(P_i)$, as a measure for the quality of the firm's accounting.

The comparability of the prices of different securities is reduced as the securities might reflect totally different proportions of owners' equity. Therefore, we rely on returns instead of on prices and on the volatility of returns instead of the volatility of prices and use the volatility of the return of a security as one of our measures.

The comparability of the share prices of different firms is also reduced if investors are oriented towards the market portfolio instead of single securities. In that case, theory suggests examining abnormal prices as is done in the next section.

Risk Measured by the Volatility of Residual Prices (Returns) of a Security

It can be argued that the variance of the prices of a security as a measure for the quality of an accounting regime is also influenced by other variables than the accounting regime. One way to react to this argument is to apply the CAPM. This model regards the price of a share as a function of the market price per unit of risk and the number of risk units included in the share. Again, we examine returns instead of prices: the risk modified return of the share.

The empirical version of this model assumes that the residual return (u_i) of a share is taken out of the share's return (R_i), the market return (R_m) and the amount of firm specific risk (β_i) that is systematically related to the market return:

$$R_i = R_f + \beta_i R_m + u_i$$

Corresponding to this model the variance of returns of a share may be separated into two parts:

$$Var(R_i) = \beta_i^2 \, Var\,(R_m) + Var\,(u_i)$$

The square root of these terms can be calculated in order to determine the corresponding standard deviations. Assuming the relevance of the CAPM, the dispersion of the residual returns, measured by its standard deviation, $s(u_i) = \sqrt{Var\ (u_i)}$, may be seen as a measure for a revised risk of returns. The larger the uncertainty of a firm's future, the larger this unsystematic risk, $s(u_i)$, will be under the market portfolio assumption.

This risk can be diminished by an investment in the market portfolio of shares. The extent of reaction to overall market influences, the systematic risk (β_i) has nothing to do with the quality of an accounting regime.[16] We apply here the standard deviation of the residual returns of a share as a further measure for the volatility of that share. Again, we aggregate this variable over all shares of the different market segments for firms applying the same accounting model.

Finally, it should be mentioned that the volatility of residual returns depends on how the market return is measured and how the regression parameters are estimated. A linear regression approach is applied with the market return being measured by a market index. The greater the number of shares in the market index, the nearer the index comes to the properties assumed by the CAPM.

Risk Measured by the Bid-Ask Spread

A difference in the prices of sellers and of buyers indicates that both parties have built different expectations. The information used by the parties has been interpreted differently, assuming that they have access to the same information.

Market participants will build their expectations with all information available to them. It is very probable that they rely on accounting information provided by the firm.[17] It is then also probable that the accounting regime will influence the participants' expectations. Whether the accounting numbers are interpreted by the sellers and by the buyers in the same way may be seen from the difference between the bid and the ask prices. If the accounting numbers allow for different interpretations, a regime that produces more homogeneous interpretations is generally superior to a regime which produces heterogeneous expectations. The regime with less differences between bid and ask prices gives less possibilities for different interpretations and therefore seems to be superior.

If we assume asymmetric information among the market participants, well informed market participants can exploit those who are less well informed.[18] This leads, as many theorists have shown, to disadvantageous consequences: the worse informed protect themselves by reducing their market activities.[19] The consequences are higher transaction costs, higher bid-ask spreads, and reduced liquidity of the market.[20] If, on the other hand, firms manage to improve public access to relevant information, transaction costs fall, the bid-ask spread declines, and higher liquidity might improve the access to capital for those firms.[21] If all firms follow such a strategy, one can assume an improvement of stock market properties.[22]

The bid-ask spread is an indicator of the transaction costs and of the liquidity of a share. The spread defines the cost which a market participant without superior information has to pay for an immediate transaction.[23] This spread provides a reasonable measure for evaluating accounting regimes and has been used for such purposes in prior research.[24]

To apply these approaches, it is necessary to estimate the difference between the prices or to know the bid price and the ask price from the order book of the stock exchange. The first approach is applied. The bid-ask spread is estimated using the Roll (1984) approach for each share per day. The estimate, (S_i), which represents Roll's ideas, results from the covariance (cov) between the prices (P_i) at two adjacent points in time:

$$S_i = 2\sqrt{-\text{cov}(P_{it}, P_{it} - 1)}$$

An equivalent expression on the basis of daily returns (R_{it}) is given by:

$$S_i = 200\sqrt{-\text{cov}(R_{it}, R_{it} - 1)}$$

The simplicity of the formula is the main advantage of the estimate of the bid-ask spread. The only assumptions are that the share is traded in an information efficient market and that the probability distribution of the price changes is stationary during the estimation period. The disadvantage is that a negative covariance is needed so that the expression under the root becomes positive. Other things being equal the accounting regime with the lowest spread will be the best.

Control of Other Influences

The stock market data may differ not only in relation to accounting regimes but also according to other variables. For example, in the period of this study, many firms entered the stock market for the first time. These initial public offerings (IPOs) were often underpriced at the beginning of their listing,[25] and the effect is certainly independent of the accounting regime. To avoid the influence from such an event on the research, IPO firm-years are excluded from the sample.

Another situation in which the stock market is led by information other than the accounting regime is corporate insolvency. To avoid effects from this second event, data are excluded for firms in their last year before insolvency.

The effects mentioned reduce the usable observations. We also leave out years in which we have less than 200 data points for the annual regression and less than 50 records for the estimation of the spread.

The results presented have been tested for their robustness. Fiscal years shorter than 12 months are excluded, the estimation intervals for the variables were varied and the number of records left out for other reasons was varied. None of these variations seriously changed the results.

EMPIRICAL RESULTS

Data

We analysed the different accounting regimes which have been used in Germany between the fiscal years 1996 and 2002, each year beginning after 1 July and ending before 30 June of the next calendar year. The population includes 4993 financial reports of which 2615 can be used after deleting IPOs and other firm-years for reasons outlined above. If the firm was organised as a group of companies with legally independent units we considered its consolidated statements. If it consisted of but one legal unit the unconsolidated statements were used. The regimes found were HGB, US GAAP and IFRS.

Before the existence of section 292a HGB in 1998, non-HGB accounting was only possible additionally to HGB accounting. During this period several firms disclosed at the same time two sets of financial statements or parts thereof.[26] Some disclosed a full additional set (parallel set), some produced in addition a report which fulfils the requirements of HGB and another accounting regime, and some produced a HGB report plus earnings and owners' equity in reconciliation. Following the existence of section 292a HGB, many firms disclosed financial reports, which followed only one regime. Table 10.1 shows the distribution of reports produced.

We distinguish between the shares traded in the Amtlicher Handel and in the Neuer Markt. A further distinction is made according to the type of information. Firms that disclose only HGB financial statements are distinguished from firms that disclose two sets of financial statements (HGB plus US GAAP or HGB plus IFRS). This group includes reconciliations. The last group of firms discloses just one financial report according to US GAAP or to IFRS.

The data stem from two sources. Stock prices and index returns have been taken from the Deutsche Finanzdatenbank.[27] The accounting data have been hand collected from the individual firms' reports.

Calculation of Variables

We calculate the return volatilities and bid-ask spreads of stock market variables for each financial report using data from the Deutsche Finanzdatenbank. Daily

Table 10.1 Accounting regimes applied by German firms with shares listed on the Amtlicher Handel and on the Neuer Markt

Year	Amtlicher Handel without single HGB					Neuer Markt without single HGB					Single HGB	Total
	US GAAP	Parallel Reports	Reconciled to US GAAP	Dual Report	Total US GAAP	IFRS	Parallel Reports	Reconciled to IFRS	Dual Report	Total IFRS		
1996	1	1	3	–	5	–	4	–	5	9	540	554
	0.18%	0.18%	0.54%		0.90%		0.72%		0.90%	1.62%	97.47%	100%
1997	3	3	4	–	10	3	7	–	8	18	542	570
	0.53%	0.53%	0.70%		1.75%	0.53%	1.23%		1.40%	3.16%	95.09%	100%
1998	16	6	10	1	33	35	6	3	6	50	535	618
	2.50%	0.97%	1.62%	0.16%	5.34%	5.66%	0.97%	0.49%	0.97%	8.09%	86.57%	100%
1999	68	8	17	2	95	114	12	9	2	137	524	756
	8.99%	1.06%	2.25%	0.26%	12.57%	15.08%	1.59%	1.19%	0.26%	18.12%	69.31%	100%
2000	149	1	8	1	159	224	10	1	–	235	459	853
	17.47%	0.12%	0.94%	0.12%	18.64%	26.26%	1.17%	0.12%		27.55%	53.81%	100%
2002	125	2	4	2	133	227	4	1	–	232	365	730
	17.12%	0.27%	0.55%	0.27%	18.22%	31.10%	0.55%	0.14%		31.78%	50.00%	100%
All Years	498	23	69	7	597	816	52	18	21	907	3489	4993
	9.97%	0.46%	1.38%	0.14%	11.94%	16.34%	1.04%	0.36%	0.42%	18.17%	69.885%	100%

returns are calculated from share prices controlling for dividends and for price changes due to capital contributions at other than market prices as well as predominant rights. The standard deviations of the returns and of the residual returns are calculated with reference to the fiscal year of each firm. The calculation of our yearly stock market variables begins three months after the beginning of the fiscal year and ends three months after the end of the fiscal year. We thus hope to capture effects induced by accounting regimes since annual reports for this group of firms have to be published within three months of the fiscal year end.

The calculation of the residual returns requires knowledge of a market index. This index should represent the stock market and its returns should be consistent with the security returns. The Dafox Index, a performance index on the basis of the capital invested in Amtlicher Handel of the Frankfurt stock exchange, seems to fulfil this requirement.[28]

The calculation of the bid-ask spread requires a short time interval. We use a three-month period, ending the third month after fiscal year end. Roll's method requires that the expression underneath the square root is positive, which is not always the case. As it does not make sense to aggregate over senseless numbers, we exclude bid-ask spreads where the sign of the expression is negative.

It can be expected that the value of the stock market risk variables varies with the size of the firms. While many large firms often produce and trade mature products, small firms are likely to be still growing and investors are confronted with higher estimation uncertainty.

The numbers in Table 10.2 are the starting point for the research. They represent the stock market values for years and for size segments without any reflection of the accounting regime used. The rows for the years show that there is a significant difference for firms traded in the Amtlicher Handel and for firms traded in the Neuer Markt. The numbers for the Amtlicher Handel as well as those for the Neuer Markt vary from the average for all firms. The numbers for Amtlicher Handel firms are much smaller than those for Neuer Markt firms. This is true for all three variables and all years.

We commence by examining the distribution over all years. The mean (median) of the variance of security returns of all companies was 3.15 (2.68). As we expect, the mean and the median for firms whose shares are traded in the Amtlicher Handel (2.40; 2.19) are significantly smaller than those of firms whose shares are traded on the Neuer Markt (5.59; 5.29). This is consistent with the prediction that there is a higher risk with estimating the future returns of growth firms.

A similar relation is true for the variances of the residual returns. While all companies reflect a mean (median) of 3.03 (2.61), firms of the Amtlicher Handel show 2.32 (2.11), and firms of the Neuer Markt show significantly higher values of 5.34 (5.04).

Table 10.2 Stock market variables of German shares ordered according to market segments and time

		All firms				Amtlicher Handel firms (G1)				Neuer Markt firms (G2)				Significance of difference between G1 and G2 (Wilcoxon)
		N	Mean	Median	Volatility	N	Mean	Median	Volatility	N	Mean	Median	Volatility	
Year 1996	$s(R_i)$	257	1.68	1.50	0.85	257	1.68	1.50	0.85					
	$s(u_i)$	257	1.64	1.48	0.86	257	1.64	1.48	0.86					
	S_i	257	-0.26	-0.44	1.27	257	-0.26	-0.44	1.27					
Year 1997	$s(R_i)$	263	2.03	2.00	0.79	261	2.02	2.00	0.79	2	3.04	3.04	0.18	2.04
	$s(u_i)$	263	1.91	1.83	0.78	261	1.90	1.82	0.78	2	2.91	2.91	0.16	2.01
	S_i	263	0.03	0.30	1.36	261	0.03	0.30	1.36	2	-0.39	-0.39	2.29	-0.29
Year 1998	$s(R_i)$	289	2.54	2.43	1.22	275	2.43	2.38	1.11	14	4.83	4.89	1.09	5.74
	$s(u_i)$	289	2.51	2.38	1.21	275	2.39	2.33	1.10	14	4.74	4.70	1.10	5.70
	S_i	289	0.09	0.30	1.77	275	0.04	0.39	1.68	14	-1,15	1,55	2.87	-1,59
Year 1999	$s(R_i)$	350	2.71	2.48	1.34	298	2.42	2.27	1.16	52	4.39	4.45	1.01	9.60
	$s(u_i)$	350	2.65	2.41	1.30	298	2.38	2.20	1.16	52	4.21	4.23	0.98	9.42
	S_i	350	0.48	0.87	1.93	298	0.53	0.86	1.84	52	0.21	1.13	2.36	0.22
Year 2000	$s(R_i)$	467	3.47	2.90	1.90	323	2.51	2.34	1.15	144	5.62	5.47	1.45	15.58
	$s(u_i)$	467	3.36	2.86	1.79	323	2.47	2.32	1.12	144	5.35	5.19	1.36	15.45
	S_i	467	0.27	0.93	2.38	323	0.69	1.02	1.73	144	-0.70	-0.92	3.22	-3.43
Year 2001	$s(R_i)$	534	3.97	3.45	2.22	315	2.58	2.32	1.20	219	5.97	5.76	1.79	17.68
	$s(u_i)$	534	3.79	3.33	2.14	315	2.48	2.21	1.18	219	5.66	5.41	1.78	17.40
	S_i	534	-0.00	0.39	2.69	315	0.34	0.76	1.85	219	-0.50	-1.46	3.52	-3.40
Year 2002	$s(R_i)$	455	4.06	3.68	2.38	269	3.04	2.66	1.73	186	5.54	4.95	2.41	13.10
	$s(u_i)$	455	3.88	3.37	2.36	269	2.87	2.43	1.73	186	5.34	4.68	2.40	13.11
	S_i	455	0.84	1.12	2.82	269	0.57	0.81	2.23	186	1.23	1.99	3.47	3.60
All Years	$s(R_i)$	2615	3.15	2.68	1.97	1998	2.40	2.19	1.24	617	5.59	5.29	1.92	33.45
	$s(u_i)$	2615	3.03	2.61	1.90	1998	2.32	2.11	1.22	617	5.34	5.04	1.89	33.13
	S_i	2615	0.22	0.71	2.37	1998	0.40	0.58	1.97	617	0.02	0.75	3.43	-0.50

$s(R_i)$ = Volatility of returns of share i; $s(u_i)$ = Volatility of residual returns of share i; S_i = Bid-ask spread (Roll); N = Number of observations

The same is true for the parameter S of the bid-ask spread. All firms have a mean (median) of 0.22 (0.71), while statistics for firms listed on the Amtlicher Handel show 0.40 (0.58) and 0.02 (0.75) for firms listed on the Neuer Markt. Additionally, we notice that the parameters of the bid-ask spread are higher for firms of the Neuer Markt than for those on the Amtlicher Handel; the volatility for S of the two being 3.43 > 1.97. It is very plausible that firms on the Neuer Markt have a less homogeneous bid-ask spread than companies on the Amtlicher Handel.

The distributions for individual years yield similar results. Additionally, we find that the values of the variables grow from year to year. This might be a consequence of the whole market, e.g., a consequence of a growing risk of estimation. Less clear is, however, the development of the value S of the bid-ask spread in 1997 and in 1999. For the rest of the data all the differences are significantly different from zero.

Results

Results for hypothesis H_1

Hypothesis H_1 predicts, that market variables indicate less riskiness for US GAAP and IFRS than for HGB reports. The results relating to hypothesis H_1 appear in Table 10.3.

Independent of the different size segments, there is clearly variation across the accounting regimes. Across all years, the values of the mean (median) for HGB firms are 2.35 (2.13) and 4.50 (4.26) for IFRS or US GAAP firms, which are different from the values in Table 10.2 (3.15 (2.68) in each case). More importantly, the values for HGB firms differ significantly from the values for IFRS firms. However, contrary to Hypothesis H_1, over all years the values for firms using HGB accounting have the lowest volatility of residual returns. The mean (median) of the volatility of residual returns for HGB firms is 3.03 (2.08). This is also lower than for IFRS and US GAAP firms (4.27 (4.06)). Also this difference is statistically significantly different from zero. While the bid-ask spread mean is higher for HGB firms relative to IFRS or US GAAP firms only (0.28 compared with 0.16), the median and standard deviation are lower (0.56 and 1.81 compared with 0.77 and 2.92). Overall, these statistics indicate higher risk levels for those firms using IFRS or US GAAP. The number of firms providing two sets of reports, reconciliations, or dual reports is very small compared to the other groups. We therefore abstain from interpreting the results. Except for the bid-ask spread, most numbers are statistically significantly different from their counterpart of a different regime. For the bid-ask spread the differences are less significant.

The yearly analyses show very similar results for the return and residual return variables. It is possible to interpret Table 10.3 as contradicting H_1, although

Table 10.3 Risk profiles of German shares ordered according to accounting regime and time with levels of significance of differences between groups

	Group G1 HGB report only				Group G2 two reports, reconciliations, dual reports				Group G3 IFRS/IAS or US GAAP report only				Significance of difference (Wilcoxon)		
	N	Mean	Median	Volatility	N	Mean	Median	Volatility	N	Mean	Median	Volatility	G1 v G2	G1 v G3	G2 v G3
Year 1996															
$s(R_i)$	252	1.68	1.51	0.86	5	1.42	1.14	0.48	2	2.35	2.35	0.39			*
$s(u_i)$	252	1.65	1.48	0.87	5	1.26	1.08	0.52	2	2.21	2.21	0.51			
S_i	252	-0.27	-0.46	1.28	5	0.25	0.32	0.36	2	1.16	1.10	0.56			
Year 1997															
$s(R_i)$	251	2.03	2.00	0.81	10	1.97	1.98	0.29							
$s(u_i)$	251	1.92	1.83	0.80	10	1.60	1.54	0.30							
S_i	251	0.02	-0.30	1.38	10	0.02	0.05	0.72							
Year 1998															
$s(R_i)$	250	2.42	2.29	1.18	13	3.40	3.05	1.31	26	3.26	2.81	1.15	***	***	
$s(u_i)$	250	2.39	2.25	1.18	13	3.34	2.97	1.30	26	3.19	2.80	1.11	***	***	
S_i	250	-0.09	0.29	1.75	13	-0.68	-0.74	2.06	26	0.18	0.86	1.85			
Year 1999															
$s(R_i)$	245	2.47	2.27	1.28	14	3.47	3.43	1.13	91	3.26	2.84	1.32	***	***	
$s(u_i)$	245	2.45	2.23	1.27	14	3.27	3.44	1.21	91	3.10	2.78	1.29	***	***	
S_i	245	0.50	0.84	1.94	14	1.16	1.29	1.77	91	0.35	0.92	1.90			
Year 2000															
$s(R_i)$	244	2.52	2.35	1.22	24	4.43	4.08	1.67	199	4.52	4.65	2.01	***	***	***
$s(u_i)$	244	2.50	2.34	1.20	24	4.20	4.05	1.64	199	4.32	4.38	1.88	***	***	***
S_i	244	0.82	1.12	1.80	24	-0.56	-0.12	2.38	199	-0.31	0.36	2.80	***	***	***
Year 2001															
$s(R_i)$	213	2.56	2.26	1.31	11	4.68	4.49	2.15	310	4.92	4.82	2.22	***	***	***
$s(u_i)$	213	2.51	2.25	1.28	11	4.32	3.94	2.20	310	4.64	4.51	2.18	***	***	***
S_i	213	0.43	0.77	1.86	11	-0.90	-1.49	2.87	310	-0.27	-0.50	3.10	**		
Year 2002															
$s(R_i)$	153	3.10	2.46	2.07	8	3.92	4.04	1.66	294	4.56	4.16	2.39		***	***
$s(u_i)$	153	3.05	2.44	2.05	8	3.67	3.72	1.79	294	4.32	3.99	2.41		***	***
S_i	153	0.82	0.96	2.45	8	0.30	-0.79	2.01	294	0.87	1.30	3.01			
All Years															
$s(R_i)$	1608	2.35	2.13	1.30	85	3.63	3.29	1.73	922	4.50	4.26	2.19	***	***	***
$s(u_i)$	1608	3.03	2.08	1.90	85	3.41	2.97	1.73	922	4.27	4.06	2.15	***	***	***
S_i	1608	0.28	0.56	1.81	85	-0.13	0.40	2.12	922	0.16	0.77	2.92			

$s(R_i)$ = Volatility of returns of share i; $s(u_i)$ = Volatility of residual returns of share i; S_i = Bid-ask spread (Roll); N = Number of observations; *, ** and *** expressing significance at the 10%, 5% and 1% level or higher respectively

161

the results from the interpretation of the bid-ask spread, *S*, are not quite as clear. This result, however, cannot be regarded as a sign of the general superiority of HGB accounting. It might be that the results vary for different size segments. Again, it is noticed that the values rise continuously between 1996 and 2002 for all types of accounting regime used. Alternatively, it is possible that there are important omitted variables that determine (a) the levels of the firm risk and (b) whether the firms use HGB only, IFRS or US GAAP, or a combination of both. For example, if firms with high growth options are more likely to seek funding on international markets, or at least to seek international funding via a German stock market, we would expect to see results similar to those reported in Table 10.3.

The results might be misleading as many IFRS or US GAAP firms have their shares traded on the Neuer Markt. Firms in this segment often have, according to the above discussion, properties that induce higher risk-related values of the variables, e.g., dynamic markets, start-up status, little historical information. In the next section an analysis of the distribution of the variables separately for the different market segments is presented.

Results for hypothesis H$_2$

Hypothesis H$_2$ predicts that for shares traded on the Amtlicher Handel, market variables indicate that US GAAP and IFRS are less risky than HGB reports. The association between firms' risk profiles and their chosen reporting regime for that group of firms are analysed in Table 10.4.

As in Table 10.3, Table 10.4 indicates that the returns and residual returns results are, on average over all years, lower for HGB firms than for firms that prepare IFRS or US GAAP reports. This is inconsistent with H$_2$ which predicts that for companies in the Amtlicher Handel the market variables are less risky for IFRS and US GAAP firms than for HGB firms. However, this difference is statistically significant only for the difference between HGB only firms and non-HGB only firms.

The yearly results are even less clear. They do not hold for every year, and there is considerable variation between the relative high/low measures for mean and medians of returns volatility and residual returns volatility. From 1999 on, there is only a small difference between the measures for those firms that disclose a US GAAP or IFRS report and those that provide only HGB reports. Table 10.4 indicates that the differences are generally not significantly different from zero.

With respect to the bid-ask spread (S$_i$), each year row in Table 10.4 reveals differences between the accounting regimes. Yearly results show that the difference between HGB and IFRS firms has switched direction since 2000, when the HGB firms started to have higher spreads. From 1999 onwards, we

Table 10.4 Risk profiles of German shares traded on the Amtlicher Handel ordered by accounting regime and time with levels of significance of differences between groups

	Group G1 HGB report only				Group G2 two reports, reconciliations, dual reports				Group G3 IFRS/IAS or US GAAP report only				Significance of difference (Wilcoxon)		
	N	Mean	Median	Volatility	N	Mean	Median	Volatility	N	Mean	Median	Volatility	G1 v G2	G1 v G3	G2 v G3
Year 1996															
$s(R_i)$	252	1.68	1.51	0.86	5	1.42	1.14	0.48	2	2.35	2.35	0.39			
$s(u_i)$	252	1.65	1.48	0.87	5	1.26	1.08	0.52	2	2.21	2.21	0.51			
S_i	252	-0.27	-0.46	1.28	5	0.25	0.32	0.36	2	1.16	1.16	0.56			*
Year 1997															
$s(R_i)$	249	2.02	1.99	0.80	10	1.97	1.98	0.29	20	2.75	2.70	0.67			
$s(u_i)$	249	1.91	1.83	0.80	10	1.60	1.54	0.30	20	2.70	2.66	0.66			
S_i	249	0.02	0.30	1.38	10	0.02	0.05	0.72	20	0.46	1.08	1.48			
Year 1998															
$s(R_i)$	245	2.38	2.27	1.14	10	2.87	2.69	0.66	48	2.29	2.20	0.64	*	**	**
$s(u_i)$	245	2.35	2.20	1.14	10	2.81	2.67	0.66	48	2.16	2.06	0.64	*	**	
S_i	245	-0.08	0.30	1.71	10	-0.14	-0.15	1.35	48	0.70	0.91	1.24			
Year 1999															
$s(R_i)$	242	2.44	2.24	1.25	8	2.81	2.82	0.78	71	2.44	2.27	0.91			
$s(u_i)$	242	2.41	2.22	1.24	8	2.62	2.48	0.85	71	2.38	2.17	0.86			
S_i	242	0.49	0.83	1.94	8	0.88	1.29	1.80	71	0.35	0.78	1.41			
Year 2000															
$s(R_i)$	244	2.52	2.35	1.22	8	2.91	3.01	0.76	98	2.64	2.44	0.94	*		
$s(u_i)$	244	2.50	2.34	1.20	8	2.61	2.36	0.75	98	2.44	2.14	0.94			
S_i	244	0.43	1.12	1.86	8	0.01	0.79	1.37	98	0.14	0.69	1.83			
Year 2001															
$s(R_i)$	213	2.56	2.26	1.31	4	2.40	2.41	0.61	67	3.01	2.91	1.21			
$s(u_i)$	213	2.51	2.25	1.28	4	2.04	1.95	0.63	67	2.70	2.41	1.23		**	
S_i	213	0.43	0.77	1.86	4	0.53	0.59	1.78	67	0.26	0.55	1.77			
Year 2002															
$s(R_i)$	151	3.06	2.44	2.04	4	2.89	2.20	1.40					*		
$s(u_i)$	151	3.01	2.44	2.02	4	2.65	2.18	1.56					*		
S_i	151	0.79	0.96	2.46	4	0.96	1.38	1.30							
All Years															
$s(R_i)$	1596	2.33	2.12	1.28	49	2.50	2.34	0.84	353	2.68	2.49	1.02	**	***	
$s(u_i)$	1596	2.29	2.07	1.27	49	2.27	2.13	0.90	353	2.49	2.31	1.00		***	
S_i	1596	0.28	0.56	1.80	49	0.27	0.49	1.29	353	0.32	0.77	1.68			

$s(R_i)$ = Volatility of returns of share i; $s(u_i)$ = Volatility of residual returns of share i; S_i = Bid-ask spread (Roll); N = Number of observations;
*, ** and *** expressing significance at the 10%, 5% and 1% level or higher respectively

Table 10.5   Risk profiles for German shares traded on the Neuer Markt ordered by accounting regime and time with levels of significance of differences between groups

	Group G1 HGB report only				Group G2 two reports, reconciliations, dual reports				Group G3 IFRS/IAS or US GAAP report only				Significance of difference (Wilcoxon)		
	N	Mean	Median	Volatility	N	Mean	Median	Volatility	N	Mean	Median	Volatility	G1 v G2	G1 v G3	G2 v G3
Year 1997															
$s(R_i)$	2	3.04	3.04	0.18											
$s(u_i)$	2	2.91	2.91	0.16											
S_i	2	-0.39	-0.39	2.29											
Year 1998															
$s(R_i)$	5	4.48	3.91	1.42	3	5.17	5.70	1.51	6	4.96	4.93	0.60			
$s(u_i)$	5	4.44	3.92	1.46	3	5.11	5.66	1.48	6	4.82	4.70	0.63			
S_i	5	-0.81	-1.24	3.52	3	-2.47	-3.10	3.31	6	-0.76	-1.54	2.72			
Year 1999															
$s(R_i)$	3	5.16	4.77	0.97	6	4.36	4.39	0.90	43	4.34	4.31	1.02		*	**
$s(u_i)$	3	5.12	4.72	1.02	6	4.18	4.14	0.79	43	4.15	4.15	0.99			
S_i	3	1.19	2.06	2.16	6	1.53	1.37	1.84	43	-0.04	1.08	2.40			
Year 2000															
$s(R_i)$					16	5.19	4.79	1.48	128	5.67	5.49	1.44			
$s(u_i)$					16	4.99	4.59	1.36	128	5.39	5.20	1.36			
S_i					16	-0.85	-1.44	2.75	128	-0.68	-0.87	3.28			
Year 2001															
$s(R_i)$					7	5.98	6.26	1.44	212	5.97	5.74	1.81			
$s(u_i)$					7	5.63	6.04	1.54	212	5.67	5.40	1.79			
S_i					7	-1.71	-2.60	3.17	212	-0.46	-1.35	3.53			
Year 2002															
$s(R_i)$	2	6.32	6.32	2.32	4	4.95	4.92	1.28	180	5.55	4.95	2.43			
$s(u_i)$	2	6.17	6.17	2.12	4	4.69	4.71	1.51	180	5.34	4.68	2.42			
S_i	2	2.91	2.91	0.44	4	-0.20	0.04	2.62	180	1.25	1.99	3.50			
All Years															
$s(R_i)$	12	4.72	4.56	1.57	36	5.18	5.14	1.39	569	5.63	5.33	1.95			
$s(u_i)$	12	4.64	4.52	1.56	36	4.96	4.80	1.35	569	5.38	5.08	1.92			
S_i	12	0.38	1.59	2.82	36	-0.68	1.40	2.83	569	0.06	0.87	3.47			

$s(R_i)$ = Volatility of returns of share i; $s(u_i)$ = Volatility of residual returns of share i; S_i = Bid-ask spread (Roll); N = Number of observations; *, ** and *** expressing significance at the 10%, 5% and 1% level or higher respectively

observe smaller values for IFRS and US GAAP firms than for HGB firms, for the residual returns variable (consistently) and sometimes for the overall returns variable, as well as for the bid-ask spread. In 2000, for example, the volatility of returns (residual returns) of HGB firms is 2.52 (2.50) and slightly higher than the volatility for the returns (residual returns) of firms using IFRS or US GAAP with 2.44 (2.38). The mean (median) of the bid-ask spread for HGB firms (0.43 (1.12)) exceeds that of the other group (0.35 (0.78)). These differences are, however, statistically significant only in a few cases.

Results for hypothesis H$_3$

Hypothesis H$_3$ deals with the prediction about advantage of US GAAP and IFRS compared to HGB on the Neuer Markt. Hypothesis H$_3$ is analysed in Table 10.5. This table commences in 1997 as the Neuer Markt was opened in March 1997. Given the very small number of firms using HGB, it is not possible to meaningfully analyse HGB firms for individual years. On average over all years, the results are similar to those reported in the previous tables, i.e., the results for returns and residual returns are very similar across the market segments. In only one case do the means, medians or variances of the overall analysis differ significantly. The same holds for yearly analyses.

This can be interpreted in the sense that on the Neuer Markt there is no statistical evidence that the choice for an accounting regime is of any importance. Further analyses were therefore not conducted.

CONCLUSION

Since 1996, many German firms have applied accounting systems other than, or in addition to, HGB to produce their consolidated financial reports. The number of German firms applying US GAAP or IFRS is growing. From the fiscal year 2005 on, the European Union required capital market orientated firms to apply IFRS. The arguments for moving towards IFRS (and formerly US GAAP) were mounted in terms of the better stock market properties produced by these standards. Whether this motivation holds in reality, has been only scarcely investigated. The present research delivers some further empirical results as part of an exploratory study.

To assess the truth of statements that adopting IFRS or US GAAP would increase the information content of financial statements, this research investigates whether market risk profiles were higher for HGB firms or for firms that reported using IFRS or US GAAP. If the information content of one set of annual reports was higher, then there would be less volatility in the returns, residual returns, and smaller bid-ask spreads for the more informative reports, *ceteris paribus*.

However, the evidence does not support the primary hypothesis, that the risk profiles would be lower for those firms using IFRS or US GAAP.

Further analysis of the results on the basis of German firms whose shares are listed on the Amtlicher Handel and on the Neuer Markt with respect to the volatility of returns, the volatility of residual returns and the bid-ask spread was conducted. The results suggest that the hypotheses, predicting higher market risk profiles for HGB firms, do not hold. Seen over all years the bid-ask spread is larger for firms using IFRS or US GAAP than for HGB accounting, and the other volatilities are also higher. Seen over individual years, the differences against HGB are generally declining.

The results are valuable to critical thinking about the suggested superiority of US GAAP or IFRS accounting over HGB accounting. However, it has to be acknowledged that the research is not free from limitations. While much has been done to control influencing factors, there are undoubtedly other uncontrolled factors that might influence the volatilities and the bid-ask spread. Such factors should be included in future research in order to avoid misleading influences from this study. In particular, it would be valuable to investigate whether there are particular attributes of firms with high risk variance, residual risk variance, and bid-ask spreads that motivate those firms to seek international finance using IFRS or US GAAP reports. Future research could investigate, for example, the possibility that there are high growth firms that are more likely to be expanding into international markets. Reflection of differences in corporate governance might be another approach.

In conclusion, while this is an exploratory study, it does provide interesting evidence that conflicts with the widely held view that IFRS or US GAAP regimes provide information that is more useful to market participants in valuing equity.

NOTES

1 The German stock exchanges have different trading for two groups of corporations. Firms whose shares are traded in the *Amtlicher Handel* have to fulfil the normal disclosure requirements of the law. Corporations whose shares are traded in the *Geregelter Markt* are generally much smaller and they have to fulfil lower disclosure requirements than the companies whose shares are traded in the Amtlicher Handel. The *Neuer Markt* has been introduced at the Frankfurt stock exchange as a subset of the Geregelter Markt, with the special requirement of the stock exchange to disclose, in addition to legal requirements in Germany, financial reports which follow US GAAP or IFRS.

2 See the results of a query among German companies in Pellens and Tomaszewski (1999), p. 203.

3 See Beaver (1998), especially chapter 4.

4 See Kieso et al. (2004), p. 31–3.

5 See Coenenberg (2005), p. 9–18.

6 See Esser (1998).

7 See Alford et al. (1993), Harris et al. (1994), Meitner et al. (2002), Leuz and Verrecchia (2000), or Leuz (2003).
8 See the results of a query by Förschle et al. (1995).
9 See Hüfner (2000).
10 See the Statement of Financial Accounting Concepts No. 5 for US GAAP, and IAS 11 for IFRS.
11 See Ball et al. (2000), p. 16–22 about the empirical relevance of this type of prudential accounting.
12 See D'Arcy (2000).
13 See Harris et al. (1994).
14 Studies include Alford et al. (1993), Harris et al. (1994), Pellens and Tomascewski (1999) as well as Leuz and Verrecchia (2000) and Leuz (2003). In 2003 and 2004 three further studies of Möller et al. were published (2003a, 2003b, 2004).
15 See Möller and Hüfner (2002).
16 See Auer (1998), p. 142.
17 See Beaver (1998).
18 See Lev (1988).
19 See Akerlof (1970).
20 See Glosten and Milgrom (1985) or Amihud and Mendelson (1989).
21 For theoretical models of such effects as a consequence of voluntary reporting, see Diamond and Verrecchia (1991), Kim and Verrecchia (1994) or Baiman and Verrecchia (1996), and for an experimental study see Bloomfield and Wilks (2000).
22 Lev (1988), p. 16–19.
23 See Schmidt and Iversen (1991), p. 210–11, or Callahan et al. (1997).
24 Harrison (2000) overviews this literature.
25 See Langemann (2000) for an analysis of this observation as well as for an overview of results.
26 Hütten and Lorson (2000).
27 Bühler et al. (1993).
28 Göppl and Schütz (1993).

ACKNOWLEDGEMENTS

The support of the Monash Institute for the Study of Global Movements is appreciated. This chapter has benefited from comments of the participants at the Globalisation of Accounting Standards Conference in Prato, Italy in May 2005.

REFERENCES

Akerlof, G.A. (1970), 'The market for lemons: Quality uncertainty and the market mechanism', *Quarterly Journal of Economics*, **84**, 488–500.

Alford, A., J. Jones, R. Leftwich, and M. Zmijewski (1993), 'The relative informativeness of accounting disclosures in different countries, *Journal of Accounting Research*, **31**, Supplement, 183–223.

Amihud, Y. and H. Mendelson (1989), 'Liquidity and cost of capital: Implications for corporate management', *Journal of Applied Corporate Finance*, **17**, 65–73.

Auer, K. V. (1998), 'Der einfluß des wechsels vom rechnungslegungsstandard auf die risikoparameter von schweizerischen Aktien', *Zeitschrift für betriebswirtschaftliche Forschung*, **50**, 129–55.

Baiman, S. and R. Verrecchia (1996), 'The relation among capital markets, financial disclosure, production efficiency, and insider trading', *Journal of Accounting Research*, **34**, 1–22.

Ball, R. and S. Kothari, and A. Robin (2000), 'The effect of international institutional factors on properties of accounting earnings', *Journal of Accounting and Economics*, **29**, 1–51.

Beaver, W.H. (1998), *Financial reporting – An accounting revolution*, 3rd ed., Upper Saddle River: Prentice Hall.

Bloomfield, R.J. and T.J Wilks (2000), 'Disclosure effects in the laboratory: Liquidity, depth, and the cost of capital', *The Accounting Review*, **75**, 13–41.

Bühler, W., H. Göppl and H.P. Möller (1993), 'Die Deutsche Finanzdatenbank (DFDB)', *Empirische Kapitalmarktforschung*, ed. by Bühler, W., H. Hax, R. Schmidt, *Zeitschrift für betriebswirtschaftliche Forschung*, **31**, 287–331.

Callahan, C.M., C. Lee and T. Yohn (1997), 'Accounting information and bid-ask spreads', *Accounting Horizons*, **11**, 50–60.

Coenenberg, A.G. (2005), *Jahresabschluss und Jahresabschlussanalyse*, 20th ed., Stuttgart.

Diamond, D.W. and R. Verrecchia (1991), 'Disclosure, liquidity, and the cost of capital', *The Journal of Finance*, **46**, 1325–59.

D'Arcy, A. (2000), 'The degree of determination of national accounting systems – An empirical investigation', *Schmalenbach Business Review*, **52**, 45–67.

Esser, K. (1998), 'Die deutsche Rechnungslegung auf dem Weg zu internationalen Standards', *Rechnungswesen als Instrument für Führungsentscheidungen – Festschrift für Adolf G. Coenenberg*, ed. by Möller, H.P. and Schmidt, F., Stuttgart, 617–31.

Förschle, G., M. Glaum and U. Mandler (1995), 'US GAAP, IAS und HGB: Ergebnisse einer Umfrage unter deutschen Rechnungslegungsexperten', *Betriebswirtschaftliche Forschung und Praxis*, **47**, 392–413.

Glosten, L.R.and P. Milgrom (1985), 'Bid, ask, and transaction prices in a specialist market with heterogeneously informed traders', *Journal of Financial Economics*, **14**, 71–100.

Göppl, H. and H. Schütz (1993), 'The Design and Implementation of a German Stock Price Research Index (Deutscher Aktien-Forschungsindex DAFOX)', *Mathematical Modelling in Economics, Essays in Honor of Wolfgang Eichhorn*, ed. by Diewert, W. E., K. Spremann, F. Stehling, Berlin et al., 506–19.

Harris, T.S., M. Lang and H.P. Möller (1994), 'The value relevance of German accounting measures: An empirical analysis', *Journal of Accounting Research*, **32**, 187–209.

Harrison, D.A. (2000), *Zur Vorteilhaftigkeit von Aktiensplits – Eine empirische Untersuchung der Nennbetragsherabsetzungen in Deutschland*, Frankfurt am Main et al.

Hüfner, B. (2000), *Fundamentale Aktienbewertung und Rechnungslegung – Eine konzeptionelle Eignungsanalyse*, Lang-Verlag, Frankfurt am Main et al.

Hütten, C. and P. Lorson (2000), 'Internationale Rechnungslegung in Deutschland (Teil 2)', *Betrieb und Wirtschaft*, **15**, 609–19.

Kieso, D.E., J.J. Weygandt and T.D. Warfield (2004), *Intermediate Accounting*, Vol. 1, 11th ed., pp. 31–3.

Kim, O. and R. Verrecchia (1994), 'Market liquidity and volume around earnings announcements', *Journal of Accounting and Economics*, **17**, 41–68.

Kyle, A. (1985), 'Continuous auctions and insider trade', *Econometrica*, **53**, 1315–1335.

Langemann, A. (2000), *Ökonomische Vorteile eines Börsengangs – Theoretische Begründbarkeit und empirische Evidenz*, Frankfurt am Main et al.

Leuz, C. (2003), 'IAS versus US GAAP: Information asymmetry-based evidence from Germany's new market', *Journal of Accounting Research*, **51**, 445–72.

Leuz, C. and R. Verrecchia (2000), 'The economic consequences of increased disclosure', *Journal of Accounting Research*, **38**, 91–136.

Lev, B. (1988), 'Toward a theory of equitable and efficient accounting policy', *The Accounting Review*, **68**, 1–22.

Meitner, M., F. Hüfner and V. Kleff (2002), 'Enron. Wirtschaftsprüfer, Bilanzierungsvorschriften und der deutsche Aktienmarkt – Ergebnisse einer Umfrage unter Analysten und institutionellen Anlegern', in: *Zeitschrift für kapitalmarktorientierte Rechnungslegung*, **2**, 139–41.

Möller, H.P. and Hüfner, B. (2002), 'Zur Bedeutung der Rechnungslegung für den deutschen Aktienmarkt – Begründung, Messprobleme und Erkenntnisse empirischer Forschung'. *Österreichisches Jahrbuch für Controlling und Rechnungswesen*, Vienna, 405–63.

Möller, H.P., B. Hüfner and M. Kavermann (2003a), Zur Tauglichkeit unterschiedlicher Rechnungslegungssysteme für den deutschen Aktienmarkt – Ein empirischer Vergleich von Jahresabschlüssen nach deutschem HGB und IAS bzw. U.S.–GAAP; in: *Finanzwirtschaft, Kapitalmarkt und Banken, Festschrift für Professor Dr. Manfred Steiner zum 60. Geburstag*; ed. by A. Rathgeber, H.J. Tebroke, M. Wallmeier; Schäffer-Poeschel Verlag Stuttgart 2003, 195–220.

Möller, H.P., B. Hüfner and M. Kavermann (2003b), 'Vorteilhafte Aktienmarktwirkung international anerkannter Rechnungslegung für große deutsche Unternehmen?'; in: *Management in multinationalen Unternehmungen, Festschrift zum 60. Geburstag von Martin K. Welge*; ed. by D. Holtbrügge; Physica-Verlag Heidelberg, 267–90.

Möller, H.P., B. Hüfner and M. Kavermann (2004), 'Zur Aktienmarktwirkung 'international anerkannter' Rechnungslegung in Deutschland', in: *Personal und Organisation, Festschrift zum 60. Geburtstag von R. Bühner*, ed. by Horst Wildemann, TCW Verlag München, p. 817–43.

Ohlson, J. (1995), 'Earnings, book value, and dividends in security valuation', *Contemporary Accounting Research*, **11**, 661–87.

Pellens, B. and C. Tomaszewski (1999), 'Kapitalmarktreaktionen auf den Rechnungslegungswechsel zu IAS bzw. US GAAP', Rechnungswesen und Kapitalmarkt, ed. by Gebhardt, G. and Pellens, B., in: *Zeitschrift für betriebswirtschaftliche Forschung*, Sonderheft 41, 199–228.

Roll, R. (1984), 'A simple implicit measure of the effective bid-ask spread in an efficient market', *The Journal of Finance*, **39**, 1127–39.

Schmidt, H. and P. Iversen (1991), Geld-Brief-Spannen deutscher Standardwerte in IBIS und MATIS', *Zeitschrift für Bankrecht und Bankwirtschaft*, **3**, 209–26.

11 Globalisation of Accounting: Implications for Australian Public Sector Entities

Keryn Chalmers, Jayne M. Godfrey, Ian Langfield-Smith and Wei Lu

INTRODUCTION

Following extensive and intense debate, the global private sector business community is being drawn inexorably towards adopting a single set of accounting standards – developed by the International Accounting Standards Board (IASB) – known as International Financial Reporting Standards (IFRS). Since IFRS are developed for the private sector, it is not surprising that most of the controversy surrounding this globalisation relates to the impact on private sector entities. Public sector adoption of IFRS receives little attention, despite the enormity of the potential political, economic and social implications from conceding sovereignty over public sector accounting standards.

For reporting periods commencing in 2005, Australian public sector reporting entities are required to adopt Australian equivalents to IFRS (AIFRS). This makes them among the first public sector entities in the world to adopt the private sector standards promulgated by the IASB.

In this chapter we examine the implications of globalisation of accounting for public sector governance and financial reporting by Australian public sector reporting entities.[1] In particular, we describe in general terms the likely impact on performance reporting and accountability, and the decisions that emanate therefrom. We also describe the frictions between private sector based accounting standards and public sector reporting needs. These are especially pertinent where, as in Australia, government reporting entities are required to not only prepare financial statements using AIFRS, but also to present budgets and prepare financial reports using the International Monetary Fund's Government Finance Statistics Framework (GFS).

REGULATORY BACKGROUND

The regulation of financial reporting by Australian entities ultimately rests with the Commonwealth, State and Territory parliaments. The various governments delegate the power to formulate Australia's accounting standards to the Australian Accounting Standards Board (AASB), a statutory body. The government also determines which entities are required to prepare AASB standards-compliant financial reports. Any entity that is a disclosing entity, public company, large proprietary company or registered scheme is required by the Corporations Act 2001 (Cwlth) to apply these standards.[2] Many public sector entities are not regulated by the Corporations Act 2001 (Cwlth). However, the various parliaments can, and generally do, direct such entities to apply AASB standards for reports on their activities.

Since AASB standards are sector neutral, there is no differential reporting according to type of reporting entity (i.e., private sector, public sector, for-profit or not-for-profit). In contrast, IFRS are developed for private sector for-profit entities, while the International Public Sector Accounting Standards Board (IPSASB), formerly the Public Sector Committee of the International Federation of Accountants (IFAC), makes International Public Sector Accounting Standards (IPSAS).[3] The decision that Australian reporting entities' financial reports for reporting periods ending on or after 1 January 2005 must be prepared using AIFRS, requires Australian public sector entities (e.g., local, state, commonwealth and territory government entities) to apply standards developed for private sector for-profit entities. Since the AASB has issued sector neutral 2005 AASB standards[4] and recognised the different objectives and functions of for-profit and not-for-profit entities, the AASB has inserted specific paragraphs for not-for-profit sector entities into some of the 2005 AASB standards. While this alleviates some of the friction between private sector and public sector participants' reporting requirements, it also evidences the difficulties that the AASB inevitably faces in aligning a multi-faceted domestic constituency's financial reporting requirements with single-faceted international reporting standards.

Australia's standard-setting approach differs from other countries that adopted IFRS in 2005. For example, the European Union's (EU) adoption policy applies only to consolidated reports of European publicly listed companies. The oft-cited benefits of IFRS adoption revolve around benefits to capital market participants (e.g., reduced investor confusion; greater facilitation of capital raisings; lower cost of capital) and reduced preparer costs for multinational companies. Such benefits do not accrue to public sector entities. Nonetheless, the shift to IFRS has ramifications for Australian public sector entities. In particular, key financial performance indicator measurements alter for some public sector entities and the borrowing cost of public sector entities may be affected.

This chapter explores the role of financial reporting as a governance tool. International and Australian developments in financial reporting regulation for public sector entities are then discussed. Consideration is given to several implications of adopting AIFRS for public sector entities. It also explains the program of Australia's convergence of GFS and GAAP as public sector entities adopt AIFRS.

FINANCIAL REPORTS: A KEY GOVERNANCE TOOL

General purpose financial reports (GPFR) users are varied and can be categorised as resource providers (e.g., employees, lenders, investors, donors, parliament, taxpayers and ratepayers), recipients of goods and services (e.g., customers, beneficiaries, taxpayers and ratepayers), and parties performing an oversight function (e.g., parliaments, governments, regulatory agencies and special interest groups).[5] As articulated in the Framework for the Preparation and Presentation of Financial Statements (AASB 2004a) the purpose of financial reports is to communicate information concerning the financial performance, position and cash flows of an entity that is both useful for decisions concerning the allocation of scarce resources and allows users to assess management's stewardship.

The stated objectives of private and public sector entities often differ. While the focus of the private sector in a democratic capitalist society is on return on equity and corporate related goals, public sector entities are orientated to risk minimisation and social related goals (Reijniers 1994). Nevertheless, managers in both sectors control scarce resources in order to provide goods and services to the community; are accountable to the providers of those resources; incur obligations; and need to be financially viable to meet their objectives (AARF 1990b, para. 15). Accordingly, the GPFR objectives apply equally to private and public sector entities.[6] Australian financial reporting regulators embrace this view in their development of a sector neutral conceptual framework and of sector neutral accounting standards.[7] Public sector entities manage considerable revenues and exert significant influence on the lives of their constituents, either individually or collectively. Their accountability commences when resources are allocated to them and ends when they report on the use of allocated resources and the outcomes achieved.

Given that it enables users to monitor and assess the efficacy of resources entrusted to management's use, financial reporting is a key governance tool (Rezaee 2004). Not surprisingly, then, many of the governance mechanisms operating within an entity aim directly at improving the integrity of the financial reports and global governance initiatives (e.g., auditor and director independence, Board sign off of financial reports) also attempt to improve the quality of financial reporting.

The IPSASB recognises the role of financial reporting as a governance mechanism for public sector entities through its focus on the accounting, auditing and financial reporting needs of the various levels of governments, related government agencies and their constituencies. Its goal is to enhance public sector entities' performance by encouraging better decision making and accountability. The IPSASB identifies three principles of governance for public sector entities: openness, integrity and accountability (IPSASB 2001). Accountability is particularly relevant to the public sector and is defined as:

> ... the process whereby public sector entities, and the individuals within them, are responsible for their decisions and actions, including their stewardship of public funds and all aspects of performance, and submit themselves to appropriate external scrutiny. ... In effect, accountability is the obligation to answer for a responsibility conferred (IPSASB 2001, p. 12).

In discharging accountability, financial reporting has four aspects: annual reporting; use of appropriate accounting standards; performance measures; and external audit (IPSASB 2001, p. 14). The annual report includes the financial reports and is a mechanism for ensuring effective communication with stakeholders. It is an 'account and assessment of the entity's activities and achievements, and of its financial position and performance and performance prospects' (IPSASB 2001, p. 51). In this context, the rules governing financial report preparation and presentation are important. Adopting AIFRS changes the rules for Australian public sector entities, and can significantly change some measures used to assess performance and determine pricing.

One important aspect of public sector global governance reforms is the reform of the public sector from traditional bureaucracies to management modelled on the private sector (Ahn et al. 2002). Associated with this is an increased focus on measurement and reporting of the results and performance of public sector entities (Jackson and Lapsley 2003), evidenced in Australia by public sector entities being required to prepare GPFR using accrual accounting, and the move to sector neutral accounting standards. Accordingly, the form and content of Australian public sector entities' GPFR are similar to those of private sector entities.

PUBLIC SECTOR FINANCIAL REPORTING

Internationally, there is a tradition of demarcation between public sector and private sector financial reporting. However, sector neutrality underlies the Australian accounting standard-setting process. Financial reporting and the role of financial reporting in discharging accountability are regarded as essentially the same for both private and public sector entities.[8] Thus, AASB standards apply equally to public and private sector entities.[9] Sector neutrality does exist elsewhere (e.g., New Zealand), although it is uncommon.

International Accounting Standard-Setting Arrangements

At the international level, there is one international standard setter for public sector and not-for-profit entities (IPSASB) and another for private sector entities (IASB). In 1986 the IPSASB (formerly the Public Sector Committee) of the International Federation of Accountants (IFAC) was established to address public sector entities' financial management, reporting, accounting and auditing needs. The IPSASB standards program has been funded by IFAC, the World Bank, the Asian Development Bank, the International Monetary Fund and the United Nations Development Program, and generates IPSAS that offer a platform of accounting standards that can be adopted by public sector entities.

The IPSASB ensures that the standards it pronounces are 'consistent with those of the IASB ... to the extent [they] ... are applicable and appropriate to the public sector' (IFAC 2004, p. 10, para. 7). IPSASB standards are based largely on IFRS although the topics covered by the IPSAS are less comprehensive. The IPSASB has embarked on a program to converge IPSASs with IFRSs. In September 2005, the IPSASB issued ED 26 Improvements to International Public Sector Accounting Standards. This exposure draft proposed changes to 11 existing accrual basis IPSASs to achieve greater alignment with the equivalent IFRSs. However, while the IPSASB pays attention to IFRS requirements, some argue that the IASB has traditionally ignored the public sector implications of its standards.

Table 11.1 lists IFRS and IPSAS as at the end of 2005, highlighting the differences in the coverage of international financial reporting requirements for the two sectors. Although the IPSAS topic coverage is less comprehensive than that of IFRS, several IPSASB working projects address topics not covered by IFRS (e.g., Presentation of Budget Information in Financial Statements).

The IPSASB view is that financial reporting credibility is best served by public sector entities adopting IPSAS (IPSASB 2001, p. 52). Member countries of the European Union (EU) adopted IPSAS in 2005 as their financial reporting system. Similarly, the Organisation for Economic Co-operation and Development (OECD) and the North Atlantic Treaty Organisation (NATO) adopted IPSAS in their 2005 financial reports. The Asian Development Bank also recommends the adoption of IPSAS for Asian countries.

Table 11.1 List of Accounting Standards Issued by the IASB and the IPSASB

International Financial Reporting Standards (IFRS) issued by the IASB		International Public Sector Accounting Standards (IPSAS) issued by the IPSASB	
Standard No.	Title	Standard No.	Title
IFRS 1	First-time Adoption of International Financial Reporting Standards	IPSAS 1	Presentation of Financial Statements
IFRS 2	Share-based Payment	IPSAS 12	Inventories
IFRS 3	Business Combinations	IPSAS 2	Cash Flow Statements
IFRS 4	Insurance Contracts see also: See also Financial Instruments – other issues	IPSAS 3	Net Surplus or Deficit for the Period, Fundamental Errors and Changes in Accounting Policies
IFRS 5	Non-current Assets Held for Sale and Discontinued Operations	IPSAS 14	Events After the Reporting Date
		IPSAS 11	Construction Contracts
IAS 1	Presentation of Financial Statements	IPSAS 18	Segment Reporting
IAS 2	Inventories	IPSAS 17	Property, Plant and Equipment
IAS 7	Cash Flow Statements	IPSAS 13	Leases
IAS 8	Accounting Policies, Changes in Accounting Estimates and Errors	IPSAS 9	Revenue from Exchange Transactions
IAS 10	Events After the Balance Sheet Date		
IAS 11	Construction Contracts		
IAS 12	Income Taxes		
IAS 14	Segment Reporting		
IAS 16	Property, Plant and Equipment		
IAS 17	Leases		
IAS 18	Revenue		
IAS 19	Employee Benefits		

Table 11.1 (continued)

Standard No.	Title	Standard No.	Title
IAS 20	Accounting for Government Grants and Disclosure of Government Assistance		
IAS 21	The Effects of Changes in Foreign Exchange Rates	IPSAS 4	The Effects of Changes in Foreign Exchange Rates
IAS 23	Borrowing Costs	IPSAS 5	Borrowing Costs
IAS 24	Related Party Disclosures	IPSAS 20	Related Party Disclosures
IAS 26	Accounting and Reporting by Retirement Benefit Plans		
IAS 27	Consolidated and Separate Financial Statements	IPSAS 6	Consolidated Financial Statements and Accounting for Controlled Entities
IAS 28	Investments in Associates	IPSAS 7	Accounting for Investments in Associates
IAS 29	Financial Reporting in Hyperinflationary Economies	IPSAS 10	Financial Reporting in Hyperinflationary Economies
IAS 30	Disclosures in the Financial Statements of Banks and Similar Financial Institutions		
IAS 31	Interests in Joint Ventures	IPSAS 8	Financial Reporting of Interests in Joint Ventures
IAS 32	Financial Instruments: Disclosure and Presentation		
IAS 33	Earnings per Share		
IAS 34	Interim Financial Reporting		
IAS 36	Impairment of Assets		
IAS 37	Provisions, Contingent Liabilities and Contingent Assets	IPSAS 19	Provisions, Contingent Liabilities and Contingent Assets
IAS 38	Intangible Assets		
IAS 39	Financial Instruments: Recognition and Measurement	IPSAS 15	Financial Instruments: Disclosure and Presentation
IAS 40	Investment Property	IPSAS 16	Investment Property
IAS 41	Agriculture	IPSAS 21	Impairment of Non Cash-Generating Assets
		(No IFRS equivalent)	

Australian Accounting Standard-Setting Arrangements

Unlike their US counterparts, Australian standard setters have developed a single conceptual framework that defines a reporting entity and the objectives of financial reporting for all reporting entities. This provides the foundation to develop accounting standards applicable to all reporting entities irrespective of public/private ownership or profit objective (Macintosh, 1995). Underpinning this approach are arguments premised on the notion that if accounting standards were developed specifically for different entities they would look very similar and the approach would be cost ineffective.

Under s. 229(2)(c) of the Australian Securities and Investments Commission Act 2001, the AASB must ensure that there are appropriate accounting standards for each type of entity required to comply with accounting standards. Recognising the similarities of the information requirements of private and public sector entities' stakeholders, Australia committed itself to standards that are applicable to all reporting entities in 2002, i.e., sector neutral standards. The concept of a reporting entity embedded in Australia's financial reporting conceptual framework, relates to users' information needs. The IASB's *Framework* does not accommodate the concept of a reporting entity as the standards are orientated to the private sector and not-for-profit entities.

Reporting entities are defined in Australia's conceptual framework as:

all entities in respect of which it is reasonable to expect the existence of users dependent on general purpose financial reports (GPFR) for information that will be useful to them for making and evaluating decisions about the allocation of scarce resources (Statement of Accounting Concepts SAC 1 'Definition of Reporting Entity' para. 40)

Any entity satisfying this definition is deemed to be a reporting entity that is required to produce GPFR in accordance with AASB standards.[10] Since they are in the public domain, many public sector entities are reporting entities and should prepare GPFR. Users of public sector financial reports include Parliaments, Parliamentary Committees, taxpayers, ratepayers, contributors, employers, creditors and voters. Such parties require information to determine whether the entity is achieving its objectives and delivering services; generating cash flows to meet its commitments; and using resources in the interests of the community.

Australia committed to harmonising private sector accounting standards with international accounting standards during the 1990s. At that stage, there were two accounting standard-setting bodies in Australia; one making public sector accounting standards (i.e. the PSASB), the other making private sector accounting standards (i.e. the AASB). In 2000, the PSASB was disbanded, with all responsibilities of developing accounting standards transferring to a newly constituted AASB. As such, the AASB's scope expanded to include public sector accounting. The AASB's policy statement on international convergence and harmonisation that was issued in April 2002 (Policy Statement 4) states:

> The AASB's international harmonisation objective is to work towards the development of accounting standards in Australia that harmonise with IFRS, and IPSAS issued by the IPSASB, where the AASB concludes that such standards are likely to be in the best interests of both the private and public sectors in the Australian economy (para. 6).

However, verbatim adoption of IFRS can make it difficult for the AASB to achieve sector neutrality. In adopting IFRS, the AASB has retained equivalent IFRS content and wording and inserted Australian not-for-profit paragraphs where deemed appropriate.[11] The inclusions cater for the unique features of not-for-profit entities, being the absence of clearly defined ownership interest and claims of residual distributions. The included paragraphs generally relate to the appropriate measurement of not-for-profit entities' assets. The use of Australian specific paragraphs in 2005 AASB standards is summarised in Table 11.2.

An alternative approach that could have been pursued in the interests of internationalisation is IFRS adoption for private sector entities and IPSAS adoption for public sector and not-for-profit entities. This is the path taken by the EU, and would have alleviated the need to add paragraphs in the AIFRS to make them suitable for public sector and not-for-profit entities.

THE IMPLICATIONS OF AIFRS ADOPTION FOR AUSTRALIAN PUBLIC SECTOR ENTITIES

The new (AIFRS) reporting requirements can potentially influence public sector entities' reported performance and position, reporting systems, budgets and funding. Entities that do not have strategies in place to implement AIFRS (e.g., a project leader to manage the task; communication with all employees and other stakeholders as to the changes being implemented and their consequences; adequate resources; and knowledgeable staff or consultants to assist with the implementation)[12] are likely to find the transition a difficult period. Some of the changes will enhance transparency and hence accountability. However, the decision to move to AIFRS arguably provides an opportunity for those who believe that different rules (for example GFS rules) should apply because they are more appropriate, to question and disturb the regulatory process.

Table 11.2 Not-for-profit Specific Provisions in 2005 AASB Standards

AASB No.	Title of the standard	Areas where there are different requirements	
		For-profit entities	Not-for-profit entities
AASB 5	*Non-current Assets Held for Sale and Discontinued Operations*	Non-current assets (or disposal group) once classified as held for sale are measured at the lower of their carrying amount and fair value less costs to sell. Depreciation (amortisation) of such assets ceases.	The requirements do not apply to: • restructuring of administrative arrangements of government departments. • restructuring of administered activities of government departments.
AASB 102	*Inventories*	Inventories to be measured at the lower of cost and net realisable value on an item by item basis.	Inventories held for distribution by not-for-profit entities to be measured at the lower of cost and current replacement cost.
AASB 107	*Cash Flow Statements*	A reconciliation of cash flow arising from operating activities with the profit or loss of the period must be reported.	Not-for-profit entities that highlight the net cost of services in their income statement must provide a reconciliation of cash flows arising from operating activities to net cost of services.
AASB 114	*Segment Reporting*	The standard requires: • the disclosure of specific information using primary and secondary segment reporting formats. Extensive disclosures are required for both primary and secondary segments, in addition to a reconciliation of segment revenue, results, assets and liabilities, and a range of other disclosures. • a reportable segment is an identified business segment (products and services) or geographical segment as defined in the Standard.	This standard does not apply to not-for-profit entities.

Table 11.2 (continued)

AASB No.	Title of the standard	Areas where there are different requirements	
		For-profit entities	Not-for-profit entities
AASB 116	Property, Plant and Equipment (PPE)	This standard requires: • an item of PPE that qualifies for recognition as an asset is initially measured at its cost. • after initial recognition the entity must choose between either the cost model or the revaluation model as its measurement basis. The policy chosen shall be applied to the entire class of PPE. Revaluations cannot be netted within a class of PPE.	This standard requires: • the initial cost of an asset acquired at no or nominal cost is its fair value at the date of acquisition. • revaluation increases and decreases relating to individual assets within a class of assets can be offset. • for each revalued class of PPE there is no need to disclose the carrying amount that would have been recognised had the cost model been applied.
AASB 120	Accounting for Government Grants and Disclosure of Government Assistance	Government grants must not be recognised until there is a reasonable assurance that • the entity will comply with the conditions of the grant and • the grant will be received. Government grants are recognised at their fair value.	AASB 120 does not apply to not-for-profit entities; AASB 1004 *Contributions* applies.
AASB 124	Related Party Disclosures	The standard requires: Related party information is disclosed in the financial report of an entity, including information in respect of the existence and identity of related parties, related party transactions, and outstanding balances between the entity and its related parties at reporting date.	Not required for not-for-profit entities.

Table 11.2 (continued)

AASB No.	Title of the standard	Areas where there are different requirements	
		For-profit entities	Not-for-profit entities
AASB 127	*Consolidated and Separate Financial Statements*	The standard requires the preparation and presentation of a consolidated financial report for a group of entities under the control of a parent.	Requirements specific to not-for-profit entities include: • where a group of entities is a reporting entity, but the parent may not be explicitly identified for financial reporting purposes, the parent is deemed not to be a separate reporting entity. Although a consolidated financial report is required, a separate financial report for the parent is not required to be prepared. The consolidated report must disclose a list of significant subsidiaries. • control in the public sector may be evidenced by legislative or executive authority or administrative arrangements.
AASB 136	*Impairment of Assets*	The standard requires that: • at reporting date that the recoverable amount of an asset to which the Standard applies (not applicable to impairments of certain types of assets such as inventories, assets arising from construction contracts and others) be determined whenever there is an indication that the asset may be impaired. • Value in use is the present value of the future cash flows expected to be derived from an asset or cash-generating unit.	When the future economic benefits of an asset of a not-for-profit entity are not primarily dependent on the asset's ability to generate net cash inflows and where the entity would, if deprived of the asset, replace its remaining future economic benefits, value in use is the depreciated replacement cost of the asset.

Table 11.2 (continued)

AASB No.	Title of the standard	Areas where there are different requirements	
		For-profit entities	Not-for-profit entities
AASB 140	*Investment Property*	An investment property, whether purchased or constructed, is initially measured at cost including transaction costs. After initial recognition, investment property is to be measured using either the fair value model or the cost model.	Requirements specific to not-for-profit entities include: • AASB 140 notes that property held to meet service delivery objectives rather than for rental or capital appreciation purposes does not meet the definition of investment property. • the cost of an investment property acquired at no cost or for nominal cost is deemed to be its fair value at acquisition date.
AASB 1004	*Contributions*	Not required for for-profit entities.	The standard requires: • Income from the contribution of an asset to an entity is measured at the fair value of the contribution received or receivable. • The gross amount of any liability forgiven by a credit provider is recognised by the borrower as income.
AASB 1031	*Materiality*	Quantitative thresholds to guide the materiality assessment are: • if the amount is equal to or greater than 10 per cent of the appropriate base amount, materiality is presumed. • if the amount is equal to or less than 5 per cent of the appropriate base amount, materiality is not presumed.	The Standard recognises that it may not be appropriate to assess the materiality of income statement items for not-for-profit entities by reference to profit or loss given that such entities do not have a profit generation objective.

Efficacy of Setting Accounting Standards for the Public Sector

Given the parallel development of IFRS and IPSAS, and the FRC's direction to adopt IFRS, is the AASB's pursuit of a single set of sector neutral accounting standards efficient and effective? Would it be preferable to adopt one set of standards for the public sector and another for the private sector? A single set of standards approach requires ensuring that the standards are applicable to for-profit and not-for-profit entities. Similarly, adopting two sets of standards – one for public sector and one for private sector – assumes that all private sector entities are for-profit and all public sector entities are not-for-profit, an assumption that does not hold. Arguably, the pursuit of sector neutral standards catering for all reporting entities offers greater potential for efficiency and effectiveness in standard setting. It will also benefit those who regularly apply accounting standards to for-profit and not-for-profit entities in both the private and public sectors.

Control and Sovereignty

By adopting AIFRS, despite the power to opt out in exceptional cases,[13] Australian governments can lose a significant level of sovereignty and control over the standard-setting process and the outcomes of that process. This is a matter of concern, if the organisation assuming sovereignty is indifferent to the financial reporting needs and challenges of public sector and private entities. The FRC directive has diminished the ability of the AASB and Australian accounting stakeholders to influence the direction and content of both IFRS and consequentially AIFRS. It has also diminished the AASB's ability to affect the direction and content of IPSAS through the absence of commitment to IPSAS implicit in adopting IFRS. Consequently, governance is likely to become more political – and more non-Australian in the process. That said, the IASB has supported the role of the IPSASB, and adopting IFRS developed by the IASB is likely to help convergence with the IPSASB standards yet to come.

Enforcement

Will the potential loss of control of standard setting negatively affect the ability and willingness of those responsible for enforcing public sector financial reporting requirements? In the Australian public sector, two enforcement mechanisms operate. The first is the Australian National Audit Office (Auditor-General's Office) for Commonwealth (State) public sector entities; the second is the public accounts committees of the Commonwealth and various state and territory Parliaments. To the extent that adopting AIFRS is seen to be inappropriate for public sector entities, there may be some reluctance to enforce them. Further, dissatisfaction with the new requirements provides an impetus for governments to lobby to exclude or modify the operation of individual standards for public sector entities.[14] Such moves can enhance accountability and improve governance or be used to decrease transparency and accountability with a consequential threat to good governance.

Financial Statements Impact

The impact of adopting AIFRS for public sector entities' financial reports is unclear. While media attention focuses on the financial reporting implications for listed entities, it pays little attention to the impact on public sector entities. As a governance tool, accounting numbers in public sector entities' GPFR are used to monitor the efficiency and effectiveness of activities and financial performance evaluation over time. For example, public sector entities can be required to generate a specified return on assets. The extension of AIFRS adoption to public sector entities will potentially affect their reported assets, liabilities and profit and therefore affect financial performance indicators and returns-based pricing. This will occur given that some of the AIFRS adopted in 2005 either cover more comprehensively the recognition and measurement of various items (e.g., financial instruments) or prescribe treatments for various items that vary from current Australian requirements.[15]

PROGRESSING THE GFS/GAAP CONVERGENCE

While Australian public sector entities are generally reporting entities that are required to prepare GPFR using AIFRS, governments ultimately have the power to determine the applicability of AIFRS to public sector entities within their jurisdiction. Exercising this power can result in some public sector entities being directed to adopt accounting practices incompatible with AIFRS. Adding to the complexity of the public sector reporting arrangements in Australia, the Australian Loan Council also requires all Australian governments to present budgets and prepare outcome reports in accordance with a Uniform Presentation Framework using the International Monetary Fund's Government Finance Statistics Framework (GFS) to allow comparison between jurisdictions and the formation of national aggregates (Challen and Jeffery 2005).

There are both conceptual and technical differences between GFS and AIFRS. Differences in conceptual issues include the scope of the reporting entity, the relationship between *ex ante* reporting and *ex post* reporting, and neutrality of requirements across sectors (AASB 2004b). The GFS report two major fiscal measures: the GFS net operating balance calculated as GFS revenue less GFS expenses; and the GFS net lending or fiscal balance which includes net capital expenditure excluding depreciation. Technical differences include timing differences such as borrowing costs and bad and doubtful debts, and permanent differences such as treatment of dividends, gains and losses on non-current assets, and treatment of outside equity interests (AASB 2004b, pp. 2–3). The differences can result in inconsistent reporting, particularly of budget items and in incomparable GFS and AIFRS prepared reports. Governance and credibility are potentially compromised within a jurisdiction that has two different sets of reporting requirements for public sector entities. Accordingly, the AASB at the direction of the FRS has pursued GFS and AIFRS convergence as an urgent priority with the objective of achieving 'an Australian accounting standard for a single set of Government reports which are auditable, comparable between jurisdictions and in which the outcome statements are directly comparable with the relevant budget statements' (FRC Bulletin 2002/5, 18 December 2002 as modified by FRC Bulletin 2003/1, 11 April 2003; AASB 2004b, p. 1).

GFS and IFRS are developed by different bodies for different sectors and for different purposes. As such, it is not surprising that there are differences in the requirements of GFS and the AIFRS based on IFRS. Given that Australia is committed to sector neutrality in its GAAP (AIFRS) accounting standards but Australian governments are also required to comply with GFS, the AASB has an interesting challenge in converging GFS and AIFRS. In this section we explain how the AASB is resolving the problem of converging approaches with differing conceptual orientations and technical solutions.

The Australian Financial Reporting Council (FRC), which gave the initial directive for the AASB to adopt IFRS by 2005, also provided a broad strategic direction for GAAP/GFS conversion to occur as a matter of urgent priority. The convergence objective should be to achieve accounting standards that yield statements that are directly comparable with relevant budget statements, and that are comparable between jurisdictions. In turn, in December 2004 the AASB interpreted the broad strategic direction as being applicable to all public sector entities, with the following implementation approaches:

- The AASB would not develop standards for budgetary reporting.
- The AASB would not replace AIFRS with GFS.
- The convergence would be implemented in three phases. The first focuses on general purpose financial reporting by State, Territory and Commonwealth governments (whole of government). This phase includes dealing with issues such as determining if the General Government Sector (GGS) constitutes a sector for reporting purposes, or a reporting entity. Phase 2 focuses upon reporting by entities within the GGS (including government departments currently within the scope of AAS 29 'Financial Reporting by Government

Departments'). The third phase focuses on general purpose financial reporting by local governments and other public sector entities such as universities and GBEs.

- Convergence needs to have regard to international activities, in particular work being undertaken by the IASB and by the IPSASB, the International Monetary Fund (IMF) and the Organisation for Economic Co-operation and Development (OECD) (AASB, 2004(b)).

As at the end of 2005, the AASB has undertaken a significant amount of work, as have other groups such as the Heads of Treasuries Accounting and Reporting Advisory Committee (HOTORAC), towards identifying key issues for convergence. The AASB classifies those issues as being either conceptual or technical. It plans that resolution of the conceptual issues will provide a context for resolving the technical issues.

The conceptual issues that the AASB has identified as potentially creating differences between GFS and AIFRS include: the objectives of financial statements (e.g., macroeconomic decision making *versus* accountability); identification of users and their information needs; the scope of the reporting entity; *ex-ante* reporting and its relationship to *ex-post* reporting; neutrality of requirements across and within profit/not-for-profit/public/private sectors; role of disclosure versus recognition in financial statements; and whether the focus is on differences in concepts or in practice (AASB 2004(b)).

Some of the technical issues to be resolved include:

- Permanent and timing differences between the AIFRS comprehensive statement of financial performance and the GFS two-statement equivalent at a whole of government level. Permanent differences include distributions to owners (dividends), which are treated as expenses under GFS and as allocations of earnings under AIFRS. Timing differences include such things as treatments of defence weapons platforms, which are expensed immediately under GFS but capitalised and depreciated under AIFRS.
- Differences between net results under AIFRS and the GFS net operating balance. Many of these differences arise from the ways in which GFS splits items between 'Statement of Government Operations', which yields a net operating balance, and its 'Statement of Other Economic Flows'; and how GAAP splits items between statements. Examples include gains and losses on non-current asset sales, which are recognised in the net result under GAAP, but treated by GFS as price changes recorded in the Statement of Other Economic Flows.
- Differences between the AIFRS Statement of Financial Position and GFS balance sheet at a whole of government level. An example of this difference

is the treatment of outside equity interest as a liability under GFS and as equity under AIFRS.

- Differences between the AIFRS and GFS Statements of Cash Flows. No such differences have been identified yet.
- Differences between GAAP financial statements and GFS equivalents at a sector level. An example of this is the calculation of net worth. AIFRS treat equity or net worth as the residual of assets less liabilities, regardless of the market value of the entity's equities; GFS measures net worth as assets less liabilities less shares (measured at market value) and contributed capital, potentially a negative net worth figure in the investments line of the parent sector.

There are numerous differences, some of which have been or will be resolved through the adoption of AIFRS that differ from previous Australian GAAP. For example, differences in the GFS and GAAP treatment of borrowing costs can disappear now that AIFRS are in place and they allow expensing of all borrowing costs. Other differences, though, will remain. It will be interesting to observe how political the GAAP/GFS convergence becomes as options to align the sets of reporting requirements necessitate either a movement away from IFRS adoption, changes to GFS, or increased disclosure. The AASB plans to continue liaising with the Australian Bureau of Statistics to identify opportunities for GFS changes that will align with AIFRS (and vice versa). Australia is a first mover in this convergence program; however international developments are occurring as a result of collaborations between the IPSASB and IMF.[16] As such, there is a five-way alignment challenge involving the public and private sector bodies: AASB, IASB, IPSASB, IMF, and ABS.

ED 142 Financial Reporting of General Government Sectors by Governments provides some indication of the potential give-and-take that will emanate over the convergence period. As mentioned earlier in the chapter, a reporting entity is defined to be an entity for which it is reasonable to expect there to be financial statement users who rely on the entity's general purpose financial reports (GPFR) for information in making and evaluating economic decisions (AARF 1990a, p. 15). Reporting entities are required to produce GPFR in accordance with AIFRS (refer to endnote 10). Recent debate has focused on the issue of what should constitute a reporting entity in the context of public sector entities, and particularly on whether the General Government Sector (GGS) is a reporting entity and thus required to produce a general purpose financial report (AASB 2005), as preferred by the Australian Heads of Treasury. The GGS consists of entities that fulfil the functions of government as their primary activity. They provide goods and services to the community on a non-market basis, make transfer payments to redistribute income and wealth, and finance their activities mainly through taxes and transfers from other sectors. Their scope 'conforms to the GFS principle that, generally, all entities funded by budget appropriations must be amalgamated into a single institutional unit. This principle is consistent with using the GGS for determining the scope of the budget sector' (Challen and Jeffery 2005, p. 73).

The ED 142 proposals require each GGS to: prepare a partial consolidated general purpose financial report; report a GAAP compliant single operating statement; use GAAP recognition and measurement principles in the determination of GAAP amounts; select GFS compliant options when GAAP contains optional treatments; and disclose selected GFS information in the financial statements or in the notes to the financial statements (AASB Project Summary – AASB GAAP/ GFS Convergence Project, last updated 28 September 2005 and viewed at www.aasb.com.au/workprog/board_papers/hot_subs/main.htm).

The ED 142 proposal that the GGS of a government is a reporting entity for which a stand-alone GPFR should be prepared is controversial given the AASB's December 2002 decision that the GGS was not a separate reporting entity (AASB 2005). Further, the exposure draft proposes that the GGS of a government should be exempted from the requirement to consolidate certain of its controlled entities: those that are classified under GFS as belonging to other sectors. Part of the reason for allowing a partial consolidation is that in some cases there are extreme constraints over the control that the GGS can exercise. Examples include the Australian government's ability to influence Telstra (a public telecommunications company with ownership held 51 per cent by the Australian government), which 'is subject to constraints due to the interests of minority shareholders and the interest of the public in how communications and other services are delivered' (Challen and Jeffery 2005). Another example is the fact that the executive government's ability to influence operating and strategic decisions of associated entities is often restricted or impaired e.g., the Commonwealth Treasurer can give specific instructions to the Reserve Bank Board about retaining operating surpluses, but the treasurer may not direct the board to change interest rates or support the Australian currency (Challen and Jeffery 2005). The exemption from the scope of GGS consolidation of statutory entities that are not subject to government control in the exercise of their day-to-day activities and their financial affairs is an exemption not available to the private sector.

Added to the additional paragraphs that are already inserted into AIFRS to ensure that they cover/exempt the public sector or not-for-profit sector from their scope, the reversal of the decision concerning the reporting entity status of GGS and the exemption of certain controlled entities from GGS consolidations indicate that there could be some future debate that is settled on grounds that are not applied within the private sector. The extent to which this potential is exacerbated or mitigated by international decisions remains to be seen.

CONCLUSION

Australia's financial reporting landscape for both private and public sector entities has changed for reporting periods ending on or after 1 January 2005. Whilst attention and resources have been directed at the management and potential economic consequences of the transition to AIFRS for large private sector entities, limited consideration has been directed at public sector entities, despite their economic importance. Good governance requires that managers of public sector entities have identified the adoption of AIFRS as a key strategic business risk and have installed mechanisms to manage the transition process and to understand and communicate the impact of adoption on their GPFR. A fully functioning governance system will promote reliable financial reports prepared in accordance with generally accepted accounting principles. Similarly, reliable financial reports will assist in monitoring the entity, an important aspect of governance.

Australia's promulgation of sector neutral accounting standards and its adoption of AIFRS extending to public sector entities is a unique stance relative to member countries of the EU. This stance has necessitated the AASB inserting paragraphs into 2005 AASB standards to render them appropriate to both for-profit and not-for-profit entities. The alternative approach was for Australia to adopt AIFRS for for-profit entities and IPSAS for not-for-profit entities. The approach pursued has arguably given Australia a more comprehensive set of accounting standards applicable to public sector entities, however the IPSASB is developing standards on a number of issues specific to public sector entities (e.g., accounting for social policies of government and budget reporting) for which there are no comparable IFRS.

Australia has assumed a leading approach in converging GFS and GAAP. This approach, which involves resolving conceptual issues and then technical matters, will be facilitated by AIFRS adoption, but will require high levels of cooperation and information sharing between the AASB, IASB, IPSASB, IMF and ABS. The extent to which the sector neutral globalisation approach is assisted by IASB and IPSASB cooperation remains to be seen.

NOTES

1 Reporting entities can be categorised in matrix form as public or private sector with a for-profit or not-for-profit objective. Hence public sector entities are not necessarily not-for-profit and private sector entities are not necessarily for-profit.
2 Corporations Act 2001 (Cwlth), sections 292(1) and 296.
3 The IFAC is the global organisation for the accountancy profession. In 2005 it had 157 member organisations in 118 countries. It aims to protect the public interest by encouraging high quality

practices by the world's accountants. IFAC members represent 2.5 million accountants employed in public practice, industry and commerce, government, and academe (www.ifac.org/About/).

4   As articulated in AASB Adoption of IASB standards by 2005 (last updated 10 August 2004 and viewed at http://www.aasb.com.au/international/2005_index.htm).

5   In July 2004, the AASB issued the Framework for the Preparation and Presentation of Financial Statements that supersedes Australia's earlier Statement of Accounting Concepts (SAC) 3 Qualitative Characteristics of Financial Information and SAC 4 Definition and Recognition of the Elements of Financial Statements. The Framework for the Preparation and Presentation of Financial Statements was issued by the AASB to ensure that there is consistency when (1) AIFRS refer to the AASB Framework (e.g. AASB 108 Accounting Policies, Changes in Accounting Estimates and Errors outlines a hierarchy to be followed in developing an accounting policy when an Australian accounting standard does not specifically address the transaction). The Framework developed by the IASB is integral to this hierarchy; and (2) the AASB evaluates proposed standards for application in Australia.

6   The US accounting standard setter, the Financial Accounting Standards Board (FASB), identifies three distinctions between for-profit and not-for-profit entities: namely not-for-profit entities have (1) significant resources from providers who do not expect to receive either repayment or economic benefits proportionate to resources provided; (2) objectives that may be unrelated to providing goods or services at a profit; and (3) the absence of defined ownership interest that is transferable or has a residual claim. Reflecting these differences, the FASB has separate statements for the objectives of financial reporting for for-profit and not-for-profit entities. Interestingly, in Australia in the mid 1980s the former Public Sector Accounting Standards Board (PSASB) issued an exposure draft stating that the proposed objective of financial reporting by public sector entities was to disclose information that is useful in making economic decisions (including those relating to matters of policy) and satisfy accountability (AARF 1984).

7   For a debate on the neutrality of accounting standards for private and public sector entities see Barton (1999), Barton (2002), Carnegie and Wolnizer (2002) and Newberry (2002).

8   Akin to the Australian accounting standard setters' philosophy, New Zealand accounting standard setters have pursued sector neutral accounting standards for many years. In implementing the decision to adopt IFRS in New Zealand, the Financial Reporting Standards Board of the Institute of Chartered Accountants of New Zealand and the Accounting Standards Review Board have, like the AASB, decided to adapt IFRS to ensure that the standards are sector neutral (see 'Adoption of International Financial Reporting Standards' viewed at www.icanz.co.nz/StaticContent/AGS/IFRSadoption.cfm).

9   Until January 2000 there were two standard setters in Australia, the Australian Accounting Standards Board (AASB) and the Public Sector Accounting Standards Board (PSASB) of the Australian Accounting Research Foundation (AARF). The two Boards worked closely together in developing accounting standards with technical support provided by AARF. In January 2000 the PSASB was subsumed by the AASB under the oversight of the FRC. Since June 2000 one series of accounting standards (AASB series) applicable to all sectors progressively replaced dual series of public sector (AAS) and private sector (AASB) standards.

10 In the Framework for the Preparation and Presentation of Financial Statements issued by the AASB (2004), paragraph 8 states 'The Framework applies to the financial reports of all commercial, industrial, and business reporting entities, whether in the public or the private sectors. The term "reporting entity" is defined in SAC 1 Definition of the Reporting Entity'. The status of the Framework for AIFRS is as follows: (1) Para 1: The Framework sets out the concepts that underlie the preparation and presentation of financial reports for external users, (2) Para 2: This Framework is not an Australian Accounting Standard and hence does not define standards for any particular measurement or disclosure issue. Nothing in this Framework overrides any specific Australian Accounting Standards, (3) Para 3: The AASB recognises that in a limited number of cases there may be a conflict between the Framework and an Australian Accounting Standard. In those cases where there is a conflict, the requirements of the Australian Accounting Standards prevail over those of the Framework. As, however, the AASB will be guided by the Framework in the development of future standards and its review of existing

standards, the number of cases of conflict between the Framework and Australian Accounting Standards will diminish through time.

11 The words used in the directive are 'standards that are the same as' IFRS (FRC 2002b, 2002c), which has been interpreted to require verbatim adoption of IFRS.

12 In 2004, the Australian National Audit Office conducted a survey of IFRS preparedness of 25 large Australian Government agencies. They found that 13 did not have an IFRS or equivalent project team or Steering Committee and 10 had no staff training strategy in place (Barrett 2004).

13 The only instance being recognition of government grants by not-for-profit entities.

14 In 2004 the Government of Victoria proposed changing the reporting framework to modify the application of accounting standards to public sector entities. This was done by replacing 'generally accepted accounting principles' with 'appropriate financial reporting frameworks as determined by the Minister' (see 'Amendments to Victoria's Financial Management Act', CPA Australia Media Release, 26 August 2004, viewed at www.cpaaustralia.com.au/cps/rde/xchg/cpa/hs.xsl/990_8935_ENA_HTML.htm).

15 In another project, we analysed the potential financial reporting ramifications for public sector entities pursuant to AIFRS adoption. Based on a sample of 100 Australian public sector entities randomly selected from the IBIS World database, we identified public sector entities affected by adopting the Australian equivalents to AIFRS for financial instruments and intangible assets, two of the accounting policies likely to affect entities' performance measures. We analysed the minimum impact on sample entities' financial statements based on divergences in the entities' 2002 accounting policies and AIFRS adopted in 2005 for financial instruments and intangibles. Thirty-eight of the 100 sample public sector entities (38 per cent) either recognised intangible assets, noted differences between the fair value and carrying amount of recognised financial instruments, or disclosed gains/losses associated with unrecognised financial instruments. Hence, the number of the 100 sample entities affected by AIFRS adoption is not inconsequential.

16 The IPSASB's program on converging IPSASs and statistical bases of financial reporting is progressing. In October 2005, the IPSASB issued ED 28 *Disclosure of Financial Information about the General Government Sector*. Concurrently, the IPSASB issued ED 27 *Presentation of Budget Information in Financial Statements*. ED 27 proposes the disclosure of comparable budgeted and actual financial information.

ACKNOWLEDGEMENTS

The support of the Monash Institute for the Study of Global Movements is appreciated. This chapter has benefited from comments offered by participants at the Globalisation of Accounting Standards Conference in Prato, Italy in May 2005, the 2005 Finance and Treasury Association Public Sector Conference and the 2005 European Accounting Association Annual Congress in Gottesburg.

REFERENCES

AARF (1984), *Exposure Draft: Proposed Statement of Accounting Concepts 'Objectives of Financial Reporting by Public Sector Entities'*, Melbourne: Australian Accounting Research Foundation, November.

AARF (1990a), *Statement of Accounting Concept 1: Definition of Reporting Entity*, Melbourne: Australian Accounting Research Foundation.

AARF (1990b), *Statement of Accounting Concept 2: Objective of General Purpose Financial Reporting*, Melbourne: Australian Accounting Research Foundation.

AASB (2004a), *Framework for the preparation and presentation of financial statements*, Melbourne: Australian Accounting Standards Board.

AASB (2004b), *Gap/GFS Convergence: Implementing the FRC Strategic Direction*, Melbourne: Australian Accounting Standards Board.

AASB (2005), *ED 142 Financial Reporting of General Government Sectors by Governments*, Melbourne: Australian Accounting Standards Board.

Ahn, B., Halligan, J., and Wilks, S. (2002), *Reforming Public and Corporate Governance*, Cheltenham, UK: Edward Elgar.

Australian Accounting Research Foundation and the Public Sector Accounting Standards Board (1984), *Exposure Draft: Proposed Statement of Accounting Concepts 'Objectives of Financial Reporting by Public Sector Entities'*, November.

Barrett, P. (2004), *Assurance Auditing in a Changing AGPS Environment*, Occasional Paper viewed 23 September 2005. www.anao.gov.au/WebSite.nsf/Publications/64914D7DF2EA0AC6CA256ED1000C16E6.

Barton, A. (1999), 'Public and private sector accounting – the non-identical twins', *Australian Accounting Review*, **9** (2): 22–31.

Barton, A. (2002), 'Public-sector accounting: A common reporting framework? A rejoinder', *Australian Accounting Review*, **12**(3): 41–45.

Carnegie, G. and P. Wolnizer (2002), 'A rejoinder', *Australian Accounting Review*, **12** (3): 45–47.

Challen, D. and C. Jeffery (2005), 'Definition of the Reporting Entity', *Australian Accounting Review*, **15** (1): 71–78.

FRC (2002a), 'Adoption of International Accounting Standards by 2005', *Bulletin of the Financial Reporting Council* 2002(4): 1–3.

FRC (2002b), *Broad Strategic Direction Provided by the Financial Reporting Council to the Australian Accounting Standards Board for 2002–2003*, Financial Reporting Council (Australia) (Minutes, September 2002 FRC meeting, Attachment B).

FRC (2002c), *Broad Strategic Direction Provided by the Financial Reporting Council to the Australian Accounting Standards Board for 2002–2003*, Financial Reporting Council (Australia) (letter to AASB 18 December 2002).

Government of South Australia (2001), *Report of the Auditor-General for the year ending 30 June 2001*, Part A: Audit Overview, Adelaide, 88.

IASC (1989), *Framework for the Presentation and Preparation of Financial Statements*, London: International Accounting Standards Committee.

IFAC (2004), *Handbook of International Public Sector, Accounting Pronouncements*, New York: International Federation of Accountants.

IPSASB (2001), *Governance in the Public Sector: A Governing Body Perspective*, IFAC International Public Sector Study, Public Sector Committee of the International Federation of Accountants: Study 13.

Jackson, A. and I. Lapslay (2003), 'The Diffusion of Accounting Practices in the New "Managerial" Public Sector', *The International Journal of Public Sector Management*, **16** (5) 359–372.

Macintosh, J. (1995), 'Finding the Right Fit', *CA Magazine*, March, 34–38.

Newberry, S (2002), 'The conceptual framework sham?', *Australian Accounting Review*, **12** (3), 47–49.

Rezaee, Z. (2004), 'Corporate Governance Role in Financial Reporting', *Research in Accounting Regulation*, **17**.

Reijniers, J.J.A.M. (1994), 'Organization of Public-Private Partnership Projects', *International Journal of Project Management*, **12**(3): 137–142.

12 Convergence of Chinese Accounting Standards with International Standards: Process, Achievements and Prospects

Wei-Guo Zhang and De-Ming Lu

INTRODUCTION

Since 1979, China has made phenomenal progress in advancing Chinese Accounting Standards (CASs[1]), with an overall trend towards convergence with accounting standards developed by the International Accounting Standards Board (IASB) and its predecessor, the International Accounting Standards Committee (IASC). These international standards, which were originally International Accounting Standards (IAS) and are now labelled as International Financial Reporting Standards (IFRS), are referred to as IFRS throughout this chapter.[2] A growing capital market is the major force driving CASs convergence with IFRS, the capital market being a primary user and beneficiary of high quality accounting standards.

When China commenced its reform program in the 1980s, foreign investment enterprises were pivotal in pushing CASs towards IFRS. However, convergence of accounting standards was limited and application of accounting standards was narrow in scope due to the fact that the Chinese capital market was still at its inception. The market only developed rapidly from 1990 when the Shanghai Stock Exchange debuted, and it was from then that convergence of CASs with IFRS fast-tracked.

Even if accounting standards are of a high standard, high quality financial information is not necessarily generated unless there are consistent and appropriate interpretations, and strict enforcement. Hence, the IASB, the European Union (EU) and the International Organisation of Securities Commissions (IOSCO) have all reiterated the importance of interpretation and enforcement, and established various schemes necessary to realise that. In China, the China Securities Regulatory Commission (CSRC) is the local capital market watchdog. It has worked jointly with the Ministry of Finance (MOF), the accounting standard setter, to stress tough enforcement of accounting standards since 1992.

There is no doubt that China has accomplished solid and effective progress both in driving convergence and in ensuring a strict implementation of accounting standards, despite no official announcement of an overall IFRS adoption policy. CASs will further converge with IFRS in the coming years. However, differences will continue to remain in a very few areas, arising from the needs of the environment specific to China as an emerging country in transition.

This chapter describes the development and achievements of the Chinese capital market. This is followed by a discussion of the interaction between accounting standards and capital markets. China's programme in converging with international accounting standards is then detailed. The chapter concludes with some comments on China's transition to IFRS.

DEVELOPMENT AND ACHIEVEMENTS OF THE CHINESE CAPITAL MARKET

Historical Perspective

Before 1949, China had probably the largest capital market in East Asia. After the Chinese Communist Party came into power and the socialist system was established in 1949, enterprises generally adopted public ownership. In the case of state-owned enterprises (SOEs)[3] the government provided capital, a central plan controlled production and business development, and profit was returned in full to the government. Under these circumstances, China dissolved its capital market and bank loans were limited to very narrow areas. However, the capital market has revived since 1979 when China introduced its reform policy. Its development from then can be divided into three stages.

Initial Stage (1979–1989)

Since 1979, in an attempt to facilitate fundraising for economic development, China began to issue treasury bonds and to allow private equity injections from employees into small enterprises for reform and development purposes. From 1984, a sweeping reform of the economic system began from rural farms to urban enterprises, and that year some enterprises in Beijing and Shanghai issued shares to the public. Open market trading was prohibited initially, regardless of private equity shares or shares offered to the public. Over-the-counter trading of shares was available to investors in 1986 as permitted by the government. But at that time there was no centralised stock exchange. Moreover, trade volumes were extremely low.

Boom Stage (1990–1998)

At the end of 1990, the Shanghai and Shenzhen stock exchanges debuted in tandem, a milestone for a national and centralised capital market. In 1992, the blueprint for establishing a market economy with Chinese characteristics was formulated by the central government. It became widely accepted among government officials and public consensus emerged that China should achieve a diversified ownership structure by restructuring SOEs into joint stock limited companies, and significantly developing the country's capital market. The number of listed companies grew sharply, accompanied by a fast growing capital market, particularly from 1992 to 1993, 1996 to 1998, and from 2000 to 2001.

In addition to shares issued in the domestic market for domestic residents (A shares), B shares were issued in the domestic market for foreign investors by companies registered in mainland China from 1992.[4] In 1993, companies registered in mainland China were permitted to issue H shares in the Hong Kong, New York, London, and other major international capital markets. Over the same period, a suite of laws and regulations passed, including the *Securities Law* and *Company Law*. In addition, the capital market accomplished a transition from segmentalised administration to centralised administration, along with the establishment of the CSRC.

Regulated Development Stage (1999–)

Probably no country's capital market has ever grown without the benefits of a securities regulatory framework. The Chinese capital market entered into a regulatory development phase in 1999. An indication of this is the implementation of *Securities Law* from mid-1999.

In China, *Securities Law* represented a new stage of legislation and regulation of the Chinese capital market. Its implementation became a cornerstone for regulating the Chinese capital market in subsequent years, with the purpose of protecting minority shareholders' interests. The CSRC also launched campaigns to underpin institutional investment growth to nurture the philosophy of investing in value and issued a set of merger and acquisition regulations to support the expansion of listed companies and to pressure management to improve efficiency and profitability. Upon China's accession to the World Trade Organisation (WTO) in 2001, the CSRC further opened the Chinese capital market in full compliance with WTO commitments, including permitting Sino-foreign joint venture securities firms and fund management companies.

Achievements

An unfledged market as it is, the Chinese capital market has undergone remarkable transformation. There were only a dozen listed companies in 1990 when the Shanghai and Shenzhen stock exchanges opened. By the end of 2004, there were 1,377 listed A share companies, with a market capitalisation of RMB 3,706 billion yuan, 27 per cent of GDP. In addition, there were 110 B share companies. Furthermore, 111 domestic companies had issued H shares overseas by the end of 2004 (see Table 12.1).

Capital markets have played a critical role in hastening industrial structure upgrade and enterprise development by helping enterprises reposition themselves in the market by means of technological innovation and production expansion; propelling a transition from sunset industries to sunrise industries; facilitating enterprises' branding strategies; driving the formation and expansion of large-scale conglomerate groups; and supporting Chinese enterprises to compete with prestigious multinational companies in international markets.

In the 1980s, China tried many business arrangements in the course of enterprise reform. The capital market has driven the establishment of the modern enterprise system with joint stock limited companies, and this has been aided by corporate governance reforms, and encouraging businesses to operate by internationally accepted standards.

At a pace synchronised with market developments, various types of market infrastructure have developed steadily. Laws and regulations accommodating capital market development needs have been issued gradually. A jump start in this regard occurred in 1992 when China issued several regulations, including *Provisional Regulations on Issuance and Trade of Stocks*, all of which were developed with a global mindset that accommodated local insights. Hence, the Chinese capital market could develop on a uniform basis nationwide. For Chinese accounting, a revolutionary event that year was the issue of *Accounting Standard for Business Enterprises (Basic)*. More importantly, China issued *Company Law* in 1993 and *Securities Law* in 1998, to facilitate development of the Chinese capital market. Additionally, in 1993 China issued *Detailed Implementation Rules on Information Disclosure by Companies Offering Shares to the Public* to provide investors with the information necessary for investment decision-making; *Provisional Regulations on Administration of Securities Investment Funds* in 1997 and *Law of Securities Investment Funds* in 2002 to boost institutional investment; *Administrative Measures on Mergers and Acquisitions of Listed Companies* to assist listed companies in their M&A activities; and *Corporate Governance Standards* in 2002 to improve listed companies' corporate governance.

At its capital market inception, China adopted a segment-based regulatory

Table 12.1 Chinese capital market statistics

	1993	1994	1995	1996	1997	1998	1999	2000	2001	2002	2003	2004
A share companies	177	287	311	514	720	825	923	1,060	1,133	1,224	1,287	1,377
B share companies	40	58	70	85	101	106	108	114	112	111	111	110
H share companies	6	13	18	25	42	43	46	52	61	76	93	111
Market cap (billion yuan)	105	369	347	984	1,753	1,951	2,647	4,809	4,352	3,860	4,246	3,706
Market cap (% of GDP)	10	8	6	15	23	25	32	54	45	37	36	27
Turnover (billion yuan)	68	813	404	2,133	3,072	2,354	3,132	6,083	3,831	2,799	3,212	4,233
Investors by account (million)	2	11	12	23	33	39	45	58	67	69	70	72

Source: CSRC (2005), *Almanac of the Chinese Securities and Futures Statistics.*

197

system. Regulatory power was separated among various government departments at the central and local level. By referring to developed economies, China established a central level market watchdog in 1992, i.e. the Securities Committee under the State Council and CSRC. The Securities Committee was to have a cross-department function to coordinate and enact policies while the CSRC was to be the executive body responsible for regulating the capital market. In 1998, the central government discontinued the Securities Committee, with all of its functions being integrated into the CSRC. The CSRC was then upgraded to the MOF and central bank level to enhance its authority. Securities regulatory offices at provincial level were all directly led by the CSRC from 1 January 1999, establishing a regulatory framework containing Chinese characteristics and consistent with developed market economies.

Parallel with the capital market growth, the number and variety of intermediary agencies (e.g., securities companies, CPA firms, law firms and asset appraisal firms) grew. Also, a new generation of talented, and ambitious professional business people emerged. They were market economy savvy and were aggressive in pursuing their careers.

There was no computerised trading tool when the Shanghai Stock Exchange debuted. Only a few years later, paperless, electronic, and network trades were all available in the Chinese capital market. Computerisation, information and network technologies have advanced to the same level as, if not beyond, other countries in many aspects.

The capital market has educated the general public, scholars, entrepreneurs and government officials about market economies, providing insight into the 'invisible hands' that operate in such economies, and why non-compliance with market economy rules inevitably will be punished. Such a change in mindset may be considered as the most profound achievement.

CONVERGENCE OF CHINESE ACCOUNTING STANDARDS

Over thousands of years, China developed a set of bureaucratic accounting systems accommodating fiscal, taxation, government audit and jurisdiction systems, as well as Chinese bookkeeping methodology. From the mid 1800s, Chinese accounting was a mixture of Chinese bookkeeping and western accounting practice. Application varied regionally and across businesses. Yang (1998) divides Chinese accounting history from 1949, when the People's Republic of China was established, into four phases: in tandem with Russia from 1949–57; eradicating superstition from 1958–78; establishing an accounting system with Chinese characteristics from 1978–91; and the IFRS convergence phase from 1992. Additionally, Qu, Chen and Yang (1999) divide the history of

Chinese accounting reform subsequent to the commencement of China's economic reform program into three phases, namely, the phase partially referring to international conventions from 1979–92; the phase implementing accounting systems for the needs of economic system reform from 1992–97; and the phase building up a standard framework to guide accounting for economic transactions.

The division of history this chapter employs is similar to that of Qu, Chen and Yang (1999), but based more on the convergence process towards IFRS. It divides the history of CASs from 1979 into the following three phases:

- Introducing and preparing (1979–91);
- Fundamental reform (1992–96); and
- Full-swing convergence (1997–).

The link between historical events in the Chinese capital market and the major developments in CASs are displayed in Table 12.2.

Introducing and Preparing Phase (1979–91)

China's reform policy commenced in rural areas in 1979. In 1984 it infiltrated the urban economic system, particularly SOEs reform, and over the next dozen years involved a wide range of actions, for example, establishing Sino-foreign equity joint ventures, restructuring some SOEs into joint stock limited companies and easing government direct control over enterprises. These actions brought huge cultural shocks, but their depth and breadth were still limited. From an accounting perspective, the environment remained open for further sweeping reforms although some had occurred, particularly the introduction of internationally accepted accounting standards into the Sino-foreign equity joint venture reporting system.

Over the same period, many Chinese scholars studied how to establish the CASs system by referring to western accounting standards. Their studies covered the foreign accounting standards frameworks and content (e.g. US GAAP and its conceptual framework) and the mode and structure of CASs. The most influential figures in this period were Jiwan Yang, Er-ying Lou, and Jiashu Ge.

In the decades after the 1949 establishment of the People's Republic of China, Yang led the national administration of accounting affairs within the MOF. During the 1950s, he led the transformation of China's accounting system into one compatible with a planned economy by adopting the former Soviet Union model. With in-depth knowledge of both capitalist and socialist accounting theory and practice, Yang published views on how to harmonise the Chinese accounting system with IFRS. He noted that comparative financial information and international convergence of financial information can only be realised via a

Table 12.2 Interaction between the Chinese capital market and CASs

Year	Historical events in capital market	Major evolutions of CASs
1979	• Reform policy introduced in China	
1980	• Enterprises permitted to raise funds from own employees	
1984	• Reform of Chinese economy system directed towards urban areas • Beijing and Shanghai companies began issuing stocks	
1985		• MOF issued *Accounting System for Sino-foreign Equity Joint Ventures*
1986	• Over-the-counter stock trade began	
1987		• China Accounting Society established study group on fundamental accounting theory and accounting standards
1988		• MOF established accounting standards group
1990	• Shanghai and Shenzhen Stock Exchanges opened	
1992	• Chinese government vowed to market economy • CSRC established • First B share issued	• MOF issued *Accounting System for Enterprises in Joint Stock Experimental Program* • MOF issued *Accounting Standards for Business Enterprises (Basic)* • MOF issued *Supplementary Regulations on Hong Kong IPO Accounting Issues for Enterprises in Joint Stock Experimental Program*
1993	• First H share issued	

Table 12.2 (continued)

	• CSRC issued *Detailed Implementation Rules on Information Disclosure by Companies offering Shares to the Public* • National People's Congress issued *Company Law*	
1994	• *Company Law* was effective	
1995		• MOF began to issue Auditing Standards • MOF issued *Provisional Regulations on Consolidated Financial Statements*
1997	• First consequential case of accounting	• MOF issued first stand-alone fraud accounting standard
1998	• National People's Congress issued *Securities Law*	• MOF issued *Accounting System for Joint Stock Limited Companies* • MOF issued suite of stand-alone accounting standards to fight profit manipulation
2000		• *Securities Law* was effective
2001	• CSRC expressed support to IPO of financial institutions	• MOF issued *Accounting System for Business Enterprises* • CSRC and MOF issued suite of accounting and disclosure rules related to IPO of financial institutions
2002	• CSRC issued *Corporate Governance Standards of Listed Companies*	
2003	• Supreme People's Court issued Certain Regulations on Civil Damages Trials arising from False Statements relative to Capital market	
2005	• National People's Congress passed amendments to Company Law and Securities Law	• MOF vowed to expedite convergence of CASs with IFRS

piecemeal process. Among the initiatives to drive this process were the focus on comparison and synchronisation of accounting standards by country and focus on improvement and spread of IFRS. He argued that it was inevitable that GAAP differences would remain between countries when their economic systems and social environments differed. Some of the many differences between CASs and IFRS would be eliminated as China's reforms continued; others would be long-lived. Nevertheless, to facilitate the production of comparative financial information and international convergence of financial information, Yang argued that countries should not overstress local accounting characteristics and conventions (Yang 1980, 1989).

Having been educated in the west, Lou had knowledge of both western accounting theory and principles and Chinese accounting practice. After China's reforms commenced, Lou (1982; 1983a,b; 1984) and other scholars conducted a series of studies comparing CASs and US GAAP, including the impact of the socio-economic systems on aspects of accounting and the relationship between accounting and society. He also published extensively on GAAP convergence.

Ge proposed that CASs be established with Chinese distinctions while as close to international conversion as possible. The former was due to the Chinese social system; the latter a necessity for China's fundamental policy of reform and openness. He suggested that on one hand, tradition and experience of CASs formation should be summarised for succession; on the other hand, appropriate experiences in foreign GAAP formation and the scientific components in foreign GAAP content should be studied and borrowed (Ge 1995).

The accounting standards groups established by the China Accounting Society and the Department of Accounting Affairs under the MOF also played an important role relating to CASs at the threshold of convergence with IFRS. With a view to enhancing the role of accounting in China's new course, the China Accounting Society established seven research groups in 1987. The most important group was on fundamental accounting theory and accounting standards. At its first seminar in Shanghai in January 1989, Lou and Zhang (1989) analysed the significance of accounting standards in China, the content and hierarchy of accounting standards, the relationship between accounting standards and other fundamental accounting concepts, the relationship between accounting standards forged in market economic environments and the accounting systems developed for planned economies, and the approaches to establishing accounting standards. The paper itself and the consensus arrived at this meeting greatly affected the MOF's determination to finalise the content, structure and strategy of its accounting standards programme.

Soon after the above group was established, the MOF Department of Accounting Affairs also set up an accounting standards group fully supported by government resources. The group's publications included an exposure draft containing the basic conceptual framework proposed by the FASB, the IASB, and those published by other national standard setters, which was revised into the *Accounting Standard for Business Enterprises (Basic)* issued at the end of 1992.

In the early stage of implementing its new policy and reforms, China made some efforts towards IFRS convergence. The most important was the issue of the *Accounting System for Sino-foreign Equity Joint Ventures*. China made significant progress in foreign direct investment (FDI) employment in the form of Sino-foreign equity joint ventures, Sino-foreign cooperative joint ventures and wholly foreign-owned enterprises ('Sanzi' enterprises in Chinese means three different kinds of foreign invested enterprises). As the Sanzi enterprises' business mode was different from that of SOEs, their accounting needs differed from SOEs in the planned economic system.

To buttress the development of Sino-foreign equity joint ventures and reinforce regulation over their accounting practices, from the end of 1979 the MOF began designing the *Accounting System for Sino-foreign Equity Joint Ventures*, that came into force on 1 July 1985.

The *Accounting System for Sino-foreign Equity Joint Ventures* was based on four guiding principles: accordance with relevant Chinese laws and regulations; relation to IFRS and other international accounting conventions; selective adoption of the accounting system for Chinese SOEs, if applicable; and reflection of the needs for macroeconomic regulation at State level and micro business management at individual enterprises level. This *System* achieved the following breakthroughs:

1. It clarified some fundamental accounting principles implicit in the accounting systems developed after 1949 and consistent with IFRS, e.g., accrual basis, matching principle.
2. By referring to internationally accepted standards, it explicitly divided accounting elements into assets, liabilities, equity interests, cost and income or loss, different from the division method of fund source versus fund application adopted by SOEs.
3. In conforming to IFRS, the primary financial statements were established as being the balance sheet, income statement and statement of changes in financial position.
4. The word 'capital' was used for the first time in post-1949 accounting. The account 'contributed capital', the 'capital maintenance' concept, the concept of intangible assets and related accounts were also introduced.
5. The principle of prudence was introduced.
6. Sales expenses and general administration expenses were to be separated from production cost of goods.

7. Audit of financial statements by a CPA licensed by the Chinese government was required pursuant to tax law for Sino-foreign equity joint ventures.

The Accounting System for Sino-foreign Equity Joint Ventures drew on many international conventions. It represented China's evolutionary economic reform process, specifically in transforming the accounting system to suit a market economy. It also established the groundwork at both theory and practice levels for the whole 1990s accounting reform programme. It is noteworthy, however, that the reform accomplished by this *System* was applicable only to the few Sino-foreign enterprises, and unable to shake the accounting system free from taxation policy.

Fundamental Reform Phase (1992–1996)

In 1992, Deng Xiaoping, China's reform policy leader and designer, proposed forward-looking views regarding some of the most controversial issues confronting China in the course of its economic progress. Consequently, the Chinese central government vowed to establish a market economic system with Chinese characteristics. Under such a political atmosphere, overwhelming changes occurred in the Chinese accounting system, the most important of which included *Accounting System for Enterprises in Joint Stock Experimental Program, Accounting Standard for Business Enterprises (Basic)* and a set of IFRS-flavoured accounting standards governing H share companies. Objectives of accounting, basic accounting equation, primary financial statements, fundamental recognition and measurement principles and other fundamental concepts and principles became closer to IFRS for all enterprises, rather than for Sanzi enterprises only.

Deng's vision energised China's reform and instigated radical change in the Chinese capital market. It was widely accepted among government officials and a public consensus emerged that China should achieve a diversified ownership structure by establishing joint stock limited companies, mainly by restructuring the SOEs and making them list on stock exchanges, and developing the country's capital market fully. Both the number of listed companies and trading volume surged. As the market expanded, the Shanghai and Shenzhen stock exchanges both developed remote communication systems to convey real-time market data across the country and to attract stock investors. Securities companies swarmed into large and medium-sized cities and opened business outlets, and investors in the country expanded in geometric progression, with many opening trading accounts at both stock exchanges. But, due to the differences in accounting systems used by different listed companies, much financial information lacked comparability, frustrating investors in their decision making.

Capital market growth necessitated a new accounting system. The advent of B shares for foreign investors in 1992, especially, meant the accounting system for joint stock limited companies needed to converge with international conventions.

Consequently, *The Accounting System for Enterprises in Joint Stock Experimental Program* was issued in June 1992. This *System* contained the accounting assumptions of business entity, going concern, accounting period and monetary unit of measurement; and specified the qualitative characteristics of financial information including truthfulness, legality, relevance, timeliness, comparability, consistency and materiality and fundamental accounting principles such as accrual, historical cost, separation of revenue expenditures from capital expenditures, and prudence. It also specified financial statement elements recognition, measurement and reporting methods. For joint stock limited companies, it required balance sheet, income statement, and statement of changes in financial position, for both parent company and consolidated financial statements.

After issuing *the Accounting Standard for Business Enterprises (Basic)* in November 1992, the MOF took account of distinctions between different industries' production and business operating modes and issued accounting systems for 13 industrial sectors. Consistent with its guiding principles for reform, which revolved around supporting a socialist market economy, the Chinese accounting system reforms made some fundamental changes similar to those in *The Accounting System for Sino-foreign Equity Joint Ventures* discussed previously. The major difference is that the newly promulgated *Accounting Standard for Business Enterprises (Basic)* and industrial sector accounting systems applied to all sorts of enterprises. In this respect, this round of reform had a profound impact on Chinese accounting systems.

In November 1992, the Securities Commission of the State Council was established and, as an affiliated executive body, the CSRS came into existence. Regional capital markets regulated by provincial level governments gave way to a national capital market governed by central government. Upon establishment, the CSRC prepared for domestic companies to offer H shares, following the B share offerings to foreign investors in the domestic market. To help those companies adapt to public offerings in the Hong Kong market, the MOF issued *Supplementary Regulations on Accounting for HK Listed Enterprises* in November 1992 and issued *Notice on Accounting System for HK Listed Enterprises, Opinion on Certain Adjustment of Financial Statement for HK Listed Enterprises* and a series of supplementary rules, in April 1993. On 15 July 1993, Tsingtao Brewery Company Limited became the first H-share mainland corporation to go public on the Hong Kong Stock Exchange. Subsequently, a succession of corporations has listed on overseas exchanges. In April 1996 the MOF issued the *Notice on Supplementary*

Regulations on Accounting of Listed Companies, requiring all H- share or B-share companies to follow the same accounting policies. In order to further converge with IFRS, these documents specify recognition and measurement principles for the following important transactions:

1. Equity accounting is to be adopted when a company can significantly influence its investee company, regardless of the level of its voting capital holding. Previously, equity accounting applied to only investments exceeding 50 per cent of voting capital.
2. Except when permanent loss is incurred, a long-term investment can be carried either at cost or at revaluation. Originally, long-term investments could only be carried at original cost.
3. Short-term investments should be presented at the lower of historical cost and market value. Previously, only historical cost was permitted.
4. Between year-end and the financial statement issuing date, significant foreign currency fluctuation effects on financial position should be disclosed in the analysis of financial position without year-end adjustment. Previously, only year-end adjustment was needed.

In addition to converging towards IFRS, these pronouncements also specify requirements for inter-period tax allocation, borrowing costs capitalisation, and contingencies. Although the regulations only apply to a few H-share companies, they act as a meaningful attempt for Chinese companies to adopt IFRS in those important areas, rather than at a conceptual level only.

Also exemplifying the capital market drive for accounting standards convergence at that time was the issue of *Provisional Regulations on Consolidated Financial Statements*. Under the planned economy, most city enterprises were state-owned. Any links between enterprises were based on the government regulatory system, not equity control. Consequently, industrialised government departments and enterprises prepared financial reports only on a combined basis, without considering minority shareholding and consolidated financial statements.

Rapid capital market growth and fierce competition meant that listed companies structured themselves into groups in order to derive economies of scale. Of the Shanghai stock exchange listed companies for instance, in 1992 10 per cent prepared consolidated financial statements, while in 1994, the percentage exceeded 90 per cent. How to regulate consolidated financial statements of listed companies became a top priority and the MOF issued provisional measures on February 9, 1995.

It is worth noting that since *Accounting Standards for Business Enterprises (Basic)* were issued in 1992, the MOF drafted many detailed accounting standards which refer to both internationally accepted standards and the situation of China, under World Bank support and expert assistance from home and abroad. But for various reasons, these draft standards were not finalised during this period. To some extent, the convergence of accounting standards lost momentum.

Full-Swing Convergence Phase (1997–)

In mid-1997, the MOF issued the first detailed accounting standard on related party disclosure, marking the start of full-swing convergence. In rapid succession, the MOF issued 16 specific accounting standards and issued *Accounting System for Business Enterprises*, *Accounting System for Financial Institutions* and *Accounting System for Smaller Business Enterprises*. These standards and systems integrated China's socio-economic features as well as IFRS. Accounting policy and practice for reporting purposes gradually separated from taxation requirements.

Meanwhile, the CSRC issued over 50 disclosure standards based on *Company Law* and *Security Law* requirements. These standards were similar in breadth and depth to those in mature markets. They not only supplemented, but also upgraded, CASs and the changes were closely related to capital market development. The Chinese government, especially the Chinese capital market watchdog, like its foreign counterparts, was conscious of the significance of high quality financial information to ensure the openness, justice and integrity of the capital market and to guarantee the interests of investors, especially public investors.

At the beginning of 1997, the Chinese capital market saw its first case of severe false financial disclosure. Mingyuan was a publicly traded stock company listed on the Shenzhen stock exchange in the early 1990s. In January 1997, the company published its 1996 annual report showing a current year profit of RMB 570 million yuan and capital surplus increase of RMB 600 million yuan. Investigation by the CSRC revealed profit and capital surplus manipulation. The legal punishment was stern: the board chairman received a three-year imprisonment; the auditors received life bans on capital market engagements; and the CPA firm was de-licensed forever. The MOF then issued the first specific accounting standard in May, 1997: *Accounting Standards for Business Enterprise – Disclosure of Related Party Relation and Transactions*, with CSRS encouragement . This standard was a milestone to indicate that after a four-year suspension, formulation and formal release of detailed accounting standards had resumed.

In February 1996, a foreign power station project contracted by Sichuan International Cooperation Co. Ltd. had difficulties, dishonoured a contract, confronted a lawsuit and recorded a huge loss. However, the 1995 annual report disclosed nothing about this event occurring after the balance sheet date. Right after the 1996 interim report revealed the losses, the company's stock price fell sharply and investors faced huge losses. There were many similar cases during this period. In response, the MOF issued *Accounting Standards for Business Enterprises – Events Occurring after the Balance Sheet Date* in May 1998.

In 1998, the CSRC found instances of fraud involving overstatements of revenue and income from investments in listed companies' 1997 accounts. The CSRC and the MOF coordinated with each other, strictly investigating and punishing those companies and related intermediaries. Later, the MOF issued accounting standards on revenue, investment, and cash flow statements with convergence towards IFRS.

Since 1998, listed Chinese companies have engaged in high levels of asset restructuring and mergers and acquisitions. However, some listed companies have faked transactions to manipulate financial information. The CSRC strengthened investigations and released regulations to deal with this problem. It also supported the MOF to build and release a series of accounting standards converging with IFRS, including standards for debt restructuring and non-monetary transactions. These measures restrained non-compliance to some degree.

Also during the mid-1990s, there was a spate of large corporate losses, possibly due to under-provisioning. In response, in 1998 the MOF required H-share and B-share companies to make sufficient provisions for short-term and long-term investments, bad debts and inventories. Other listed companies may also apply these regulations. The CSRC 1998 review of listed companies' annual reports revealed that some companies underprovided for expenses while others overprovided, intentionally exaggerating their losses. To combat the non-comparability of different firms' financial statements, at the end of 1999 the CSRC and the MOF required all listed companies to record bad debt and other provisions based on facts. Consequently, in the annual reports of 1999 the additional and supplementary provisions summed to more than RMB50 billion yuan, two thirds of the aggregate current year profit for all listed companies. Along with later regulations, this contributed to edging out artificialities in the financial data and to improving its accuracy.

However, the number of modified audit reports focused on provisions increased. To address that situation, the MOF successively released specific regulations through Q&A on accounting standards. Some were stricter than IFRS. Although these helped restrain the profit manipulations, they also induced listed companies to create other manipulation methods.

When the Chinese capital market was established, several finance institutions were listed. Later, the government tightened its monetary policy and strengthened finance industry regulation. As one of the policies, financial institutions were not allowed to offer shares to the public. Under approval from the State Council, in the first half of 2000 the CSRC clarified that financial institutions were again encouraged to list. Considering the situation where Chinese financial institutions did not provide enough for non-performing loans and other assets, net asset values were unrealistic and risk management systems were unsound before listing, the CSRC and the MOF strictly regulated accounting, audit and disclosure. These regulations included the requirement for financial institutions to provide sufficiently for potential losses, fully disclose off-account liabilities, and to request internationally well-known CPA firms to perform supplementary audits according to IFRS and to assess their internal control systems. After applying the new regulations, bad debt provisions increased sharply, while net assets declined significantly.

Although annual reports prepared using the new regulations improved considerably, they were still quite different from IFRS annual reports because the managers of listed financial institutions used lower provision rates for their CASs based financial statements than for their IFRS based financial statements. At the end of 2001, the CSRC specified that management could not make different accounting estimates for the same event during the same accounting period. Thereafter, the accounting differences declined considerably.

Reviewing the development of CASs from 1992 to 2004 indicates that:

1. In this period, China's accounting system underwent transition to a modern accounting system that works for a market oriented economy, with significant convergence with IFRS.
2. The vigorous and expanding capital market was the ultimate driving force of this reform.
3. No matter whether the accounting standards are principle-based or rule-based, companies can still manipulate profits, a problem common to all countries.

Since the publication of *Accounting Standard for Business Enterprises (Basic)* in 1992, at the end of 2005, China had successively issued 16 specific accounting standards and three accounting systems for business enterprises referring to internationally accepted accounting practice. During the process, China has gradually shaped up general ideas on accounting standards convergence. These are embodied in the speeches of two chief officials in charge of accounting affairs in the MOF.

Feng Shuping, now Deputy Director of the Budget Commission of National People's Congress, has suggested that business transactions in China can be classified into four categories and that different convergence strategies can apply to different transactions:

1. Where business transactions are identical to those regulated by IFRS and so are the environments, China should actively improve convergence with IFRS, and even directly adopt IFRS.
2. Where business transactions are identical to those regulated by IFRS but due to the special environment in China, the economic substance is not exactly the same, China should not duplicate IFRS principles, but should establish standards based on the transactions' economic substance.
3. Where business transactions regulated by IFRS are common in countries with developed market oriented economies, but not in China, China should not directly duplicate IFRS until such transactions are more common.
4. Where business transactions are specific to the Chinese environment and/or are not addressed by IFRS, China needs to develop specific accounting standards or rules to regulate the related accounting practices (Feng, 2004).

On the topic of accounting standards convergence, Wang Jun, the current Vice Minister in charge of accounting affairs in the MOF, maintains:

1. Convergence involves advancement, orientation, and international cooperation in GAAP convergence: attributes also required for economic globalisation. Any country or organisation that does not want to be dropped from the global economic system should not overlook this trend.
2. Convergence does not mean identical outcomes. If a country's specific situation is overlooked, convergence will become meaningless.
3. Convergence takes time.
4. Convergence is interactive. It is the mutual communication, learning and recognition among countries, and between the IASB and regional accounting bodies, bilateral or multilateral. Global diversity determines that the nature of convergence is interaction (Wang, 2005a).

With the fast development of the Chinese economy and its convergence trend, early in 2005 the MOF established standard-setting programme targets for the establishment and modification of standards that will not only be adaptable to China's economic development, but also be consistent with IFRS and cover all kinds of business transactions.

CAS convergence with IFRS is one of the projects the IASB is focused on. Based on the Joint Statement of the Secretary General of CASC and the Chairman of the IASB after convergence meetings between the China Accounting Standards Committee (CASC) and the IASB, IASB resolutions are as follows:

- Establishing and improving a single set of high quality global accounting standards is the logical consequence of the economic globalisation trend and will be pursued by the IASB.
- China stated that convergence is one of the fundamental goals of its standard-setting programme, with the intention that enterprises applying CASs should produce financial statements that are the same as those of an enterprise that applies IFRS. How to converge with IFRS is a matter for China to determine.
- The IASB and China agree that, in converging their national standards with IFRS, China adding provisions and implementation guidance not included in IFRS to reflect national circumstances is a pragmatic and advisable approach.
- The two parties acknowledged that differences between CASs and IFRS still exist on a limited number of matters. Both parties agreed to work to eliminate those differences quickly. However, these are relatively small impediments to convergence.
- The IASB identified accounting issues for which China, because of its unique circumstances and environment, could be particularly helpful in finding high quality IFRS solutions. The CASC has agreed to assist the IASB in researching and providing recommendations on these issues. Similarly, the IASB will assist the CASC.
- The CASC and the IASB will meet periodically and strengthen exchange and cooperation to achieve convergence of CASs with IFRS.

As a member of IOSCO, the CSRC brings forward its own opinion on IFRS, reflecting the particular issues China faces, in order to obtain understanding by international communities.

IMPLEMENTATION AND ENFORCEMENT

Even if an accounting system is harmonised with IFRS, it is ineffective if enforcement is ineffective. Accordingly, China strives to ensure the implementation of its accounting standards and punish non-compliance. Concrete measures have been exerted mainly in the following areas: emphasising listed companies' management responsibility in relation to disclosure; establishing sound information disclosure standards; using independent directors and the media to promote quality financial information disclosure by listed companies; promulgating auditing standards and other rules of conduct consistent with international conventions; applying a special licence system for CPA firms providing services in the capital market; annual report scrutiny; and penalising non-compliance.

According to Chinese *Company Law* and *Securities Law*, from 1993 the CSRC began to stress board responsibility for the accuracy, reliability and integrity of disclosed information, and sanctioned board members responsible for false or misleading disclosure. In addition, laws such as *Accounting Law* in China prescribe that CEO equivalents and those who govern accounting practice and finance functions should sign the financial report. When the CSRC finds false or misleading financial disclosure, the responsible people are to be punished, and always more severely than ordinary directors.

The Chinese capital market has now established a complete, multi-layered set of disclosure standards based on the *Securities Law, Company Law* and other related regulations. They include disclosures of company financing, regular reports such as annual, half-year and quarterly reports, as well as temporary disclosures as the company meets with special situations. Not only the principle matters, but also the operation; not only the content, but also the form and the method all must meet international standards.

Besides, the CSRC coaches the Shanghai and Shenzhen stock exchanges to establish their 'Listing Rules', and strengthen the responsibility of supervising information disclosure, suspension of listing and e-listing. The Listing Rules also require listed companies to disclose published information on the internet to ensure investors obtain timely information. It is complementary to CASs that disclosure is reasonable, and systematically and efficiently enforced. It also helps to ensure that the CASs are properly implemented.

Every country's corporate governance issues vary because of different structures of stockholder's rights. The conflict between stockholders and management is the main governance problem in many western countries. However, in China, stockholdings are more concentrated. The greatest concern is that controlling stockholders and their representatives in a management team may manipulate financial data to cheat public investors through connected inter-company transactions. To combat this potential, the CSRC has established a system of independent directors. The CSRC also endeavours to use the mass media to ensure implementation of CASs. Indeed, there are many cases of severe disclosure issues that have been revealed by the media in the first instance and then traced by the CSRC, and the responsible parties have been severely punished.

The role of the Chinese Institute of Chartered Accountants (CICPA) has been promoted by capital market development. In just 20 years since the CICPA was restored, not only the scope, but also the quality of CICPA activities has improved dramatically. China holds the establishment of auditing practice guidelines in high regard. Since auditing standards and other practice guidelines are basically procedural, China has referred to standards set by the International Federation of Accountants (IFAC) and other related standards in mutual markets. From

1996, the MOF promulgated four sets of auditing standards. Meanwhile, standards on professional ethics, quality control and continuing professional development have been promulgated, too. China has in 2006, at the time of writing, formed its system of auditing practice, which basically corresponds with international conventions.

In a mature market, the audit work of a listed company is mainly undertaken by a 'Big-Four' accounting firm. But in China, because the CPA system was only restored in the 1980s and the national CPA examination began much later (1992), the quality of CPAs and their firms was not satisfactory. In order to ensure the quality within the capital market, China started a special licence system for security businesses at the beginning of the development of China's capital market. Under this system, when providing audit service or other assurance services to listed companies, security companies, fund management companies, exchanges, CPAs and CPA firms need to have not only an ordinary licence, but also a special licence issued jointly by the CSRC and the MOF. There are only 75 out of 4,000 CPA firms (2,000 out of 60,000 CPAs) with the qualification.

Penalties for not applying appropriate standards include cancellation of licences temporarily or permanently. In addition, the reputation effects of losing the licence are dire for CPAs or CPA firms that in the event would probably have to exit the industry.

The CSRC, the MOF, and other Government departments supervise accounting and other related information disclosures. Commensurate with developments in these areas, their powers are significant and they severely penalise misdemeanour or negligence. In the supervisory process, the CSRC can treat non-compliance that does not warrant more severe penalties by punishments including forced corrections, internal criticism and issuing supervising attention letters. These punishments will be sent not only to the offending parties, but also to other supervisors. Stock Exchanges are also empowered to sanction listed companies by issuing and publishing condemning letters.

The CSRC has the power to punish listed companies and audit firms whose related leaders commit severe non-compliance with accounting standards and audit criteria or provide false financial information. The punishment can include warning, penalty, confiscating illegal goods and revenue, forcing shutout and revoking licenses.

By the end of 2004, the CSRC had completed investigating about 851 cases and 953 related persons had been punished, most for disobeying the accounting standards and showing false information in their reports.[5]

CONCLUSION

Twenty years since China introduced its reform policy, and especially after capital markets were established there, China has come a very long way in the development, adoption, and enforcement of high quality accounting and financial information. Accounting standards are increasingly converged with IFRS.

China will continue to accelerate the convergence of its accounting standards. There are several key reasons for IFRS convergence. Firstly, since 1992, China has decided to take the market economy as its orientation. In 2002, joining the WTO sped up marketing the economy even more than internal reforms. This orientation will not change. Therefore, China will inevitably accept IFRS, which is important to developing the nation's market economy environment.

Secondly, the Chinese economy is rapidly joining the economic globalisation tide. This naturally requires accounting standards to hasten towards international standards. Thirdly, China is still a developing country. Further, China's political system and its economic and cultural traditions are also quite different from comparable developed countries. Nevertheless, China is diligently behaving consistently with its world image of a responsible and significant nation by joining the WTO, signing the Kyoto protocol, and complying with the tide of accounting standards internationalisation. Finally, although China has chosen a step-by-step path to reform, in little more than 20 years China has achieved more than many countries could achieve with regard to the internationalisation of accounting standards. China has already absorbed, and will continue to absorb, the essence of IFRS rapidly and efficiently.

It is expected that as the breadth and depth of the Chinese economy develop, CASs and IAS differences will diminish even further. At the same time, China has determined that it will continue to set its own accounting standards rather than adopt IFRS. This approach is mainly determined by China's special national condition. For instance, accounting regulations are part of China's written law. Thus, their style and force in implementation differ from IFRS applied in unwritten law. Further, as China's capital market is still not fully developed, relative to developed markets the proportion of listed companies and the contribution of listed companies and the capital market to the national economy is not high. As a result, the need for high quality accounting standards to inform external stakeholders is also limited. Further, China's economic development is still in a preliminary stage, thus many transactions still lack the reliable market values required under IFRS.

Accounting standards are not developed solely from conceptual underpinnings. Instead, they are the result of political compromise amongst various lobbying interest groups (Zeff 1978). China has to consider the economic consequences of accounting standards convergence. Despite its extremely positive approach to IFRS, China is not rushing to adopt these standards and concede its own sovereignty over standard setting. The major developed markets such as the US, the UK, Japan, France and Germany have been involved in accounting standards internationalisation and have sometimes criticised China for not adopting IFRS, yet these countries themselves neither assimilate IFRS totally nor cancel their own standards timetables. Given this, China is not likely to make the decision to fully adopt IFRS.

While assimilating IFRS, China encounters some cases with obvious Chinese characteristics. Similarly, the IASB has to deal with special circumstances of countries and areas, while promoting the establishment of a high quality accounting standards. The IASB possibly faces an embarrassing situation if the scope of IFRS does not accommodate individual country characteristics. The IASB has the option to incorporate country-specific situations and to contain some exceptional principles. Alternatively, if the IASB hands over country specific issues to national standard setters, the national standard setters may act to enlarge their own standard-setting programmes. Considering that various countries all possibly have some unique issues, it might be reasonable for the whole world to allow GAAP differences in a few areas and require reconciliation disclosures while approaching full convergence.

No matter how high the quality of an accounting standard, there will not be high quality and comparable accounting information without reasonable and consistent interpretation, and strict enforcement. With the greater assimilation of CASs and IFRS, China needs to guarantee the effective implementation of standards. In particular, the IFRS principle basis and fair value orientation will provide challenges to preparers, users (including regulators), and auditors of financial information in China because these two orientations rely more on judgement than the traditional Chinese approach. If China does not strengthen training, raise judgement skills and enhance consciousness of the true and fair view, this might cause serious earnings management problems. Such a result would counteract the ultimate objective of the whole convergence endeavour.

NOTES

1   In a broad sense, in addition to accounting standards, a uniform set of account titles, financial statements and guidance on use are also part of the regulations governing accounting recognition, measurement and reporting in China. All of these are within the scope of this chapter. For the sake of convenience, unless otherwise specified, all of these standards or rules are referred to as accounting standards. The regulations concerning CPA practices and filing of accounting information, issued in China by the Ministry of Finance (MOF) are not within the scope of this chapter.

2   In developing its own set of accounting standards, China has also referred to the standards of the United States, the Hong Kong SAR, Taiwan and other countries and regions.

3 Enterprises in cities were mainly formed as SOEs. By contrast, enterprises in rural areas were mainly formed as collective entities.
4 From 2001, local residents were also allowed to invest in B shares.
5 Additionally, listed companies, CPAs and CPA firms and other intermediaries may also be sued in civil and criminal litigations. To protect shareholders' rights, the Supreme People's Court issued the *Circular on Verdicts on Civil Indemnities arising from False statement relative to Capital Market* in 2002, specifying that the promoters of listed companies, de facto controlling shareholders, issuers or listed companies, underwriters, sponsors, CPA firms, law firms, CPV firms and other intermediaries, and directors, supervisors, managers and other senior management and people having direct responsibility in the above parties are all liable for civil charges brought by investors whose interests are damaged as a result of false statements by such parties. In 2003, the supreme People's Court issued the *Certain Regulation on Verdicts on Civil Indemnities arising from False statement relative to Capital Market*, specifying the lawsuit proceedings in this regard. Pursuant to *Company Law, Securities Law* and *Criminal Law*, listed companies, firms, other intermediaries and their responsible person shall be sued if false statements by them are regarded as crimes. As for securities-related crimes, CSRC will redirect the relative cases to justice departments for inspection and follow-up. In addition, CSRC set up an inspection force on securities-related crimes. By the end of 2004, 59 people had been penalised.

REFERENCES

CSRC (2005), *Almanac of the Chinese Securities and Futures Statistics*.

Feng, Shuping (2004), 'China's basic attitude towards the international convergence of accounting standards and related issues', *Accounting Research*, **1**.

Ge, Jiashu (ed.) (1995), *On the Basic Accounting Theory and Method in Market Oriented Economic Environment*, Beijing, China: Chinese Finance and Economics Publishing House.

Guo, Yongqin (2003), *Evolvement of Accounting System for Business Enterprises in the New China*, Dalian, China: Publishing House of the Northeast University of Finance and Economics.

Jiang, Yihong (2001), 'The evolution of accounting system for China's joint stock companies (1990–2000)', Listed Companies.

Lin, Zhijun (1985), *Accounting Postulates, Assumptions, and Principles*, Doctoral dissertation, Xiamen University.

Lou, Er-Ying et al. (1982), 'The influence of social economic system – the 1st report on comparative research on Sino-US accounting system', *Accounting Research*, **1**.

Lou, Er-Ying et al. (1983a), 'Accounting objectives, assumptions, concepts and principles – the 2nd report on comparative research on Sino-US accounting system', *Accounting Research*, **2**.

Lou, Er-Ying et al. (1983b), 'The comparison of balance sheet and income statement in China and the US – The 3rd report on comparative research on Sino-US accounting system', *Shanghai Accounting*, **1–3**.

Lou, Er-Ying et al. (1984), 'The relationship between accounting and society – the 4th report on comparative research on Sino-US accounting system', *Accounting Research*, **2**.

Lou, Er-Ying and Wei-Guo Zhang (1989), 'A study on accounting standards and fundamental accounting theory to promote accounting practice in China', *Accounting Research*, **2**.

Lou, Er-Ying and Wei-Guo Zhang (1992), 'A Comparative Study on Sino-Foreign Accounting Standards', *Accounting Research*, **2**.

Qu, Xiaohui, Chen, Shaohua, and Yang, Jinzhong (1999), *Research on Accounting Standards: Learning from other countries experiences and looking back*, Xiamen, China: Xiamen University Publishing House.

Tang, Yunwei (1987), *On Replacement Cost Accounting*, Doctoral dissertation, Shanghai University of Finance and Economics.

Tang, Yunwei (2000), 'Bumpy Road Leading to Internationalization: A Review of Accounting Development in China', *Accounting Horizons*, **14** (1) March: 21–36.

Wang, Jianx (1990), *China's Joint Stock Economy and the Related Accounting Issues*, Doctoral dissertation, Institute of Research on Public Finance, MOF.

Wang, Jun (2005a) 'Active Innovation and Vigorous Promotion: International Convergence of Accounting and Auditing Standards', 125th Anniversary Conference, ICAEW, London, June 28.

Wang, Jun (2005b), 'Deliberate carefully, catch the opportunity, and improve CASs', *Accounting Research*, **10**.

Winkle, G.M., Huss, H.F. and Chen, Xi-Zhen (1994), 'Accounting standards in the People's Republic of China: responding to economic reforms', *Accounting Horizons*, **8** (3): 48–57.

Wei, Minghai (1991), *Structure of Basic Accounting Theory*, Doctoral dissertation, Xiamen University.

Wu, Yanpeng (1990), *Theory of Asset Measurement*, Doctoral dissertation, Shanghai University of Finance and Economics.

Yang, Jiwan (1980), 'On the inquiry into accounting theory in China', *Accounting Research*, **1**.

Yang, Jiwan (1989), 'Issues in accounting standards', *Accounting Research*, **1**.

Yang, Shizhan (1998), *Evolution of Accounting System in China: 1949–1992*, Beijing, China: Chinese Finance and Economics Publishing House.

Zhang, Wei-Guo (1996), 'The controversy over the establishment of accounting standards', in Liu, Kin Cheung and Wei-Guo Zhang (eds), *Contemporary Accounting Issues in China: An Analytical Approach*, Singapore: Prentice Hall, pp. 3–26.

Zhang, Wei-Guo (1989), *Accounting Objectives and Accounting Reform*, doctoral dissertation, Shanghai University of Finance & Economics.

Zeff, S.A. (1978), 'The rise of "economic consequences"', *Journal of Accountancy*, **146** (12): 56–63.

Zeff, S. A. (1987), 'Setting accounting standards: some lessons from the US experience', *The Accountant's Magazine*, December, 26.

Zeff, S.A. (2005a), 'Evolution of US Generally Accepted Accounting Principles (1)', *The CAP Journal,* January: 18–27.

Zeff, S.A. (2005b), 'Evolution of US Generally Accepted Accounting Principles (2)', *The CPA Journal*, February: 18–29.

13 Accounting Harmonisation and Diffusion of International Accounting Standards: The Japanese Case

Chitoshi Koga and Gunnar Rimmel

INTRODUCTION

Much has been written since the 1980s about successful Japanese firms revolutionising worldwide production processes, a revolution that has faltered in recent years. The Japanese financial reporting system has also been studied internationally and appreciated as a system designed to suit Japan's national business system. However, with the rapid pace of the globalisation of business and of accounting standards, it is surprising that little is known about Japan's attitude towards the globalisation of accounting standards or about attitudes to adoption of International Financial Reporting Standards (IFRS) within Japanese firms. As in other countries, Japan's accounting is closely aligned with the nation's most common form of business organisation. The Japanese business system is unique, dominated by intertwining main banks with Keiretsu (a group of affiliated companies, such as the Mitsubishi group or Sumitomo group), informal business groups and stakeholders. The importance of banks in the Japanese economy has been critical, and has led to close aspects of business control, including large cross-holdings which still continue. The multi-faceted system adds complexity when it comes to international accounting harmonisation.

Over the last decade the shiny façade of Japanese business success stories has been tarnished as the world has learned of a number of business scandals and as bad loans hit Japan hard in the 1990s. The economic benefit of Japan's unique business system has been questioned internationally, as well as within Japan.

From an international perspective, the unique characteristics and the behaviour of Japanese firms have been criticised severely for being closed and secretive. This closed and secretive character is also reflected in Japanese corporate accounting policy choice and disclosure practices. Accordingly, questions have been raised, within Japan, as to what extent former accounting practices are suitable for the future of Japanese business in a global economy (Koga, Houghton and Tran 2001). Internationally, concerns have been expressed that Japan's accounting standards are inferior to IFRS (Sharp 1997). If this concern is well-founded, such criticism should provide a strong stimulus for Japan to enhance its accounting standards and disclosure practices in ways that may or may not be consistent with IFRS.

Meetings between Japanese standard setters and members of the International Accounting Standards Board (IASB) in 2005 have indicated that Japanese accounting will move towards IFRS. If that is to occur successfully, it is important that Japanese senior financial managers support the direction that their accounting takes. This chapter helps to assess the Japanese business community's attitude towards IFRS adoption. Using a survey of Japanese senior financial managers, the study described in this chapter assesses the respondents' views regarding the costs and benefits of IFRS adoption.

The next section of the chapter offers an overview of the conservative nature of Japan's accounting standards, explaining them as an artefact of the closed traditional Japanese business system. Thereafter, the movement towards Japan's accounting harmonisation is outlined, highlighting some areas where differences between Japanese GAAP and IFRS remain. The following section provides a discussion about the theory of diffusion of innovations, particularly in relation to IFRS. This analysis raises questions that our questionnaire survey study addresses. Finally, the chapter presents some empirical evidence on the attitudes of Japanese senior financial managers toward adopting IFRS.

Our survey indicates that senior Japanese financial managers do not hold unified views regarding the potential costs and benefits of IFRS adoption. However, very few believe that the benefits significantly outweigh the costs. The main benefits they perceive relate to international capital markets and the international image of their business. Applying diffusion theory to Japanese accounting developments, we argue that for IFRS adoption to occur successfully throughout Japan, there is a need for strong champions of accounting globalisation in the form of opinion leaders and change agents.

JAPAN'S ACCOUNTING STANDARDS AND THE JAPANESE TRADITIONAL FINANCIAL SYSTEM

Traditionally there have been several features common to Japan's accounting standards (Koga et al 2001). First, Japanese accounting is often characterised as 'conservative'. With the principle of conservatism declared as one of seven general principles underlying Japanese GAAP, conservatism is inherent in both the structure of historical cost and in substantially under-reported earnings (Cooke 1993). Income reducing practices are common in Japan (Haskins, Ferris and Selling 1995). For example, Japanese firms generally use short estimated lives for depreciable assets, and declining balance depreciation is the most prevalent depreciation method. Also, Japanese GAAP permits firms to establish contingency accounts for various future expenses.

In addition to conservatism, the disclosure requirements in Japan lack the detail and depth of those in the West. As Sharp (1997) pointed out, concerns have been expressed that:

> Japan's accounting standards are inferior to IAS. Financial reporting in Japan does not result in transparent financial information on which commercial decisions can be made. The international capital markets do not rely on Japanese financial reporting. This can result in a 'Japanese premium' which increases the cost of capital (Sharp 1997).

As at 2005, Japanese financial statements have been used primarily to indicate the results of managerial stewardship, which is mainly influenced by company law. It is noteworthy that in Japan the concept of decision usefulness has been peripheral to the stewardship function (Koga et al 2001). This is in sharp contrast to typical contemporary Western views on accounting standards where decision usefulness is a key objective of financial reporting.

Traditionally, there have been substantial differences between the accounting measurement and disclosure practices common in Japan and those in the West. As previously noted, the conservative practices in Japan are driven in part, at least, by the legal requirements of company law and, more importantly, by tax law. However, they also originate because of differences in commercial and corporate structures and management styles between Japan and the West.

Japan's business and economic system has given rise to several unique factors (see Sheard 1994, Aoki 1994, Ide 1996, Fukao and Morita 1997, Koga et al 2001). Three of these factors are listed below:

- A typical Japanese firm has about 70 per cent of its shares held by other corporations, and only about 20 per cent are held by individuals. The remaining 10 per cent are held by foreign investors.
- The corporate shareholders with whom the company has a long-term business relationship hold large portions of the shares of listed companies. The shareholdings are also reciprocal among the 'corporate families' (*Keiretsu*). As a result, firms hold each others' shares.
- Main banks are also major shareholders. They play a significant role in loan funding, monitoring business affairs and providing financial rescue operations where required. Business failures have, at least until recently, been rare. Arranged financing and/or mergers have been more common.

Bearing in mind these unique factors, one could argue that there is less incentive for the Japanese capital and debt markets to be well informed than there is for Western capital and debt markets. The Japanese system relies more on internal rather than external information sources. Hence, there is much greater information asymmetry between internal and external users of financial information in Japanese firms than in the West. The consequence is fewer information sources about Japanese firms and significantly lower levels of disclosure and consequently, one might argue, lower levels of public ongoing accountability. This can affect the real or perceived usefulness of Japanese firms' external accounting reports in at least one of two ways. Either they are seen as low value because they do not, or are perceived not to, convey a complete picture of the economic characteristics of the firms they purport to describe. Alternatively, it may mean that they are seen as more important since they are the principal means for outside parties to glean information about these firms.

The different characteristics of investors in Japan and the West reflect differences in the fundamental objectives of their respective investment decisions. In the West, investment decisions are largely motivated by financial goals (for example the maximisation of a financial return via dividends and capital gains), whereas in Japan the objective is not necessarily a financial goal. Non-financial objectives, such as maintaining a good business relationship, are often seen as more important. The Japanese business community has ways of dealing with any challenges this may cause. For example, if cross-holding results in low profitability of the firm, then this can be accommodated by the use of understated asset bases, resulting in an acceptable return on investment (Ide 1996). It is argued that a long-term and interlocking relationship helps firms to obtain a competitive advantage in terms of the cost of capital.

Another key aspect of the interlocking shareholdings is the effect of risk sharing and corporate longevity. As many authors suggest (Aoki 1994; Sheard 1994), these stable shareholdings have a role in insulating the management of Japanese firms from the risk of takeover raids. More importantly, the use of stable shareholdings is closely related to the relatively common lifetime employment system in Japan (Sheard 1994). For the lifetime employment system to continue, it is assumed that the firm will also continue to operate. In other words, as long as the incumbent management of the firm is insulated from exposure to the risk of a takeover, employees of that firm can expect to enjoy a guarantee of lifetime employment. 'The risk-sharing aspect of interlocking shareholdings can be seen in this light as a device that indirectly enhances the capacity of the firm to offer meaningful lifetime employment guarantees to its employees' (Sheard 1994).

These characteristics have two consequences. One relates to disclosure and the other to the accountability of management. The sharing of information between interlocked companies and the main bank (Ide 1996; Aoki 1994) is the main and, perhaps, only necessary financial disclosure commitment required in many cases to discharge fiscal accountability. As a business partner, the main bank plays a significant role in monitoring business affairs and supplying financial assistance where appropriate. The close relationship requires companies to provide full and continuous access to this small group (alone). In such a business environment, full public disclosure of information is seen as economically unnecessary.

In the case of financial distress, the limitations of financial disclosure and the fact it is handled within the group (often by the main bank funding a reserve and reorganising the firm) mean that there are low levels of management accountability. In Japan, business matters appear to be handled behind closed doors, without loss of face by any parties.

MOVEMENT TOWARDS JAPAN'S ACCOUNTING HARMONISATION

The preceding discussion suggests that there is uniqueness about Japan's business system. Both international and domestic criticisms have been levelled at this system since the rise in the value of the Japanese yen in 1985. Furthermore, the emergence of global markets and cross-border financing has compelled Japan to conform to the standards of the more widely accepted Western system (Ide 1996). In addition, recent concerns about national trade imbalances and friction between Japan and other trading partners have led to further pressure for change. For instance, the traditional Japanese Keiretsu and closed markets were key concerns at the US-Japan Structural Impediments Initiative Talks in the 1990s. From a domestic point of view, the downturn in the growth of the economy and financial deregulation has generated a push for change in Japanese firms (Poeth and Nemoto 1992). Moreover, the downturn in the Japanese economy in the 1990s had a distressing impact on Japanese firms. For example, much of the Japanese management style is premised on assumptions of high growth (e.g., the seniority lifetime employment system); now these assumptions are no longer certain. Also, the financial deregulation implemented in the past few years has had the effect of providing firms with an incentive to move from the traditional relationship-based system towards a more performance-oriented operating style (Poeth and Nemoto 1992).

Some early signs of the move away from the traditional Japanese business system have been noted. Changes in the 1990s linked to low economic growth mean that Japan's low cost of capital advantage may have largely disappeared and the cost of maintaining the cross-ownership arrangement is seen as increasingly expensive. Due to the substantial amounts of bad and non-performing loans, banks began to realise capital gains on their cross-holding equity portfolios and have been trying to move away from the 'main bank system' (Ide 1996, Fukao and Morita 1997). Moreover, as the relative weight of bank loans among total funds has declined (31.7 per cent in 1985, 25.6 per cent in 1995), the role of main banks as delegated monitors for their client firms is starting to show signs of stress. Also, there are signs that some Japanese firms are beginning to recognise that the profitability of Japanese firms should be a key objective. If these signs of change are indicative of the future, they are suggestive of a fundamental shift toward the Western open market approach and signal a move from the current insular approach.

Japanese accounting and disclosure standards have been considerably revised through the so-called 'Financial Big-Bang' since 1996. Included in the revisions are accounting standards for consolidated financial statements, retirement benefits, tax effect accounting, financial instruments, impairment of assets and business combinations. Significant efforts have been made towards international accounting harmonisation of Japanese GAAP with IFRS and the substantial differences between Japanese and IFRS accounting standards in consolidated financial statement, retirement benefits, tax effect accounting and impairment of assets have been reduced. However, significant incompatibilities between the IFRS and/or FASB standards for financial instruments, business combinations and some others still exist (Ministry of Economy, Trade and Industry 2004), as indicated in the following descriptions.

1) Standards for financial instruments: According to the new Japanese standards for financial instruments (1999), the official introduction of fair value in the measurement of derivatives and trading securities and the adoption of hedge accounting under certain circumstances reflects great progress towards international harmonisation. However, the differences from IFRS in the following points still remain.

 • Under IFRS 39, available-for-sale securities are measured at fair value with changes in fair value charged directly to equity through the Statement of Changes in Equity. In contrast, under Japanese GAAP, the corresponding 'other securities' are valued at market value. The difference is to be accounted for in either of the following ways: (a) All of the changes in value are to be charged in equity; or (b) Increases in value are to be added to equity, or decreases in value are to be accounted for as losses in the accounting period when they occur.[1]

 • Under IFRS 39, receivables are assessed for impairment and the book value should be adjusted to no more than the discounted present value of expected future cash flows, while under Japanese GAAP, receivables are classified into three categories such as normal receivables, doubtful receivables, and bankruptcy receivables according to the bad debt estimation method, and bad debts (potential credit losses) are estimated in this way.[2]

- In relation to hedge accounting, IFRS 39 allows both the fair value hedge and the cash flow hedge. In contrast, Japanese GAAP adopts deferred hedge accounting as its standard method, with the market value (fair value) hedge accounting method being permitted as well (Accounting Standards for Financial Instruments, 1999). Still, as an exception, Japanese GAAP admits that the net amount received or paid out from the interest rate of a swap may be added to, or deducted from, the interest on the relevant assets or liabilities (Ibid., Note 14).

2) Standards for business combinations: Accounting treatments of goodwill differ between Japanese GAAP and IFRS.

- According to Japanese GAAP, Accounting Standards for Business Combinations (2003), business combinations are classified as 'acquisitions' and 'uniting of interests'. In the case of the former, the purchase method is applied and in the latter, the pooling of interests method is adopted. Japanese GAAP permits the pooling interests method only when specific requirements are met. In contrast, IFRS 3, Business Combinations (2004) requires the application of the purchase method to all business combinations and it prohibits the pooling of interests method.

- Under Japanese GAAP all goodwill, positive or negative, is strictly and regularly amortised over an appropriate period within 20 years. Under the IFRS approach, positive goodwill is not amortised. Instead, it is tested for impairment every year with any impairment written off against earnings. IFRS standards do not recognise negative goodwill.

3) Standards for lease transactions: In principle, finance lease transactions, under Japanese GAAP, are to be accounted for in a similar way to ordinary sales and purchase transactions. However, as an exception to the rule, where it is not expected that the ownership of the leased asset will be transferred to the lessee, finance lease transactions may be accounted for as rental transactions. According to IAS 17, Accounting for Leases (1997), finance lease transactions under any condition are required to be accounted for the same way as ordinary sales and purchase transactions (paras.18,19).

4) Standards for government subsidies: Generally, Japanese GAAP recognises a government subsidy as profit in the period when it is acquired. In practice,

accounting treatments may be influenced by the tax rules (Business Accounting Principles 1974, Note 24). In contrast, in order to match the government subsidy with related expenses, IFRS recognises it regularly as profit over a period of time.

These are just some examples of the types of difference between Japanese GAAP and IFRS. Broadly speaking, substantial differences still remain in some areas, particularly in relation to financial instruments and business combinations. However, the gap between Japanese accounting standards and IFRS has been dramatically narrowed due to the sequence of accounting reforms in recent years. Under these circumstances, should Japanese accounting standards be regarded as a quasi-Japanese edition of IFRS? And if so, should efforts be made to dissolve the inconsistencies with IFRS? Or should Japanese accounting standards be kept distinct, with only individual IFRS requirements introduced? In the next section, the issue of adopting IFRS is discussed from the perspective of the theory of diffusion of innovation.

DIFFUSION OF INNOVATIONS AND INTERNATIONAL ACCOUNTING STANDARDS

From the perspective of Rogers (1995), not only do IFRS themselves matter, but so do the contextual conditions in which they are presented, adopted, rejected or modified (E*Know-Net, 2003). Diffusion theory provides a useful tool for sorting data and discussing the conditions for the spread of IFRS. In relation to diffusion theory, diffusion is defined as 'the process by which an innovation is communicated through certain channels over time among the members of a social system' (Rogers 1995, p. 5). An innovation is an idea, practice, or object that is perceived as new by an individual (Ibid., p. 11). If IFRS are deemed to be new to the individual, they are an innovation, and the Rogers framework can be applied.

Based upon their readiness to adopt innovations, adopters fall into five categories: innovators, early adopters, early majority, late majority, and laggards (Ibid., pp. 263–6). Both innovators and early adopters are eager to adopt a new idea. The early and the late majority adopt new ideas with deliberate willingness and with some scepticism, respectively. Laggards tend to be suspicious of innovations and the past is their point of reference. On the international scene, Japan is likely to be viewed as either a later majority or a laggard in relation to IFRS adoption.

Two groups play significant roles in the diffusion process of an innovation. One is opinion leaders, the other is change agents. An opinion leader is an individual who 'is able to influence other individuals' attitudes or overt behaviour informally in a desired way with relative frequency' (Ibid., p. 27). Leaders of the professional accounting organisations, such as the Japanese Institute of Certified Public Accountants (JICPA), have a decisive role in the diffusion of IFRS. They are in a position to influence members who will, in turn, influence their employer or client firms to adopt or not to adopt IFRS.

A change agent is an individual who influences clients' innovation decisions in a direction deemed desirable by the change agency. In Japan, the Financial Services Agency, which is in charge of monitoring financial institutions and securities markets, is assumed to be the change agent. It can seek to obtain the adoption of IFRS, but may alternatively attempt to slow down the diffusion of IFRS.

So far, we have assumed that adoption of an innovation means the exact copying or imitation of how the innovation was used previously in a different setting (Ibid., p. 174). However, the new idea changes and evolves during the diffusion process. The concept of re-invention means that an innovation is changed or modified by a user in the process of its adoption and implementation (Ibid.).

Some flexibility in the process of adopting an innovation is needed to enhance customisation of the innovation to fit it appropriately to social situations or changing conditions (E*Know-Net 2003, p. 5). In other words, ideas and innovations should be changed and influenced by local conditions, belief systems, and needs.

In relation to the theory of diffusion of innovations, several questions arise in relation to the perception of the IFRS innovation:

1) Are there differences in the perception of the relative advantage of adopting IFRS?
2) What impacts do specific conditions have on perceptions?
3) What development of the Japanese approach to IFRS adoption does analysis suggest?
4) What are the roles of the opinion leader and the change agent?

RESULTS OF QUESTIONNAIRE

The questions above are the foundation of a postal questionnaire, which we sent to the 500 largest companies (based on sales) of the Tokyo Stock Exchange. In order to assure an economically significant empirical setting for this study, we selected the 500 largest companies to ensure that the information obtained was based on large firms with economic substance. The questionnaire was addressed to senior financial managers of the firms in March 2005. By the end of March 2005, we had received 123 usable responses. The response rate was 24.6 per cent, which may be considered satisfactory for a postal survey. Overall, the data seem to offer a representative sample of the Japanese economy, since the respondents are spread across a range of different industries, including firms like SONY (home electronics), Toyota (automobile) and Mitsubishi Heavy Industry (heavy industry).

The respondent percentages reported in this chapter are based upon the total number of responses to the questions. The design of the questionnaire allowed multiple answers for some questions. Consequently, the combined responses for some questions exceed 100 per cent. Transcribing the questionnaire responses shows that the questionnaire was answered either by the Chief Financial Officer (CFO) directly, or by senior managers from accounting and treasury departments under the direction of the CFO. This implies that the intended target group for the sample of this study was met.

The first question sought to establish the senior finance managers' views of the importance of the stock market and bond market to their firms, and also the importance of domestic and overseas markets, using a five point Likert scale ranging from 1 = not important, 3 = not so important and 5 = very important. From Figure 13.1 it can be observed that the domestic markets are by and large deemed to be the most important markets.

The largest category, 67.5 per cent of the respondents, attributed the domestic stock market as being very important for the operation of their business. The domestic bond market was regarded by 35 per cent (38.2 per cent) of the respondents as being very important (important). The overseas markets were noticeably assessed as less important relative to domestic markets. Only 31.1 per cent (32.5 per cent) of respondents rated the overseas stock market (overseas bond market) as either important or very important. The majority of respondents rated the overseas markets as being not so important relative to the domestic markets.

Senior finance managers' views of a significant difference in the relative importance of domestic and overseas markets might reflect the contemporary Japanese business attitude towards domestic and international users of financial statements and the relative lack of attention to external users of financial statements. In keeping with this observation, the questionnaire sought senior views, using the Likert scale as previously described, on the importance of financial statements to users.

Overall, Figure 13.2 illustrates that the respondents think that the majority of users do believe that financial statements are important. Generally, respondents expressed an assessment of more importance for domestic investors compared to overseas investors. Sixty-two per cent of senior financial managers rate

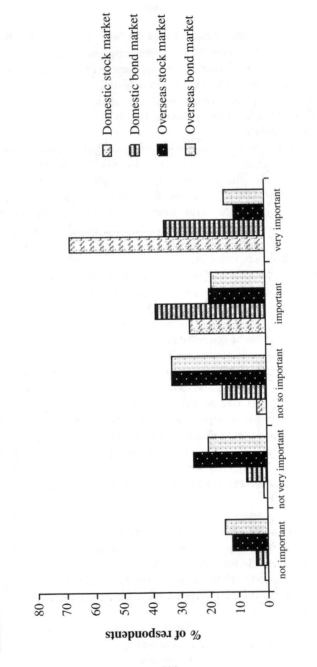

Figure 13.1 Importance of markets for Japanese business operations

Figure 13.2 Importance of Japanese financial statements to users

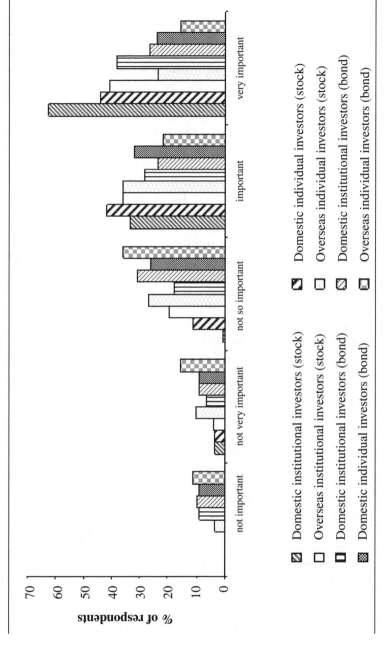

229

financial statements as very important to domestic institutional investors in the stock market, as do 43.9 per cent of the senior financial managers in relation to domestic individual investors in the stock market. Over 40 per cent of senior financial managers believe that financial statements are very important to overseas institutional investors while only 23.4 per cent believe they are very important to overseas individual investors.

We also asked respondents to state the rate of overseas investments in relation to all their securities investments. Nearly 41 per cent of the respondents stated that their rates of overseas investments are 0 per cent in relation to their securities. The second largest category with 31.7 per cent was a rate ranging from 1–10 per cent of securities investments. An overseas investment rate between 11–20 per cent was stated by 9.2 per cent of the respondents, and an overseas investment rate relative to all securities investments of between 21–40 per cent was stated by only 5.8 per cent. Twelve per cent of respondents answered that the overseas investment relative to total securities investment exceeded 40 per cent.

The survey asked respondents to select one of three options indicating how IFRS should be adopted: (1) international accounting standards only, (2) both international (for overseas use) and domestic accounting standards and (3) domestic standards with supplementary international accounting standards reports. The majority of respondents (51.1 per cent) selected a preference for adopting only IFRS as the basic financial statement standard. The second preference, with 35.6 per cent of the responses, was for the use of IFRS as supplementary to domestic standards. Respondents did not support adopting international standards for overseas use only with domestic accounting standards for local use. Only 13.3 per cent of respondents rated this as their preferred choice.

The survey also addressed Japanese senior financial managers' opinions of the importance of the difference (using the five-point Likert scale previously described where 5 = very important) between IFRS and Japanese GAAP in eight areas (R&D expenses, leases, real estate investment, business combinations, financial instruments, foreign currency transactions, consolidation and goodwill, and allowances). These different items represent an assortment of topics that have been discussed in an earlier section of this chapter. As Figure 13.3 indicates, the differences between IFRS and domestic standards were generally regarded as not so important by the majority of respondents across many of the topic areas. However, respondents did identify differences in Japanese and IFRS lease accounting and accounting for business combinations as areas of important difference.

A reasonably stable ranking in the level of importance can be traced for the following items: leases (important = 32.5 per cent, very important = 30.8 per cent), consolidation and goodwill (important = 34.2 per cent, very important =

Figure 13.3   Importance of IFRS versus Japanese GAAP differences by areas of accounting

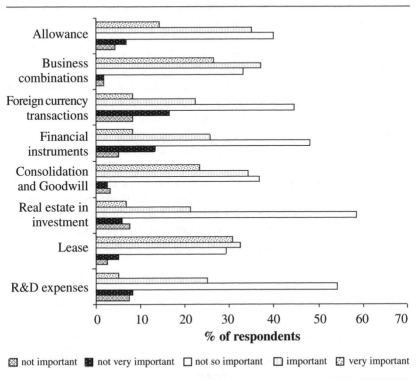

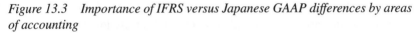

23.3 per cent) and business combinations (important = 37.1 per cent, very important = 26.4 per cent). For these differences between Japanese GAAP and IFRS, Japanese financial managers believed that, on average, the difference was at least important, and often very important.

Regarding R&D expenses, 25 per cent of respondents deemed the differences to be important, but only 5 per cent regarded them as very important. The same assessment patterns can be seen for real-estate investments (important = 21.2 per cent, very important = 6.8 per cent), financial instruments (important = 25.6 per cent, very important = 8.3 per cent), foreign currency transactions (important = 22.3 per cent, very important = 8.3 per cent) and allowances and reserves (important = 35 per cent, very important = 8.3 per cent).

We also asked respondents to articulate their beliefs about changes concerning the application of international accounting standards five years from now. Most of the respondents expect that there will be an increase in the use of IFRS for the full set of financial statements including both consolidated and parent entity accounts, particularly consolidated accounts, and for disclosure purposes. A minority considered that IFRS would be adopted for the parent entity accounts only. If these Japanese senior financial managers' expectations are correct, then those managers will need to plan for the switch to IFRS. This is not necessarily a simple task, as accountants and managers in countries that are currently adopting IFRS can attest.

Respondents were also asked whether they agreed with the statement that it would be difficult to change from Japanese GAAP to IFRS. Figure 13.4 illustrates that 70 per cent of the respondents are of the opinion that the changeover from Japanese GAAP to IFRS would be difficult. Interestingly, though, almost 50 per cent of the respondents only slightly agreed that the transition would be difficult.

The questionnaire asked if the respondents' firms were currently adopting IFRS for reporting purposes. Only two respondents out of 121 usable responses reported that IFRS were being adopted. One further respondent indicated that IFRS were not yet being adopted, but that adoption is intended. However, the vast majority (97.5 per cent) of the respondents noted that IFRS were not being adopted, and

Figure 13.4   Responses to whether changing from Japanese GAAP to IFRS will be difficult

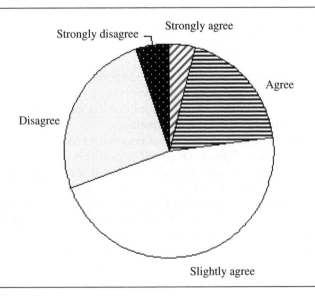

that it still remains unclear whether they will be adopted in the future.

To establish the motives for firms not adopting IFRS, we asked respondents indicating that IFRS were not being adopted, why this was the case. Possible reasons presented to respondents were: the cost is too high, inadequate staff training, incompatibility with Japanese government policy, and the benefits do not outweigh the costs. Respondents could cite other reasons also and could select multiple answers. Only 10 respondents (7.4 per cent) answered that their reason for not adopting IFRS is that the cost is too high. Forty-one respondents (30.5 per cent) indicated that the reason was associated with the inadequate training system for the accounting staff. The fact that IFRS does not conform to Japanese GAAP was mentioned by 18 respondents (13.2 per cent). Only three respondents (2.2 per cent) stated that there are few benefits for their firm as being the motive for not adopting IFRS. The majority of respondents not adopting IFRS (46.7 per cent) cited other reasons for the non-adoption. The reasons noted included: IFRS is not legally required; US GAAP has been adopted; Japanese GAAP is more suitable to the Japanese business environment and Japanese GAAP is equivalent or convergent with the IFRS.

This was a logical lead-in to questioning why firms would adopt IFRS. We asked the respondents to indicate on a five-point Likert scale, the importance of the following factors, should IFRS be adopted: improve the trust and understanding of securities investors; improve the trust and understanding of bond investors; make it easier to issue securities in international markets; reduce the cost of raising bond capital; improve the international image of the company; reduce barriers to list in overseas securities markets and reduce financial statement preparation costs. The majority of respondents perceived that the most important benefits (based on a 4 or 5 rating on the level of importance scale) of IFRS adoption were making it easier to issue securities in international markets (61.7 per cent), reducing barriers to list in overseas securities markets (56.2 per cent) and improving the international image of the company (53.7 per cent). Clearly, the most important perceived benefits all relate to international markets, international status and international fund-raising. The cited benefit of reducing the cost of preparation of financial statements was not regarded as important by respondents. Only 5 per cent of respondents rated this as important or very important.

Finally, the questionnaire elicited responses of senior Japanese financial managers to whether they expected the benefits of IFRS adoption to exceed the costs should IFRS be adopted. Figure 13.5 demonstrates that respondents were sceptical about the benefits of IFRS adoption. Indeed, 69.5 per cent of respondents indicated a belief that the costs would exceed the benefits, 26 per cent indicated that adoption would be cost-benefit neutral and 4.2 per cent of respondents believed that the benefits would exceed the costs.

Figure 13.5   Benefits versus costs of IFRS adoption

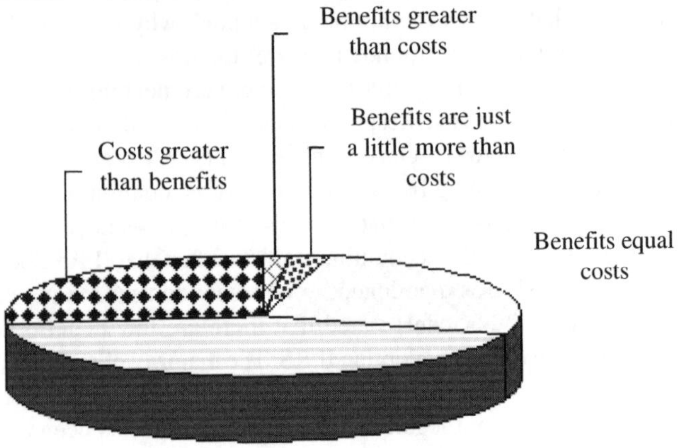

CONCLUSION

This study explores the views of senior financial managers of Japanese firms regarding the harmonisation and diffusion of IFRS. These views were sought by way of a questionnaire that dealt with the attitudes towards IFRS adoption, problems perceived with IFRS adoption, and potential benefits for firms if and when they adopt IFRS reporting. The responses reveal a rather sceptical attitude towards IFRS adoption, with nearly 70 per cent of respondents indicating that the costs were likely to exceed the benefits.

However, at the turning of the twenty-first century, with intensified competition in global markets, Japanese firms are compelled to raise funds in more effective ways than in the past. Therefore, it is essential for many of them to secure the trust of both domestic and overseas investors in Japanese markets. To do this will require efforts to maintain the Japanese market infrastructure, in which accounting standards are included, and efforts to harmonise with the major overseas capital markets.

Globalisation of accounting standards is likely to be most successful if it is promoted with adequate attention paid to the distinct cultural background of each country and the specific conditions of the business activities in various countries. As IFRS 3 shows, for example, for business combinations accounting, the purchase method is gradually being adopted almost all over the world, while Japan permits the application of pooling of interests method where it is not possible to identify an acquirer. Given the extensive degree of corporate cross-holdings and the cooperative nature of those cross-holdings, such a circumstance is not rare in Japan. This implies that a uniting of interests approach should not be ignored (Business Accounting Council 2001). However, as the cross-holding approach to investment diminishes, it is to be expected that so will potential reservations about a complete adoption of the purchase method.

In the event of accounting standards diffusion, will the concept of re-invention, which requires certain modifications to the original models, be realistic? According to diffusion theory, innovation is not imitated and accepted directly as it is. Instead, there is a tendency for continuous modification of the innovation to some degree according to specific needs and particular contexts during the diffusion process. This kind of flexibility improves the application of the innovation to particular environments and circumstances and makes it easier to implement it (E*Know-Net 2003). While international harmonisation of Japanese accounting is tending now towards the point where no substantial differences exist between Japanese standards and the IFRS, nonetheless, the survey results reported in this chapter indicate that there are differences in the perceptions of the cost-benefit of introducing IFRS. According to diffusion theory, IFRS will be more quickly adopted as senior financial managers recognise the relative advantages of IFRS adoption. At present, almost no enterprise has adopted IFRS without modification. As shown in the results of the questionnaire on the benefits of adopting IFRS, some firms can become early adopters or early majority relative to others in the country, whereas many others are likely to be labelled as late majority and laggards.

Throughout Japan's foray into the globalisation of accounting standards, the role of opinion leaders – in leading firms, accounting professional organisations and the media – is noteworthy in the diffusion of IFRS. Especially remarkable progress can be made if the JICPA promotes the diffusion of IFRS with support from the government and in cooperation with large firms. However, it has been the basic stance of the Financial Services Agency, the JICPA and Japanese Accounting Standards Council that Japanese accounting standards are already substantially in accord with IFRS with no remarkable differences (Financial Services Agency 2004). This contradicts the views of senior Japanese financial managers, who indicate a view that there are significant differences between Japanese GAAP and IFRS, particularly in relation to the key standards relating to leases, business combinations and goodwill.

Diffusion of IFRS in Japan is likely to involve the diffusion of revised Japanese accounting standards as the re-invention of the innovation (IFRS). Therefore, it is indispensable to corroborate whether there are substantial differences between Japanese standards and IFRS and to try to remove any significant differences that do exist. It is also important to make an active appeal for the significance of culture and the individuality of these differences, and to address the costs of change. Globalisation, furthermore, will require greater championing by opinion leaders and change agents if it is to be successful. To date, that championing has not occurred to the same extent in Japan as in countries such as Australia, UK and parts of Europe.

The International Accounting Standards Board (IASB) and the Accounting Standards Board of Japan (ASBJ) have begun to work together towards convergence of accounting standards. At the first meeting held in March 2005, representatives of both boards exchanged views on the basic philosophies or frameworks underlying their respective accounting standards for mutual understanding. They also informed each other of their deliberations on five topics for the first phase; measurement of inventories, segment reporting, related party disclosures, unification of accounting policies applied to foreign subsidiaries, and investment property (http://www.aia.org.uk//News/IAfull Story.php?id=50466).

In the context of achieving convergence of accounting standards, the Committee of European Securities Regulators (CESR) has completed its assessment of the equivalence of Japanese GAAP with IFRS in accordance with the mandate of the European Commission. After an in-depth analysis and discussion of the significant differences CESR proposes to the Commission to consider that Japanese GAAP can be assessed as equivalent subject to remedies of additional disclosures (CESR 2005, paras 132-47). Through this process of remedies, Japanese GAAP would have high comparability with IFRS.

NOTES

1   The firm may choose either (a) or (b) on a consistent basis.
2   Potential credit losses on normal receivables should be estimated by applying rational standards, such as the historical rate of credit losses. Those losses on doubtful receivables should be estimated by applying either the financial state valuation method or the cash flow estimate method. Also, the losses on bankruptcy receivables should be estimated by applying the valuation method based on the financial state (Practical Guidelines on Accounting Standards for Financial Instruments, paras 110–115).

ACKNOWLEDGEMENTS

This paper is based on a two-day Globalisation of Accounting Standards Conference held in May 2005 in Prato, Italy. The authors would like to acknowledge the sponsorship of the conference by the Monash Institute for the Study of Global Movements. The authors also would like to thank the participants at the conference for their inspiring input to the chapter.

REFERENCES

Aoki, M. (1994), 'The Japanese Firm as a System of Attributes: A Survey and Research Agenda', in M. Aoki and R. Dore (eds), *The Japanese Firm*, Oxford University Press.

Business Accounting Council (2001), 'Issues Summary on the Accounting Standards for Business Combinations', July.

The Committee of European Securities Regulators (CESR), Consultation Paper, 'Technical advice on equivalence of certain third country GAAP and on description of certain third countries mechanisms of enforcement of financial information', April 2005.

Cooke, E. (1993), 'The impact of accounting principles on profits: The US versus Japan', *Accounting and Business Research*, 23–92.

E*Know-Net (2003), (A European Research Arena on Intangibles), *Report of Workpackage* 2.

Financial Service Agency (2004), 'Evolving Japanese GAAP: High Quality Accounting Standards', co-supported by Accounting Standards Board of Japan and the Japanese Institute of Certified Public Accountants.

Fukao, M. and Y. Morita (1997), Kigyo Governance kouzou no Kokusaihikaku (International Comparison of the Corporate Governance Structure), Nihon Keizai Shinbunsha.

Haskins, ME, K.R. Ferris and T.I. Selling (1995), *International Financial Reporting and Analysis*, Irwin.

Ide, M. (1996), 'The Financial System and Corporate Competitiveness', in P. Sheard (eds), *Japanese Firms, Finance and Markets*, Melbourne: Addison-Wesley.

Koga, C., K. Houghton and A. Tran (2001), 'International harmonisation and the Japanese accounting system', *Asian Review of Accounting*, **9** (2), 99–116.

Ministry of Economy, Trade and Industry (2004), 'Wagakuni Kigyoukaikei no Kokusaika ni kansuru Houkoku' (Report on globalisation of Japanese Corporate Accounting).

Poeth, G. and T. Nemoto (1992), *Companionship Capitalism: The Evolution of Management in Japan*, Delft: Eburon Delft.

Rogers, E. et al. (1995), *Diffusion of Innovations*, The Free Press.

Sharp, M. (1997), 'International Accounting Standards', presentation paper at the Tokyo Conference for Japanese Firms.

Sheard, P. (1994), 'Interlocking Shareholdings and Corporate Governance', in Aoki, M. and R. Dore (eds), *The Japanese Firm*, Oxford University Press.

14 The Impact of Globalisation of Accounting Standards on India

R. Narayanaswamy

INTRODUCTION AND BACKGROUND

This chapter explains India's approach to the globalisation of financial reporting, examines the effects of globalisation on Indian capital markets and explores the implications of these effects for Indian firms' investment, financing and operating decisions. It also illustrates the changes in corporate governance mechanisms that have occurred as part of India's economic reforms of recent decades and indicates the future course of Indian accounting in the context of the pressures of globalisation of capital, product and labour markets on reporting by Indian firms. It addresses the following basic research question in the Indian context: How does the globalisation of financial reporting standards impact Indian accounting standards and related regulations and what are its economic, social, legal and political implications?

This question assumes importance due to the rapid entry of India into the global economy in the 1990s. From the early 1950s to the early 1990s, India had followed a centralised, inward-looking model of development that discouraged domestic competition and impeded foreign investment. The sweeping economic reforms initiated by the government in the early 1990s have dramatically changed India's approach to economic development. India is now regarded by many as an emerging economic giant similar to China. A report prepared in 2003 by Goldman Sachs on Brazil, Russia, India, and China predicts that in US dollar terms India's economy could be larger than all but the US and China in 30 years. The report further notes that India has the potential to show the fastest growth over the next 30 to 50 years and that growth could be higher than 5 per cent over the next 30 years and close to 5 per cent as late as 2050, if development proceeds successfully. The country's sophisticated manufacturing base, skilled workforce and expanding markets are particularly attractive to large global corporations.[1] The question is important to many individuals and organisations including accounting firms, fund managers, brokers and analysts, investment banks, multinational corporations, foreign stock exchanges interested in listing Indian securities, Indian firms interested in foreign listings, accounting standard setters, securities market regulators, and academics. Financial reports are a product of the larger environment – corporation laws, securities markets, stock ownership, accounting profession, and culture – in which they are produced.

Narayanaswamy (1997) analyses the development of accounting regulation in India since the 1950s. Since then, the environment of financial reporting in India has undergone significant changes. A number of well-recognised frameworks (e.g., Choi and Mueller 1986; Puxty et al. 1987; and Gray 1988) provide multiple perspectives for investigating the research question, and Sunder and Yamajih (1999) and Sunder (2002) explore the role of accounting in labour, capital and product markets.

Prior research on financial reporting in India is limited. In an early study, Singhvi (1967) compared corporate disclosure in annual reports in India with those in the United States. Using an index of disclosure consisting of 34 items, Singhvi found that the quality of disclosure in India was inferior to that in the United States during 1964–65. Similarly, Marston (1986) provided evidence to show that disclosure in the United Kingdom was better than in India and Das Gupta (1977) concluded that most of the firms in India provided only the minimum information required by law. A study by the accounting profession, however, concluded that published reports gave more information than strictly required by law (ICAI 1981). Many of the ICAI study companies that had made voluntary financial disclosures were in the public sector. Chander (1992) found an improvement in the disclosure practices of a set of companies in 1984–85 compared with 1980–81, with disclosure by government-owned companies showing more improvement than private-sector companies. Bhattacharyya (2004) refers to efforts to improve corporate financial reports, especially increasing the quantum of voluntary disclosure. In earlier research using a case study approach, Narayanaswamy (1996) examined the decision of Infosys Technologies Limited to voluntarily adopt US GAAP financial statements and disclosures in 1994–95 and concluded that the company's decision was influenced by the company's (a) private placement of equity with foreign institutional investors, (b) deriving a very large part of its software revenues from the US and (c) seeking a NASDAQ listing in the near future.

This is the first attempt at a detailed analysis of the effect of India's ongoing economic reforms and globalisation on the country's accounting standards and governance systems. It examines changes in Indian accounting standards since the late 1990s and corporate management's responses to the changes. Significant advances have been made in addressing gaps in the country's financial reporting regulations. As a result, Indian accounting standards are now much more comparable to international benchmarks, such as US GAAP and International Financial Reporting Standards (IFRS) promulgated by the International Accounting Standards Board (IASB, previously the International Accounting Standards Committee, IASC). Nonetheless, some differences still remain. This chapter contributes to understanding Indian accounting reforms in the context of the radical change in the country's economic development model from an inward-looking and government-controlled command economy to a globally competitive market-driven economy.

The rest of this chapter is organised as follows. An overview of the Indian economy provides a perspective on the on-going economic reforms in India with globalisation at the centre of the reform agenda. The connections between changes in Indian financial reporting with India's economic reforms and globalisation are then established. The institutional framework for setting accounting standards in India, focusing on recent developments, is described and the reasons for the issue of a spate of new accounting standards beginning in the late 1990s are discussed. The chapter concludes by linking the development of accounting regulation to the influence of national and international capital markets and market regulators.

INDIA'S ECONOMIC REFORMS AND FIRST STEPS IN GLOBALISATION[2]

Soon after India's independence from Britain in 1947, there was a conscious attempt to make the country a modern industrial power with a large manufacturing base. The government adopted the vision of a 'socialistic pattern of society' as the guiding philosophy of the country's economic development. National priorities were laid down in five-year plans formulated by the Planning Commission. The goal was to become self-sufficient in every area of economic activity, and import substitution became an important means to achieve this goal. Private foreign investment was looked upon with suspicion because of fears of re-colonisation. Growth with equity and abolition of poverty became the slogans of successive governments.

During 1950 to 1991, the state assumed a major role in determining the economic life of the country. A mixed economy system, with the state occupying the commanding heights of the economy and the private sector playing a supportive role, was put in place. State regulation extended to most areas of economic decision making; for example, detailed rules existed for matters such as capital raising, investment in industries and regions, foreign trade, prices and distribution, size of industrial units and industrial houses, receipt and use of foreign exchange, and appointment and remuneration of company directors. Over the years, the government nationalised major banks and all insurance companies in the country. Investment and lending policies of banks and insurance companies were laid down by the government. The state issued licences, permits and quotas for a large number of industrial and consumer goods and nearly half of the total loans and advances were to be made to 'priority sectors' identified by the government. Economic and political commentators coined the derisive term 'licence *raj*' to refer to the country's comprehensive and suffocating regime of micro-level controls. The Indian economy was arguably one of the most regulated economies in the world outside the Communist bloc.

The period from 1974 to 1991 was marked by selective deregulation driven by the collapse of the Bretton Woods system of fixed exchange rates in 1971 and the oil price hikes of 1973 and 1979. This period saw some relaxation of the rigour of industrial licensing and changes in trade policy but the fundamentals of the old economic order remained unchanged. India paid a heavy price for its state-controlled and inward-looking model of economic development. During the period 1950 to 1973, India's exports grew at an average of 2.7 per cent per annum, while world exports increased at 7 per cent per annum. The ratio of exports to GDP declined to about 4 per cent from a high of 7.3 per cent in 1951. During the period 1950 to 1991, the growth rate of the economy was below 4 per cent. India's share of world exports declined from more than 2 per cent in the early 1950s to about 0.7 per cent in 2000.

Its serious balance of payments crisis in 1991 forced India to radically reform its economic policies. That year, for the first time in its history, India was close to defaulting on its international commitments. India's international credit ratings were downgraded and external credit was completely denied. A programme of macroeconomic stabilisation was initiated with support from the International Monetary Fund. Simultaneously, the government initiated structural reforms in foreign trade, taxation and industrial policy. Many of the numerous controls on firm-level economic decision-making were dismantled. Free floatation of the Indian rupee within limits, permission to Indian companies to raise capital abroad, liberalisation of the rules for foreign direct investment and permission for portfolio investment by foreign financial institutions are particularly significant in the context of reforms in accounting standards. Successive governments have not only continued the early economic reforms but also broadened the reform agenda.

Since 1991 when the reforms began, India has been integrating closely with the global economy. Exports have increased from 5.8 per cent of GDP at market prices in 1991 to 10.8 per cent in 2004 and imports have increased from 8.8 per cent of GDP at market prices in 1991 to 13 per cent in 2004. The invisibles

Table 14.1 Selected Indicators for India's Economy

Indicator	2001–02	2002–03	2003–04	2004–05
Panel A: Absolute values				
Gross domestic product at factor cost (at 1993–94 prices)				
Indian rupees billion	12,679	13,184	14,305	15,294
Index of agricultural production				
1981–82 = 100	178.8	154.1	180.1	179.2
Index of industrial production				
1993–94=100	167.0	176.6	189.0	199.4
Consumer price for industrial workers				
1982 =100	468	487	504	521
Value of imports US$ million	51,413	61,412	78,149	83,442
Value of exports US$ million	43,827	52,719	63,843	60,754
Foreign investment, US$ million				
Foreign currency assets,				
US$ million	51,049	71,890	107,448	123,654
Panel B: Percent changes over previous period				
Gross domestic product at factor cost				
(at 1993–94 prices)	5.8	4.0	8.5	6.9
Index of agricultural production				
1981–82 = 100	7.9	-13.8	16.9	-0.5
Index of industrial production				
1993–94=100	2.7	5.8	7.0	8.4
Consumer price for industrial workers				
1982 =100	5.2	4.1	3.5	3.8
Value of imports	1.7	19.4	27.3	34.7
Value of exports	-1.6	20.3	21.1	25.6

Source: Ministry of Finance, Government of India, *The Economic Survey*, 2004–2005.

balance as a percentage of GDP at market prices has dramatically increased from 0.1 per cent in 1991 to 4.3 per cent in 2004. This improvement has come from, among others, the rapid rise in software services exports and remittances from Indians working overseas. In 2005, India's share of world exports improved to 0.8 per cent. The improvement of 0.1 percentage points over a decade of economic reforms may not look highly impressive. It should be viewed in the context of the steady decline in the earlier decades when India was becoming increasingly insular in its economic interaction with the rest of the world. Also, the economic reform programme is only now beginning to gather momentum insofar as it relates to international trade.

Table 14.1 gives an overview of the major indicators of the Indian economy in recent years.

FINANCIAL REPORTING IN THE CONTEXT OF ECONOMIC REFORMS AND GLOBALISATION

There have been major changes in financial reporting in India since the aforementioned economic reforms and globalisation, which began in the early 1990s. Among others, the following factors have contributed to these changes:

- Market pressures;
- Company law and securities law changes in India; and
- International accounting and securities regulations.

Market Pressures

Pressures in a firm's capital, product and labour markets affect its financial reporting, as explained below.

Capital market pressures

Stock exchanges have existed in India for more than a century.[3] But the capital market could not play an effective role in channelling savings into investments because of a number of factors. First, the importance of stock exchanges in financing corporate investments was greatly reduced by the expanding operations of government financial institutions (development banks and insurance companies) that came into existence in the 1950s and 1960s and continued to play a major role until the mid-1990s. Second, the government controlled issuance and pricing of equity and preference capital and debentures. Finally, the stock markets themselves were plagued by extensive insider trading and there were other serious deficiencies in their trading and settlement procedures that undermined investor confidence in their functioning. As a result, there were inadequate mechanisms for price discovery. The capital markets lacked breadth, depth and liquidity. As a result, prior to 1991, companies depended on state-owned and state-controlled banks and financial institutions for their capital requirements. However, since 1991 Indian companies have depended to a greater extent on the capital market for raising resources.

Table 14.2 Highlights of the Performance of Indian Capital Markets

	(Amounts in billions of Indian rupees)			
	2001	2002	2003	2004
Panel A: Primary Market New Capital Issued				
Debt	492	345	379	238
Equity	73	237	289	3,348
of which IPOs	53	198	194	2,261
Total	564	583	668	3,586
Panel B: Secondary Market Turnover				
NSE spot	6,956	62,432	90,788	117,516
BSE spot	4,752	33,281	40,916	53,325
NSE derivatives	3,985	34,544	143,114	258,674
BSE derivatives	208	93	910	1,917
Indian equity turnover	121,274	130,351	275,729	431,432
Panel C: Equity Returns, Market Capitalisation, Volatility, and Price/ Earnings Ratio for Nifty Stocks (50 most liquid stocks)				
Returns (per cent)	-16.2	3.3	71.9	10.7
End-year market capitalisation	2,85,007	3,52,943	6,34,248	9,02,831
Daily volatility	1.62	1.07	1.23	1.73
End-year P/E	15.35	14.83	20.73	15.32

Source: Ministry of Finance, Government of India, *The Economic Survey*, 2004–2005.
NSE = National Stock Exchange
BSE = Bombay Stock Exchange

Both the primary market and the secondary market have grown rapidly in recent years. The volume of public issues rose by roughly five times to a level of Rs 359 billion in 2004. The bulk of this was made up of equity issuance, which amounted to Rs 335 billion. In the secondary market, total Indian equity turnover has gone up from Rs 12,127 billion in 2001 to Rs 43,143 billion in 2004. One international ranking in the area of finance, where India figures, is the size of securities exchanges, as measured by the number of transactions. In 2002, the National Stock Exchange (NSE) displaced Shanghai to take the third place, and the Bombay Stock Exchange (BSE) moved up from the eighth rank in 2001 to the fifth rank in 2003. NSE and BSE were stable at ranks 3 and 5 respectively in 2003 and 2004. Table 14.2 gives highlights of activity in the

Table 14.3 Foreign Investment in India

Panel A: Foreign Institutional Investment

			(Amounts in billions of Indian rupees)	
	2001	2002	2003	2004
End-year number of foreign institutional investors	527*	490*	502*	637
End-year number of sub-accounts	–	1,372*	1,361*	1,785
Spot market activity				
Gross buy	5,177.90	2,875.90	9,441.20	18,567.20
Gross sell	3,865.10	2,525.70	6,395.40	14,670.70
Net	1,312.80	350.20	3,045.80	3,896.50

Panel B: Total Foreign Investment in India

								(Amounts in US$ million)		
Net figures	1990–1991	1997–1998	1998–1999	1999–2000	2000–2001	2001–2002	2002–2003	2003–2004	2003–2004	2004–2005#
Foreign Investment	103	5,353	2,312	5,117	5,862	6,686	4,161	14,776	5,122	2,554
(i) foreign direct investment	97	3,525	2,380	2,093	3,272	4,734	3,217	3,420	1,610	2,042
(ii) foreign institutional investors	0	979	-390	2,135	1,847	1,505	377	10,918	3,287	339
(iii) Euro equities and others	6	849	322	889	743	447	567	438	225	173

Source: Ministry of Finance, Government of India, *The Economic Survey*, 2004–2005.
* As at 31 March.
# April 2004–September 2004.

245

Indian capital market in recent years.

Foreign institutional investors hold a significant portion of equity in major listed firms.[4] These investors make international comparisons of financial reporting standards and corporate governance systems in various countries and may increase their weights for countries that have superior accounting standards and governance quality (e.g., Bradshaw et al. 2004; Aggarwal et al. 2003). Foreign institutional investors have been net buyers over the last four years. Also, the volume of business transacted has gone up substantially. In 2004, out of the total institutional turnover of Rs 5,475 billion, foreign institutional investors accounted for about 92 per cent. Table 14.3 provides details of foreign institutional investors' activity in India. As may be expected, the level of investment by foreign institutional investors closely follows the movement of the major stock market indices.

As Table 14.3 demonstrates, foreign direct investment has also been increasing over the years. In 2004, foreign direct investment was US$3.42 billion, much of it in the form of setting up wholly-owned subsidiaries or joint ventures with Indian companies. Presenting the financial statements of Indian operations in accordance with the accounting system that the overseas parent uses is important for performance evaluation and preparation of consolidated financial statements. From 1995 onwards, India has made considerable progress in terms of greater trade integration and entry of foreign investors. This should have led to higher correlations between Indian stock market indices and those of the outside world. However, as yet the extent of global integration is still quite small, with a correlation between Nifty and the US S&P500 index of 0.327 in calendar years 2003 and 2004. The Korean Kospi index serves as a proxy for 'other emerging markets'. Korea had high trade integration as of 1995, but had many barriers to portfolio flows. This gave a Korea-US correlation of 0.316. In the period after the East Asian Crisis, Korea further liberalised portfolio flows. This has given a higher correlation of 0.509 in 2003 and 2004. In India, the second tier of the next 50 less liquid stocks, Nifty Junior, has an even lower correlation of 0.195 against the S&P500 index. At the same time, the correlation between Nifty and the Korean Kospi has risen from 0.288 to 0.425, which suggests that India is now more integrated with the factors that affect all emerging markets such as fluctuations in world trade, portfolio flows, and foreign direct investment.

Partial privatisation (referred to as 'disinvestment' in India), in which non-controlling shares of state-owned firms are sold on the stock market to private investors, and privatisation create demand for high quality financial reporting from these firms as a means of monitoring and rewarding managerial performance even when the government remains the controlling owner.[5] Also, it has been argued that investor confidence in companies is bound to increase if they comply with internationally accepted standards (e.g., Ball 2001; Kothari

2000). This view is the same argument that has been applied around the world, particularly in countries whose accounting standards might be considered less developed, or less likely to ensure the provision of high quality financial information to investors. Both full and partial privatisation of Indian business has increased since the economic reforms began (see annual report for 2004–2005 of the Government of India, Department of Disinvestment available at http://www.divest.nic.in). Proceeds from full and partial privatisation totalled over Rs 478 billion (approximately US$10 billion).

Consistent with the trend towards privatisation and internationalisation, several Indian firms have listed on overseas stock exchanges. They are subject to detailed disclosure requirements, as specified by the relevant exchanges. Since 2000, eight Indian companies have listed on the New York Stock Exchange with a total market capitalisation of US$37 billion. These companies are from the following industries (number of companies): banking (2); technology (2); telecommunication (2); pharmaceuticals (1); and automobile (1). Three companies, all in technology, are listed on the NASDAQ. A further 19 companies are listed on the London Stock Exchange. Annual reporting of financial statements based on accounting standards adopted and/or trusted in the country of listing reduces investors' costs of monitoring the listing company, and should therefore reduce the companies' cost of capital.[6]

Product market pressures

Since the commencement of the economic reforms, Indian firms have enjoyed greater interactions with overseas markets in the form of exports and imports of goods and services. Overseas customers, dealing with Indian firms are concerned with the firms' financial performance, especially when long-term relationships are involved. Increasingly, they demand high quality financial reports to monitor the firms' performance. To a slightly lesser extent, the same comment applies to suppliers. Also, high quality financial reporting contributes to the reputation of a firm in its product market as a dependable organisation to transact business with. Using the case of Infosys Technologies, Narayanaswamy (1996) illustrates how a company modifies its financial reporting in response to the needs of its product market.[7] In 1994–95, the company voluntarily provided unaudited US GAAP financial statements. At the time, 73 per cent of the company's revenue came from the United States. As at 31 March 2005, the company provides financial statements (consolidated income statement and consolidated balance sheet) prepared in accordance with the national accounting requirements in Australia, Canada, France, Germany, Japan and the United Kingdom.[8] The company has operations in all of these countries. A major objective for overseas listing is to create brand equity in the company's international product markets (Bancel and Mittoo 2002).

Similar considerations apply to domestic listing. For example, India's largest software services firm, TCS, has long been privately held by the Tata group but in 2004 the company's shares were offered for sale to the public. Clearly, the motivation for going public was not any immediate need for additional capital, as the company is cash rich. Being a listed company carries greater prestige when it comes to dealing with present and potential customers. We would expect TCS to seek overseas listing in due course, given its significant exposure to the US software market. Again, financial reporting under accounting standards recognised internationally will assist that transition.

Exports and imports as percentages of GDP have been rising over the period in which economic reforms were implemented indicating India's increasing integration with the global economy.[9] Software exports have grown at an annual compound growth rate of around 36 per cent between 1995–96 and 2003–04. By 2008, the IT industry is projected to grow to 7 per cent of GDP (from 2.64 per cent in 2003–04) and account for 35 per cent of total exports (from 21.3 per cent in 2003–04). An export potential of US$57–65 billion for the software and services sector can be realised, with the ITES-BPO sector contributing US$21–24 billion by 2008.[10] The rapid globalisation of the services sector of India explains why technology and software services firms are in the forefront of adopting international financial reporting standards. The evidence from Infosys and other IT firms is persuasive in concluding that potential benefits in product markets provide significant incentives to Indian firms to accept high quality accounting and disclosure systems.

Labour market pressures
Indian firms need talent to stay ahead of the competition in their product and capital markets. Pagano et al. (2002) refer to labour market spillover of foreign listing. Superior financial reporting could be useful in convincing a firm's present and potential employees of its financial soundness, so that as key users of a firm's accounting information they can trust the firm as a dependable employer offering good long-term prospects of growth. Also, some firms (mainly, but not only, in the technology sector) have employee stock ownership plans.[11] Employees in these firms demand financial information in order to make decisions about their claims. Sunder (2002) states that strong pay-performance links in US managerial contracts make demands on US accounting systems that are largely absent in seniority-based systems elsewhere. In India, prior to the 1990s the government regulated and approved remuneration of top management. However, since the 1990s Indian companies have been moving in the direction of relating management compensation to financial performance.[12] Again, since professional employees have worldwide mobility, they are likely to benefit from making investments that have cross-border mobility that results from

international listing of their companies' stocks. Further, firms with large overseas operations employ foreigners who are generally more comfortable with financial reporting and disclosure standards that are followed around the world. These arguments build on the point in Desai (2004) that firms with employees abroad might be interested in listing their stock in these foreign markets as an employee incentive program.

National Regulations

In the last decade there have been significant changes to Indian laws and regulatory requirements relating to accounting and governance. The major developments are discussed below.

National advisory committee on accounting standards

In 1999, the Companies Act was amended to provide for setting up a National Advisory Committee on Accounting Standards (NACAS) to advise the government on the formulation of accounting standards. This amendment was largely in response to an international groundswell of interest in the globalisation of accounting standards, and as part of India's economic reforms to facilitate international trade and capital movements. As a result of the amendment, the government has been given the authority to prescribe accounting standards in consultation with NACAS. The chairman and members of NACAS are appointed by central government and are drawn from the accounting and allied professions (chartered accountants, cost and works accountants and company secretaries), the Central government, the Reserve Bank of India, the Comptroller and Auditor-General of India, academe, chambers of commerce and the Securities and Exchange Board of India. Prior to the amendment, there was no legal recognition for accounting standards. The Committee was first constituted in September 2001 and was given a term of one year. The press release issued by the government stated that 'the Committee shall advise the Central government on the accounting standards to be followed, evolved and practised in the country ... to meet the challenges of emerging globalisation of Indian economy'.[13]

Securities legislation and the stock exchange listing agreement

The Securities and Exchange Board of India (SEBI) was established by Parliament in 1992 'to protect the interests of investors in securities and to promote the development of, and to regulate, the securities market'.[14] Over the years, and more so since the late 1990s, SEBI has played an active role in requiring compliance with accounting standards and provision of additional disclosures. It mandated half-yearly reporting of financial results and later required quarterly reporting. In 1995, SEBI amended the listing agreement to require annual report publication of the statement of cash flows by listed companies, although the Companies Act did not (and even now does not) require the statement. In 2001, SEBI amended the listing agreement to require segment performance reporting in listed companies' quarterly results.

Corporate governance reforms

Over the years, a number of initiatives have been taken by the government, regulators and the private sector on reforming corporate governance in India. The recommendations made by the various committees have had an impact on financial reporting in India. These are described briefly below.

The Narayana Murthy Committee on Corporate Governance established by SEBI in 2003 was mainly concerned with issues related to audit committees, audit reports, independent directors, related parties, risk management, directorships and director compensation, codes of conduct and financial disclosures. The recommendations were applicable to listed companies. The major recommendation concerning financial reporting is that in case a company has followed an accounting treatment different from that prescribed in an accounting standard, management should justify why they believe such alternative treatment is more representative of the underlying business transaction. Management should also clearly explain the alternative accounting treatment in the footnotes to the financial statements. These changes have been incorporated in the new clause 49 in the Listing Agreement. SEBI also requires a certificate from the company's external auditor on compliance with this clause.

The Government of India, Ministry of Finance and Company Affairs established the Naresh Chandra Committee on Corporate Audit and Governance Committee in 2002 in the wake of a series of corporate scandals that shook the US in 2001 and 2002 and the enactment of the Sarbanes-Oxley Act (SOX) in July 2002. The Committee made several recommendations on strengthening the mechanism of corporate audit as an effective tool for monitoring the quality of financial statements.

SEBI set up the Kumar Mangalam Birla Committee on Corporate Governance in 1999. This was the first official committee to examine corporate governance in India. It was motivated, among others, by 'the financial crisis in emerging markets', a reference to the 1997 East Asian Crisis. The Committee emphasised the effect of globalisation of accounting standards by saying that India has 'to move speedily towards the adoption of international standards. This is particularly important from the angle of corporate governance' (para. 12.1). The Committee recommended presentation of consolidated financial statements, segment reporting and disclosure of related party transactions. In 2000, the recommendations of the Committee resulted in a major change in the Listing Agreement.

International Accounting and Securities Regulations

The restructuring of the International Accounting Standards Board (IASB) and the International Organization of Securities Commissions' (IOSCO) acceptance of the IASB's 'core set of standards' for the purpose of cross-border listing have improved the acceptability of IFRS within India. SEBI is a member of IOSCO and is on several of its key committees. As such, it would be difficult for SEBI to defend Indian accounting practices that are not in accordance with international standards and practices. The changes in Indian accounting described in this chapter are mostly the result of pressure felt by SEBI because of being a part of a body of international securities regulators. In turn, SEBI required major changes in Indian accounting.

The effect of international influence or pressure becomes clear when we look at the role played by SEBI and the Government of India's Department of Company Affairs (DCA). The latter is less susceptible to international influence and has generally followed SEBI's lead. SEBI appears to be relatively more concerned with international developments. Consider, for example, the following statement on the effect of the East Asian crisis in 1997 in SEBI's 1998–99 annual report:

> The financial crisis in East Asia which has re-emphasised the need for strong supervision and regulation of capital market and its further developments from the point of view of investor's protection, trade guarantee, transparency, better payment system, safe transactions and international accounting standards should serve as guiding indicators for FIIs to invest in Indian equity (p. 14).

In contrast, the annual reports of the Department of Company Affairs do not contain references to international developments affecting Indian markets. Interestingly, the Companies Act is yet to be amended to require consolidated financial statements and cash flow statements, even though SEBI requirements on these have existed for many years. The DCA appears to have woken up to this regulatory competition when SOX was enacted in the US in 2002 by quickly setting up the Naresh Chandra Committee. Apparently not to be left behind, SEBI established the Narayana Murthy Committee that examined not only accounting and auditing but also the role of analysts and other market participants.

Even though SEBI and the DCA could be said to be broadly interested in disclosure and accounting respectively, the lines of distinction have been blurred, at least by SEBI. For example, it was SEBI that first set up an Accounting Standards Committee in 1998–99 as a Standing Committee with the following objectives:

- To review the continuous disclosure requirements under listing agreements;
- To provide input to the ICAI for introducing new accounting standards in India; and
- To review existing accounting standards, where required, and to harmonise these accounting standards and financial disclosures on a par with international practices.

In 2001, the DCA entered the scene with the idea of the National Advisory Committee on Accounting Standards.

Despite the DCA's activism, necessary amendments to the Companies Act have not been made on many of the matters on which recommendations were made by the Naresh Chandra Committee. SEBI's competitive advantage is that it is less politicised, it deals with listed companies via stock exchanges and has to worry less about the implementation costs of its requirements, since listed companies do not apparently succeed much in stalling stock exchange regulations despite protest.[15] On the other hand, the DCA has to work with several ministries and departments in the Government of India and any changes it wants to bring about require the approval of Parliament. Therefore, the process is slow and sometimes politicised.

It is significant that international developments produce ripples quicker in India than was the case earlier. For example, the 1987 stock market crash in the rest of the world left India relatively unaffected. In fact, many commentators then argued that India was safe because it was not a part of the international securities markets. Even more to the point was the securities scam in 1992 in India that wiped out a large part of investors' wealth in many companies.[16] The response to the scandal was considered slow and half-hearted and many commentators felt that fundamental reforms were needed to avert a similar scam in the future.[17] Contrast this with the developments in the late 1990s and later when major events such as the bursting of the dotcom bubble, corporate accounting scandals, corporate governance reforms in the US and elsewhere, and SOX, were followed up more quickly in India. This, more than any other measure, captures the effect of globalisation of the Indian economy on standards of accounting and corporate governance.

Impact of economic reforms and globalisation on accounting and governance

A recent study on corporate governance in ten countries in Asia indicates that in conformity to the IASB's standards, India is ranked fourth in the region; Singapore, Hong Kong and Malaysia are ahead of India; South Korea, Taiwan, Thailand, Philippines, China and Indonesia are behind. In enforcement, only Hong Kong and Singapore are ahead of India. Indian investors are willing to pay a governance premium of 23 per cent, conceivably for lower agency costs (Barton et al. 2004).

ACCOUNTING STANDARDS SETTING IN INDIA

Prior to 1998, accounting standards were prepared by the Institute of Chartered Accountants of India (ICAI), a professional accountancy body established by the Chartered Accountants Act 1949. The ICAI is governed by a council comprising 24 persons elected by its members (both practising and non-practising) and six persons nominated by the government of India. In 1977, the ICAI established the Accounting Standards Board (ASB) to harmonise the diverse accounting policies and practices in use. As a committee of the council, the ASB consisted of a few members of the council but included invitees from government and industry.

The function of the ASB was to prepare the draft of a proposed accounting standard, circulate it to interested parties and individuals for comment, and send the final version of the proposed standard to the council for approval. The accounting standards were issued by the council. The ICAI required that its members auditing the financial statements of companies comply with its accounting standards. But the standards were not mandatory on companies, as the Companies Act did not require compliance. Consequently, the standards could not be enforced.[18]

Furthermore, under the Chartered Accountants Act the function of the ICAI was 'to regulate the profession of chartered accountants'. Hence, there was a view that accounting standards should be formulated by a body that was independent of the accounting profession with representation for the various stakeholders in financial reporting. This is an issue that has dogged standard setters in many countries during their histories of standard setting.

As a result of an amendment in 1999, the Companies Act requires that the profit and loss account and balance sheet be prepared in compliance with Indian accounting standards. Any deviation from the accounting standards, reasons for such deviation, and the financial effect must be disclosed.

At the time of writing, the NACAS has recommended 23 accounting standards to the government. However, the government has not issued any notification prescribing the standards.[19] The Companies Act provides that until the accounting standards are prescribed by the government, the standards specified by the ICAI shall be deemed to be the accounting standards. For this purpose, the ICAI has specified all the standards that were mandatory on its members.

In summary, accounting standards now have a legal status and can be enforced on companies and their auditors. The flip side is that control over establishment of accounting standards has moved from the private sector to the public sector, at least in theory. In the years to come, government control over financial reporting and disclosure is likely to increase. At the time of writing (2005) however, standards are all the product of the ICAI's standard-setting process.

NEW INDIAN ACCOUNTING STANDARDS

Issuance of Accounting Standards Gathering Pace

Accounting standards issued since 2000 are frequently referred to as the 'new accounting standards'. The ICAI issued 13 accounting standards between 2000 and 2004, as compared to 16 standards issued from 1977 (when it was established) to 1999. The new accounting standards cover several complex recognition and disclosure issues, such as segment reporting, leases, deferred taxes, consolidated financial statements, intangible assets and impairment of assets.

These standards cover matters for which there were mostly no prior pronouncements. As a result, they have tended to follow the IASB promulgations more closely than the previous generation of standards. For example, when accounting standards for matters such as depreciation and inventory valuation were issued, the ICAI had in place a set of accepted pronouncements that was being followed by auditors and preparers.[20] The relevant international accounting standards were modified to conform to the existing Indian pronouncements and issued as Indian accounting standards. Nevertheless, there are substantial differences between the new accounting standards and the corresponding IASB standards.

Some of the new accounting standards came to be issued because of the pressure brought to bear on the ICAI by SEBI.[21] In turn, SEBI was under pressure from the IOSCO to improve Indian accounting standards and bring them in line with the IASB.[22] SEBI backed up its pressure by tightening the Listing Agreement with companies for listing their securities on stock exchanges. Some of the matters that SEBI required were not then reporting requirements under the Companies Act 1956. As such, the accounting standards globalisation movement in which IOSCO was a key player led to SEBI's influence to hasten India's involvement in the globalisation process. For example, an amendment to the Listing Agreement required companies to present consolidated financial statements even though such a requirement did not exist then in Indian law, and does not exist even now. Also, companies were required to publish quarterly segment financial results although the Companies Act has no requirement for segment reporting.[23]

Greater Convergence with International Accounting Standards

Increasingly, Indian accounting standards are getting closer to IFRS than was the case until the 1990s. To begin with, the ASB sticks faithfully to the language of standards with few exceptions. This contrasts sharply with the earlier ASB practice of making inconsequential verbal changes. Also, in the past Indian accounting standards were tacitly influenced by tax considerations. The ASB was implicitly concerned with the effect of standards on reporting for income tax, despite the fact that shareholder reporting and tax reporting are different in India, as in other British Commonwealth jurisdictions. For example, it is understood that an accounting standard on leases was not issued until 2001, even though there was a tax-driven leasing boom in the 1980s and early 1990s. The fear was that if leases were capitalised, tax authorities could refuse the benefit of capital allowances to lessors and lessees. In recent times, there is recognition that financial reporting should not be coloured by tax considerations. An enabling factor for this development is the steady drop in income tax rates resulting in taxation being less important now than it was.

Another trend in India's movement towards accepting the globalisation of accounting standards is the adoption in some cases of the benchmark treatment rather than the allowed alternative treatment in the relevant IFRS. For example, when AS 11 dealing with the effects of foreign exchange rates was revised in 2003, the ASB decided to adopt the international benchmark treatment that requires recognition in the current period of all exchange differences arising from transactions. The alternative treatment that allows carrying the additional liability arising from a severe devaluation as part of the cost of the related fixed asset was not accepted. This was despite the fact that the Companies Act requires that the cost of fixed assets be adjusted for exchange differences arising from foreign exchange liabilities related to acquisition of fixed assets.

Moving Towards International Accounting Standards

The differences between Indian accounting standards and IFRS have been narrowing, especially in the case of standards issued since the late 1990s. Some of the differences are attributable to the need for conformity with the Companies Act. Some others exist because there is no corresponding Indian standard on the subject (e.g., financial instruments and business combinations). A general perception is that financial reporting practices have improved over the past five years; however, significantly strengthened enforcement mechanisms are needed to further improve the quality of corporate financial reporting (World Bank 2004).

Some of the new accounting standards are far-reaching in their impact on firms' balance sheets and income statements and are therefore expected to have significant economic consequences. These provide opportunities for research. Mizuno (2004) provides evidence that Japanese companies' adoption of new accounting standards produced significant economic impacts on decision making by corporate management. It is possible that India, too, will experience some effects. The following are illustrations of possible economic consequences that may arise from implementing the accounting standards.

Consolidated Financial Statements

In the past, companies were required to attach the financial statements of subsidiaries to the parent's financial statements. There was no requirement for equity accounting or proportionate consolidation of joint ventures. Consequently, companies could keep loss-making businesses as subsidiaries rather than as divisions of the parent and not recognise the subsidiaries' losses in the parent's financial statements. With the advent of consolidation, companies have incentives to divest unprofitable subsidiaries and associates. Changes in the structure of corporate holdings since the initiation of consolidated financial statements in 2001–02 can be studied. Another issue is whether consolidation has led to companies changing their criteria for performance evaluation. Given the significant role of family-controlled corporate groups in India, the requirement for consolidated financial statements may lead to significant improvement in transparency and considerable restructuring activity. Also, the question of capital market value relevance of consolidated financial statement numbers can be examined.

Deferred Tax Accounting

The effect of deferred tax accounting is to capture the tax effect of differences between accounting profit and taxable income. The need to create deferred tax liabilities for temporary differences will result in lower net profit. This could impact firms' tax planning strategies. According to some commentators, deferred tax accounting is a major change with far-reaching consequences.[24]

Foreign Exchange Transactions

In the past, companies were allowed to adjust their foreign exchange gains and losses arising from change in foreign exchange liabilities related to acquisition of fixed assets. AS 11 (revised) provides for recognition of such differences in the period in which they arise. Management would likely reduce the resulting volatility in reported profit by entering into suitable hedging arrangements.[25]

The new accounting standards on consolidated financial statements and leases became effective from fiscal years beginning on or after 1 April 2001 and the revised accounting standard on foreign exchange transactions became effective from fiscal years beginning on or after 1 April 2004. It is early to assess the effect of these standards, but exploratory studies can be considered.

CONCLUSION

This chapter summarises the developments in Indian accounting in the context of the on-going globalisation of the Indian economy. Indian accounting standards and corporate governance requirements are now more in line with international practices. The developments that have taken place can be attributed to the operation of economic forces arising from capital, product market and labour market pressures and to regulatory initiatives in response to overseas developments, such as the East Asian Crisis and SOX. Foreign financial institutions and listing in international stock exchanges are playing a major role in speeding the pace of raising Indian standards to international levels. India is still in the early stages of its involvement in the globalisation of accounting standards. As in other countries, the stock exchange and the securities regulator have been very significant in influencing this process. This is consistent with SEBI's role in increasing the external focus of India's economic activity and development.

NOTES

1 See, for example, the following recent articles and write-ups on India's changing economic scene: Amadeo M. Di Lodovico, William W. Lewis, Vincent Palmade, and Shirish Sankhe, 'India – From emerging to surging', *The McKinsey Quarterly*, 2001 No. 4; Aude Lagorce, 'Outsourcing to India vs. China', *Forbes*, 16 February 2004; Robin Meredith, 'Giant sucking sound', *Forbes*, 29 September 2003; 'BPO Providers Are Moving Up the Value Chain', *Knowledge@Wharton*, 24 September–7 October 2003; Amy Waldman, 'How India's mother of invention built an industry', *The New York Times*, 16 August 2003; Thomas Friedman, 'What Goes Around …', *The New York Times*, 26 February 2004.

2 See Srinivasan and Tendulkar (2000) for a history of India's economic development since 1950.

3 The Bombay Stock Exchange was established in 1875 as 'The Native Share and Stockbrokers Association' which has evolved over the decades in to its present status as the premier Stock Exchange in India. It is one of the oldest in Asia having preceded even the Tokyo Stock Exchange which was founded in 1878.

4 Sowmya Sundar, 'Foreign shareholdings in India Inc – Tugging at market strings', *Business Line*, 14 April 2004.

5 Gupta (2005) finds that partial privatisation in India has a positive impact on profitability and productivity. She interprets the finding as an indication of the role that the stock market can play in monitoring and rewarding managerial performance even when the government remains the controlling owner.

6 Sources: Mark Yarm, 'India on the Cusp', *NYSE Magazine* 2004; 'Nasdaq keen to list more Indian cos', *Business Line*, 26 May 2005; 'Indian mid-cap cos catch LSE's fancy', *Business Line*, 7 November 2004.

7 Khanna et al. (2004) suggest that cross-border economic interactions are associated with similarities in disclosure and governance practices. See also Palepu and Khanna (2001).

8 These statements are also in the languages of the respective countries. For example, the statements prepared in accordance with Japanese accounting requirements are in Japanese.

9 Source: Ministry of Finance, Government of India, The Economic Survey, 2004–2005.

10 The term ITES-BPO refers to IT-enabled services and business process outsourcing.

11 Prerna K. Mishra, 'New breed of tech firms creating millionaires through ESOPs', *The Hindustan Times*, 29 December 2003.

12 See for example: Suresh Krishnamurthy, 'Directors' pay rises faster than staff's', *Business Line*, 15 August 2004; Ajita Shashidhar, 'In corporate India, it pays to reward performers', *Business Line*, 14 March 2003; 'TCS: Double clicking EVA', http://www.tata.com/tcs/articles/20030326_double_clicking_eva.htm.

13 http://pib.nic.in/archieve/lreleng/lyr2001/rsep2001/12092001/r120920015.html.

14 From the preamble to The Securities and Exchange Board of India Act 1992.

15 In contrast, despite statutory backing, accounting standards have become the subject matter of litigation. Several companies have approached courts for staying the operation of accounting standards. For example, an interim injunction was granted against the application of AS 22 Accounting for Taxes on Income (M. Padmakshan 'India Inc. gets time to rethink deferred tax provision', *The Economic Times*, 22 June 2002).

16 In 1992, there was a major financial scandal that resulted in losses running to several billions of rupees involving a number of Indian and foreign banks. The scandal related to, among others, transactions in government securities entered into between banks and stock brokers. A Joint Parliamentary Committee was set up to enquire into the scandal. The Committee's report was critical of the role played by regulatory agencies and statutory auditors.

17 For example, Barua and Varma (1993) argue that the origins of the scam lie in over-regulation of Indian markets. For a review of the development of the securities markets in India in the 1990s, see Shah and Thomas (2001).

18 The ICAI lobbied for recognition of its accounting standards for the purpose of financial reporting by companies. In the absence of an amendment to the Companies Act granting such recognition, the ICAI required auditors to qualify their reports on financial statements in the event of non-compliance with its standards. Some companies took the view that in the absence of a legal requirement, they were under no obligation to comply with these standards. As a result, compliance was largely voluntary and some companies chose not to comply. Also, the ICAI did not have any monitoring mechanism for enforcing compliance.

19 'DCA in a fix over notifying ICAI's accounting norms', New Delhi , 30 July 2003.

20 These include the Statement on Auditing Practices and various other Statements and Guidance Notes.

21 The following excerpt from SEBI's annual report for 1999–2000 indicates the role played by SEBI in bringing to bear pressure on the ICAI (p. 19): 'Major recommendations of the Committee that have been implemented by the SEBI are given below :
  • The [Accounting Standards] Committee [of SEBI] has emphasized the need for formulation of accounting standards on Consolidation of Accounts, Segmental Reporting, Deferred Taxation and Related Party Disclosures and has urged the ICAI to expedite the issue of Accounting Standards on the above.'

22 For example, the annual report of SEBI for 1998–99 states (p. 120): 'India stands committed to the various measures and efforts undertaken by IOSCO in order to improve transparency in the functioning of the international capital markets and increasing the efficiency of the global securities markets.' In its 1999–2000 report, SEBI states (p. 59): 'The IOSCO has issued a set of 30 principles of securities regulation, which are based upon three objectives of securities regulation. These objectives are:
  • The protection of investors
  • Ensuring that markets are fair, efficient and transparent
  • The reduction of systemic risk.'
Principle 30 states: 'Accounting and auditing standards should be of a high and internationally acceptable quality.'

23 World Bank (2004) provides a review of the corporate financial reporting regime in India.

24 Aarati Krishnan, 'Deferred tax accounting: Debit companies, credit investors', *Business Line*, 4 May 2003; S. Murlidharan, 'ICAI proposes, court disposes?', *Business Line*, 19 August 2002.

25 'Adjustment of exchange differences — ICAI revises accounting standards', *Business Line*, 7 February 2003.

ACKNOWLEDGEMENTS

I am grateful to Keryn Chalmers, Jayne Godfrey, Sidney Gray and the participants at the Globalisation of Accounting Standards Conference in Prato, Italy, in May 2005, for their valuable comments and suggestions. I appreciate financial support from the Monash Institute for the Study of Global Movements for my participation in the Conference.

REFERENCES

Aggarwal, R., L. Klapper and P.D. Wysocki (2003), 'Portfolio preferences of foreign institutional investors', World Bank Working Paper # 3101.

Ball, R. (2001), 'Infrastructure requirements for an economically efficient system of public financial reporting and disclosure', Brookings-Wharton Papers on Financial Services.

Bancel, F. and U. Mittoo (2002), 'European managerial perceptions of the net benefits of foreign stock listings', *European Financial Management* 7 (2), 213–236.

Barton, D., P. Coombes and S. Wong (2004), 'Transparency: Asia's governance challenge', *The McKinsey Quarterly*, Issue 2, 54–61.

Barua, S. and J. R. Varma (1993), 'Securities Scam: Genesis, Mechanics and Impact', *Vikalpa* 18 (January-March), 3–12.

Bhattacharyya, A, (2004), 'Corporate financial reporting', in Darryl Reed and Sanjoy Mukherjee (eds), *Corporate Governance, Economic Reforms, and Development: The Indian Experience*, New Delhi, India: Oxford University Press.

Bradshaw, M.T., B.J . Bushee and G.S. Miller (2004), 'Accounting choice, home bias, and US Investment in non-US Firms', *Journal of Accounting Research* 42 (December): 795–841.

Chander, S. (1992), *Corporate Reporting Practices in Public and Private Sectors*, New Delhi: Deep & Deep Publications.

Choi, F.D.S., and G.G. Mueller (1986), *International Accounting*, Englewood Cliffs, NJ: Prentice Hall.

Das Gupta, N. (1977), *Financial Reporting in India*, New Delhi: Sultan Chand & Sons.

Desai, M.A. (2004), 'Cross-border listings and depositary receipts.' Harvard Business School Note 9-204-022.

Goldman Sachs (2003), *Dreaming With BRICs: The Path to 2050*, New York: Goldman Sachs.

Gray, S.J. (1988), 'Towards a theory of cultural influence on the development of accounting systems internationally', *Abacus* (March): 1–14.

Gupta, N. (2005), 'Partial privatization and firm performance', *The Journal of Finance* 60(2): 987–1015.

Institute of Chartered Accountants of India (ICAI) (1981), 'Precedents in Published Accounts', New Delhi: ICAI.

Khanna, T., K.G. Palepu and S. Srinivasan, (2004), 'Disclosure practices of foreign companies interacting with US markets', *Journal of Accounting Research* **42** (May): 475–508.

Kothari, S.P. (2000), 'Role of Financial Reporting in Reducing Financial Risks in the Market', in Eric Rosengren and John Jordan (eds), *Conference on Building an Infrastructure for Financial Stability*, Federal Reserve Bank of Boston.

Marston, C. (1986), *Financial Reporting in India*, London: Croom Helm.

Mizuno, M. (2004), 'The impact of new accounting standards on Japanese companies', *Pacific Economic Review*, **9** (4): 357–369.

Narayanaswamy, R. (1996), 'Voluntary US GAAP disclosure in India: The case of Infosys Technologies Limited', *Journal of International Financial Management and Accounting*, **7**: 137–166.

Narayanaswamy, R. (1997), 'The development of accounting regulation in India', *Research in Accounting Regulation*, Supplement 1: 331–365.

Pagano, M., R.A. Ailsa A and J. Zechner (2002), 'The geography of equity listing: Why do companies list abroad?', *The Journal of Finance*, **57** (6): 2651–2694.

Palepu, K. and T. Khanna (2001), 'Product and Labor Market Globalisation and Convergence of Corporate Governance: Evidence from Infosys and the Indian Software Industry', SSRN working paper.

Puxty, A.G., H.C. Wilmott, D.J. Cooper and A. Lowe (1987), 'Modes of regulation in advanced capitalism: Accountancy in four countries', *Accounting, Organisations and Society*, **12**: 273–291.

Shah, A. and S. Thomas (2001), 'The evolution of the securities markets in India in the 1990s', Working paper, Indira Gandhi Institute for Development Research.

Singhvi, S. (1967), 'Corporate disclosure through annual reports in the USA and India', Ph.D. dissertation, Graduate School of Business, Columbia University.

Srinivasan, T.N. and S.D. Tendulkar (2000), *Reintegrating India with the World Economy*, New Delhi: Oxford University Press.

Sunder, S. (2002), 'Accounting: Labor, Capital And Product Markets', Yale ICF Working Paper No. 03-10.

Sunder, S. and H. Yamaji (1999), *The Japanese Style of Business Accounting*, Westport, CT: Greenwood Publishing.

World Bank (2004), *Reports on the Observance of Standards and Codes: India: Accounting and Auditing*, Washington D.C.: The World Bank Group.

15 Globalisation of Financial Reporting: An Islamic Focus

Norita Mohd Nasir and Aniza Zainol

INTRODUCTION

Accounting thought and practices are influenced by culture and religion. Due to global diversity in culture and religion, it is unclear whether a common accounting language is possible. Some regard International Financial Reporting Standards (IFRS) as the common language of accounting and the number of countries adopting these standards is growing. However, IFRS are often viewed as being dominated by Anglo-American accounting thought and practices, which raises questions as to the suitability of IFRS compliant financial reports in countries with cultural or religious attributes dissimilar to Western economies.

The objectives of individuals and organisations operating in Western economies tend to be economically orientated. In contrast, organisations and individuals operating in Islamic economies adhere to Shariah requirements[1] which emphasise socio-economic objectives. Thus, the financial reporting needs of Islamic economies' constituents are not necessarily served by IFRS compliant financial reports. Islamic accounting is an alternative accounting system and promotes the preparation of financial reports that enable organisations and individuals to assess Shariah compliance. In particular, the emergence of Islamic financial institutions has prompted the development of international accounting and auditing standards specifically for Islamic financial institutions. To achieve financial reports that are compliant with Shariah requirements necessitates that these standards address issues that IFRS do not address. The standards also prescribe accounting treatments that are dissimilar to those prescribed by IFRS.

The country setting for this chapter, Malaysia, provides an interesting study of how to manage support for the globalisation of accounting standards concurrently with support for accounting and auditing standards of Islamic financial institutions. The objectives of the study are threefold. Firstly, the chapter discusses how Islamic accounting differs from conventional accounting. Secondly, the chapter focuses on the history and role of the Accounting and Auditing Organization for Islamic Financial Institutions (AAOIFI) in fulfilling the need for financial reports prepared in adherence to Shariah requirements. Thirdly, the chapter explores how the adoption of accounting standards for Islamic financial institutions is accommodated in Malaysia, given Malaysia's commitment to convergence with IFRS.

ISLAMIC ACCOUNTING VERSUS CONVENTIONAL ACCOUNTING

The differences in transactions under the Islamic and conventional accounting systems are due to differences in the function of the economic entity and the financial reporting needs of users. In particular, the need for Shariah-compliant economic entities to demonstrate compliance with Shariah requirements justifies a need for differential financial reporting standards.

Function of the Economic Entity

Shariah are Islamic laws derived from the Quran and Sunnah (MASB FRSi-1, para 6).[2] Shariah requirements emphasise a balance between the interests of the individual and society. Accordingly, Shariah-compliant business entities are encouraged to apply the concept of social responsibility, particularly for the welfare of society and the prevention of harm. Therefore, any activities that can cause harm to oneself, others, the environment or society in the pursuit of material returns are strictly prohibited. Examples of Shariah-prohibited (haram) activities are usury (riba), gambling (maisir) and activities involving uncertainty, risk and speculation (gharar). Shariah-compliant business entities must carry out their social responsibilities by avoiding the above-mentioned activities in order to protect the rights of all parties. In addition, as a player in a society, a business entity must carry out its social obligations by giving out a certain portion of the net assets or business income to the Zakah recipients.

Zakah literally means blessing, purification, increase and cultivation of good deeds. Zakah is defined as obligatory contributions based on assets owned by a Muslim that satisfy certain conditions and is to be distributed to a specified category of beneficiaries referred to as Zakah recipients (MASB FRSi-1). According to Islamic requirements, wealth is not owned in absolute terms by man. A certain portion of the wealth belongs to a group of people, the Zakah recipients. There are seven categories of Zakah recipients: the poor, the needy, the wayfarer, the heavily indebted, freedom of slaves, new converts to Islam, and the cause of Allah. In Shariah, Zakah is an obligation in respect of funds paid for a specified purpose (Zakah) and for specified categories[3] such as income, business, savings, shares income, superannuation contributions, gold, silver, wealth, crops, paddy, or livestock. Since Shariah requirements emphasise the concept of social responsibility and the welfare of society, Zakah plays an important role in protecting the rights of the Zakah recipients.

Users' Requirements for Financial Reporting

The objective of conventional financial reports is to provide information to users, which is useful for making and evaluating decisions about the allocation of scarce resources. While this objective is similar to the financial reporting under the Shariah requirements, those who transact with Shariah-compliant business entities, or who are otherwise stakeholders in such entities, are concerned with the business entities' compliance with Shariah requirements in their financial and other dealings. Therefore, some of the information required by the users of Shariah-compliant business entities' financial reports differ from the information needs of users of conventional business entities' financial reports.

Given that the Shariah requirements emphasise the concept of social responsibility and recognise the business entity as an important player in the economy, financial reports of Shariah-compliant business entities should disclose how the entities discharge their social obligations. Zakah is an item that demonstrates the importance of social responsibility in Shariah requirements and is a compulsory payment. It is a crucial and unique item that requires special disclosure and reporting. Similar to taxation agencies, the Zakah agency is a body responsible for calculating the Zakah payment. To do so, it requires detailed information about certain elements in the financial statements, for example fixed assets.[4] In addition, to calculate the Zakah amount, the trading assets, for example inventories and accounts receivable, are to be valued at their market selling price.[5] Accordingly, the information needs of the users of Shariah-compliant financial reports and conventional financial reports differ. Taxation does not rule out the Zakah obligation because of differences in the nature, criteria and recipients. While both taxation and Zakah are compulsory payments, the criteria differ as the former is based on a percentage of taxable income (that differs among countries), while the latter is calculated as 2.5 per cent[6] from the Zakah base (Para 2.1, AAOIFI 2003b). In terms of benefits for which Zakah and tax are spent, Zakah should be fully distributed in the year of collection to the seven specific categories of recipients, while tax collection forms part of the Government funds. Nevertheless, Zakah is also similar to a donation as some of the recipients are the needy and the poor. However, Zakah should strictly come from funds earned in a manner that complies with the Shariah requirements, while for donation purposes, the funds can be taken from funds earned in a manner that fails to comply with Shariah requirements (AAOIFI 2003b, Appendix D).

Reporting on Compliance with Shariah Requirements

Since Shariah-compliant business entities follow the Shariah requirements in their dealings and operations, differences in financial reporting between the Shariah and conventional systems are expected. Some items may be recognised under the Shariah requirements but not recognised under conventional rules. In general, the Shariah requirements entail that business entities provide information about compliance with the concepts of Shariah in their dealings and operations and that their financial reports should provide information on their compliance with these requirements. Accordingly, Shariah-compliant business entities should provide a clear and precise description of the significant accounting policies used for the preparation and publication of their financial statements. In the event of any of the accounting policies adopted by management being inconsistent with the Shariah requirements, management should disclose, by way of notes to the accounts, clear descriptions of the accounting policy and its inconsistencies. Additionally, information about the role of the Shariah advisor[7] in supervising the activities of the entities, and the nature of the advisor's authority in accordance with the entities' by-laws and in actual practice should also be disclosed.

Since Zakah is an important item for Shariah-compliant business entities, comprehensive disclosures ranging from the determination of the Zakah base, the method of calculating Zakah and the treatment of Zakah in the financial statements should be made. Zakah should appear in all three financial statements: the Balance Sheet, the Income Statement and the Statement of Cash Flows. The amount of unpaid Zakah (liability) should be disclosed under 'other liabilities' in the Balance Sheet, as a deduction from net income in the Income Statement and as a cash outflow in the Cash Flow Statement. Information about the Zakah base, the Zakah due for the financial period and the declared, but not yet distributed Zakah, is also required to be disclosed. Additionally, the AAOIFI standard also requires the presentation of two additional statements: Statement of Sources and Users of Funds in the Zakah and Charity Funds; and a Statement of Sources and Uses of Qard[8] Funds. Other requirements include general disclosures on Zakah, such as information on the determination of Zakah, where it will be spent and the responsibility of the Shariah-compliant business entities in paying and distributing Zakah on behalf of the shareholders and investment account holders.

Shariah requirements strictly prohibit the use of interest[9] in business dealings. Therefore, there is a major difference between Islamic and conventional banks, where the conventional banks borrow (lend) money and pay (earn) interest associated with the borrowing (lending) activities. In conventional reporting, interest is recognised as an income expense item that needs to be disclosed separately in the Income Statement and Statement of Cash Flows. However, under the Shariah requirements, since interest is a prohibited item, it needs to be separated from permitted items and dealt with differently. Shariah-compliant financial statements should disclose the amount and nature of earnings that have been realised from sources not permitted by Shariah. Similarly, disclosures should also be made of the amount and nature of expenditures for purposes not permitted by Shariah. In the case where the component of earnings or expenditure consists of permitted and prohibited items, the business entity should segregate the prohibited and permitted income earnings. Additionally, the Shariah-compliant business entities should disclose how they intend to dispose of the assets generated by the prohibited income or acquired through prohibited expenditure. Practically, since the income or assets generated from the prohibited items cannot be used for business purpose and Zakah, they are frequently disposed of by way of donations (charity).

ISLAMIC ACCOUNTING AND AUDITING STANDARDS

The claim that financial reports premised on Anglo-American accounting thoughts and practices inadequately service the needs of Islamic economies was first made in the 1980s (AAOIFI 2003, p. xxiii). Claims of inadequacy persist given that approved standards do not address Islamic accounting issues. Hence, although the approved standards are useful in providing a structural framework for reporting, they are inadequate to accommodate Shariah requirements which form the basis of all Islamic transactions. This creates the need to have accounting and auditing standards for Shariah-compliant business entities (AAOIFI 2003, p. xxiii).

The need to disclose information relating to matters that comply with the Shariah requirements has resulted in the issuance of international Islamic standards by the AAOIFI.[10] The AAOIFI, an international autonomous non-profit-making corporate body, was formed in 1991 in the State of Bahrain, with the primary objective being to develop accounting, auditing, governance and ethical thought relating to the activities of Islamic financial institutions that comply with Islamic Shariah requirements. To date, the AAOIFI has issued 56 standards on accounting, auditing, governance, ethical and Shariah standards including a statement on capital adequacy.[11]

The interest in developing financial accounting standards for Islamic financial institutions commenced in 1987 (AAOIFI 2003c, p. 4). The Islamic banking and finance industry was concerned that the then International Accounting Standards (IAS) which were unable to incorporate the Shariah requirements related to the business entities' activities, the differences in the economic substance of many of the Islamic-compliant business entities' operations and the different needs of users of the Islamic-compliant financial reports (AAOIFI 2003, pp. xxiii–xxiv). Consultative groups and experts[12] recommended the urgent need to have the objectives, concepts and standards of financial reporting fully compliant with the Shariah requirements. The lack of approved standards to be applied by Islamic financial institutions has a negative effect on the confidence of users of the financial statements and impedes the comparability of financial reports. For instance, if prohibited items, such as interest, are not separated from permitted items, users are skeptical about the amount and status of the reported earnings (AAOIFI 2003, p. xxiii). Further, prior to application of the AAOIFI standards, Islamic financial institutions differed in the treatment of the accounting profit on profit-sharing investment accounts (Karim, 2001). For instance, financial institutions in Malaysia, Egypt and Sudan used the on-balance sheet approach, whereas institutions in Bahrain, Saudi Arabia and Lebanon treated the item as an off-balance sheet (Karim, 2003).

The objectives of the AAOIFI (AAOIFI 2003, p. x–xi) are to:

- Develop accounting, auditing, governance and ethical thought relating to the activities of Islamic financial institutions taking into consideration the international standards and practices which comply with Shariah requirements.

- Disseminate accounting, auditing, governance and ethical thoughts relating to the activities of Islamic financial institutions and its application through training seminars, publication of periodical newsletters, preparation of reports, research and through other means.

- Harmonise the accounting policies and procedures adopted by Islamic financial institutions through the preparation and issuance of accounting standards and the interpretations of the same to the said institutions.

- Improve the quality and uniformity of auditing and governance practices relating to Islamic financial institutions through the preparation and issuance of auditing and governance standards and the interpretation of the same to the said institutions.

- Promote good ethical practices relating to Islamic financial institutions through the preparation and issue of codes of ethics applicable to these institutions.

- Achieve conformity or similarity, to the extent possible, in concepts and applications among the Shariah supervisory boards[13] of Islamic financial institutions to avoid contradiction and inconsistency between the fatwas[14] and the applications by these institutions, with a view to activate the role of the Shariah supervisory boards of Islamic financial institutions and central banks through the preparation, issue and interpretations of Shariah standards and Shariah requirements for investment, financing and insurance.

- Approach the concerned regulatory bodies, Islamic financial institutions, other financial institutions that offer Islamic financial services, and accounting and auditing firms in order to implement the standards, as well as the statements and guidelines published by the AAOIFI.

The AAOIFI effort has gained international recognition as the standards have been used either as guidelines by the regulators (capital market or accounting bodies), or implemented by the leading Islamic banking and finance centres globally. Among countries that apply AAOIFI standards are Sudan, Bahrain, Jordan, Malaysia, Qatar and Saudi Arabia. To encourage the application and enforcement of the Islamic standards globally, the AAOIFI ensures that the standard setting process constitutes strong cooperation among interested parties and that the standards are of high quality. The membership of AAOIFI has grown tremendously since its establishment. The organisation's membership consists of 115 institutional members from 27 countries.[15]

GLOBALISATION OF ACCOUNTING STANDARDS: THE MALAYSIAN APPROACH

Malaysian Institutional Background

Generally, countries have their own particular accounting systems based on their economies, politics and social customs. Ball et. al. (2003) cites variations in accounting standards across countries being due to the interplay of market and political forces. The market forces refer to the economic variables (such as the size of businesses and capital market and the level of accounting information required) which set the country's economic policy. Political forces refer to the government's intervention in prescribing the accounting standards applicable in the country. Therefore, it is crucial to examine the market and political factors in the study of the development of accounting practices in Malaysia.

Malaysian accounting regulations are different from many capitalist countries due to the dominant role played by the government. Ball et al. (2003) indicates that the Malaysian government has taken more interventionist roles in standard setting and financial reporting practices through the establishment of several government agencies operating for the welfare and benefit of the government.

The Development of Accounting Standard Setting in Malaysia

The development of accounting standard setting in Malaysia commenced with its independence from Britain in 1957. Since then, the development of accounting standards in Malaysia has progressed in several phases. Interestingly, the earliest development was initiated by the professional accounting bodies and has only recently been shifted to an independent body with the mandate to develop, review and approve the accounting standards in Malaysia. This section focuses on the development of accounting standard setting and highlights several factors that have contributed to Malaysia's economic growth.

The development of standard setting in Malaysia began with the establishment of the Malaysian Certified Public Accountants (MACPA) in 1958.[16] This initiative was seen as the collective efforts of practising accountants to protect their interests. However, the role of MACPA became crucial when the Malaysian economy grew significantly in the 1960s. Since MACPA was the only active local accountancy body, it was responsible for meeting the demands for qualified accountants in Malaysia. A problem arose when there were many accountants in Malaysia with different academic and training backgrounds, for example UK, US and Australian. Hence, the establishment of the Malaysian Companies Act in 1965 and the enactment of the Accountants Act 1967 were pivotal in regulating and controlling the accounting profession. The former set up the scope for financial reporting which highlights the legal and regulatory framework that governs company legislation in Malaysia, while the latter is to provide assistance for the registration of qualified accountants. This constitution was established by the Malaysian government as it recognised the importance for the local authority to regulate and control accounting practice. Hence, the 1967 Accountant's Act led to the establishment of the Malaysian Institute of Accountants (MIA) as a statutory accounting body responsible for ensuring that only suitable qualified persons are admitted to the accounting profession. For many years, the development of Malaysian accounting practice resided with these two professional accounting bodies (MIA and the then MACPA). Generally, the MIA dominated the statutory aspect of the accounting profession while the then MACPA dominated the development of accounting practices through conducting local examinations for qualified accountants and the adoption of the IAS.

The winds of change began with the establishment of the Financial Reporting Act (FRA) 1997. The new era of financial reporting is facilitating the development of accounting standards setting in Malaysia with the establishment of a two-tier framework, comprising the Financial Reporting Foundation (FRF) and the Malaysian Accounting Standard Board (MASB) under the enactment of FRA 1997. Within this framework, the FRF and the MASB are responsible for the development, review and approval of accounting standards in Malaysia.

Generally, the new framework comprises a single national body of accountants (MASB) that takes over the role of accounting standards setting which was previously dominated by the professional accounting bodies. The FRF comprises prominent members of the accounting profession and the industry, and acts as the trustee body to oversee matters concerning performance and funding arrangements of the MASB.

Currently, the MASB is fully responsible for the development of accounting standards in Malaysia. It has the sole authority to set legally binding accounting standards and to develop and promote high quality accounting and reporting standards that are consistent with international practices. The MASB has prescribed the policy of convergence with standards issued by the International Accounting Standards Board (IASB). In line with the policy of convergence, the MASB Standards are generally numbered the same as the equivalent IFRS, but with a FRS prefix.[17] However, the MASB has issued additional standards which are relevant to meeting the needs of a particular industry or the local reporting or statutory requirements. When there is no equivalent IFRS, the MASB will issue a specific standard to fulfill these needs. The issue of Islamic Accounting Standards (e.g., MASB FRS*i* -1) to meet the local requirements for Islamic financial institutions is an example of this. To date, the MASB has issued 33 standards as approved accounting standards for application by business entities in Malaysia.[18]

Malaysian cultural diversity had also contributed to the policies underlying accounting regulation. Malaysia adapts the capitalist economic approach that is based on the mixed economic system of private enterprises with strong government support. However, government interventions are rare in Malaysia because the government chooses to interfere through separate statutory bodies but they are monitored closely by government agencies. For example, the operations of the Central Bank of Malaysia (Bank Negara Malaysia – BNM) and the Securities Commissions (SC) are mainly due to the Government's directives but operated as separate entities and their operations are closely monitored by the Ministry of Finance.

Malaysia's Approach to the Globalisation of Shariah-Compliant Accounting Standards

The Islamic Capital Market (ICM) refers to the market where activities are carried out in ways that do not conflict with Islamic requirements, or are free from Shariah prohibited activities such as usury (riba), gambling (maisir) and speculation (gharar). The ICM today is part of the overall capital market in Malaysia, functioning as a parallel market to the conventional capital market for capital seekers and providers. It also has played a complementary role to the

Islamic banking system in broadening and deepening the Islamic financial markets in Malaysia.[19]

In recent years, there has been a rapid growth in the demand for the identification of capital market transactions that are free from Shariah-prohibited activities. Accordingly, the Shariah-compliance counter in the local market was established to meet the public demand for capital transactions that are Shariah-compliant. The Kuala Lumpur Shariah Index (KLSI) was launched on 17 April 1997 to meet demands from local and foreign investors seeking to invest in securities which are consistent with Shariah requirements. The index identifies Shariah-compliant firms and acts as a benchmark for tracking the performance of Shariah-approved securities. Shariah-compliant firms are Bursa Malaysia listed firms whose activities conform to the Shariah requirements.[20] In the Malaysian equity market, 857 securities or 85 per cent of Bursa Malaysia's total listed securities are classified as Shariah-compliant securities.[21] Currently, although listed as Shariah-compliant securities, firms are not required to apply the MASB FRS*i*, but are encouraged to do so (MASB FRS*i*-1, paras 1–2).

In conjunction with the Shariah-compliance demand, Malaysia has experienced a tremendous growth in the Islamic financial institution industry, comprising Islamic banking, Islamic insurance (takaful) and the Islamic capital market within the global financial market.[22] Recognising the growing awareness of, and global demand for, investing in accordance with Shariah requirements, the Malaysian government has played a major role in the development of the Islamic capital market. Through the BNM, the National Shariah Advisory Council on Islamic Banking and Takaful (NSAC)[23] was established on 1 May 1997, with three primary objectives. First, to act as the sole authoritative body to advise BNM on Islamic banking and takaful operations; second, to coordinate Shariah issue with respect to Islamic banking and finance, and third, to analyse and evaluate Shariah aspects of new products or schemes submitted by the banking institutions and takaful companies. The SC also supported the Government's effort and formed an Islamic Capital Market Unit (ICMU), with the mandate to carry out research and development activities including formulating and facilitating a long-term plan to strengthen the Islamic capital market in Malaysia.[24] The Shariah Advisory Council (SAC) of SC was established on 16 May 1996 to ensure that the running of the Islamic capital market complies with Shariah requirements. The Council is a focal point of reference on all issues relating to the Islamic capital market and Shariah, such as Islamic trust funds and other Islamic capital market products, schemes and institutions. In addition, the Islamic Financial Accounting Working Committee (IFAWC) which was formed by the MICPA, provides technical support and advice in respect of Islamic reporting and accounting standards to the SAC (Majid 1997).

With the development of the Islamic banking and financial system, the growth in Islamic-based transactions and the promotion of the Islamic capital market, Malaysia recognised the need for financial reporting standards to service users' needs. In the absence of a comprehensive set of accounting standards, Islamic financial institutions (IFIs) and conventional banks providing Islamic banking services relied on guidelines issued by the BNM, through the then NSAC, and on Shariah rulings issued by Shariah advisors appointed by the respective banks.[25] The absence of a specific set of accounting standards for the recognition, measurement, and disclosure of Islamic-based transactions complicates or hinders comparability of the financial statements among banks or between periods for individual banks.

Recognising the need to have a standard that could cater for Shariah-compliant financial reporting and also the market forces that demand Islamic reporting of financial transactions, Malaysia fully supports the AAOIFI's efforts in issuing accounting standards for IFIs. The standards issued by AAOIFI serve as a reference for countries establishing accounting and auditing norms and requirements for Shariah-compliant financial reports. Adoption of AAOIFI standards by Islamic financial institutions will facilitate financial reporting comparability. However, considering the needs of Islamic financial practices, and the regulatory as well as economic structure in Malaysia, a local accounting standard for financial institutions is needed that serves to bridge the gap in areas that the IFRS and AAOIFI's Islamic Accounting Standards have not been able to address (Summary of MASB FRS*i*-1).

In formulating the standard for Islamic financial institutions in Malaysia, the MASB has given careful consideration to the substance of the AAOIFI standards. The MASB also gives due cognisance to various local and international aspects: the existing regulatory framework in Malaysia; the accounting standards issued by other international bodies, namely the IFRS issued by the IASB; the requirements of the Companies Act 1965; the Basle requirements and the requirements of GP8 Guidelines on the Specimen Financial Statements for the Banking Industry issued by the BNM. The MASB also recognises the fundamental importance of Shariah requirements in developing the standard and has established a formal structure that allows for issues relating to Shariah to be referred to the SAC of BNM.

As the first step to achieve Shariah-compliant standards for financial reporting in Malaysia, the MASB FRS*i*-1 Presentation of Financial Statements of Islamic Financial Institutions was developed, based on a careful consideration of the substance of the AAOIFI standard. The objective of MASB FRS*i*-1 is to prescribe the presentation and disclosure of financial statements of Islamic financial institutions conducting Islamic banking activities. Apart from providing guidelines for the structure and content of the financial reports, the standard aims to harmonise accounting practices especially in areas where Shariah requirements allow for different accounting treatments and alternatives, for example, the allocation and distribution of profits to depositors.[26] Being the first Shariah-compliant accounting standard in Malaysia, MASB FRS*i*-1 serves to bridge the gap for areas not addressed by the IAS and AAOIFI's Islamic Accounting Standards (Summary of MASB FRS*i*-1). Currently, the MASB FRS*i*-1 is mandatory only for IFIs and conventional banks and other financial institutions that participate in the Islamic Banking Schemes (IBS). Recognising future needs and demand for Islamic banking and capital markets in Malaysia, the MASB has approved a structural framework and due process to develop Islamic accounting standards for application, initially by IFIs, and hopes to extend the standards to all entities, for example clients of IFI, at a later stage (MASB FRS*i*-1, Appendix A).

CONCLUSION

The AAOIFI was registered on 11 Ramadhan 1411H (27 March 1991) in the State of Bahrain, as a response to the claim that existing international standards were inadequate to cater for the Islamic banking and finance industry needs. As an international autonomous non-profit-making corporate body, the AAOIFI is responsible for pronouncing accounting, auditing, governance, ethics and Shariah standards for Islamic financial institutions. The fundamental differences in the underlying requirements, along with the distinctive nature of Islamic financial practices, result in the application of conventional accounting standards irrelevant to Shariah-compliant business operations. The demand for Shariah-compliant financial reports justifies a need for differential financial reporting standards.

Malaysia is supportive of the AAOIFI's efforts in issuing international accounting standards for Islamic financial institutions. However, based on the needs of Islamic financial practices, and the regulatory as well as economic structure in Malaysia, there is a need for local accounting standards for financial institutions to bridge the gap between IFRS and the AAOIFI's Islamic Accounting Standards. To do this, the MASB issued MASB FRS*i*-1 Presentation of Financial Statements of Islamic Financial Institutions with a mandatory application dating from 1 January 2003 for all financial institutions that conduct Islamic banking business. Recognising the need for a set of comprehensive guidelines and accounting standards to cater for the growth in Islamic-based transactions in Malaysia, the MASB has approved a structural framework and due process to develop Islamic accounting standards for all business entities. Other issues relating to the recognition, measurement and disclosure of specific Islamic-based transactions and events will be dealt with by the MASB, in other forthcoming Islamic standards.

NOTES

1 *Shariah* requirements refer to Shariah principles, rules and regulations, as used by MASB FRS*i*-1 Presentation of Financial Statements of Islamic Financial Institutions.
2 Quran is the Holy book for Muslims, Sunnah are the acts or sayings of Prophet Muhammad (peace be upon him).
3 *Zakah* is due on different types of assets/items.
4 Under the Shariah requirements, only trading assets are subject to Zakah. Fixed assets are not considered as trading assets, unless they are subsequently sold in trading and Zakah becomes due if other conditions for Zakah are fulfilled (AAOIFI 2003b, Appendix D).
5 Fatwas of the Seventh Seminar on Contemporary Issues of Zakah, Kuwait, 1997.
6 2.5 per cent for a lunar calendar year and 2.5775 per cent for a solar calendar year (AAOIFI, 2003b, para. 2).
7 Shariah advisors are a group of people who are knowledgeable in Shariah requirements, and appointed by the respective business entities to advise on Shariah rulings pertaining to the business operations.
8 Qard literally means loan.
9 Interest is known as Riba under the Shariah requirements.
10 The founding members of AAOIFI are the Islamic Development Bank, Dar Al-Maal Al-Islami (Switzerland), Al Rajhi Banking and Investment Corporation (Saudi Arabia), Dallah Albaraka Group (Saudi Arabia) and Kuwait Finance House (Kuwait).
11 As at November 2005.
12 Those studies were financed by the Islamic Development Banks in 1987, and were discussed by four different committees comprising several Shariah and accounting scholars, officials from Islamic banks, representatives of regulatory agencies, certified public accountants and other relevant parties.
13 A Shariah supervisory board is an independent body of specialised jurists in Islamic commercial jurisprudence and (may include) experts in the field of Islamic financial institutions with knowledge of Islamic commercial jurisprudence. The board is entrusted with the duty of directing, reviewing and supervising business activities in order to ensure that they comply with Islamic Shariah rules and requirements.
14 Fatwa is a legal statement in Islam, issued by a mufti or a religious lawyer, on a specific issue. Fatwas are asked for by judges or individuals, and are needed in cases where an issue of fiqh is undecided or uncertain.
15 www.aaoifi.com, accessed 18 April 2005.
16 Currently known as the Malaysian Institute of Certified Public Accountants (MICPA), effective from 29 January 2002.
17 For example, IAS 116 Property, Plant and Equipment is known as MASB FRS 116 Property, Plant and Equipment.
18 As at 14 December 2005.
19 www.sc.com.my/eng/html/icm/icmmain.html, accessed 3 October 2005.
20 The general criteria in evaluating the status of Shariah-approved securities are that the companies are not involved in financial services based on riba; gambling, manufacture or sale of non-halal products or related products; conventional insurance; entertainment activities that are not permissible according to Shariah; manufacture or sale of tobacco-based products or related products; stockbroking or share trading in Shariah non-approved securities; and other activities deemed non-permissible according to Shariah.
21 As at 20 October 2005. The breakdown of Shariah-compliant securities to total securities according to sectors are 91 per cent Consumer Product, 94 per cent Industrial Product, 100 per cent Mining, 100 per cent Construction, 81 per cent Trading/Services, 81 per cent Properties, 91 per cent Plantation, 95 per cent Technology, 78 per cent Infrastructure, 7 per cent Finance, 0 per cent Hotel, 0 per cent Close End Fund.

22 As at 30 June 2004, there were 65 Islamic funds with net asset value of RM5.4 billion and a market share of 7.2 per cent. Since 1993, the net asset value of the Islamic funds has been growing at a staggering 47.6 per cent whilst the total industry grew at 9.6 per cent annually (Mahmood, 2004).
23 Currently known as Shariah Advisory Council (SAC) of BNM.
24 www.sc.com.my/eng/html/icm/icmmain.html.
25 Consistent with AAOIFI (2003a) requirement, MASB FRS*i*-1 Para 71 requires Islamic financial institutions to appoint and disclose the role and authority of the Shariah advisor or board in monitoring the entity's activities pertaining to Shariah matters.
26 Most fuqaha are of the opinion the distribution of profit shall be made at gross level (before deductions for indirect expenses, for example salaries, rental), while some are of the view that indirect expenses can be deducted from the funds (MASB FRS*i*-1, Appendix B). MASB FRS*i*-1 adopts the first method.

ACKNOWLEDGEMENTS

We gratefully acknowledge the support from the Monash Institute for the Study of Global Movements and Monash University Malaysia and comments of the participants at the Globalisation of Accounting Standards Conference in Prato, Italy in May 2005. We also thank Jayne Godfrey and Keryn Chalmers for their patience and support throughout the process.

REFERENCES

AAOIFI (2003), *Accounting, Auditing and Governance Standards for Islamic Financial Institutions*, Bahrain: AAOIFI.
AAOIFI (2003a), 'Financial Accounting Standard No. 1: General Presentation and Disclosure in the Financial Statements of Islamic Banks and Financial Institutions', in AAOIFI (2003), pp. 6–11.
AAOIFI (2003b), 'Financial Accounting Standard No. 9, Zakah', in AAOIFI (2003), pp. 274–95.
AAOIFI (2003c), 'Statement of Financial Accounting No. 1: Objectives of Financial Accounting for Islamic Banks and Financial Institutions', in AAOIFI (2003), pp. 2–19.
Ball. R., Robin, A. and Wu, J.S. (2003), 'Incentives versus standards: Properties of accounting income in four East Asian countries', *Journal of Accounting Economics*, **36**(1-3), 235–70.
Karim, R.A.A. (2001), 'International accounting harmonization, banking regulation, and Islamic banks', *The International Journal of Accounting*, **36**, 169–93.
Karim, R.A.A. (2003), Interest, morality and Islamic banking, Keynote Address at the International Islamic Banking Conference, Italy, September 9-11.
Mahmood, N.R. (2004), 'Legal and Shariah Issues in Islamic Capital Market', National Seminar on Corporation, Corporate Law and Corporate Governance: Islamic Perspective, www.sc.com.my/eng/html/resources/speech/sp_20040914.html.
Malaysian Accounting Standard Board (MASB) (2005), FRS*i*-1: Presentation of Financial Statements of Islamic Financial Institutions, Kuala Lumpur: MASB.
Majid, M.M.A. (1997), Public Hearing of Islamic Accounting and Auditing Standards (www.sc.com.my/eng/html/resources/speech/1997/sp_97402.pdf).

16 Globalisation and Accounting Reforms in an Emerging Market Economy: A Case Study of South Africa

Iain Edwards, Peter Schelluch, Adel Du Plessis, Jean Struweg and Andrew West

INTRODUCTION

This chapter highlights the results of extensive literature searches and structured interviews conducted with technical and training partners of accounting firms as well as other senior officials, business executives and educators during 2005. Areas covered include the political, cultural and economic impacts of transformation in South Africa on the accounting profession and its adoption of global accounting standards; the role of the profession in harmonising South African and International Financial Reporting Standards as well as the pragmatic problems associated with the adoption of IFRS. It also looks at how the adoption and implementation of IFRS has impacted on the educational needs of practitioners, clients and higher education and the increasingly pivotal role of the South African government and the South African accounting profession in economic developments in Africa as a whole.

THE CHALLENGES OF POST-APARTHEID GLOBALISING SOUTH AFRICA

Since the late 1980s South Africa has been fundamentally transformed by two processes of rapid macro-change. The first process is the politically-driven transition from Apartheid which, formally beginning in 1990, culminated in the formation of the first democratically elected government in 1994. Contemporaneously, after decades of economic and political isolation, South Africa is becoming incorporated into the now globalising international economy.

This dual-pronged character is reflected in post-Apartheid South Africa's political and economic goals. First, to transform a crisis ridden and isolated racial capitalist economy, which provided rich benefits to a white minority, into a more sustainable economy offering tangible material benefits to the majority of its citizens. The second task has been to shape state, state-owned enterprises and private corporate policies and practice to gain strategic advantage within global and not simply national contexts. The direct consequence of this has been the dramatic transformation of many of the fundamental structural characteristics of the South African political economy.

However, the two ongoing processes of post-Apartheid restructuring and global economic incorporation and insertion are neither simply mutually inclusive nor exclusive. Key characteristics of the post-Apartheid South African state, political parties and the corporate and civil society sectors hinge on how imperative elements of these two processes have joined or collided, either promoting or impeding particular forms of political stability, economic growth and social change. Indeed, as South Africa moves steadily away from Apartheid and its racial capitalist foundations, public discourses are being shaped more and more by highly contested debates over the relationships between sought-after social policy and the strengths and weaknesses of globalisation (Bezuidenhout 2000; Biggs and Abedian 1999; Bond 2004 and Harris 2005; *This Day* 2004).

Ten years after democracy South Africa looks less back to rid itself of the vestiges of Apartheid than forward into a globalised future.

IFRS and Accounting Transformation in South Africa

In a little over ten years, the accountancy profession in South Africa has undergone rapid and significant changes. These changes reflect closely integrated aspects of the dual-pronged state-driven processes of change. Although largely hidden from public scrutiny and debate, the role of the accounting profession in the structural transformations of post-Apartheid South Africa, and in particular the processes of globalisation, should not be underestimated. The centerpiece in this process, as driven by the South African government, has been South Africa's adoption of new Statements of Generally Accepted Accounting Practice (GAAP) based to a large extent on the International Financial Reporting Standards (IFRS), formerly known as the International Accounting Standards (IAS), as promulgated by the International Accounting Standards Board (IASB) and the International Federation of Accountants (IFAC) (South African Institute of Chartered Accountants 2003 and Werksmans 2005). This transformation applies to publicly listed companies, parliament, all three levels of government and state-owned enterprises (SOEs). Transformation commenced in 1993 and was effectively completed by 2004. With effect from 1 January 2005 all companies on the JSE Securities Exchange South Africa (JSE), previously the Johannesburg Stock Exchange, are required to comply with IFRS (*The Sunday Times* 2005).

Beginning in the mid 1990s this transformation to IFRS was known as the 'harmonization project'. This project was coordinated by the South African Institute of Chartered Accountants (SAICA) through its Accounting Practices Committee in conjunction with the government's own transformation of public sector accounting standards. The goal was a rapid and smooth transformation of accounting standards in both the public and private sectors (Boshoff and Carstens). This process was all but complete by 1 January 2005, when the IFRS were adopted and became applicable to all listed companies in South Africa with a financial year end on or after 31 December 2005.

The internationalisation of both accounting and auditing standards has been described by David Damant, a former board member of the IAS Committee as 'the most revolutionary development in accounting in our professional careers' (*The Sunday Times* 2005). Some envisage a future where, with a convergence between IFRS and the FASB (US standard setter), there will be one set of global accounting standards (De Beer 2003). As an emerging new market economy, it is very significant that South Africa took such a step to implement the IFRS long before many far more powerful globalised economies.

The comparisons are stark and significant and have been noted by international analysts. South Africa's decisions to globalise its accounting and auditing standards place it well ahead of the European Union which requires that all listed companies complied with IAS by 2005. In 2003, New Zealand was still considering such a step as were the Asian standard setters. Other developing countries are still struggling to align their national standards with the new international codes.[1] Ian Mackintosh, chairman of the IFAC's Public Sector Committee has applauded South Africa's decision to adopt international public sector accounting standards. Indeed South Africa is the first country to use the IPSASs for the development of GAAP in its governance structures (IFAC 2001). Noting the leading role of the JSE, David Damant has commented that as a result 'South Africa was in a better position than other countries to adopt the new standard [and that] unlike any other country in the world, South Africa won't have to make many changes 'in implementing new "fair value" accounting principles' (*The Sunday Times* 2005).

IFAC has clearly recognised the urgent need for the accountancy profession in developing countries to move rapidly to adopt the new international standards. In so doing IFAC operates very closely with both the World Bank and the United Nations Conference on Trade and Development (Uctad) to ensure that new accounting standards are an inextricable component of wider development projects including capital investment and aid and the implementation of appropriate standards of good governance.[2] These interlinked goals were also highlighted at the World Economic Forum's 'African Economic Summit' held in South Africa in 2003 (World Economic Forum 2003). In its recent study of the accountancy profession in Sub-Saharan Africa the World Bank noted the convergence between accounting standards, good governance and African economic development:

> In many countries in Sub-Saharan Africa (SSA), accounting and auditing performance has been unsatisfactory over the past many years. This is due primarily to a critical shortage of accountants at all levels, the lack of recognised and accepted accounting and auditing standards, and the inadequacy of accounting development. ... Numerous studies of accounting in SSA have concluded that sustained economic growth cannot be maintained without a sound accounting infrastructure and an appropriately trained accounting profession (The World Bank Group 1996).

In steering African states into a globalised future, it is remarkable to note how institutions of global governance and finance and the IFAC have identified the strategic importance of the South African government and South Africa's economic sectors and accountancy profession.

State Policies and Strategies: Regional, National and Global

There are six significant reasons why and how South Africa adopted these standards when they did. The reasons are the need for the post-Apartheid government to restructure and gain control of public accounts; the need to restructure the legal regimes of public and private business; the need for foreign direct investment (FDI); global demands for good governance protocols; South Africa's foreign polices; and crises within the late-Apartheid accountancy profession. These reasons provide illuminating insights into the nature of the accounting profession in Apartheid South Africa and globalising processes in late-developing democracies; in particular the powerful role which nation states can play in influencing the trajectories of globalisation.[3]

In the late 1980s, as the exiled African National Congress (ANC) prepared for negotiations and ultimately accession to power, the ANC's London office, under the leadership of Thabo Mbeki, approached KPMG for advice on future macroeconomic policy (*Accountancy Age* 2001). Despite its anti-free market capitalist public statements, the ANC was gradually quietly pursuing quite contrary agendas, often through pressure from organised business (ANC 1990; Bond 2005; Natrass 1994).

In similar vein, despite much anti-globalisation public rhetoric and political discourse, the South African government's responses to globalisation have been complexly nuanced and highly strategic. The South African government does not see globalisation as simply and essentially postcolonial exploitation by northern hemisphere multinationals. For the South African government globalisation is not an externally driven process which impinges and reshapes the parameters in which South Africa has to move from its Apartheid past (*Afrikaanse Handelsinstituut* 2001; Loots 2001). Instead the government believes that if approached strategically, well-placed initiatives will influence the character of the globalisation process and enhance the country's strategic position in a globalising world.[4] This strategic outlook is clearly evident in key areas of state policy throughout the first ten years of democracy. These areas are the need for FDI, the restructuring of public accounts, good governance, the restructuring of state assets and the major South African foreign policy initiative: the New Plan for African Development (NEPAD). This plan is now the cornerstone of African inter-state discourse and the founding principles of the Pan African Parliament, inaugurated in March 2004 and headquartered in Johannesburg.

It has been through this overall strategic outlook and its multifaceted policy that the South African government is intent upon accomplishing its two main tasks: developing the structural base of a post-Apartheid South Africa and inserting the country into and influencing the processes of globalisation to its benefit. So, as the South African government pursues the NEPAD policies, the government is using international financial reporting standards and equity legislation aimed at increasing the role of a black professional and business elite. The Black Economic Empowerment (BEE) policy and legislation serves as the central thrust to gain control of, restructure and legitimate SOEs and alter the regulatory framework of the public and private economic sectors (Van der Westhuizen 2002).

In order to effect these substantial policy directions the government has moved steadily, often after close consultation with institutions of global finance and other organised business interests, to alter the regulatory frameworks of the public and private economic sectors. A cornerstone of these strategic initiatives has been South Africa's active participation in assisting with the formulation and adoption of IFRS. Simply put, the introduction of IFRS is central to the ANC government's initiatives to achieve global, continental and specifically South African strategic objectives.

South Africa is now a major player in the globalisation of Africa (African Development Bank 2003; Ayittey 2005; Cheruzed 2002). Indeed the South African government is intent upon influencing strategies other African governments use in adapting to a globalising world.[5] Gradually African states are now resisting processes of globalisation less than embracing them (Stevenson 2002).[6] South Africa is the uncontested economic powerhouse of southern Africa.

South Africa is also one of the top three economic engines of Africa, along with Nigeria and Egypt. After decades of economic and political isolation during the Apartheid period, the democratic South African government has steadily and persistently focused on an ambitious foreign policy initiative. This is to integrate and expand into and gain political legitimacy within not only southern Africa but the wider continent, particularly Sub-Saharan Africa. Ten years on, the South African government is now in a position where it provides leadership, represents and is actively seeking to develop other countries in Sub-Saharan Africa.

A central feature of this initiative is the increasingly powerful role which South African SOEs and the private sector are now playing in investing in, developing and restructuring state and private economies and regulatory regimes in the rest of Africa (Melber 2004). Overall, in political and economic terms these initiatives have been extremely successful, but with often contradictory side effects. On the one hand, for example, through deals brokered between the South African and Angolan governments, 140 South African companies are active in Angola with future billion US dollar joint ventures in the pipeline. Similarly Eskom, South Africa's SOE power utility has investments in some 31 other African countries and is currently upgrading and linking up the Sub-Saharan African power grid in a three phase US$500 million project funded by the World Bank. South African BEE consortia are becoming increasingly powerful economic forces in Sub-Saharan Africa. On the other hand, African states do express a concern over being 'colonised' by Africa's post-Apartheid South African powerhouse.[7] Similarly, as the chief economist of the International Finance Corporation (IFC), the private-sector arm of the World Bank recently noted, many African and southern hemisphere governments still seem 'hell-bent on discouraging the very trade and investment that would benefit their own economies and their own home-grown companies'.[8]

In order to provide a massive boost to Africa's private sector, the IFC is to treble its support for continental initiatives over the next five years to more than one billion US dollars a year. A substantial amount of these funds are to be allocated to smaller South African companies in order to assist such companies in investing in other parts of Africa. The central emphasis in the overall project will be on infrastructural investment and development. It is highly significant that this IFC initiative comes at the same time as the World Bank and IFAC have recognised the need to raise accounting standards in Africa: an issue now formally recognised as an objective within the NEPAD protocols. The World Bank recognises SAICA as having to play a pivotal role. In its efforts to encourage the development and transformation of African economies the World Bank and the IFC are clearly adopting a carrot and stick approach, with South Africa at the cutting edge: the World Bank will provide capital for infrastructure and require that African countries upgrade their standards of accounting and embrace global standards of good governance.[9]

ACCOUNTANCY IN SOUTH AFRICA: POWER AND TRANSFORMATION

In effecting structural changes to the South African economy the government has worked exceptionally closely with the 'Big Five' and now 'Big Four' global accounting and assurance services and consulting and advisory services firms. All these international firms all have offices not only in South Africa but also southern Africa and throughout Africa. Of these, Deloitte & Touche has 21 offices located in all but one of the South African Development Community (SADC) countries: namely Angola, Botswana, Malawi, Mozambique, South Africa, Swaziland and Zimbabwe. The majority of the current Big-Four have historic origins with some of South Africa's oldest and most prestigious accounting firms that go back to early patterns of modern global economic development through cumulative mergers and incorporations (Hopkins 2003). The global firm Ernst & Young has historic associations with South African commercial agencies dating back to 1850. Deloitte & Touche's South African origins also date back to the nineteenth century and since 1990 through a series of mergers with prominent South African accounting firms.

The power of these global firms in South African accounting and auditing is notable. In 2003 approximately 67 per cent of South African publicly traded companies used the services of the Big Four. Four South African firms have international affiliation and audit approximately 19 per cent of the country's publicly traded companies. The remaining 14 per cent of auditing services is taken by 52 South African national firms (World Bank 2003).

The Big Four's power is attributable to four factors. First, power came from the extended global reach of these firms. Second, all these firms had diversified their operations from accounting and auditing into a range of nationally and globally sought-after financial and advisory services. South African firms had neither the resources, experience nor, until the 1990s, the reasons to provide such services. Third, the Big Four had more compellingly professional public profiles than did many purely South African firms. Finally, and most importantly, the global accounting firms quickly assumed an increasingly powerful role as corporate advisors to the South African government. In September 1995, Deloitte & Touche prepared one of the first reports on the privatisation of state assets with Deloitte & Touche partner Jeff van Rooyen becoming a government advisor. Deloitte & Touche were also consultant advisors in the transformation of the South African National Defence Force. KPMG Global Edge, Ernst & Young,

Price Waterhouse and Coopers and Lybrand (now PricewaterhouseCoopers) have advised on aspects of privatisation, labour relations, the provision of government services and other central aspects of state restructuring. The close professional associations between the Big Four and the South African government have caused continual tensions within the ANC and between the ANC and its alliance partners, the Congress of South African Trade Unions, the South African Communist Party and within ANC-aligned non-governmental organisations. Despite such pressure from its own organised political constituents the links between the South African government and the Big Four continue to grow.

During the process of adopting global accounting and auditing standards, the South African accounting profession has accepted the need for the substantial transformation of accounting standards, membership of the profession and professional ethics, the need to gain government legitimacy and the benefits of government's policies and initiatives. Over the years SAICA, the major professional body, has moved to both gain acceptance of the problem areas within the profession and adopt polices and plans to follow national frameworks in resolving these issues. Under the aegis of adopting global standards the profession has moved to resolve six related issues. These are poor public perceptions of the standards and services of the profession; the need for new ethical good governance protocols, arising from both local and worldwide examples of poor accounting and auditing performances; the need for reforms of legal statutory frameworks; reviewing educational qualifications; the need for BEE in a traditionally white and male dominated profession; and southern African regional institutional professional affiliation and collegial involvement). These cover the entire ambit of the activities of the accounting profession. It is significant that the profession has managed to effect substantial changes in a short space of time under the aegis of a pace and framework set by government. Further, it is most significant that the accounting profession quickly saw the government's strategic wisdom in moving quickly to gain competitive advantage in being an early participant in the process of adopting IFRS (*Accountancy – SA* 1998–2000).

The Ambiguities of Transformation

This is by no means to state that these initiatives have all been successful or undertaken without conflicting developments. The very implementation of IFRS has also thrown up new challenges. As the South African government well knows, globalisation cannot be controlled by late developing emerging market democracies. Whilst restructuring the regulatory regimes for public and private economic activity to suit the needs of global capital markets is a necessary precondition for FDI, FDI is not an automatic consequence of such restructuring. South Africa has significant economic and related social problems: the state's delivery record is poor, unemployment has increased as have levels of poverty amongst the African majority and rural-urban quality of life figures reveal deep and growing disparities. As the South African government pursues its policies these conditions have deepened. This is not an uncommon characteristic in the globalising world (Mansbach and Rhodes 2000).

As has been the case for decades, South Africa has two economies: what President Mbeki refers to as the 'first' and 'second' economies. The first economy is increasingly less white and involves increasing numbers of the growing black capitalist and professional middle classes. For this economy, globalisation has largely been hugely lucrative. The second economy is almost totally African, and is characterised by low levels of skills, productivity, income and access to basic facilities. These structural features, originating in the political economy of racial capitalism during Apartheid, now have less to do with that past than the neo-liberal globalising policies followed by the South African government since 1994 (Harris, Zegeye and Auderdale 2005; ILO 2001; Love 1999). As a result, the main public discourses over the relationship between the state and its citizens and discourses within the ruling ANC alliance all continue to centre on challenges to state policies. And the state appears to be heeding such critiques – at least in part. SOEs are now seen not as organs to be privatised but as state engines for economic growth. In line with significant international thinking the South African government is now recognising the need for a developmental state.[10]

Transforming Accountancy: The Balance Sheet

The profession's response to the IFAC harmonisation process was rapid and deliberate, to ensure that the rewards of globalisation can be taken advantage of by the South African corporate sector as well as government policy initiatives. Over the last decade the South African accounting profession has made considerable efforts to achieve the goals of this 'harmonisation process'. However, despite and because of these efforts, a number of important issues remain unanswered. There are several related reasons for this state of affairs. These are the very rapid process of change itself; institutional weaknesses within the South African accounting profession as revealed by the process; and inherent tensions and contradictions between global and national needs and their reflection in accounting standards. These issues have manifested themselves in particular ways. All these issues reflect particular combinations of principled and technical professional accounting issues and more widely cultural institutional characteristics.

In early 2005, a survey by Ernst & Young revealed that 96 per cent of South Africa's listed companies polled were not on track to meet IASB 'improvements project' requirements on time.[11] Clearly South African companies have largely underestimated the enormity of the tasks required to achieve IFRS harmonisation and improvement. Indeed some practitioners claim that the implications of effecting IFRS implementation were downplayed within accounting circles. Despite the fact that considered opinion correctly holds that most South African companies are now still in a better IFRS compliance position than companies in many other countries where no equivalent of a harmonisation process was followed, the issues highlighted in the survey are undeniable.

There are two significant issues relating to accounting principles which have led to technical and implementation frustrations. First, appears to be the practicalities of implementing IFRS 1. This is a global phenomenon and not unique to South Africa. Even though there appears to be little or no difference between the local and international standards, interpretive differences do exist between South African practitioners and the international body. The second point of frustration for South African practitioners, highlighted from the implementation of IFRS 1 onwards, is the extreme normative nature of the international standards. Although the South Africa standards are very close to the international standards, more room for judgment was allowed in South Africa. Internationally, very little room is left for professional judgment and the letter of the standard is applied, even when reason dictates otherwise.

The harmonisation process has also thrown up inconsistencies and tensions between IFRS requirements and long-standing operational characteristics of leading South African economic sectors and national economic policies and plans. The adoption of IFRS has not suited all of South Africa's economic sectors. Two are particularly notable, and they span both ends of the economic scale.

First, at one end is the mining industry – historically since the late nineteenth century South Africa's major global economic sector. An extremely powerful player in South Africa's political economy, the mining industry initially did not get involved in the harmonisation process. However, given the increasingly global nature of South African mining interests, the mining sector later did become part of the process. Second, at the other end of the economic scale are small and medium-sized enterprises: SMEs. Both the South Africa state and private sector view this sector as playing a pivotal role in ameliorating poverty and increasing the links between the 'first' and 'second' economies.

Given the costs involved in applying IFRS, as well as the extensive disclosure requirements, many practitioners have been calling for a differential reporting framework for SMEs. This is common practice in many countries around the world. Many practitioners feel that South Africa will find itself in a situation where most small business financial statements are not fully compliant with IFRS. This adds to the risk that if a differential reporting framework is not introduced a culture of partial compliance may develop. On the other hand, implementing differential reporting standards for smaller business raises a range of different issues. These include the definition of an SME for accounting purposes as well as legislative issues. At the time of writing the reform of South African corporate legislation is underway, and it is hoped that the amended legislation will address the issues.

In South Africa the responsibility for IFRS compliance is frequently outsourced to the external auditor. As part of the annual audit the auditor is required to ensure that the relevant accounting standards are adhered to. In practice, where the accounting standards are not met, the auditors usually make recommendations for the client to implement in order to ensure compliance. Many companies in South Africa do not have the resources available to employ a knowledgeable person to ensure IFRS compliance, with this function becoming the responsibility of the financial manager or accountant. Most often such employees have neither the time nor knowledge to ensure proper IFRS compliance. The client then relies on the external auditor to ensure IFRS compliance, as part of the audit, but with the auditor having to prepare the information. This raises serious questions about the external auditor's independence to the client. It also increases the levels of risk for the auditor as information is prepared by the same entity that performs the external audit, effectively reducing the assurance value of an audit. Since the global accounting and financial scandals of the 1990s the need to separate accounting from external auditing has been made a priority in terms of the criteria for good governance.

Very few professionals in South Africa have a thorough grasp of IFRS requirements and the expectation is that, bar very few exceptions, only the big four firms have these skills at this stage. Practitioners have expressed concern that, due to a lack of knowledge, financial statements will be prepared to be as close to IFRS as possible, as opposed to being fully compliant. The profession runs a risk that a culture of partial compliance will develop within the accounting fraternity in South Africa. That would obviously have a negative impact on the profession in South Africa, as the quality of reporting will suffer, and reflect badly on the profession.

In addition to these issues of principle and technical reporting standards, there are a host of institutional issues relating to resources, professional skills, education and training and, in general, institutional characteristics of the accountancy profession in South Africa. If nothing else, the rapid pace of the harmonisation process has been fruitful in highlighting these issues. Some of these issues have long roots in South Africa's Apartheid past. Others relate to the particular mix of global, regional and national institutional characteristics in the post-Apartheid South African accountancy profession. Adapting these institutional characteristics in order to create a more global approach is a complex and potentially contradictory issue. The ways forward promise to be rather more long-term than many would have supposed or wished and will most probably embrace elements of global, national and regional features. Many of these features and their resolution are less within the powers of the accounting profession *per se* than characteristics of the changing South African and regional political economy.

EDUCATION AND TRAINING[12]

The Big-Four firms operating in South Africa share a common view of the issues of education and training. In the words of one partner, the Big Four's approach to global standards and training is readily summarised as 'global quality and consistency'. In their views, the critical period for improving accounting education and training in South Africa and moving them towards global standards occurred four to five years ago when South Africa commenced the harmonisation process. However, the need for such changes only became fully recognised as a pressing issue much later; prompted in large part by the JSE's listing requirement that all listed companies with year-ends commencing on or after 1 January 2005 must be IFRS compliant. Most of the Big Four's clients are listed on the JSE. As a result of the JSE's compliance requirements this resulted in these clients being over-reliant on the technical expertise of their auditors.

In South Africa up to 2004, as with most other countries, only a few professional accountants, primarily at partner and accounting technical manager level, have a detailed knowledge of IFRS and the requisite skills to apply these standards. All the Big-Four firms have set up in-house training schemes focused on IFRS training to both partner and manager levels. However, amongst the Big-Four educational strategies vary.

Big-Four firm (a) has appointed global accounting training consultants, focusing on the interpretation and implementation of IFRS in the global firm. In 2004 they also set up their own global policy board, with one of its main areas of focus being the development of an in-house IFRS training curriculum. So, personnel from their South African operations are selected to be trainers and sent to Europe for a specific 'train the trainer' course and then return to South Africa to train more trainers for their South African and African branches. All training had to be complete by December 2004. Their programme was reviewed by their own global policy board in February 2005. The firm operates ongoing tuition and updates.

At Big-Four firm (b) the approach is different. In-house training material is developed by the global firm, which can be accessed on the intranet by any employee in their own time. The technical department writes their own national IFRS material for the South African and other African offices. This material is based on the global training material but adjusted for specific South African circumstances. Training focuses on partners and managers with bi-weekly training sessions. Training to the other levels is done twice a year with 'technical updates'. The trainers are all in-house trainers from the South African Johannesburg office. Attendance is a competency requirement for performance evaluation. This firm also has intranet update facilities and has developed a global conversion methodology. This is regularly updated with new tools and guidance to be used in conversions. Due to their own policies on professional independence the firm does not assist their clients with the IFRS conversion but does provide opinions that the client requires regarding IFRS compliance. In contrast, Big-Four firm (c) has a national technical division that provides local IFRS training. The trainers participated in the firm's IFRS function, attended global IFRS training sessions in Europe and use the global IFRS training curriculum as a basis when developing IFRS material for their firm. The training is to provide skilled in-house trainers for all their southern African operations. Big-Four firm (d) has its own technical division and writes its national IFRS training modules, using the global IFRS training curriculum as a basis. Training is compulsory for all partners, managers and trainee accountants. Training sessions are filmed with copies made available to all SA and African branches.

Some South African accounting firms have recently started conversion consulting departments. These firms provide services to non-audit clients on IFRS conversion. All these firms experienced high set-up costs, later redeemed by new business contracts. The experiences of two smaller South African accounting and auditing firms are illustrative. At SME firm (a) both partners attended external IFRS training courses late in 2004. This information was then shared by them at intensive training sessions with all their managers and clerks in the first weeks of January 2005. Due to costs and the small client base these training sessions were specifically aimed at tailoring IFRS standards relevant to this client base. At SME firm (b) all three audit partners attended an IAS course run by a private accounting education provider in South Africa. No training sessions will be provided to managers and clerks. This is because most of the staff are currently engaged with tertiary courses which teach IFRS compliant material, cost factors and a belief in in-house hands on learning rather than training. All small firms make use of software packages updated for IFRS standards and reviewed by the Public Accountants and Auditors Board of South Africa.

Many of South Africa's publicly listed companies have not managed to develop their own internal IFRS compliant accounting expertise. Such education and skills upgrading is expensive and time diverted to training diminishes time for professional duties. Due to the largely prohibitive costs of operating their own in-house training, firms either employed new technical and training staff or sought outside professional advice and support. Some firms are becoming more dependent on their auditors.

SMEs make use of external IAS training, due to their own limited in-house training resources. The view of two audit partners dealing with SMEs is that the nature of their client's business made the training needs of IFRS at their firms less intense. They emphasised that the harmonised South African accounting standards with IFRS in 2004 also contributed to the less intense training needs. SMEs receive minimum support from SAICA regarding IFRS training for the smaller business types and audit firms in South Africa. According to two partners at SME audit firms in South Africa, the main role of SAICA for SMEs is the annual practice quality review and the annual review of the training contracts of their trainee accountants. They emphasised that the training challenges in relation to SMEs are generally far more extensive than those for large audit firms. The challenge for SMEs is that the IFRS update seminars run by SAICA do not cater for their specific training needs. For many SMEs the SAICA half day update seminars are too expensive, too short and impersonal, due to large numbers attending the seminars, and are focused on listed clients.

Tertiary and professional institutional education and training remains a huge challenge. At one level, the volume and speed of changes have made it impossible for educational facilities to adapt quickly enough. Many educators are not yet familiar with new standards and nor have they experience of standard application. As a result, many tertiary institutions hire partners from private firms with the necessary technical and application knowledge of IFRS.

PROFESSIONAL TRANSFORMATION: EQUITY AND CULTURE

The accountancy profession in South Africa is still largely white and male dominated. In 1975 there were seven African articled clerks. In that year the PAAB and the National Board of Chartered Accountants developed a proactive policy to increase the number of black accountants. Despite this, more than a decade later the total number of black articled clerks had only increased to 11. In 1988 SAICA supported voluntary employment codes to increase the numbers of black chartered accountants. However by 1990, the political turning point in South Africa's modern history, there were still only 25 black chartered accountants, out of a population of 32 million. The warning bells were sounded from within the profession in 1998 with the then chief executive officer of SAICA stating that the future of the profession hinged on its ability to meet the changing needs of society. The number of professionals entering the field was too small and the racial imbalances too severe to ensure any social legitimacy. In 1998 SAICA developed an equity development programme. However, by 2001 the number of African members of SAICA had only increased from 141 to 209: a 1.1 per cent increase over total SAICA membership.

The accountancy profession in South Africa has also not yet fully embraced the South African government's NEPAD initiatives. Surveys of the accountancy profession indicate that whilst a majority favour increased professional involvement in the rest of Africa, what is stated is not commensurate with it actually happening. Similarly, whilst statements of the need for the organised South African accountancy to be active assisting and developing agents with their collegial organisations in other parts of Africa, much of this is lip service. Nevertheless, considerable progress has been made. Mr Ignatius Sehoole, the incoming executive president of SAICA has committed the organisation to expanding its training and collegial contacts throughout the NEPAD region in order to 'meet and implement global standards in general and international federation standards and NEPAD objectives in particular'. SAICA is currently working with professional institutes in, *inter alia*, Namibia, Swaziland and Zimbabwe in order to develop common teaching materials and qualifications, with reciprocal accreditation, which take account of individual country's tax and company law differences. SAICA is currently discussing similar approaches with other African countries with the eventual goal being the formation of an 'African accountancy profession'. Of SAICA's currently 23,263 members, over 5,000 currently work outside of South Africa.[13]

The processes of globalisation do not only affect political and economic institutions. Similarly, as Western democracy and culture spread seemingly ascendant throughout the world, so concerns over 'cultural imperialism' and the perceived erosion of national or indigenous cultural practices and values have become powerful politicised forces within globalisation and debates over the benefits of globalisation. Consequently, one of the responses to the potentially homogenising effects of globalisation and the 'one size fits all' approach is the rediscovery and reinterpretation of local traditions and practices. As South Africa emerges from its racially fragmented past to be an African powerhouse, traditional African cultural practices have been revived and given state legitimacy with President Mbeki's enunciation of an 'African Renaissance'.

Culture remains a relevant force in the globalisation process. An investigation into the relationships between culture and accounting systems is thus worthwhile. Some African countries, including South Africa, Botswana and Kenya have adopted IFRS prior to their acceptance in 'developed' countries. Similarly such African countries have acknowledged accounting qualifications administered by foreign bodies, such as ACCA and CIMA, in some cases due simply to the costs involved in setting up and administering local accounting institutions themselves. However, given this seemingly unambiguous and often strategic process of incorporation within a globalised setting, it is important to speculate on how this process may result in the re-emergence of interest in traditional accounting practices and if cultural differences may actually mean more in terms of the practical application of IFRS than is typically expected.

The links between culture and organisations have been demonstrated by Hofstede's classic investigations into the variables of values in one institution – IBM – across 50 different countries (Hofstede 1983, 1984 and 2001). Hofstede suggested five dimensions by which cultural values within organisations could be differentiated across countries, and across certain distinct clusters of countries: power distance, individualism, uncertainty avoidance, masculinity and long-term versus short-term orientation. Gray extended the original model with hypotheses that correlate the dimensions with four significant characteristics of accounting systems: professionalism, uniformity, secrecy and conservatism, where the 'accounting values' of professionalism and uniformity tend to relate to mechanisms of authority and enforcement, while those of conservatism and secrecy tend to relate to the measurement and disclosure aspects of accounting systems (Gray 1988).

South Africa was the only African country to be considered separately in Hofstede's study although his results made clear that there were significant differences between the West and East African regions and Britain and the USA on all dimensions. Perhaps reflecting its multi-cultural makeup, South Africa fell between the other African and the British and USA scores. Hofstede's cluster analysis, used to group countries together, reinforces this 'middle ground' perception as it placed South Africa with Italy, Switzerland and Germany – countries with which it has very limited historical, let alone geographical, ties.

It is difficult to correlate developments in accounting in South Africa with the predictions from these models. Although government is taking a greater role, this is not significantly different to measures taken in developed countries in response to the corporate collapses and consequent mistrust in accountants, corporate management and auditors of recent years. The harmonisation project and alignment with IFRS all but eliminates any cultural vestiges (although the recently developed AC500 series of statements and interpretations intended to provide guidance for South African issues not dealt with by IFRS offers hope). Despite these difficulties, Hofstede and Gray's models provide both useful dimensions through which local accounting practices and institutions, and changes in these, can be examined and an alternative lens through which the globalisation of accounting can be viewed.

A more successful indication of how culture may impact on accounting systems is found in the locally developed King II report on Corporate Governance in South Africa. The King II report attempts to extend the philosophy of interdependence into the corporate environment in that it advocates an 'inclusive' stakeholder approach to corporate governance, in contrast to the more individualistic shareholder approach more evident in Western countries:

The modern approach is for a board to identify the company's stakeholders, including its shareowners, and to agree policies as to how the relationship with those stakeholders should be advanced and managed in the interests of the company.[14]

Drawing on corporate law and recent events, the report requires that the directors act in the best interests of the company as a separate legal person and thereby rejects the typically Western notion that the shareholder's interests are paramount. The report goes on to state that 'companies ... must recognise that they co-exist in an environment where many of the country's citizens disturbingly remain on the fringes of society's economic benefits'.[15] The report also diverges from the pattern of corporate governance reforms in 'developed' countries by including a chapter dedicated to 'Sustainability Reporting', which includes recommendations of increased disclosure for issues such as employment equity, occupational health and safety and the impact of HIV/AIDS, environmental impact and social investment practices (with particular regard to black economic empowerment). It appears then that in contrast to Gray's model, a collective approach is not inconsistent with less secrecy. The introduction to the report closes by mentioning certain aspects of African culture (that are by implication then considered significant for corporate governance), including collectiveness, an inclination towards consensus, humility and helpfulness and co-existence with others.[16]

These aspects of the King II report originate in South Africa and embody the communitarian outlook and concern for economic equality that can be identified with black South African cultural values. This thus presents an example of how accounting practices may be 'reinterpreted' for local practices that is in contrast to prevailing Western patterns. At the same time, however, two problems can be identified: First, the King II report provides recommendations and the resultant disclosures that are not mandatory. Second, the mandatory accounting practices for South African companies are found in IFRS, which therefore precludes any possibility of genuinely adapting accounting practices to reflect South African cultural concerns. It is possible to conclude that, given room, culture may have a role to play in determining preferred accounting practices and that the 'one size fits all' approach of IFRS may not be appropriate when the values and concerns of specific cultural groups are considered.

CONCLUSION

The move away from the political economy of Apartheid and into a rapidly globalising world has produced very substantial changes in South Africa and in this country's relations with both the continent and the rest of the world. The South African state has driven a process of restructuring and transformation that is bent upon overcoming the long legacies of Apartheid and re-inserting the country into the modern world. This world is a globalising world. Emerging from decades of international isolation, the South African government has developed polices aimed at attaining strategic advantages within the processes of globalisation.

A central role in this has been the dramatic and fundamental transformation of the structural fundamentals of the South African economy. Key to this has been the South African government's decision to push for the adoption of IFRS. The internationalisation of South African accounting and auditing standards has, unlike many countries, been an ongoing process beginning in the mid 1990s. That this process of globalisation has been driven by the state and in an emerging market economy is highly significant. That the South African government, in tandem with major institutions of international governance and finance is using compliance to international accounting standards as central features in the development and transformation of other African economies is also highly significant. This has placed the South African accounting profession and economy on favourable terms relative to other nations. However, it is clearly evident that to meet the pace of economic growth and equity in employment, key characteristics in both the educational system and the accounting profession still remain as challenges requiring urgent attention.

NOTES

1   See *The Russia Journal* (on-line), 'Russia Rethinks transition to International Accounting System', accessed 12 April 1999.
2   See *Zimbabwe Independent*, 18 February 2005.
3   For the debate on the role of the nation state in globalisation, see Bhagwati 2004; Dunn 1995; Fukuyama 2004; Hirst 1995; Stiglitz 2003) and Wolf 2004.
4   See, for example, speech by the South African Minister of Trade and Industry, 'South African Company Law for the 21st Century: Guidelines for Corporate Law Reform', May 2004; South African Commission on Globalization and the Prospects for Investment and Growth summit, (nd) and South African Ministry of Foreign Affairs, Briefing by Deputy Minister Aziz Pahad at the Government Communications and Information Service Media Briefing, 15 September 2000.
5   Statement of the President of South Africa, Thabo Mbeki, at the 35th Ordinary Session of the OAU Assembly of Heads of State and Government, Algiers, Algeria, (nd) and Manuel (2004).
6   See Stevenson, 2002.
7   See *This Day*, 9 and 10 March 2004.
8   See *Business Day*, 14 November 2005.
9   See *Business Day*, 18 November 2005.
10 The vice-president and chief economist at the (South African) Industrial Development Corporation as writing in the *Sunday Times*, 20 November 2005.
11 See *Finance Week*, 20 April 2005.
12 This section is based on structured interviews with Big-Four training and technical partners and a sample of non-Big-Four partners.
13 See *Business Day*, 11 November 2005.

14 IOD (2002), Introduction, para 51.
15 IOD (2002), *Ibid*, para 36.
16 IOD (2002), *Ibid*, para 38.

REFERENCES

Accountancy Age (2001), 20 June.
Accountancy – SA, 'SAAS for the Public Sector – Are We Winning', March 1998; 'The Auditing Standards Committee – an Overview of 1997', March 1998; 'The Road Ahead', May 1998; 'Legal and Ethical', July 1998; 'Poor GAAP Compliance', July 1999; 'Accounting Standards: Avoid Becoming a Tower of Babel', July 1999; 'Creating Harmony', October 1999; 'Views on Southern African Co-operation', October 1999; 'A Question of Ethics', January 2000; 'Executalk: Newsletter from the Chief Executive', February 2000; and 'Newsletter from the Executive president', May 2000.
African Development Bank (2003), African Development Report 2003 'Africa in the World Economy: Globalization and Africa's Development: Economic and Social Statistics on Africa'.
African National Congress (ANC) (1990), Discussion Document on Economic Policy.
Afrikaanse Handelsinstituut (2001), 'The globalization of the South African Economy', March.
Ayittey, G.B.N. (2005), *Africa Unchained: The Blueprint for Africa's Future*, Palgrave Macmillan.
De Beer (2003), 'Improvements, convergence and other buzz words', *CFOweb*, 29 January.
Bezuidenhout, A. (2000), 'How could a global social movement type unionism emerge in South Africa?', *International Labour Organization*.
Bhagwati, J. (2004), *In Defence of Globalization*, Oxford: Oxford University Press.
Biggs, M. and I. Abedian (1999), *Economic Globalization and Fiscal Policy*, Oxford: Oxford University Press.
Bond, P. (2004), *Against Global Apartheid. South Africa meets the World Bank, IMF and International Finance*, Zed Books.
Bond, P. (2005), *Talk left, Walk right. South Africa's Frusrated Global Reforms*, University of Natal Press.
Boshoff, A. and Carstens, A., 'Apartheid's Influence on South African Accounting Education', unpublished paper (nd).
Business Day (2005), 11,14 and 18 November.
Cheruzed, F. (2002), *African Renaissance: Roadmaps to the Challenge of Globalization*, Zed Books.
Dunn, J. (1995), *Contemporary Crisis of the Nation-State?*, Oxford.
Fukuyama, F. (2004), *State Building: Governance and World Order in the 21st Century*, Cornell University Press.
Gray, S.J. (1988), 'Towards a Theory of Cultural Influence on the Development of Accounting Systems Internationally', *Abacus*, **24** (1), p. 1–15.
Harris, R. et al, (2005), *Globalization and Post-Apartheid South Africa*, De Sitter.
Harris, R., Zegeye, A. and Auderdale, P. (eds) (2005), *Globalization and Post-apartheid South Africa*, Westview.

Hirst, P. (1995), 'Globalization and the future of the nation-state', *Economy and Society*, **24** (3).

Hofstede, G. (1983), 'National Cultures in Four Dimensions: A Research-based Theory of Cultural Differences among Nations', *International Studies of Man and Organisations*, **13** (1–2), p. 46–74.

Hofstede, G. (1984), 'Cultural Dimensions in Management and Planning', *Asia Pacific Journal of Management*, **1**, p. 81–90.

Hofstede, G. (2001), *Cultures Consequences*, 2nd ed., California, Sage.

Hopkins, A.G. (ed.) 2003, *Globalization in World History*, London: Pimlico.

International Federation of Accountants (IFAC) (2001), 'South African Government adopts IFAC's Public Sector Accounting', 22 August.

International Labour Organisation (ILO) (2000), 'Towards Global Social Movement Unionism? Trade Union responses to globalisation in South Africa', ILO.

International Labour Organisation (2001), 'Studies on the Social Dimensions of Globalization: South Africa', ILO.

Institute of Directors (IOD) (2002), *King Report on Corporate Governance for South Africa – 2002*, Johannesburg: Institute of Directors.

Loots, E. (2001), 'Globalization, Emerging Markets and the South African Economy', unpublished paper presented at the International Jubilee Conference of the Economic Society of South Africa, September.

Love, J. (1999), *Globalization, Regionalism, and Nationalism in Southern Africa*, Perseus.

Mansbach, R.W. and Rhodes, E (eds) (2000), *Global Politics in a Changing World*, New York, Chapter 10.

Manuel, T. (2004), 'Globalization and the African State', *This Day*, 11 March.

Melber, H. (2004), 'NePAD: South Africa, African Economies and Globalisation', www.pambazuka.org 29 January.

Natrass, N. (1994), 'Politics and Economics in ANC Economic Policy', *African Affairs*, **93** (372), July.

South African Institute of Chartered Accountants (2003), 'Exposure Draft 167', September.

Stevenson, R.W. (2002), 'Seeking Trade, Africans Find Western Barriers', *New York Times*, 26 May.

Stiglitz, J. (2003), *Globalization and Its Discontents*, WW Norton.

The Sunday Times (South Africa) (2005), Business Report on-line, 9 February.

This Day (2004), exert from South African Minister of Finance Trevor Manuel's speech to the Oxford University Inaugural Global Economic Governance Lecture, 11 March.

Werksmans (2005), *Business Guide to South Africa*.

World Bank (2003), 'Report on the Observance Standards and Codes (ROSC): South Africa', 15 April.

The World Bank Group (1996), 'Education and Training of Accountants in Sub Saharan Africa', *Findings Africa Region*, no. 60, April, p 1.

Wolf, M. (2004), *Why Globalization Works*, New Haven: Yale University Press.

World Economic Forum (2003), 'Africa Economic Summit', *Africa Agenda*, Durban, June.

Van der Westhuizen, J. (2002), *Adapting to Globalization: Malaysia, South Africa and the Challenges of Ethnic Redistribution with Growth*, Praeger.

Index

Feb 27/08